token

by Alisa Kwitney and Joëlle Jones

with lettering by Steve Wands

CHAPTER ONE: SOME LIKE IT HOT

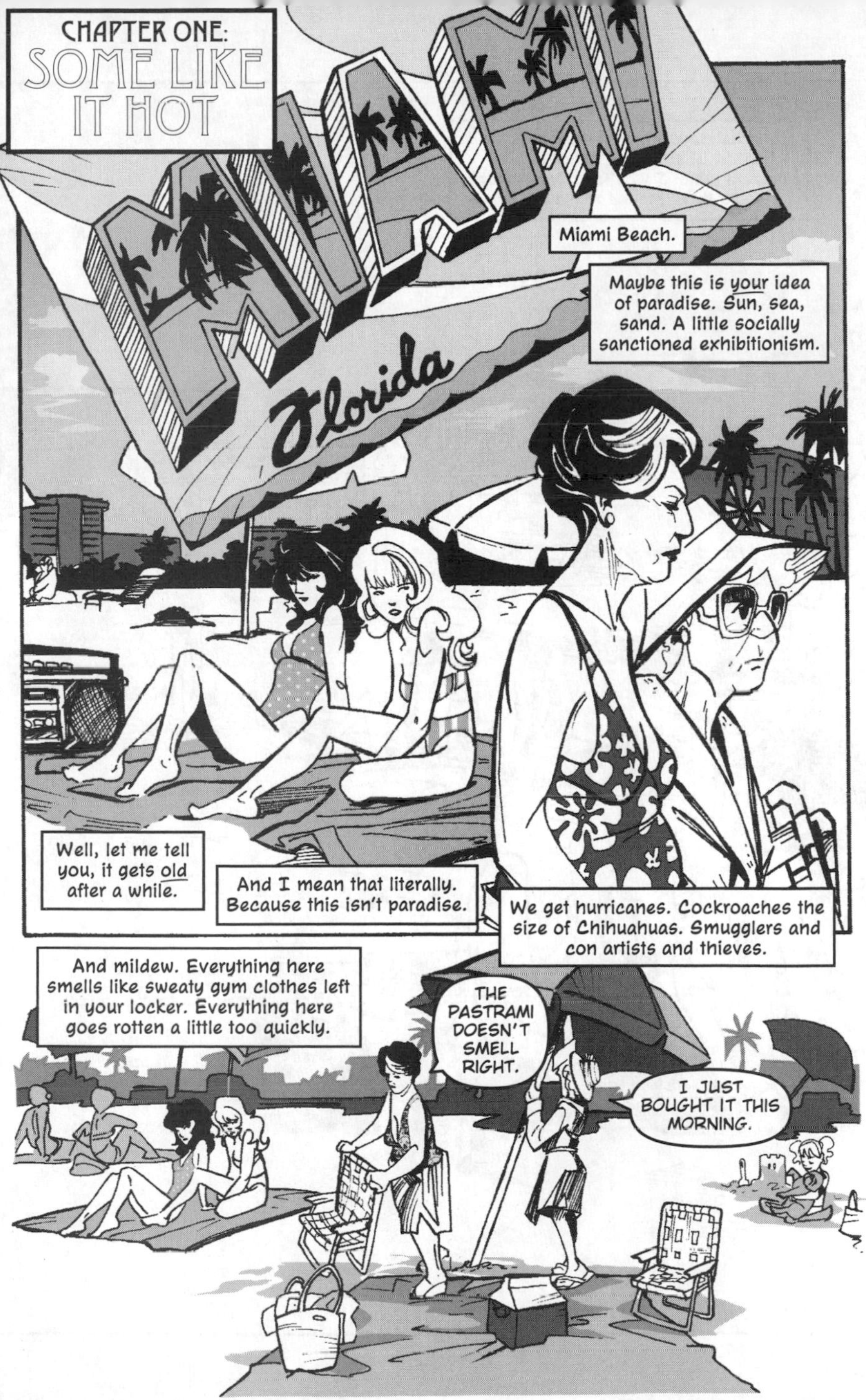
MIAMI
Florida
Miami Beach.
Maybe this is your idea of paradise. Sun, sea, sand. A little socially sanctioned exhibitionism.
Well, let me tell you, it gets old after a while.
And I mean that literally. Because this isn't paradise.
We get hurricanes. Cockroaches the size of Chihuahuas. Smugglers and con artists and thieves.
And mildew. Everything here smells like sweaty gym clothes left in your locker. Everything here goes rotten a little too quickly.
THE PASTRAMI DOESN'T SMELL RIGHT.
I JUST BOUGHT IT THIS MORNING.

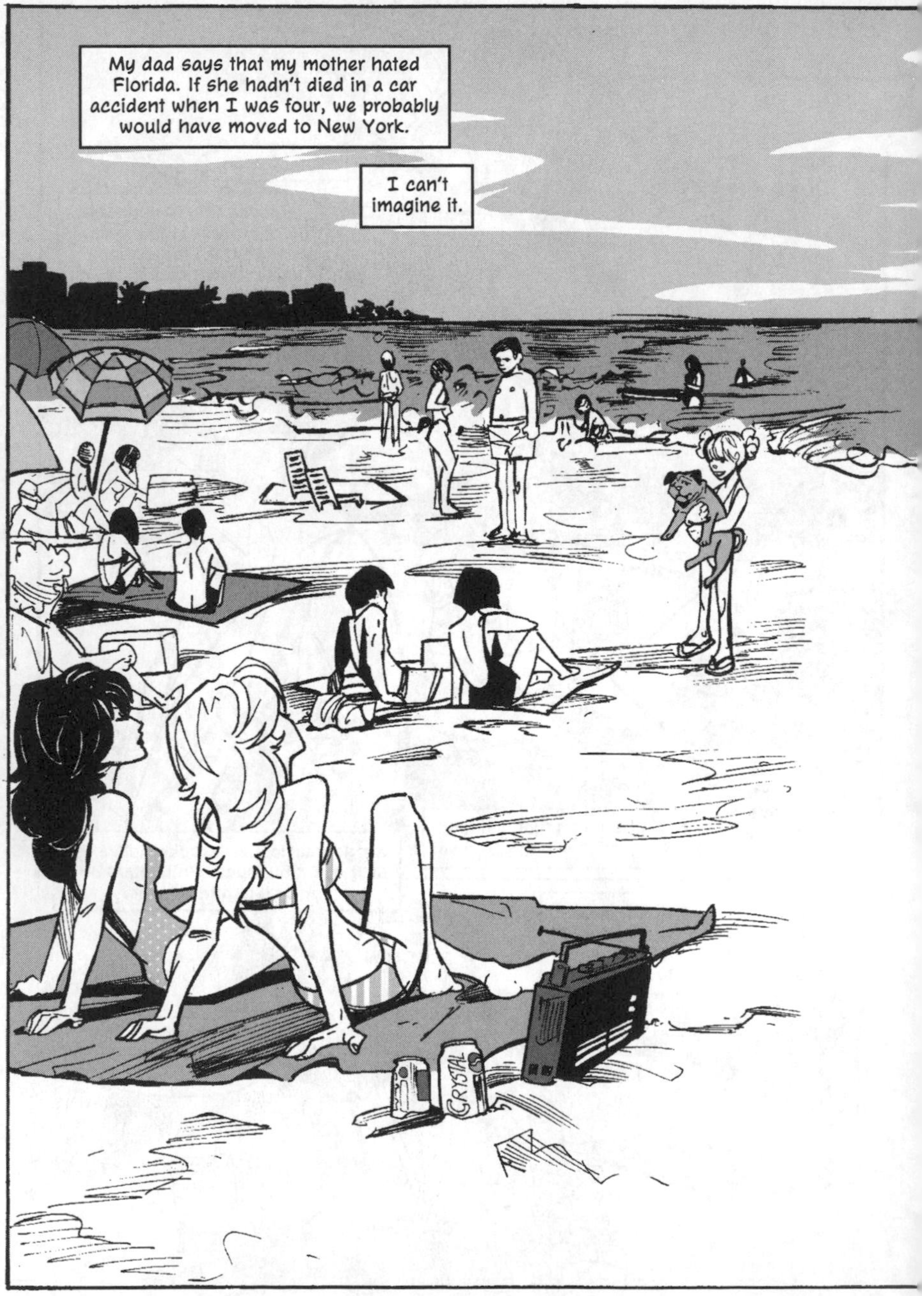
My dad says that my mother hated Florida. If she hadn't died in a car accident when I was four, we probably would have moved to New York.
I can't imagine it.
CRYSTAL

TOKEN

Published by DC Comics,
1700 Broadway, New York, NY 10019.

Printed in Canada.
DC Comics, a Warner Bros.
Entertainment Company.

ISBN: 978-1-4012-1538-5

Cover by Joëlle Jones

Karen Berger, Sr. VP-Executive Editor Shelly Bond, Editor Angela Rufino, Assistant Editor
Robbin Brosterman, Sr. Art Director Paul Levitz, President & Publisher Georg Brewer, VP-Design & DC Direct Creative
Richard Bruning, Sr. VP-Creative Director Patrick Caldon, Exec. VP-Finance & Operations
Chris Caramalis, VP-Finance John Cunningham, VP-Marketing Terri Cunningham, VP-Managing Editor
Amy Genkins, Sr. VP-Business & Legal Affairs Alison Gill, VP-Manufacturing David Hyde, VP-Publicity
Hank Kanalz, VP-General Manager, WildStorm Jim Lee, Editorial Director-WildStorm Gregory Noveck, Sr. VP-Creative Affairs
Sue Pohja, VP-Book Trade Sales Steve Rotterdam Sr. VP-Sales & Marketing Cheryl Rubin, Sr. VP-Brand Management
Alysse Soll, VP-Advertising & Custom Publishing Jeff Trojan, VP-Business Development, DC Direct Bob Wayne, VP-Sales

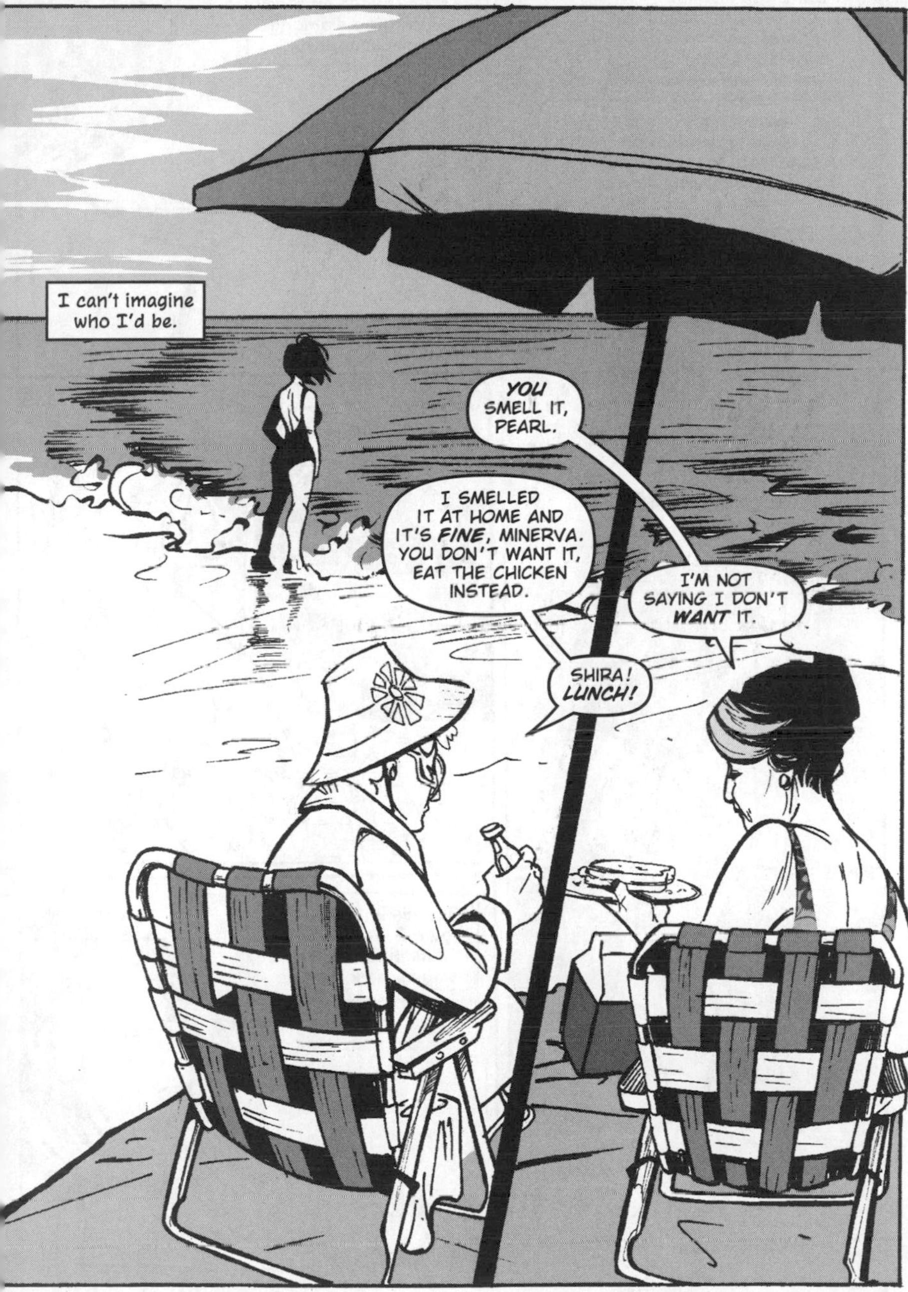
I can't imagine who I'd be.
YOU SMELL IT, PEARL.
I SMELLED IT AT HOME AND IT'S FINE, MINERVA. YOU DON'T WANT IT, EAT THE CHICKEN INSTEAD.
I'M NOT SAYING I DON'T WANT IT.
SHIRA! LUNCH!

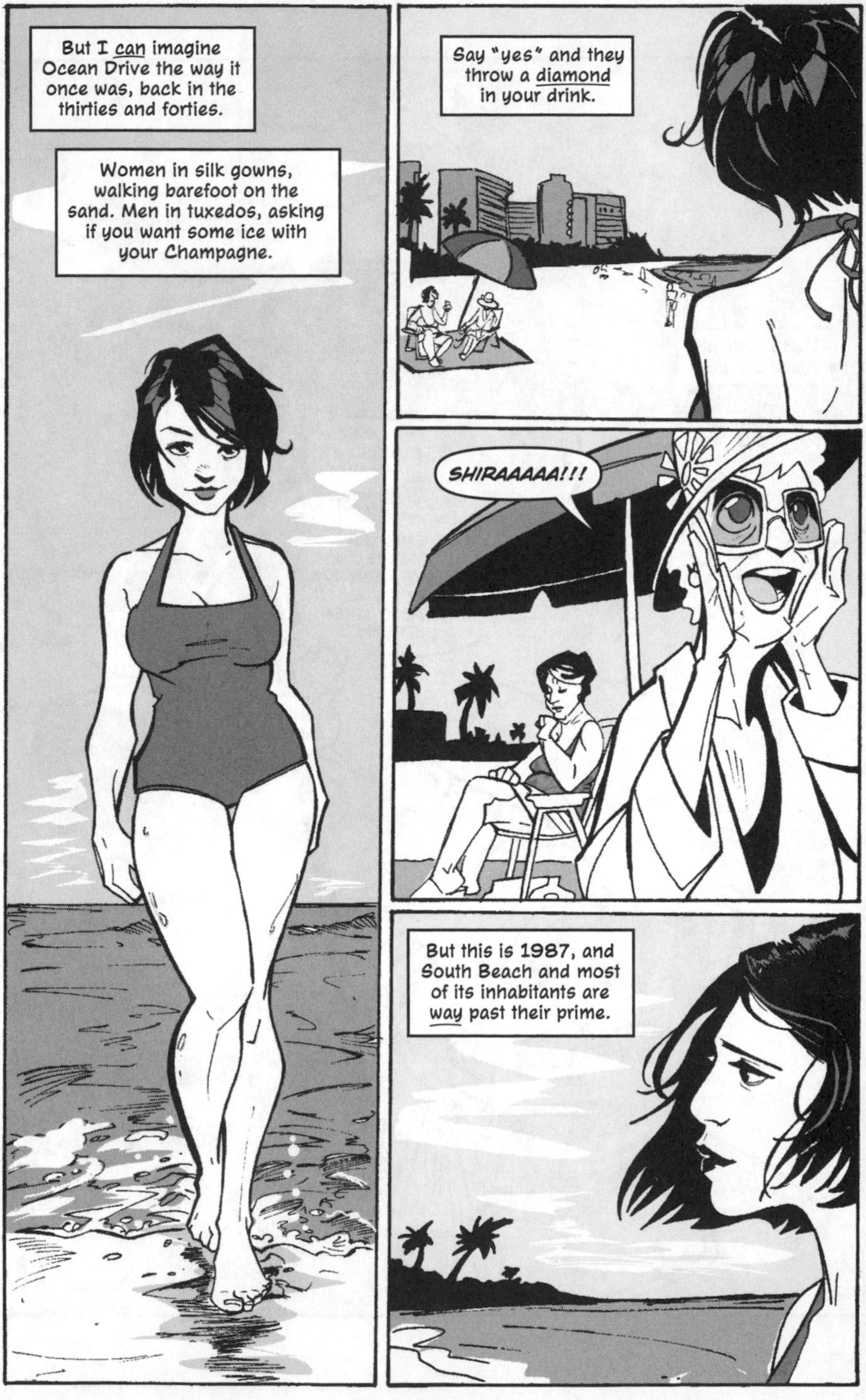

But I can imagine Ocean Drive the way it once was, back in the thirties and forties.
Women in silk gowns, walking barefoot on the sand. Men in tuxedos, asking if you want some ice with your Champagne.
Say "yes" and they throw a diamond in your drink.
SHIRAAAAA!!!
But this is 1987, and South Beach and most of its inhabitants are way past their prime.

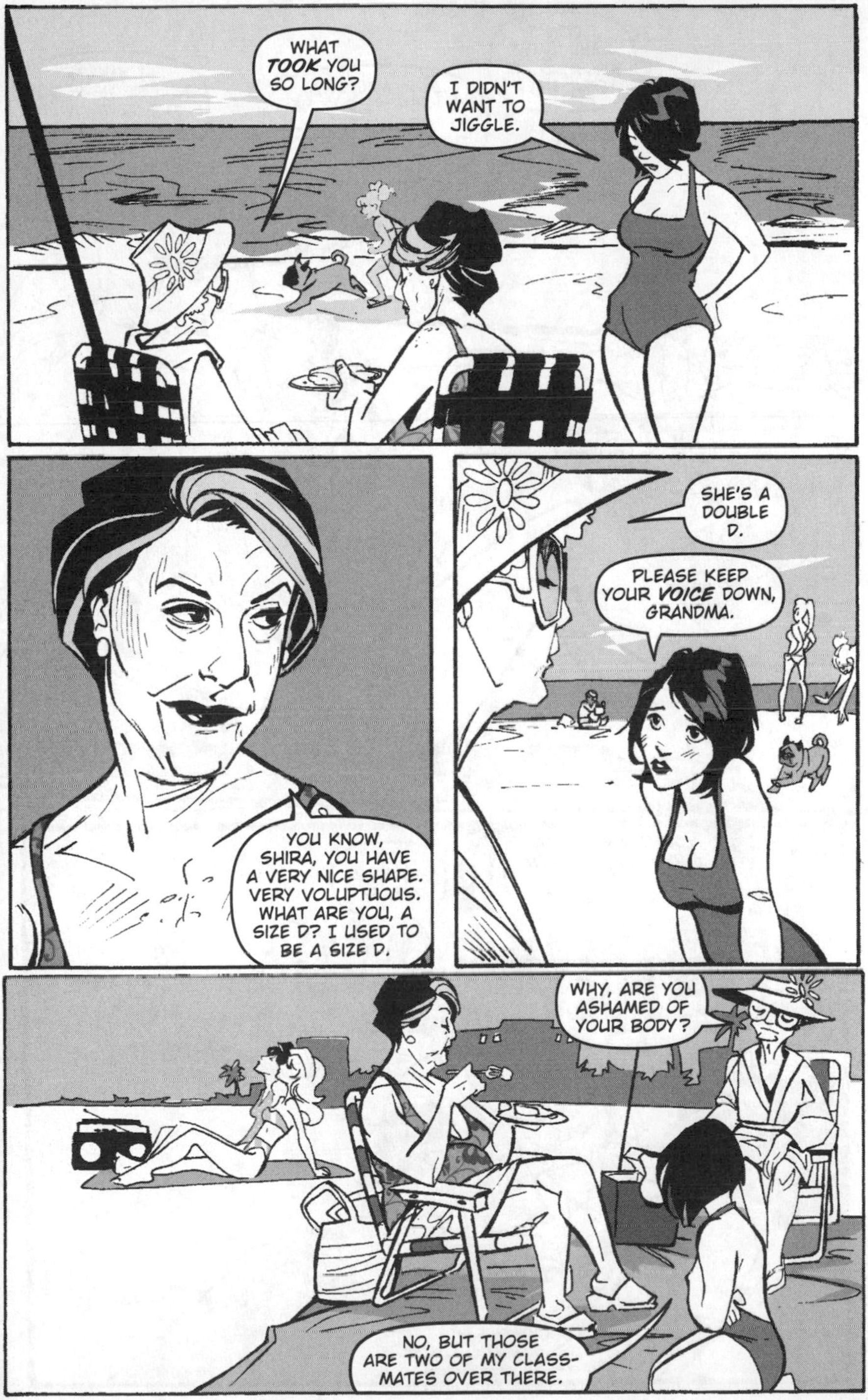
WHAT TOOK YOU SO LONG?
I DIDN'T WANT TO JIGGLE.
YOU KNOW, SHIRA, YOU HAVE A VERY NICE SHAPE. VERY VOLUPTUOUS. WHAT ARE YOU, A SIZE D? I USED TO BE A SIZE D.
SHE'S A DOUBLE D.
PLEASE KEEP YOUR VOICE DOWN, GRANDMA.
WHY, ARE YOU ASHAMED OF YOUR BODY?
NO, BUT THOSE ARE TWO OF MY CLASS-MATES OVER THERE.

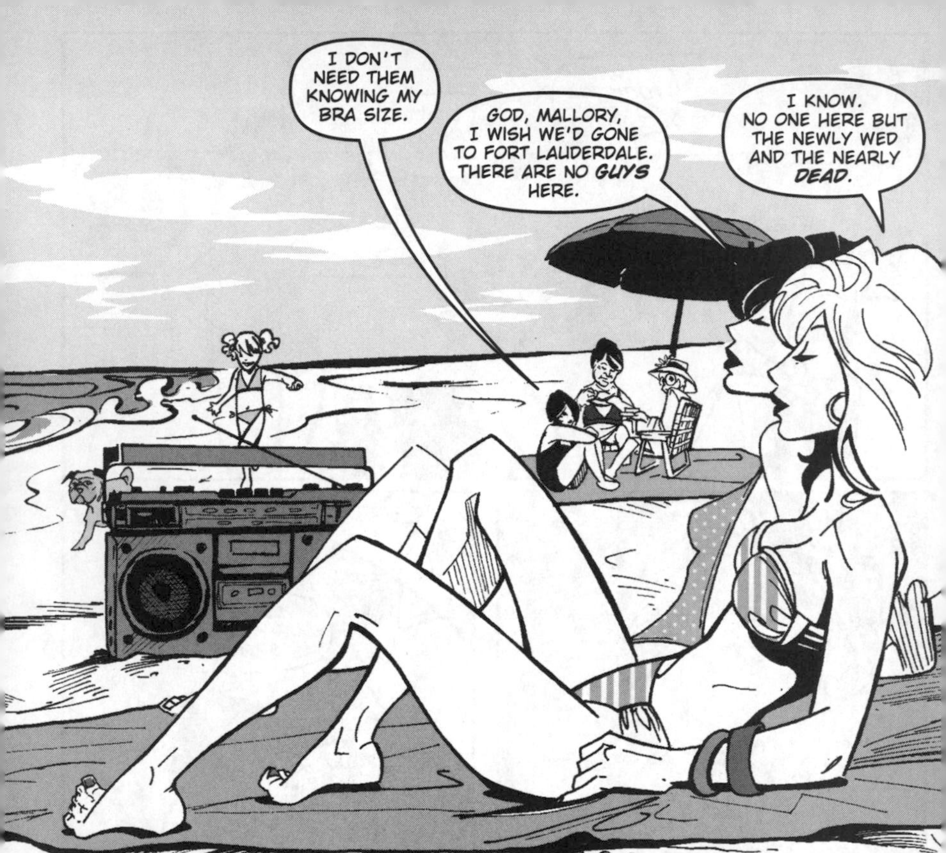
I DON'T NEED THEM KNOWING MY BRA SIZE.
GOD, MALLORY, I WISH WE'D GONE TO FORT LAUDERDALE. THERE ARE NO GUYS HERE.
I KNOW. NO ONE HERE BUT THE NEWLY WED AND THE NEARLY DEAD.

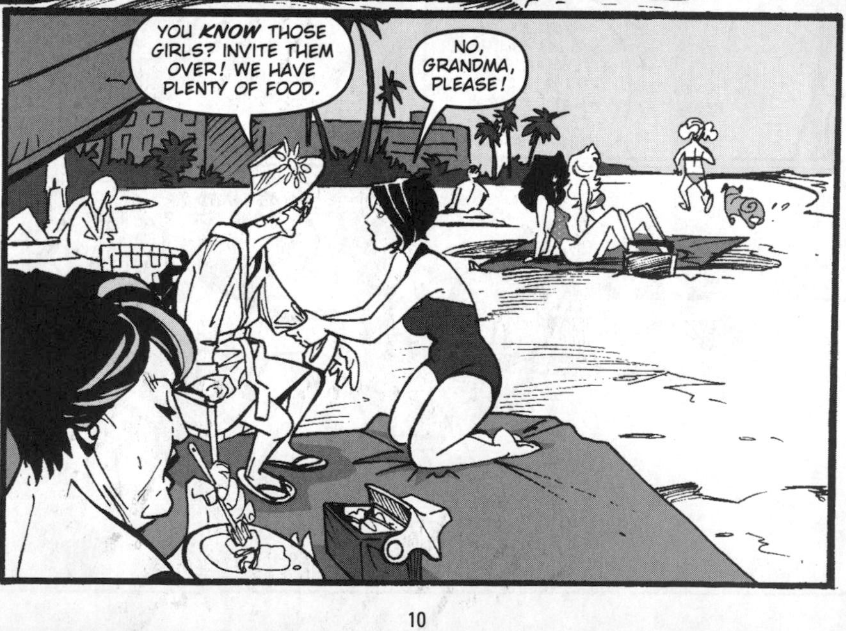
YOU KNOW THOSE GIRLS? INVITE THEM OVER! WE HAVE PLENTY OF FOOD.
NO, GRANDMA, PLEASE!

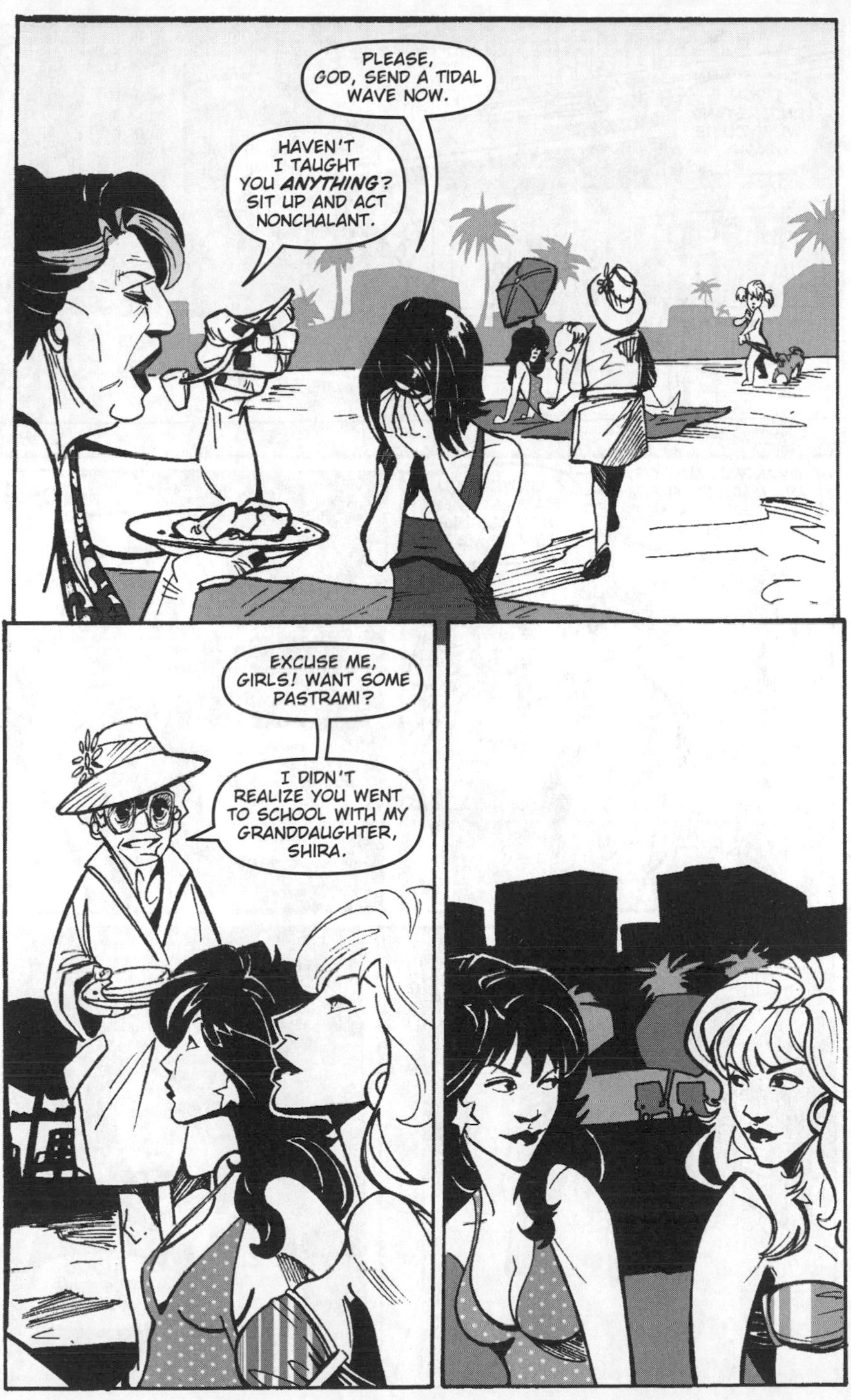
HAVEN'T I TAUGHT YOU *ANYTHING*? SIT UP AND ACT NONCHALANT.
PLEASE, GOD, SEND A TIDAL WAVE NOW.
EXCUSE ME, GIRLS! WANT SOME PASTRAMI?
I DIDN'T REALIZE YOU WENT TO SCHOOL WITH MY GRANDDAUGHTER, SHIRA.

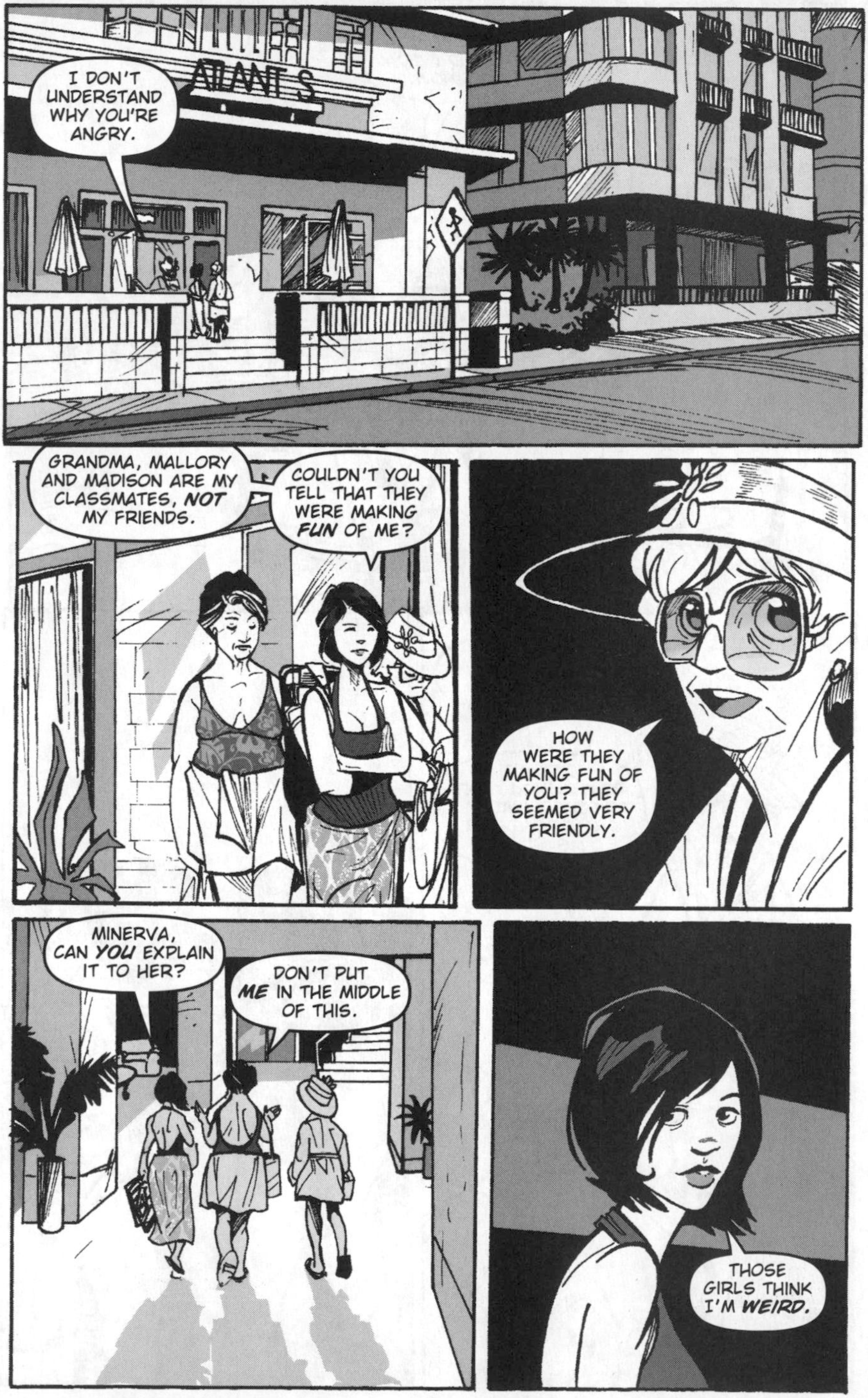
ATLANT S
I DON'T UNDERSTAND WHY YOU'RE ANGRY.
GRANDMA, MALLORY AND MADISON ARE MY CLASSMATES, NOT MY FRIENDS.
COULDN'T YOU TELL THAT THEY WERE MAKING FUN OF ME?
HOW WERE THEY MAKING FUN OF YOU? THEY SEEMED VERY FRIENDLY.
MINERVA, CAN YOU EXPLAIN IT TO HER?
DON'T PUT ME IN THE MIDDLE OF THIS.
THOSE GIRLS THINK I'M WEIRD.

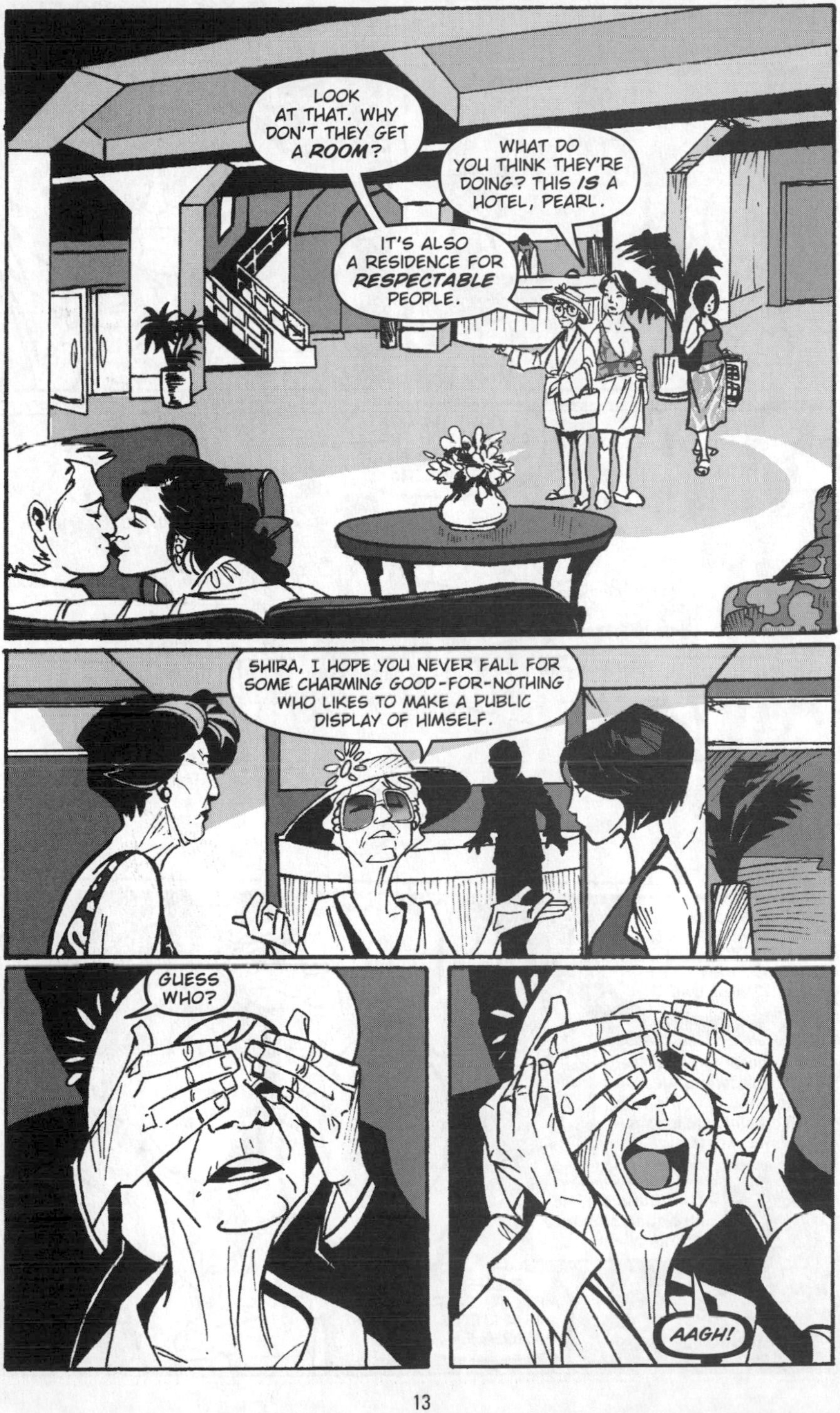
LOOK AT THAT. WHY DON'T THEY GET A *ROOM*?
WHAT DO YOU THINK THEY'RE DOING? THIS *IS* A HOTEL, PEARL.
IT'S ALSO A RESIDENCE FOR *RESPECTABLE* PEOPLE.
SHIRA, I HOPE YOU NEVER FALL FOR SOME CHARMING GOOD-FOR-NOTHING WHO LIKES TO MAKE A PUBLIC DISPLAY OF HIMSELF.
GUESS WHO?
AAGH!

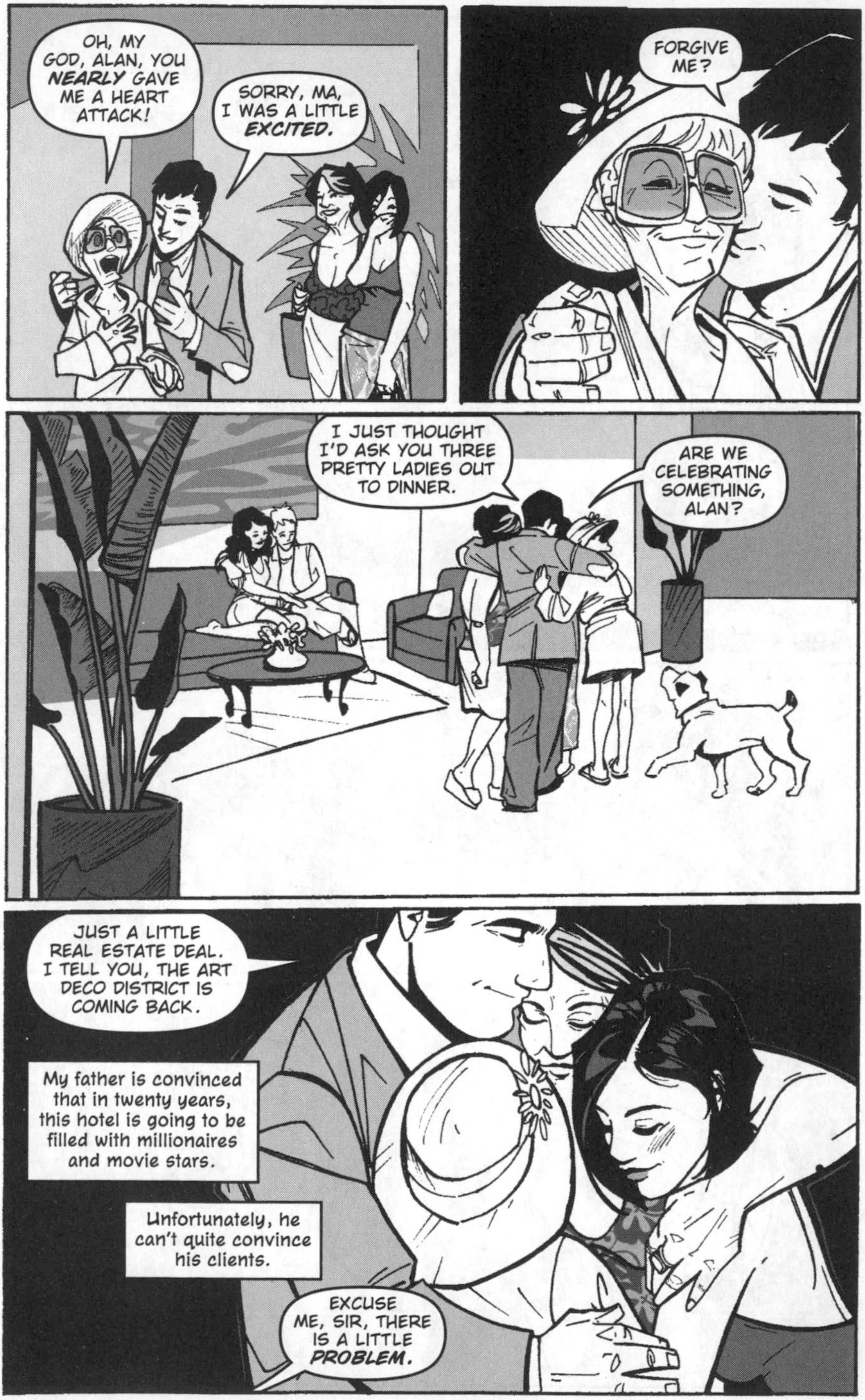

OH, MY GOD, ALAN, YOU NEARLY GAVE ME A HEART ATTACK!
SORRY, MA, I WAS A LITTLE EXCITED.
FORGIVE ME?
I JUST THOUGHT I'D ASK YOU THREE PRETTY LADIES OUT TO DINNER.
ARE WE CELEBRATING SOMETHING, ALAN?
JUST A LITTLE REAL ESTATE DEAL. I TELL YOU, THE ART DECO DISTRICT IS COMING BACK.
My father is convinced that in twenty years, this hotel is going to be filled with millionaires and movie stars.
Unfortunately, he can't quite convince his clients.
EXCUSE ME, SIR, THERE IS A LITTLE PROBLEM.

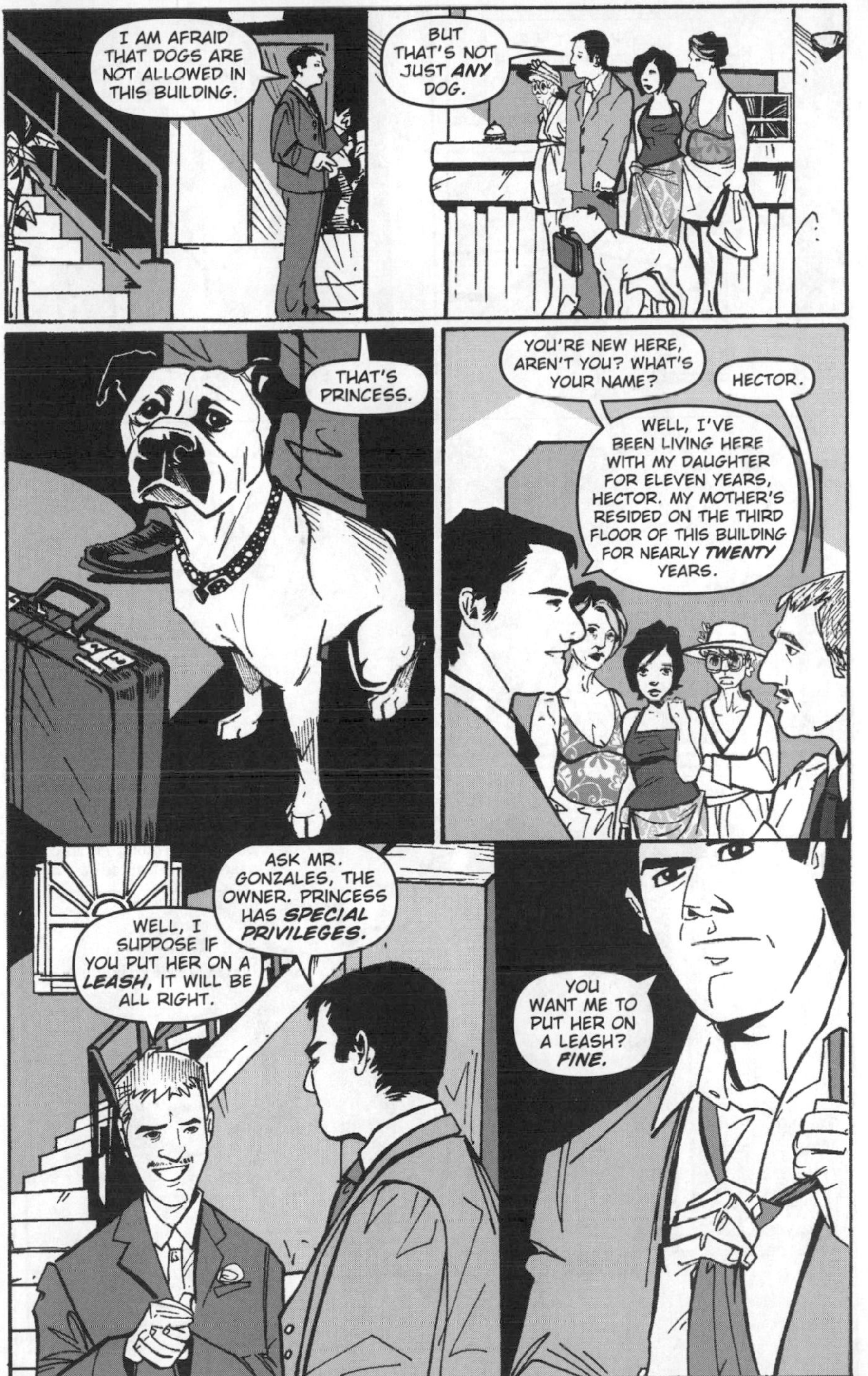
I AM AFRAID THAT DOGS ARE NOT ALLOWED IN THIS BUILDING.
BUT THAT'S NOT JUST ANY DOG.
THAT'S PRINCESS.
YOU'RE NEW HERE, AREN'T YOU? WHAT'S YOUR NAME?
HECTOR.
WELL, I'VE BEEN LIVING HERE WITH MY DAUGHTER FOR ELEVEN YEARS, HECTOR. MY MOTHER'S RESIDED ON THE THIRD FLOOR OF THIS BUILDING FOR NEARLY TWENTY YEARS.
ASK MR. GONZALES, THE OWNER. PRINCESS HAS SPECIAL PRIVILEGES.
WELL, I SUPPOSE IF YOU PUT HER ON A LEASH, IT WILL BE ALL RIGHT.
YOU WANT ME TO PUT HER ON A LEASH? FINE.

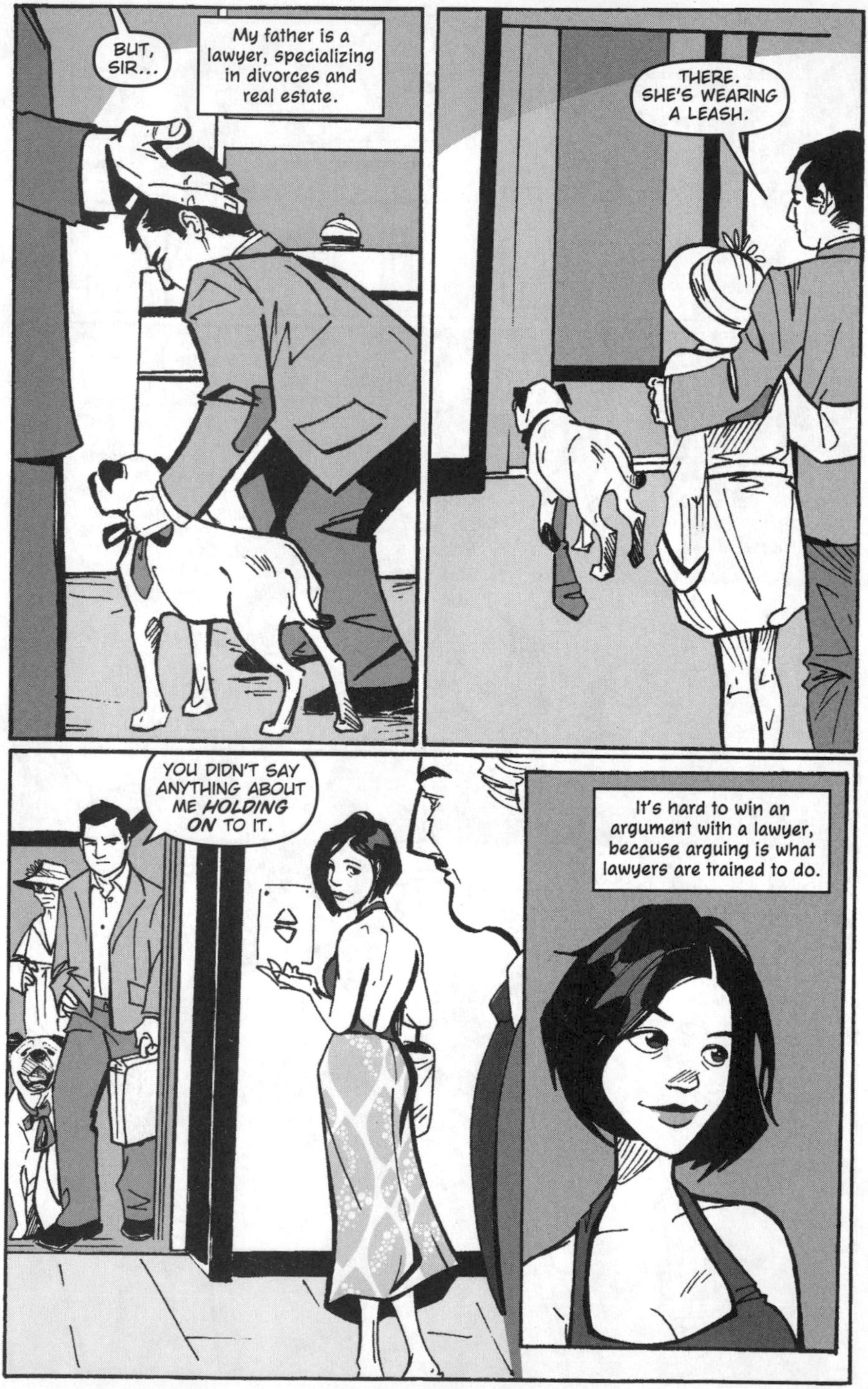
BUT, SIR...
My father is a lawyer, specializing in divorces and real estate.
THERE. SHE'S WEARING A LEASH.
YOU DIDN'T SAY ANYTHING ABOUT ME *HOLDING ON* TO IT.
It's hard to win an argument with a lawyer, because arguing is what lawyers are trained to do.

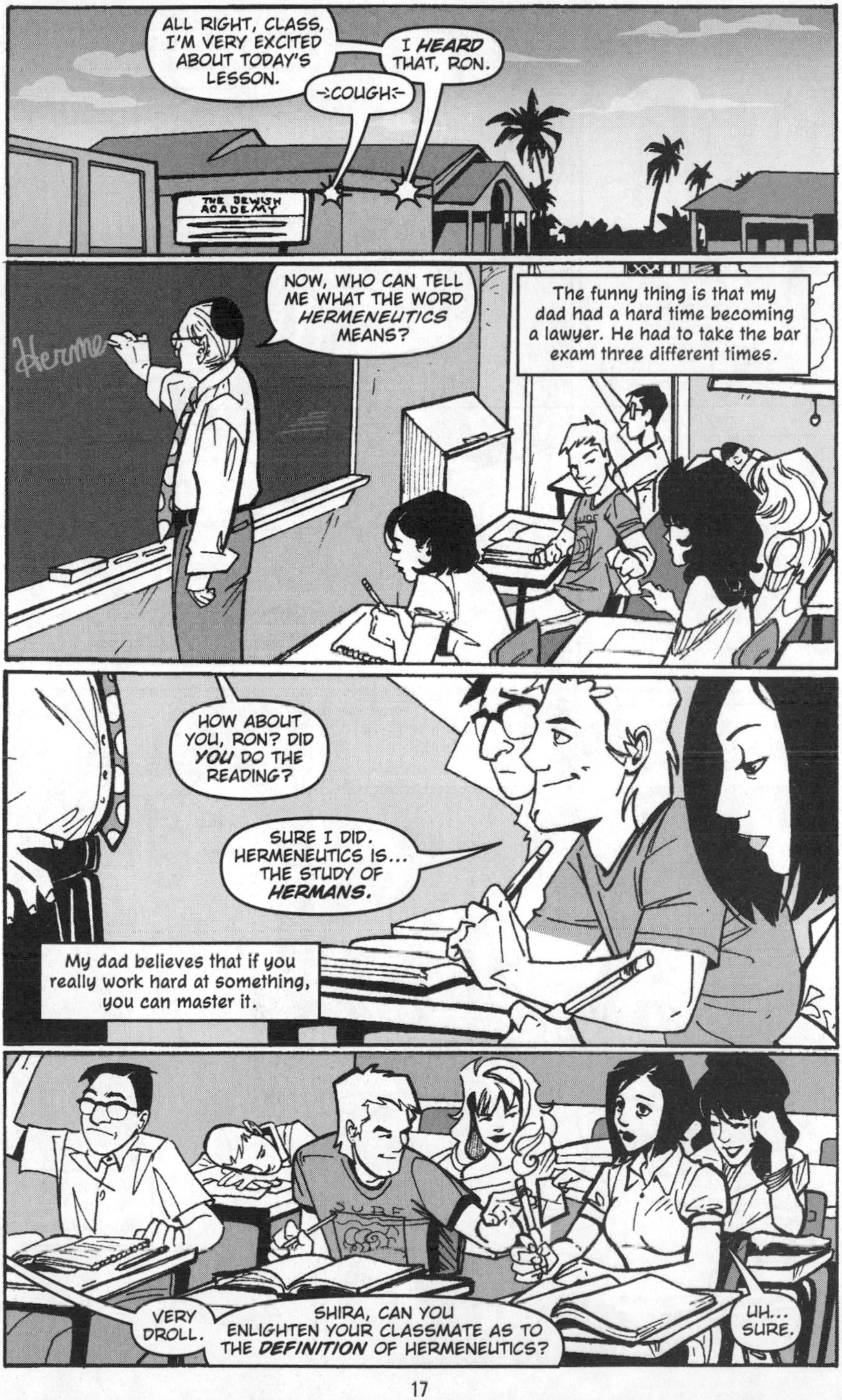
ALL RIGHT, CLASS, I'M VERY EXCITED ABOUT TODAY'S LESSON.
-COUGH-
I HEARD THAT, RON.
THE JEWISH ACADEMY
NOW, WHO CAN TELL ME WHAT THE WORD HERMENEUTICS MEANS?
The funny thing is that my dad had a hard time becoming a lawyer. He had to take the bar exam three different times.
HOW ABOUT YOU, RON? DID YOU DO THE READING?
SURE I DID. HERMENEUTICS IS... THE STUDY OF HERMANS.
My dad believes that if you really work hard at something, you can master it.
VERY DROLL.
SHIRA, CAN YOU ENLIGHTEN YOUR CLASSMATE AS TO THE DEFINITION OF HERMENEUTICS?
UH... SURE.

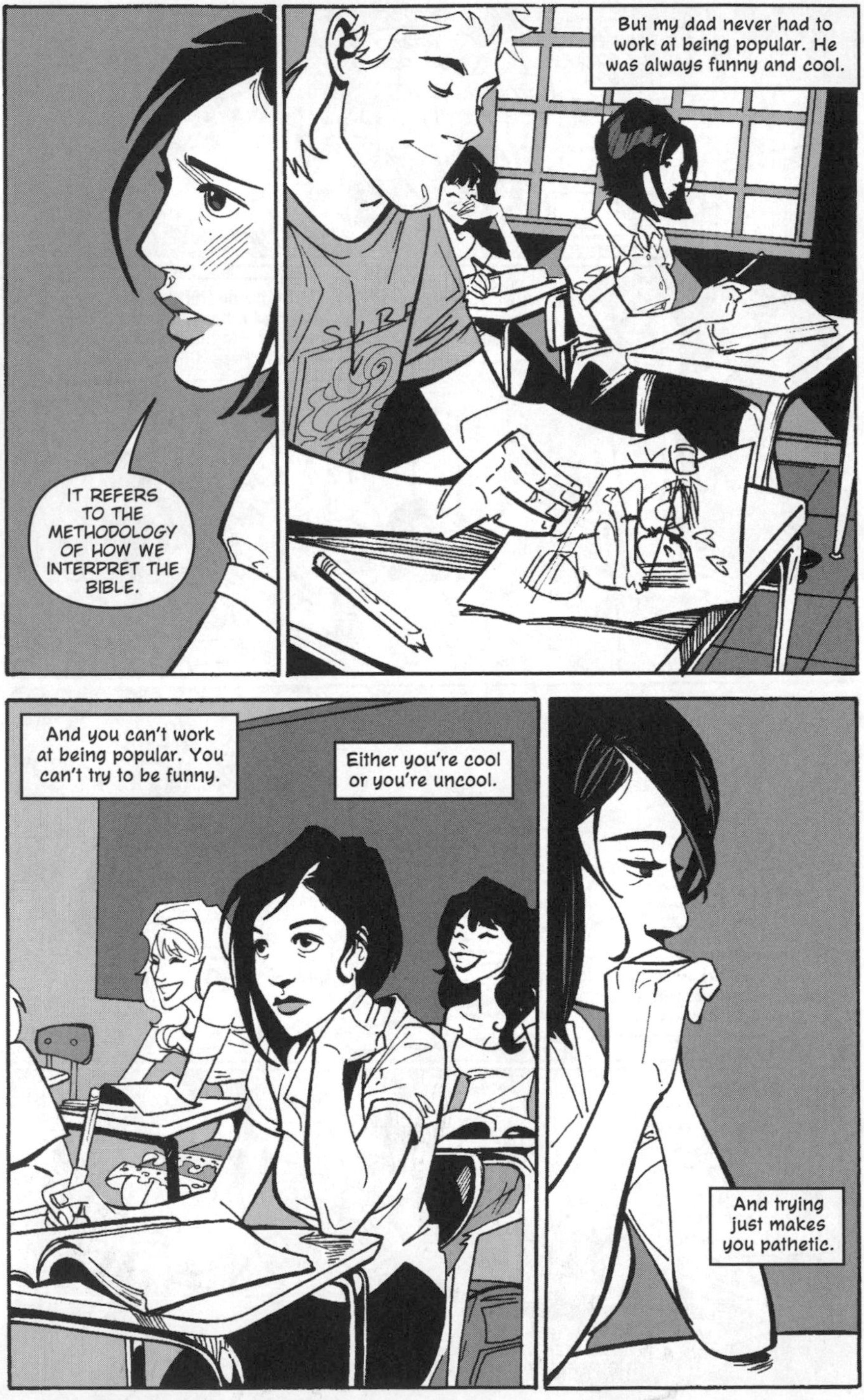
IT REFERS TO THE METHODOLOGY OF HOW WE INTERPRET THE BIBLE.
But my dad never had to work at being popular. He was always funny and cool.
And you can't work at being popular. You can't try to be funny.
Either you're cool or you're uncool.
And trying just makes you pathetic.

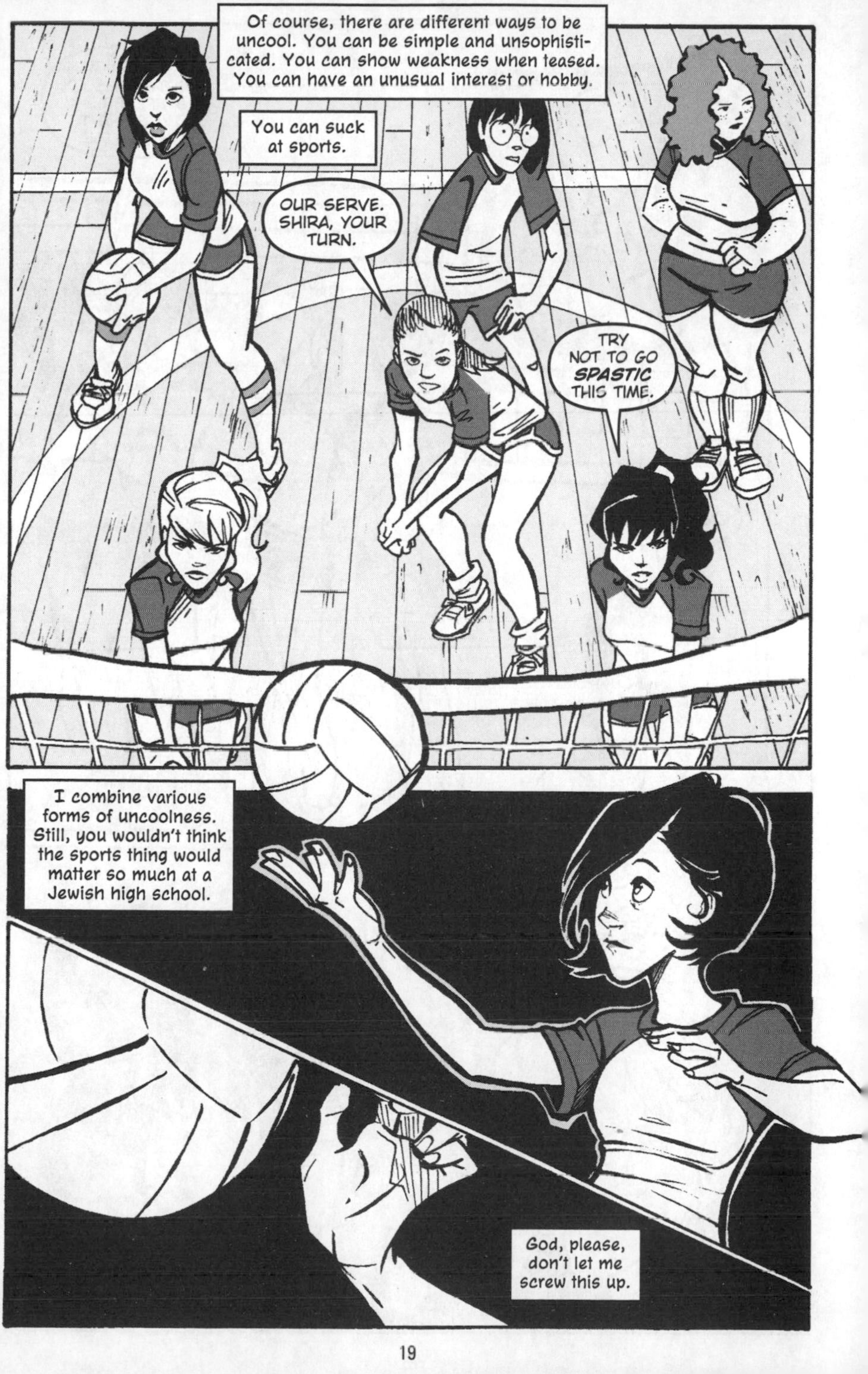
Of course, there are different ways to be uncool. You can be simple and unsophisticated. You can show weakness when teased. You can have an unusual interest or hobby.
You can suck at sports.
OUR SERVE. SHIRA, YOUR TURN.
TRY NOT TO GO SPASTIC THIS TIME.
I combine various forms of uncoolness. Still, you wouldn't think the sports thing would matter so much at a Jewish high school.
God, please, don't let me screw this up.

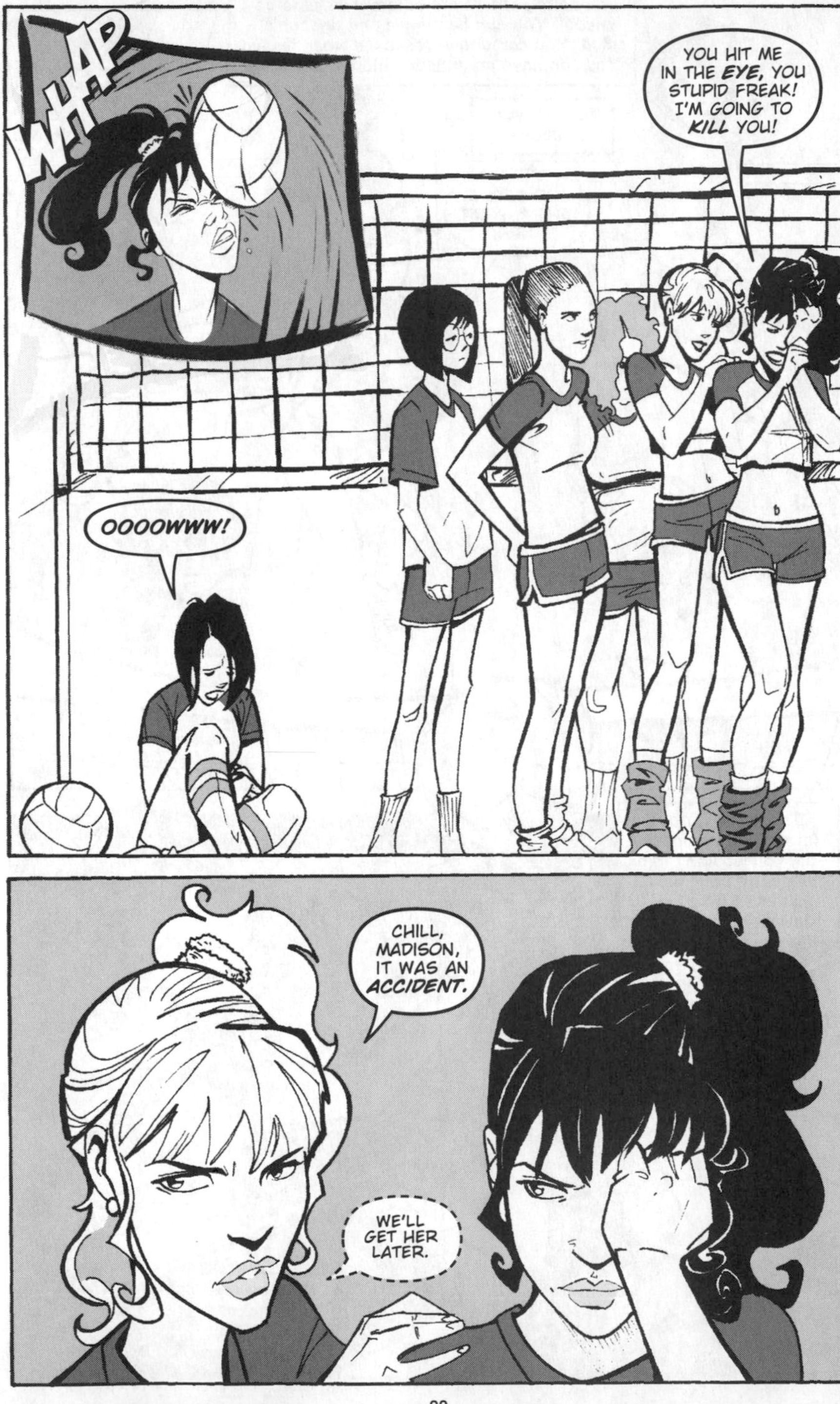
WHAP
YOU HIT ME IN THE *EYE,* YOU STUPID FREAK! I'M GOING TO *KILL* YOU!
OOOOWWW!
CHILL, MADISON, IT WAS AN *ACCIDENT.*
WE'LL GET HER LATER.

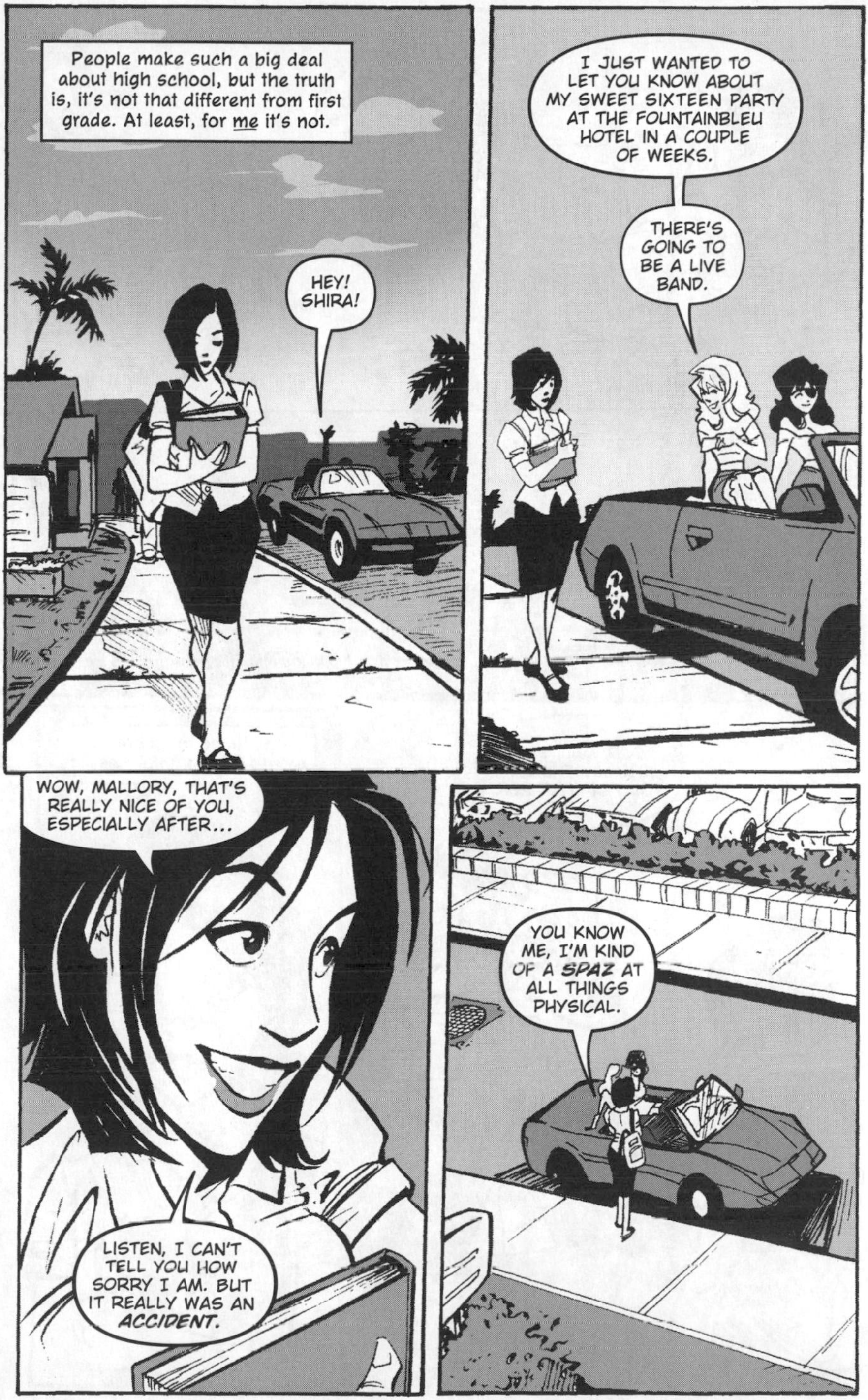
People make such a big deal about high school, but the truth is, it's not that different from first grade. At least, for me it's not.
HEY! SHIRA!
I JUST WANTED TO LET YOU KNOW ABOUT MY SWEET SIXTEEN PARTY AT THE FOUNTAINBLEU HOTEL IN A COUPLE OF WEEKS.
THERE'S GOING TO BE A LIVE BAND.
WOW, MALLORY, THAT'S REALLY NICE OF YOU, ESPECIALLY AFTER...
LISTEN, I CAN'T TELL YOU HOW SORRY I AM. BUT IT REALLY WAS AN ACCIDENT.
YOU KNOW ME, I'M KIND OF A SPAZ AT ALL THINGS PHYSICAL.

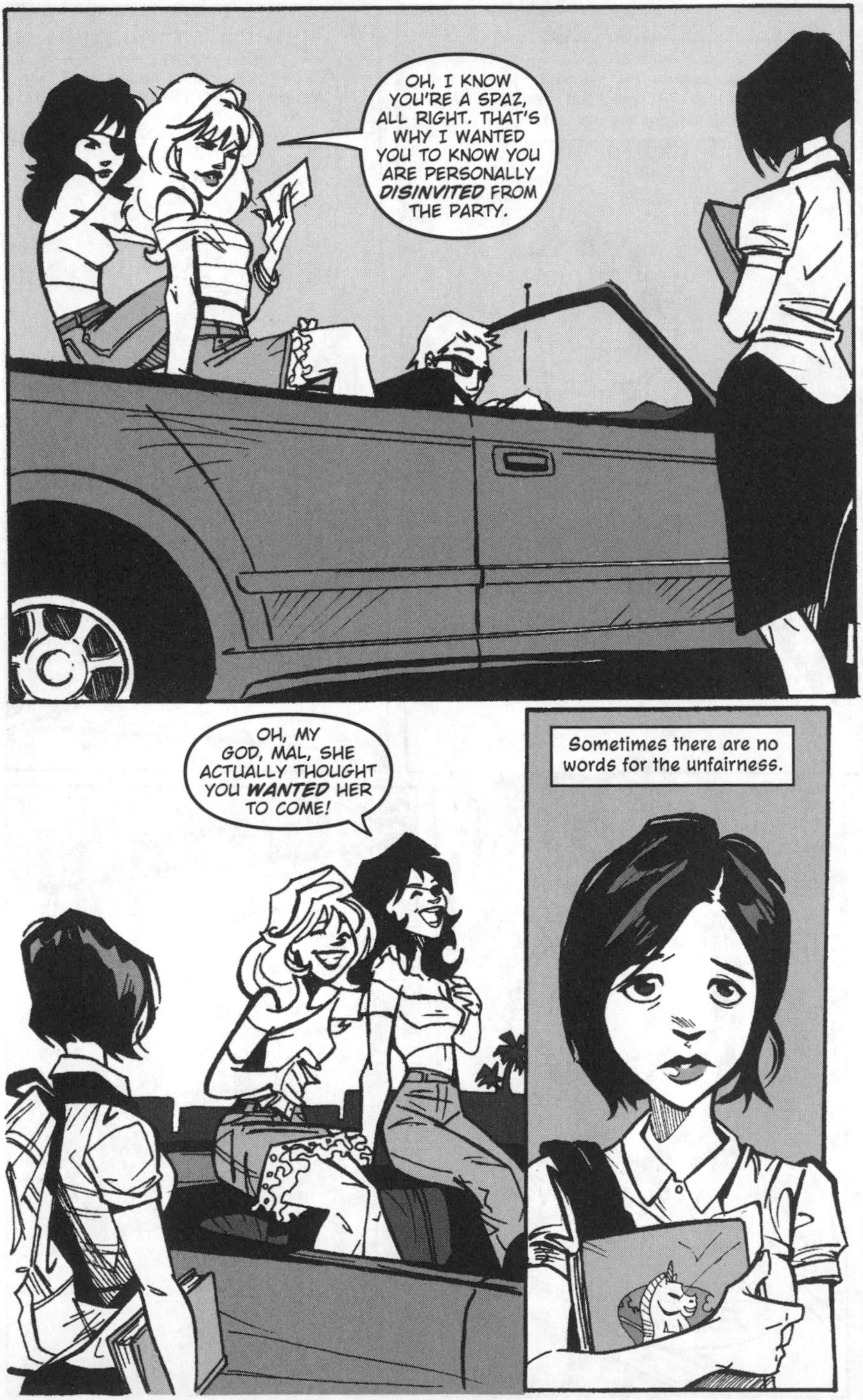
OH, I KNOW YOU'RE A SPAZ, ALL RIGHT. THAT'S WHY I WANTED YOU TO KNOW YOU ARE PERSONALLY ***DISINVITED*** FROM THE PARTY.
OH, MY GOD, MAL, SHE ACTUALLY THOUGHT YOU ***WANTED*** HER TO COME!
Sometimes there are no words for the unfairness.

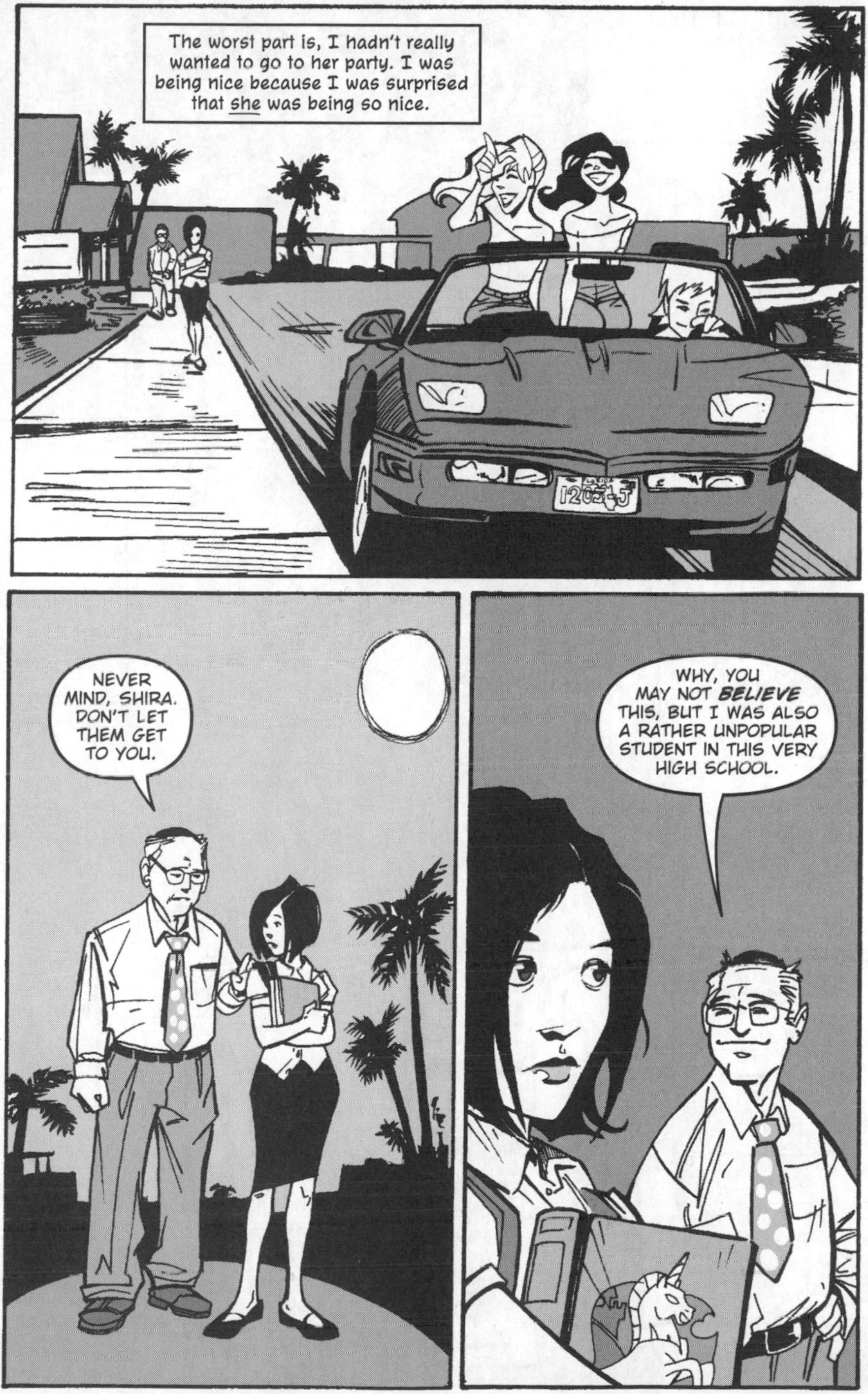
The worst part is, I hadn't really wanted to go to her party. I was being nice because I was surprised that she was being so nice.
NEVER MIND, SHIRA. DON'T LET THEM GET TO YOU.
WHY, YOU MAY NOT BELIEVE THIS, BUT I WAS ALSO A RATHER UNPOPULAR STUDENT IN THIS VERY HIGH SCHOOL.

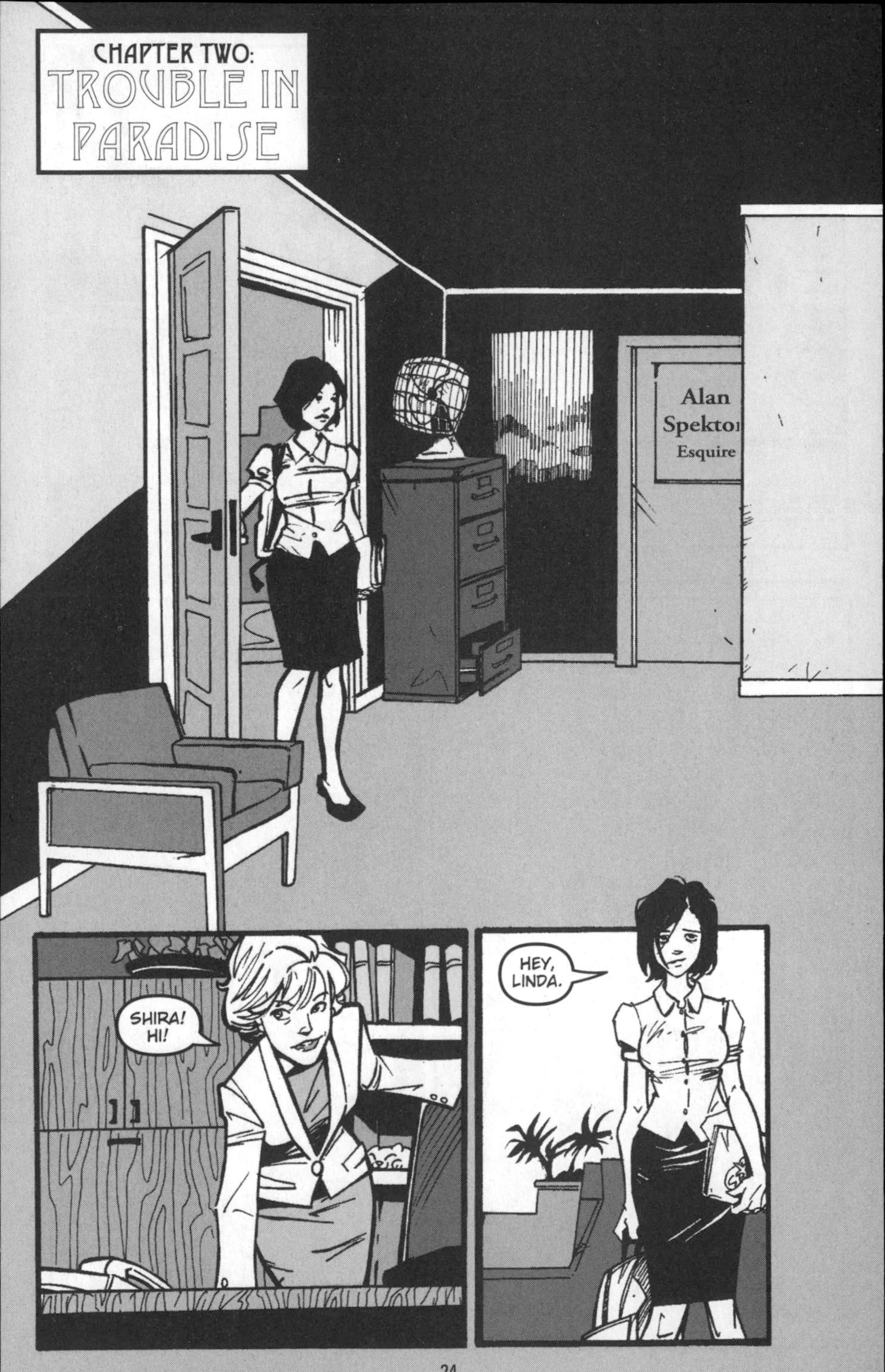
CHAPTER TWO:
TROUBLE IN PARADISE
Alan Spekto Esquire
SHIRA! HI!
HEY, LINDA.

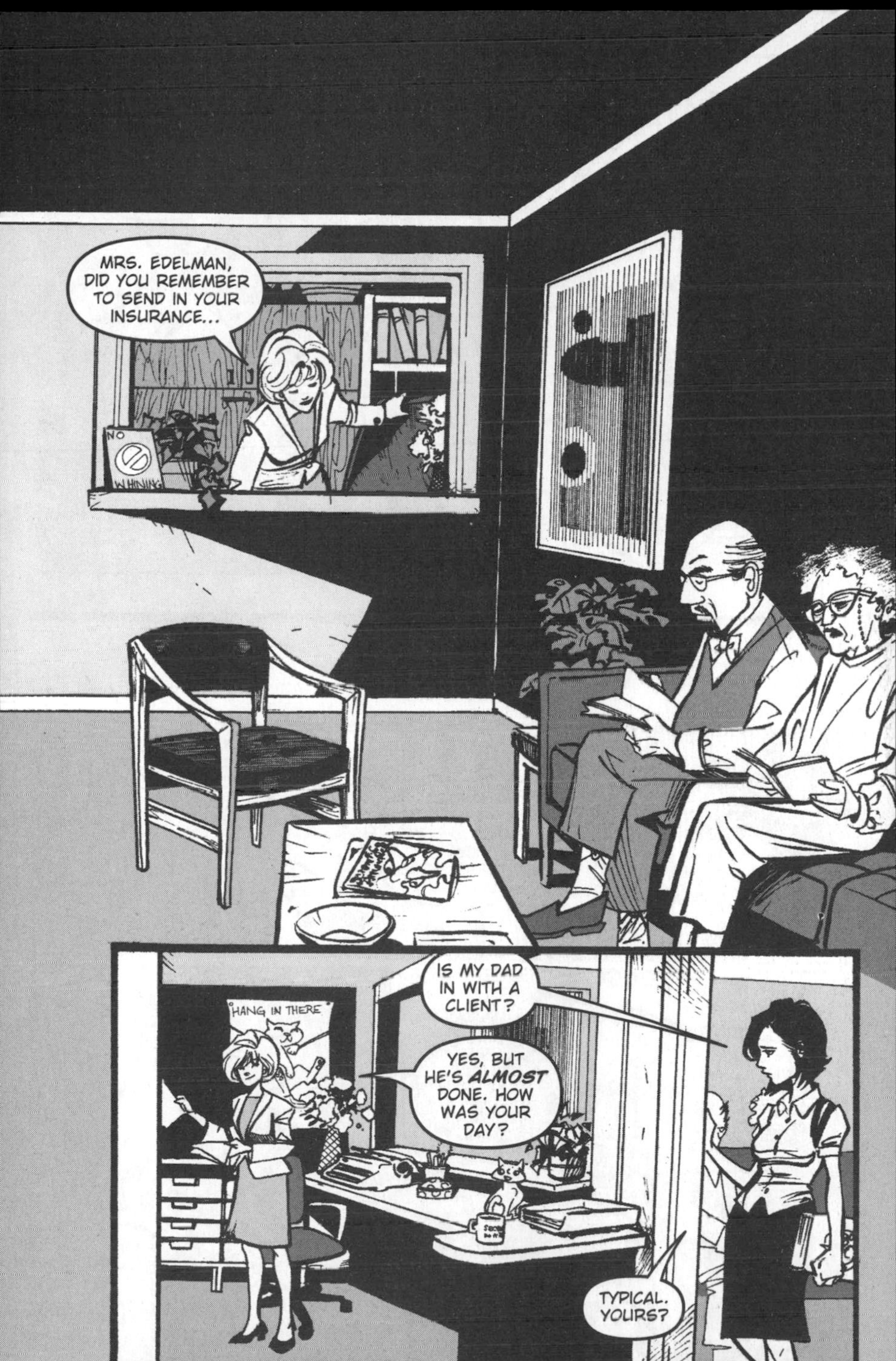
MRS. EDELMAN, DID YOU REMEMBER TO SEND IN YOUR INSURANCE...
NO WHINING
HANG IN THERE
IS MY DAD IN WITH A CLIENT?
YES, BUT HE'S ALMOST DONE. HOW WAS YOUR DAY?
TYPICAL. YOURS?

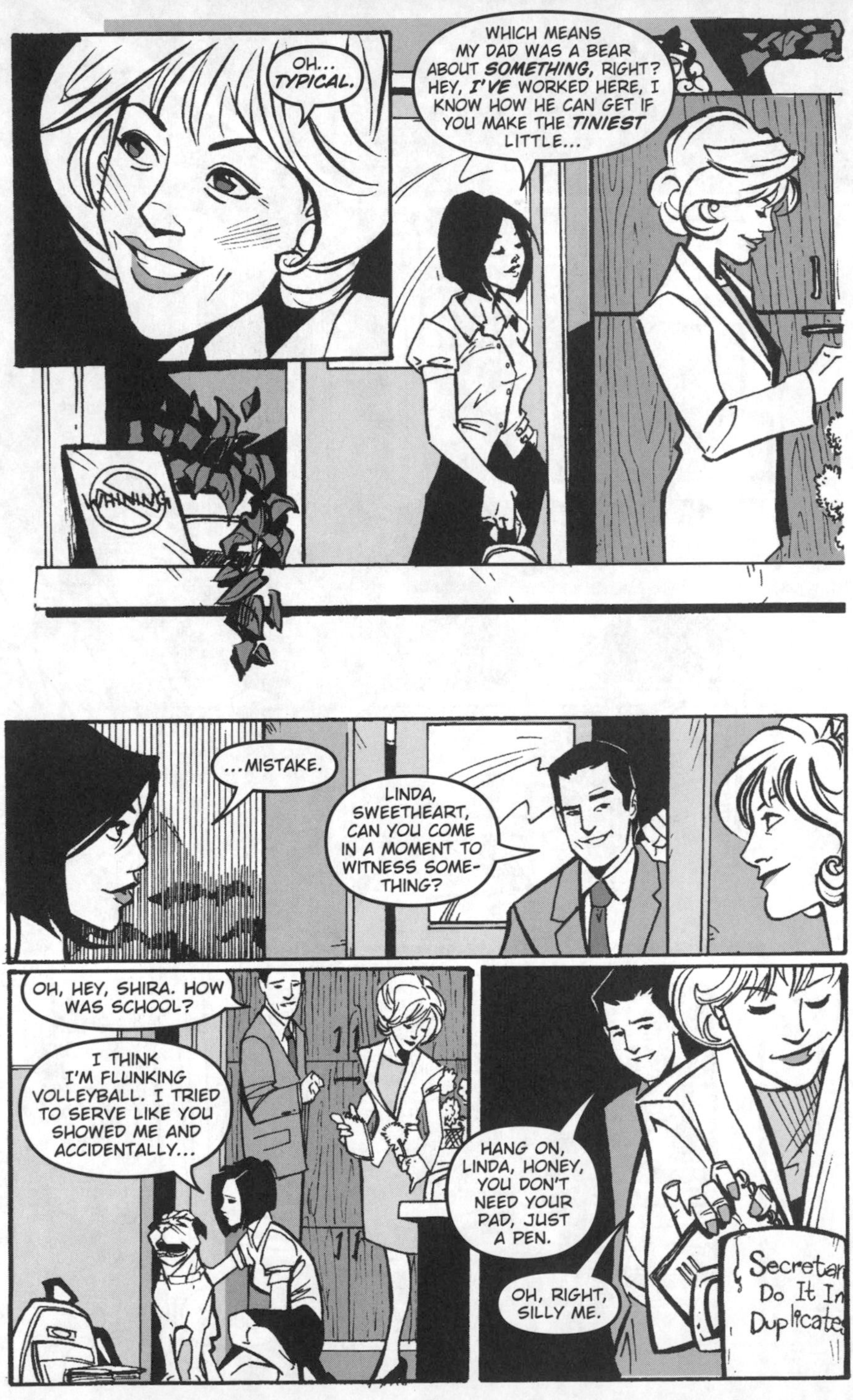
OH... TYPICAL.
WHICH MEANS MY DAD WAS A BEAR ABOUT SOMETHING, RIGHT? HEY, I'VE WORKED HERE, I KNOW HOW HE CAN GET IF YOU MAKE THE TINIEST LITTLE...
WHINING
...MISTAKE.
LINDA, SWEETHEART, CAN YOU COME IN A MOMENT TO WITNESS SOME-THING?
OH, HEY, SHIRA. HOW WAS SCHOOL?
I THINK I'M FLUNKING VOLLEYBALL. I TRIED TO SERVE LIKE YOU SHOWED ME AND ACCIDENTALLY...
HANG ON, LINDA, HONEY, YOU DON'T NEED YOUR PAD, JUST A PEN.
OH, RIGHT, SILLY ME.
Secretar Do It In Duplicates

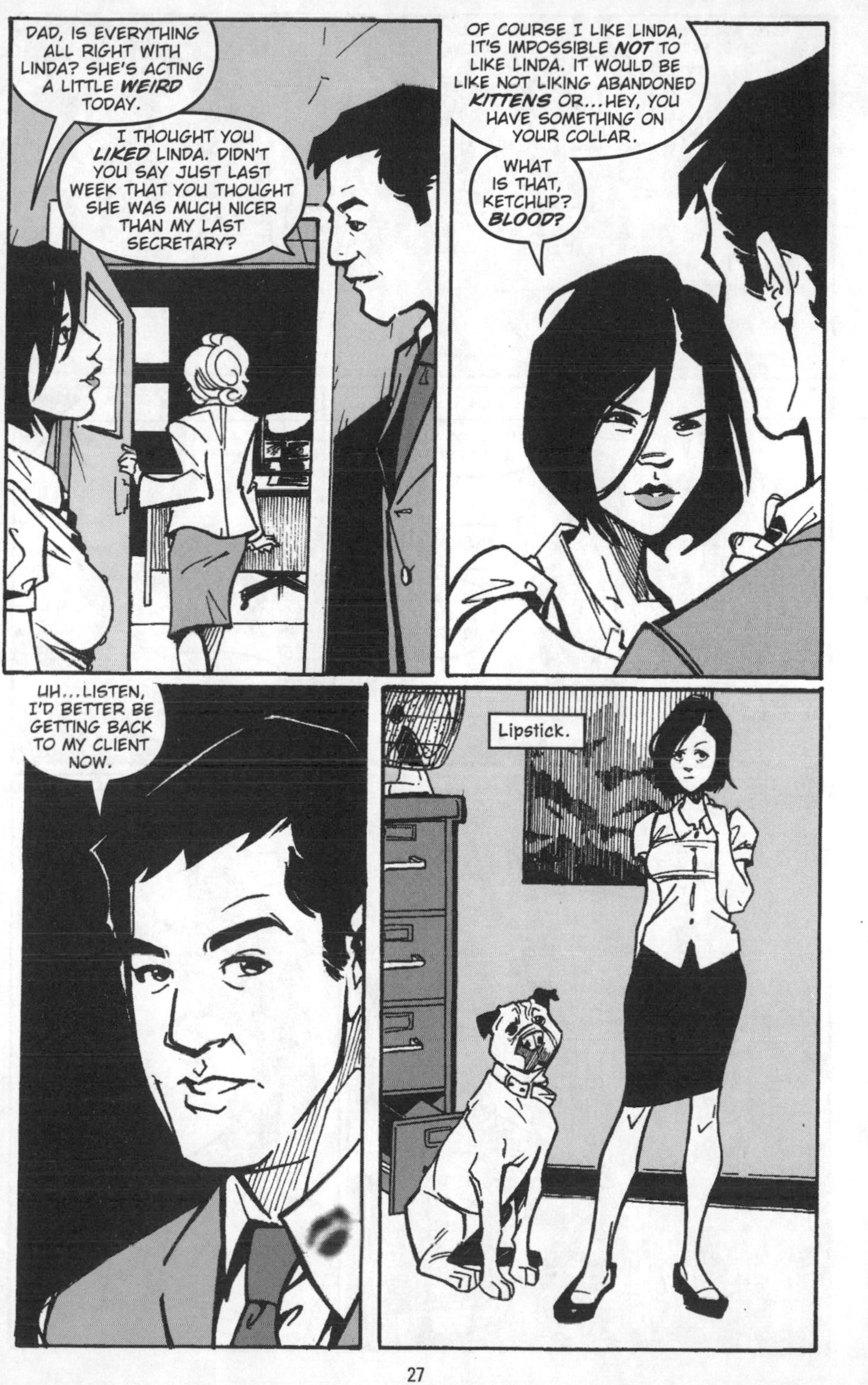
DAD, IS EVERYTHING ALL RIGHT WITH LINDA? SHE'S ACTING A LITTLE *WEIRD* TODAY.
I THOUGHT YOU *LIKED* LINDA. DIDN'T YOU SAY JUST LAST WEEK THAT YOU THOUGHT SHE WAS MUCH NICER THAN MY LAST SECRETARY?
OF COURSE I LIKE LINDA, IT'S IMPOSSIBLE *NOT* TO LIKE LINDA. IT WOULD BE LIKE NOT LIKING ABANDONED *KITTENS* OR...HEY, YOU HAVE SOMETHING ON YOUR COLLAR.
WHAT IS THAT, KETCHUP? *BLOOD?*
UH...LISTEN, I'D BETTER BE GETTING BACK TO MY CLIENT NOW.
Lipstick.

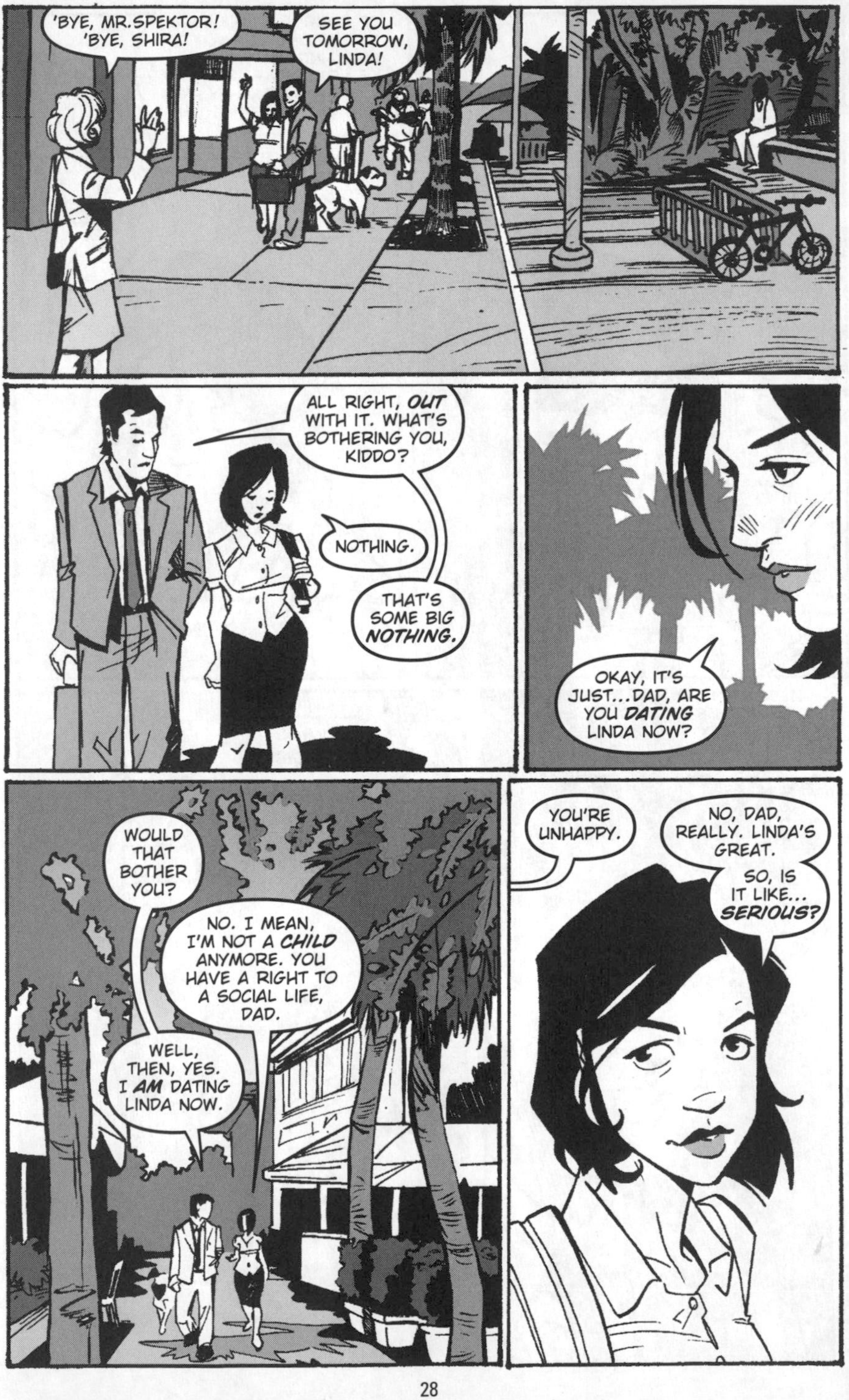
'BYE, MR.SPEKTOR! 'BYE, SHIRA!
SEE YOU TOMORROW, LINDA!
ALL RIGHT, OUT WITH IT. WHAT'S BOTHERING YOU, KIDDO?
NOTHING.
THAT'S SOME BIG NOTHING.
OKAY, IT'S JUST...DAD, ARE YOU DATING LINDA NOW?
WOULD THAT BOTHER YOU?
NO. I MEAN, I'M NOT A CHILD ANYMORE. YOU HAVE A RIGHT TO A SOCIAL LIFE, DAD.
WELL, THEN, YES. I AM DATING LINDA NOW.
YOU'RE UNHAPPY.
NO, DAD, REALLY. LINDA'S GREAT.
SO, IS IT LIKE... SERIOUS?

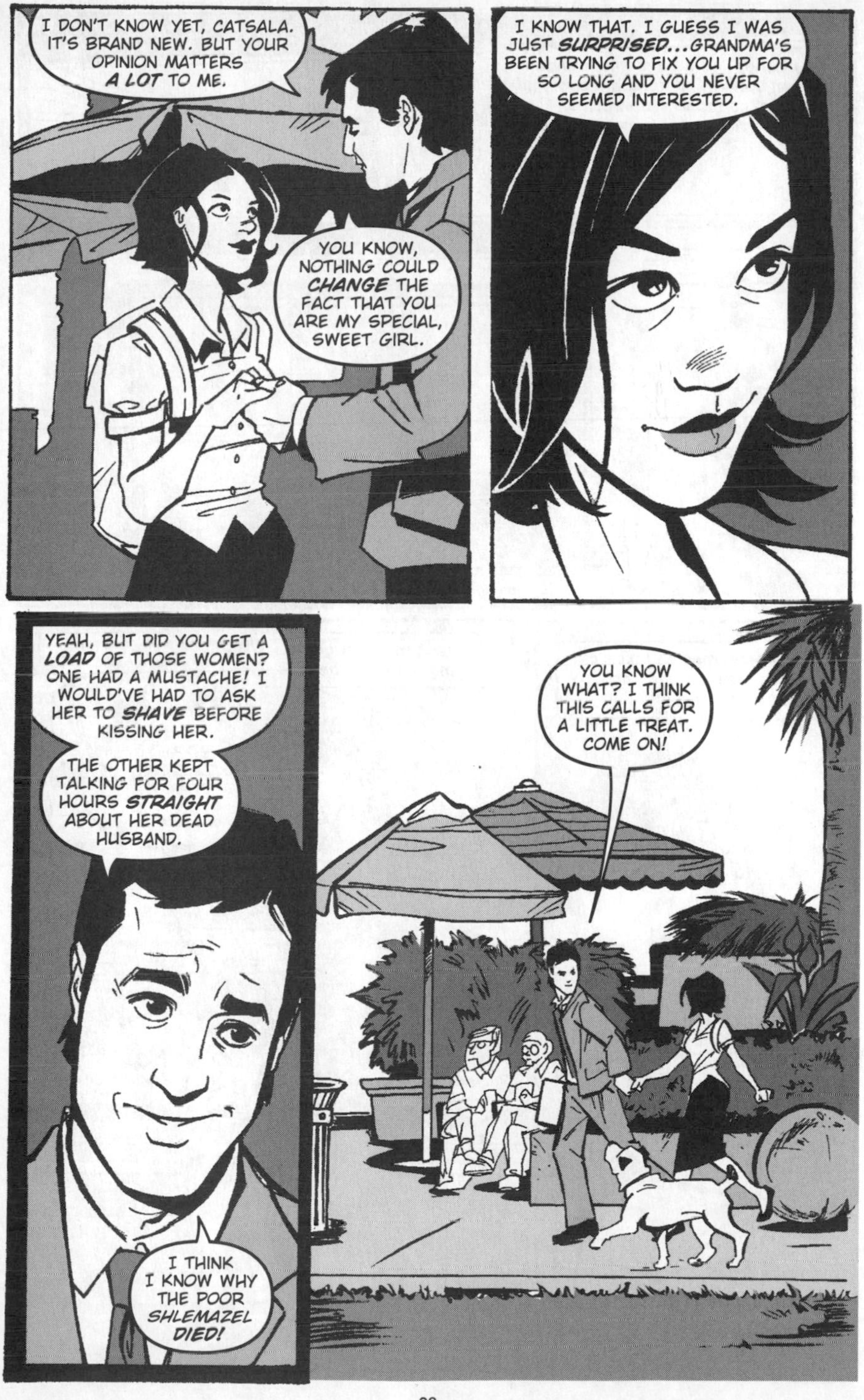
I DON'T KNOW YET, CATSALA. IT'S BRAND NEW. BUT YOUR OPINION MATTERS A LOT TO ME.
YOU KNOW, NOTHING COULD CHANGE THE FACT THAT YOU ARE MY SPECIAL, SWEET GIRL.
I KNOW THAT. I GUESS I WAS JUST SURPRISED...GRANDMA'S BEEN TRYING TO FIX YOU UP FOR SO LONG AND YOU NEVER SEEMED INTERESTED.
YEAH, BUT DID YOU GET A LOAD OF THOSE WOMEN? ONE HAD A MUSTACHE! I WOULD'VE HAD TO ASK HER TO SHAVE BEFORE KISSING HER.
THE OTHER KEPT TALKING FOR FOUR HOURS STRAIGHT ABOUT HER DEAD HUSBAND.
I THINK I KNOW WHY THE POOR SHLEMAZEL DIED!
YOU KNOW WHAT? I THINK THIS CALLS FOR A LITTLE TREAT. COME ON!

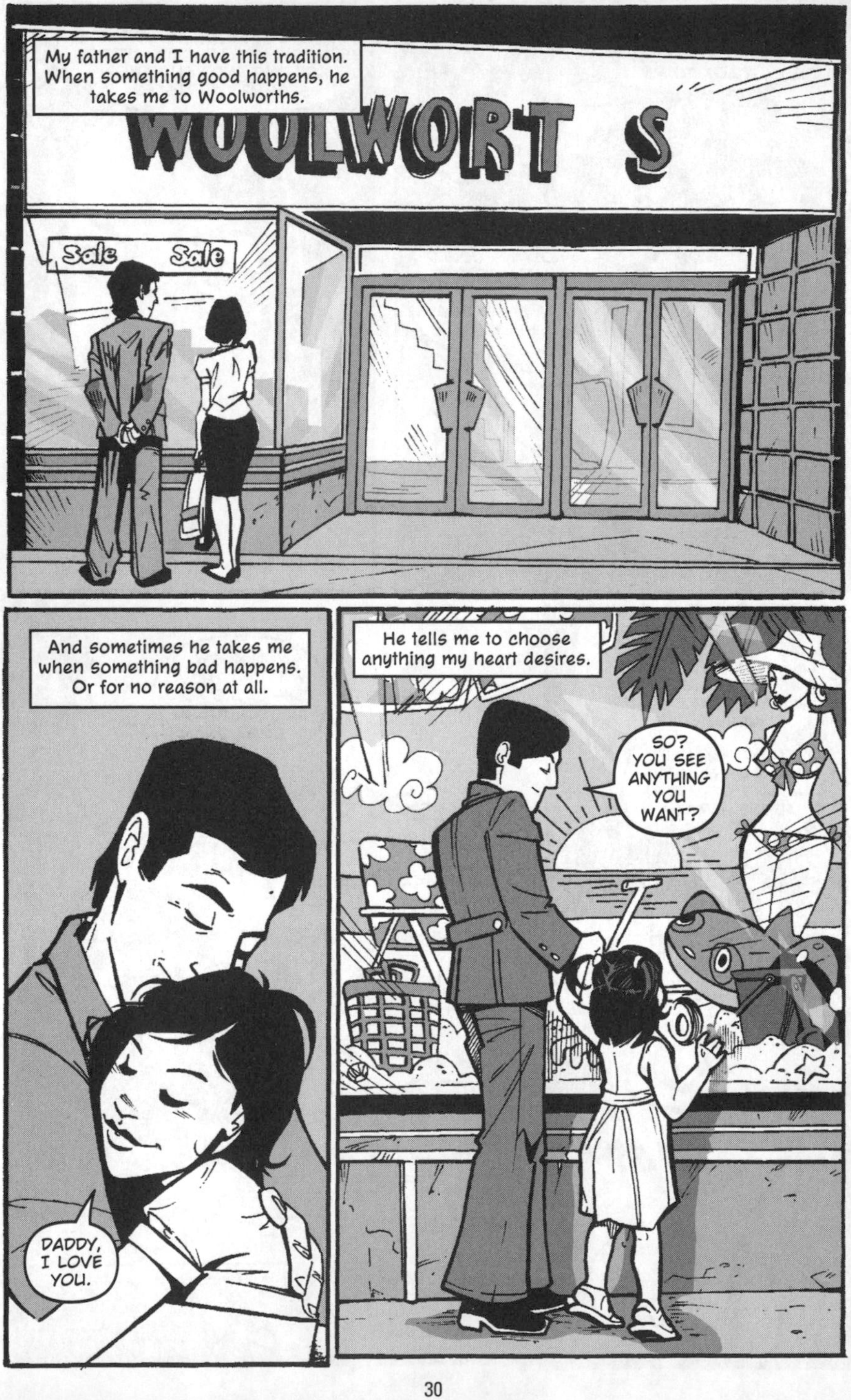
My father and I have this tradition. When something good happens, he takes me to Woolworths.
WOOLWORT S
Sale
Sale
And sometimes he takes me when something bad happens. Or for no reason at all.
DADDY, I LOVE YOU.
He tells me to choose anything my heart desires.
SO? YOU SEE ANYTHING YOU WANT?

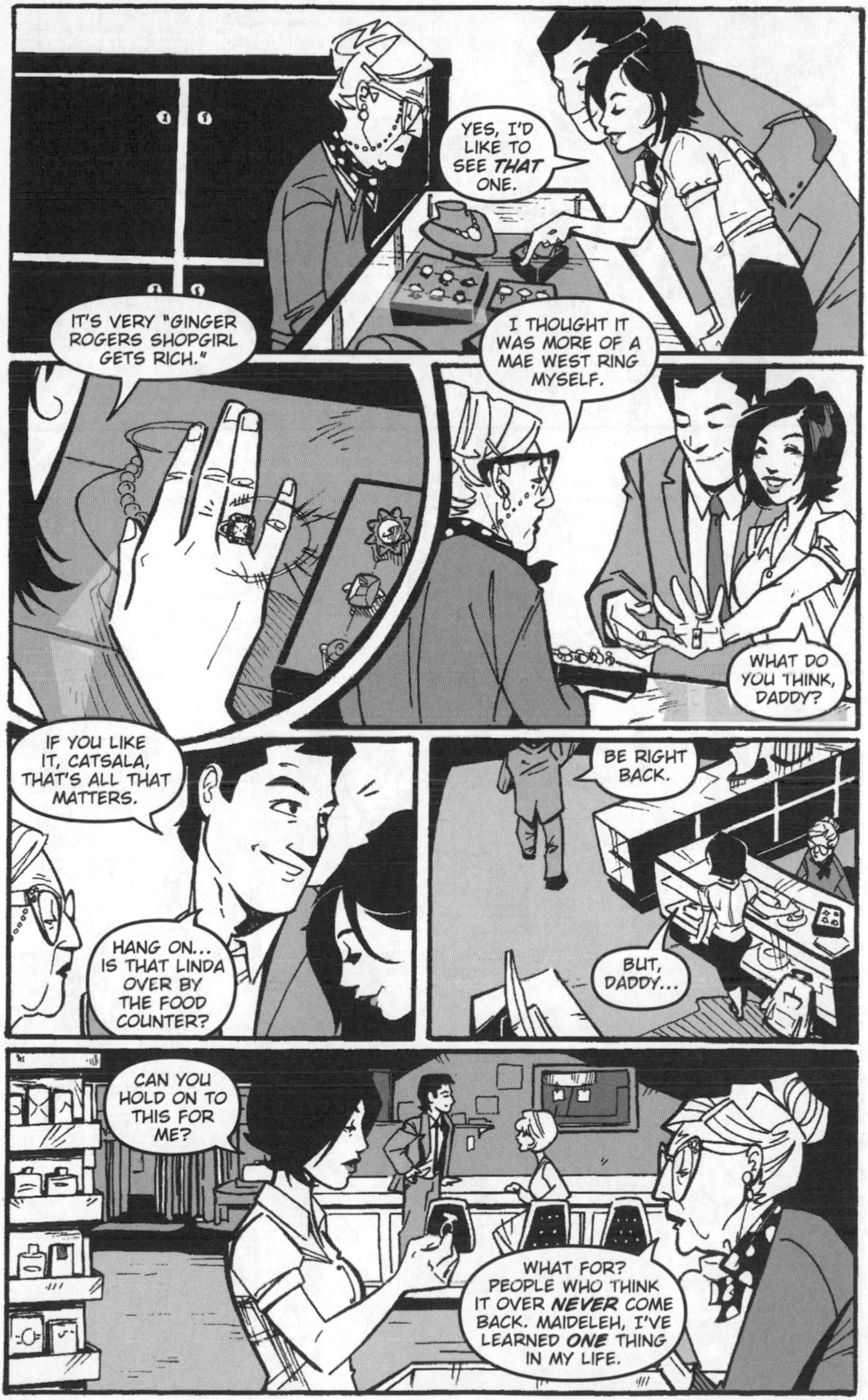
YES, I'D LIKE TO SEE THAT ONE.
IT'S VERY "GINGER ROGERS SHOPGIRL GETS RICH."
I THOUGHT IT WAS MORE OF A MAE WEST RING MYSELF.
WHAT DO YOU THINK, DADDY?
IF YOU LIKE IT, CATSALA, THAT'S ALL THAT MATTERS.
HANG ON... IS THAT LINDA OVER BY THE FOOD COUNTER?
BE RIGHT BACK.
BUT, DADDY...
CAN YOU HOLD ON TO THIS FOR ME?
WHAT FOR? PEOPLE WHO THINK IT OVER NEVER COME BACK. MAIDELEH, I'VE LEARNED ONE THING IN MY LIFE.

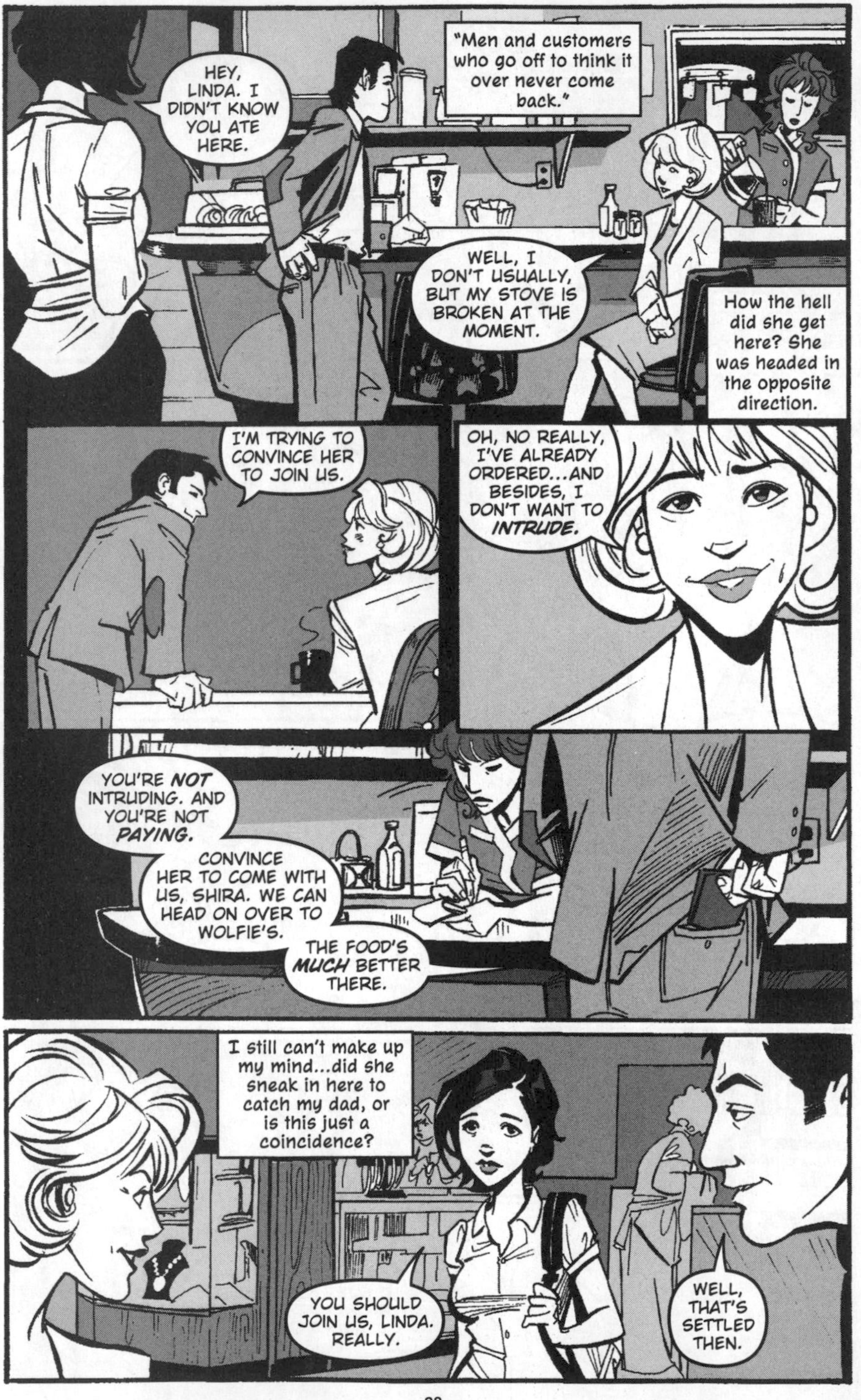
HEY, LINDA. I DIDN'T KNOW YOU ATE HERE.
"Men and customers who go off to think it over never come back."
WELL, I DON'T USUALLY, BUT MY STOVE IS BROKEN AT THE MOMENT.
How the hell did she get here? She was headed in the opposite direction.
I'M TRYING TO CONVINCE HER TO JOIN US.
OH, NO REALLY, I'VE ALREADY ORDERED...AND BESIDES, I DON'T WANT TO INTRUDE.
YOU'RE NOT INTRUDING. AND YOU'RE NOT PAYING.
CONVINCE HER TO COME WITH US, SHIRA. WE CAN HEAD ON OVER TO WOLFIE'S.
THE FOOD'S MUCH BETTER THERE.
I still can't make up my mind...did she sneak in here to catch my dad, or is this just a coincidence?
YOU SHOULD JOIN US, LINDA. REALLY.
WELL, THAT'S SETTLED THEN.

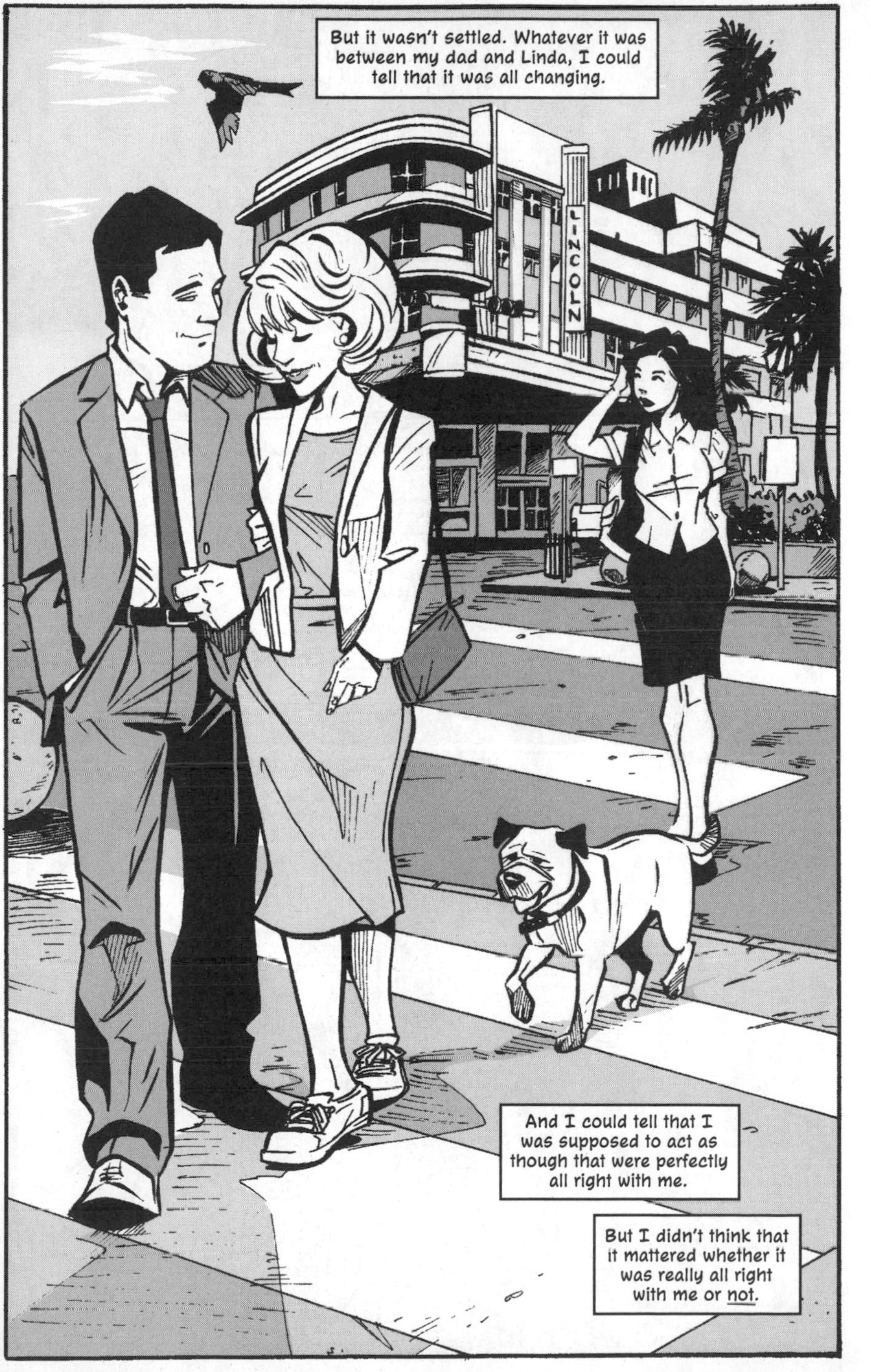
But it wasn't settled. Whatever it was between my dad and Linda, I could tell that it was all changing.
LINCOLN
And I could tell that I was supposed to act as though that were perfectly all right with me.
But I didn't think that it mattered whether it was really all right with me or not.

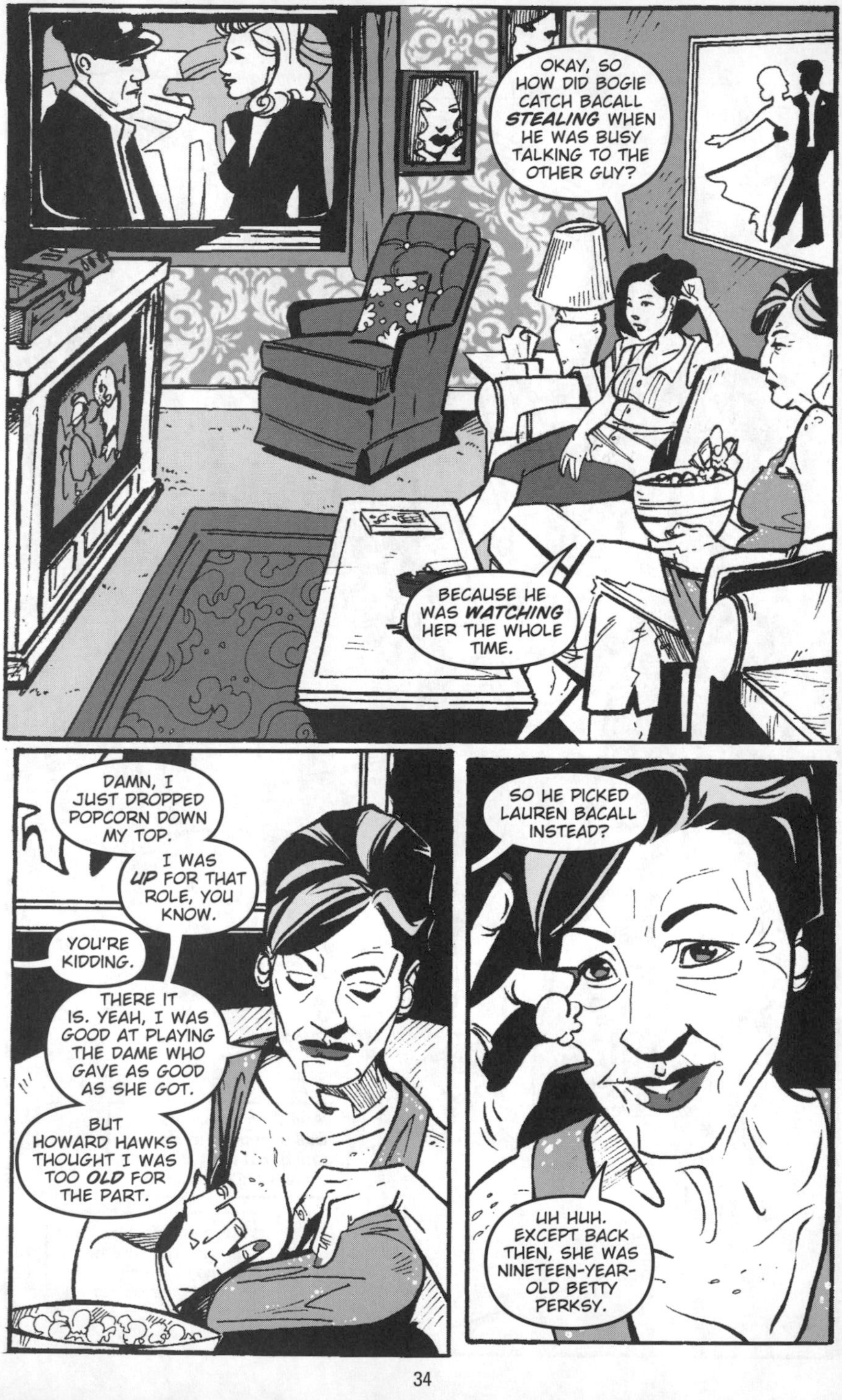
OKAY, SO HOW DID BOGIE CATCH BACALL STEALING WHEN HE WAS BUSY TALKING TO THE OTHER GUY?
BECAUSE HE WAS WATCHING HER THE WHOLE TIME.
DAMN, I JUST DROPPED POPCORN DOWN MY TOP.
I WAS UP FOR THAT ROLE, YOU KNOW.
YOU'RE KIDDING.
THERE IT IS. YEAH, I WAS GOOD AT PLAYING THE DAME WHO GAVE AS GOOD AS SHE GOT.
BUT HOWARD HAWKS THOUGHT I WAS TOO OLD FOR THE PART.
SO HE PICKED LAUREN BACALL INSTEAD?
UH HUH. EXCEPT BACK THEN, SHE WAS NINETEEN-YEAR-OLD BETTY PERKSY.

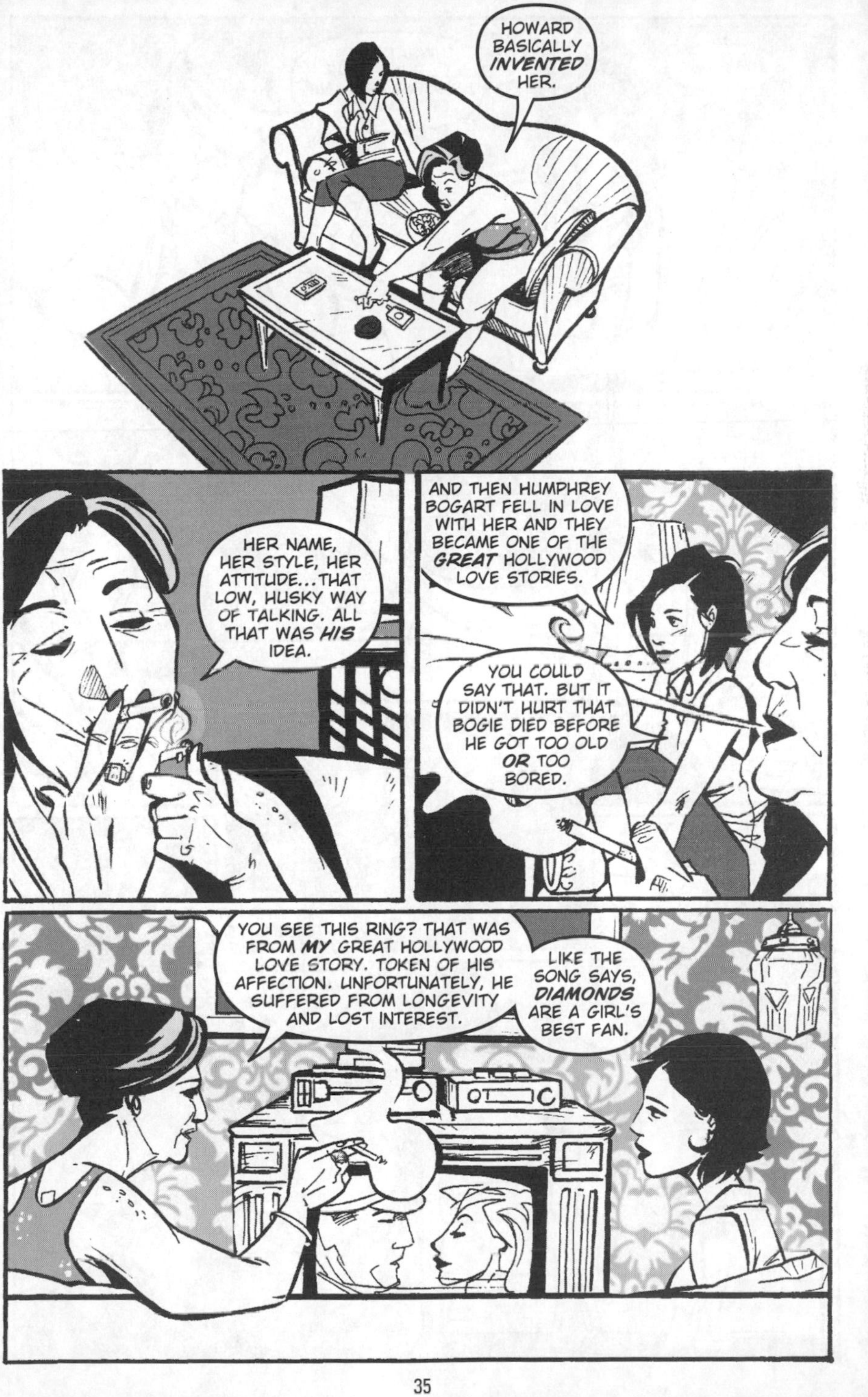
HOWARD BASICALLY INVENTED HER.
HER NAME, HER STYLE, HER ATTITUDE...THAT LOW, HUSKY WAY OF TALKING. ALL THAT WAS HIS IDEA.
AND THEN HUMPHREY BOGART FELL IN LOVE WITH HER AND THEY BECAME ONE OF THE GREAT HOLLYWOOD LOVE STORIES.
YOU COULD SAY THAT. BUT IT DIDN'T HURT THAT BOGIE DIED BEFORE HE GOT TOO OLD OR TOO BORED.
YOU SEE THIS RING? THAT WAS FROM MY GREAT HOLLYWOOD LOVE STORY. TOKEN OF HIS AFFECTION. UNFORTUNATELY, HE SUFFERED FROM LONGEVITY AND LOST INTEREST.
LIKE THE SONG SAYS, DIAMONDS ARE A GIRL'S BEST FAN.

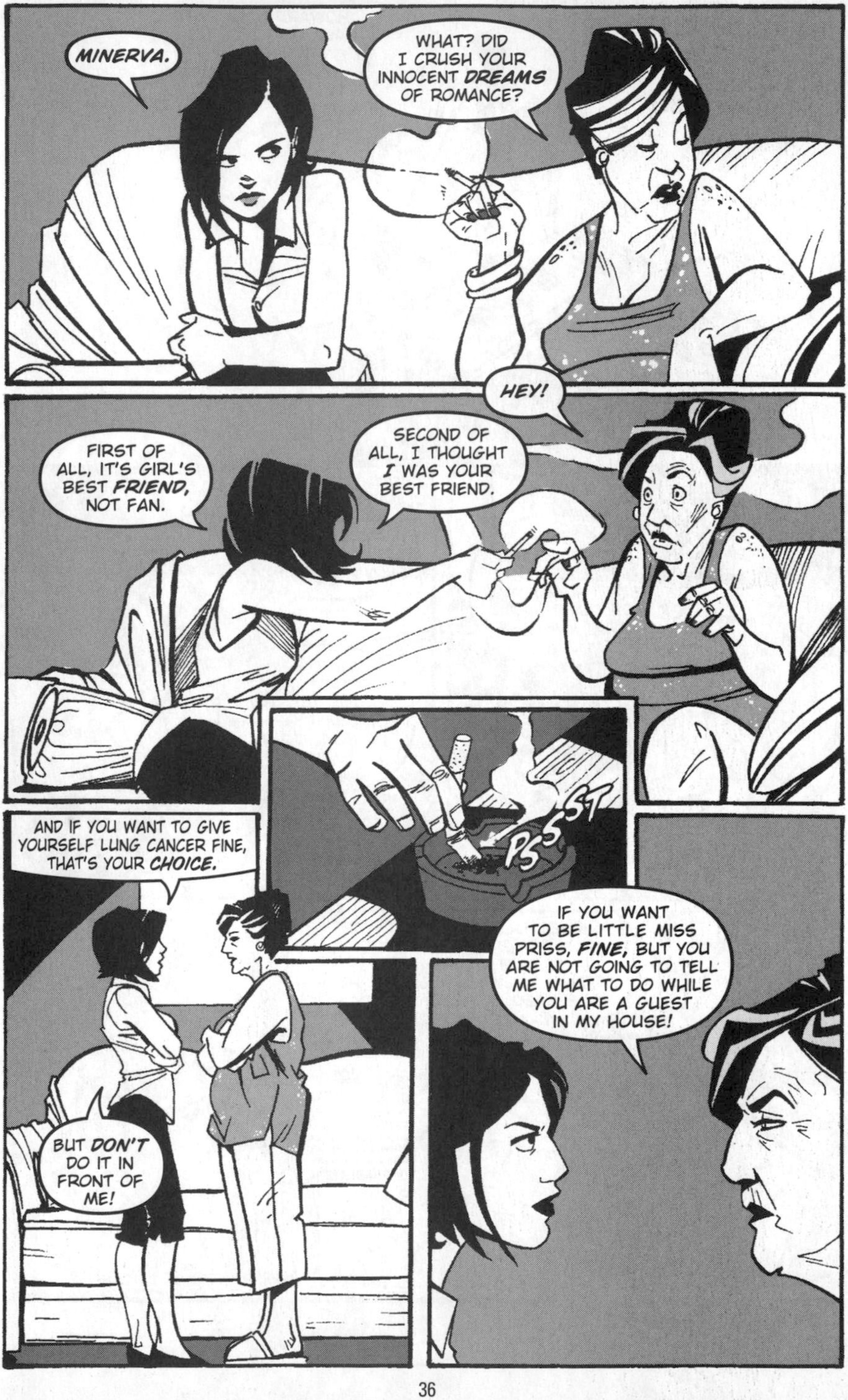

MINERVA.
WHAT? DID I CRUSH YOUR INNOCENT DREAMS OF ROMANCE?
HEY!
FIRST OF ALL, IT'S GIRL'S BEST FRIEND, NOT FAN.
SECOND OF ALL, I THOUGHT I WAS YOUR BEST FRIEND.
PSSSST
AND IF YOU WANT TO GIVE YOURSELF LUNG CANCER FINE, THAT'S YOUR CHOICE.
BUT DON'T DO IT IN FRONT OF ME!
IF YOU WANT TO BE LITTLE MISS PRISS, FINE, BUT YOU ARE NOT GOING TO TELL ME WHAT TO DO WHILE YOU ARE A GUEST IN MY HOUSE!

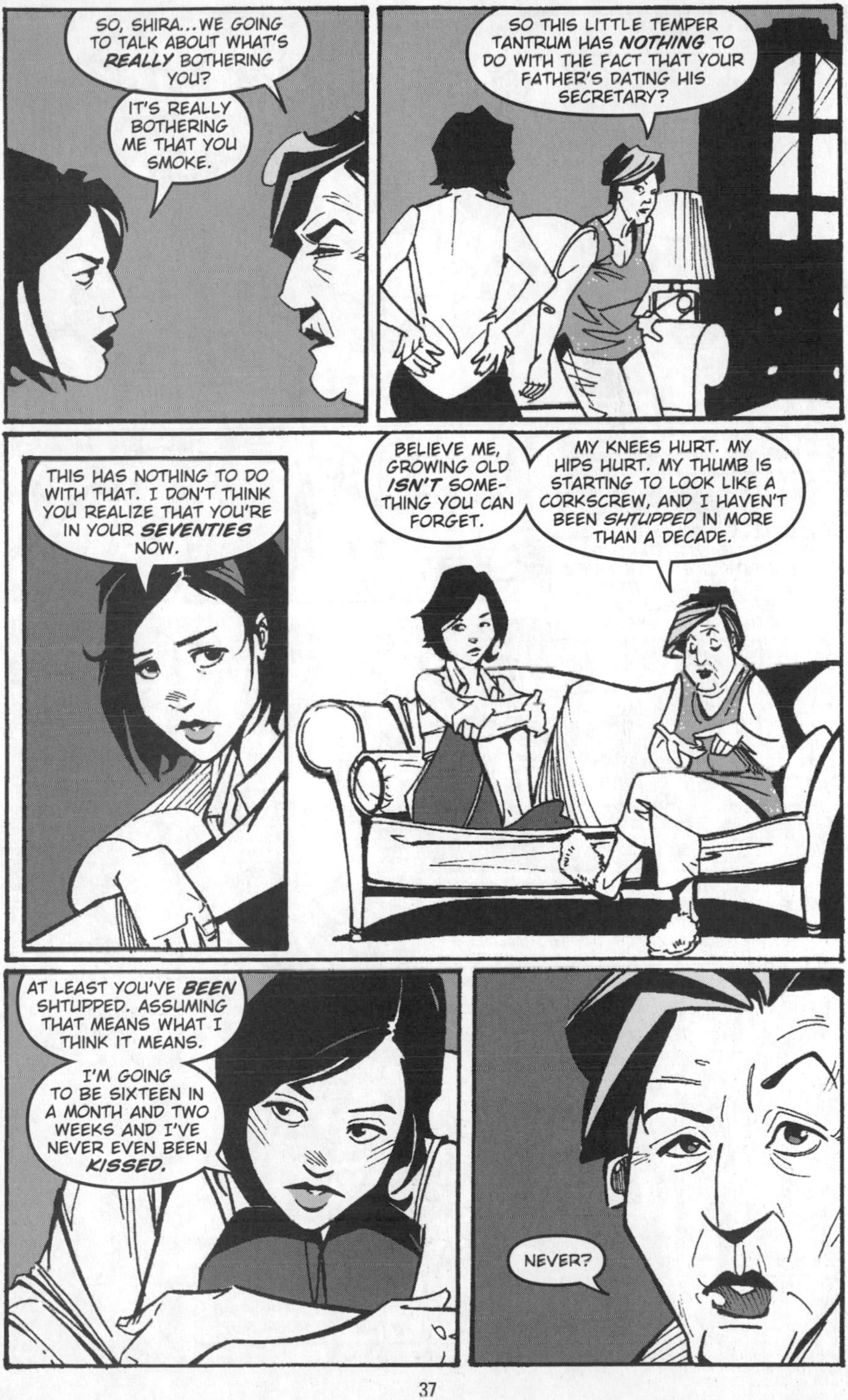
SO, SHIRA...WE GOING TO TALK ABOUT WHAT'S REALLY BOTHERING YOU?
IT'S REALLY BOTHERING ME THAT YOU SMOKE.
SO THIS LITTLE TEMPER TANTRUM HAS NOTHING TO DO WITH THE FACT THAT YOUR FATHER'S DATING HIS SECRETARY?
THIS HAS NOTHING TO DO WITH THAT. I DON'T THINK YOU REALIZE THAT YOU'RE IN YOUR SEVENTIES NOW.
BELIEVE ME, GROWING OLD ISN'T SOMETHING YOU CAN FORGET.
MY KNEES HURT. MY HIPS HURT. MY THUMB IS STARTING TO LOOK LIKE A CORKSCREW, AND I HAVEN'T BEEN SHTUPPED IN MORE THAN A DECADE.
AT LEAST YOU'VE BEEN SHTUPPED. ASSUMING THAT MEANS WHAT I THINK IT MEANS.
I'M GOING TO BE SIXTEEN IN A MONTH AND TWO WEEKS AND I'VE NEVER EVEN BEEN KISSED.
NEVER?

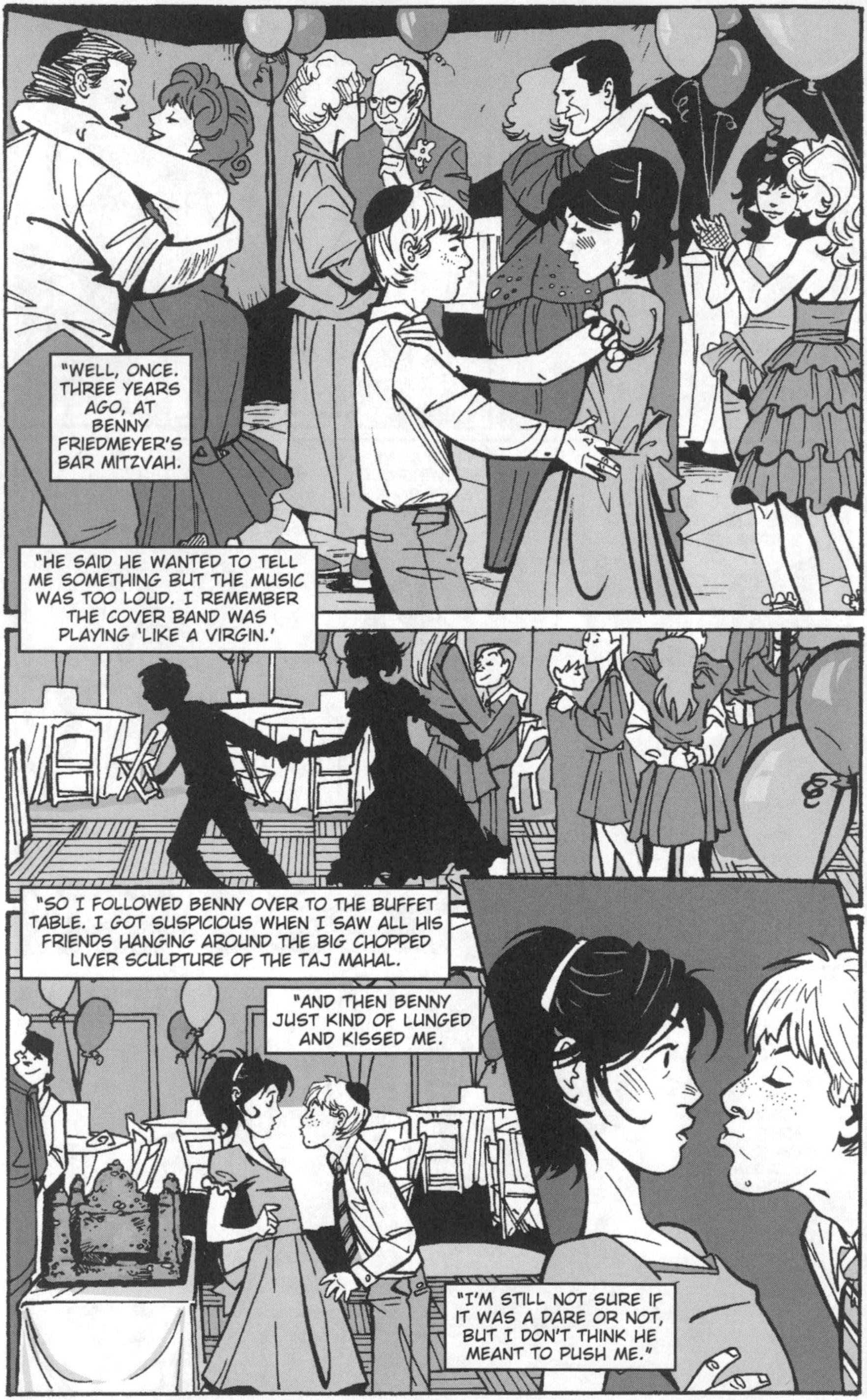
"WELL, ONCE. THREE YEARS AGO, AT BENNY FRIEDMEYER'S BAR MITZVAH.
"HE SAID HE WANTED TO TELL ME SOMETHING BUT THE MUSIC WAS TOO LOUD. I REMEMBER THE COVER BAND WAS PLAYING 'LIKE A VIRGIN.'
"SO I FOLLOWED BENNY OVER TO THE BUFFET TABLE. I GOT SUSPICIOUS WHEN I SAW ALL HIS FRIENDS HANGING AROUND THE BIG CHOPPED LIVER SCULPTURE OF THE TAJ MAHAL.
"AND THEN BENNY JUST KIND OF LUNGED AND KISSED ME.
"I'M STILL NOT SURE IF IT WAS A DARE OR NOT, BUT I DON'T THINK HE MEANT TO PUSH ME."

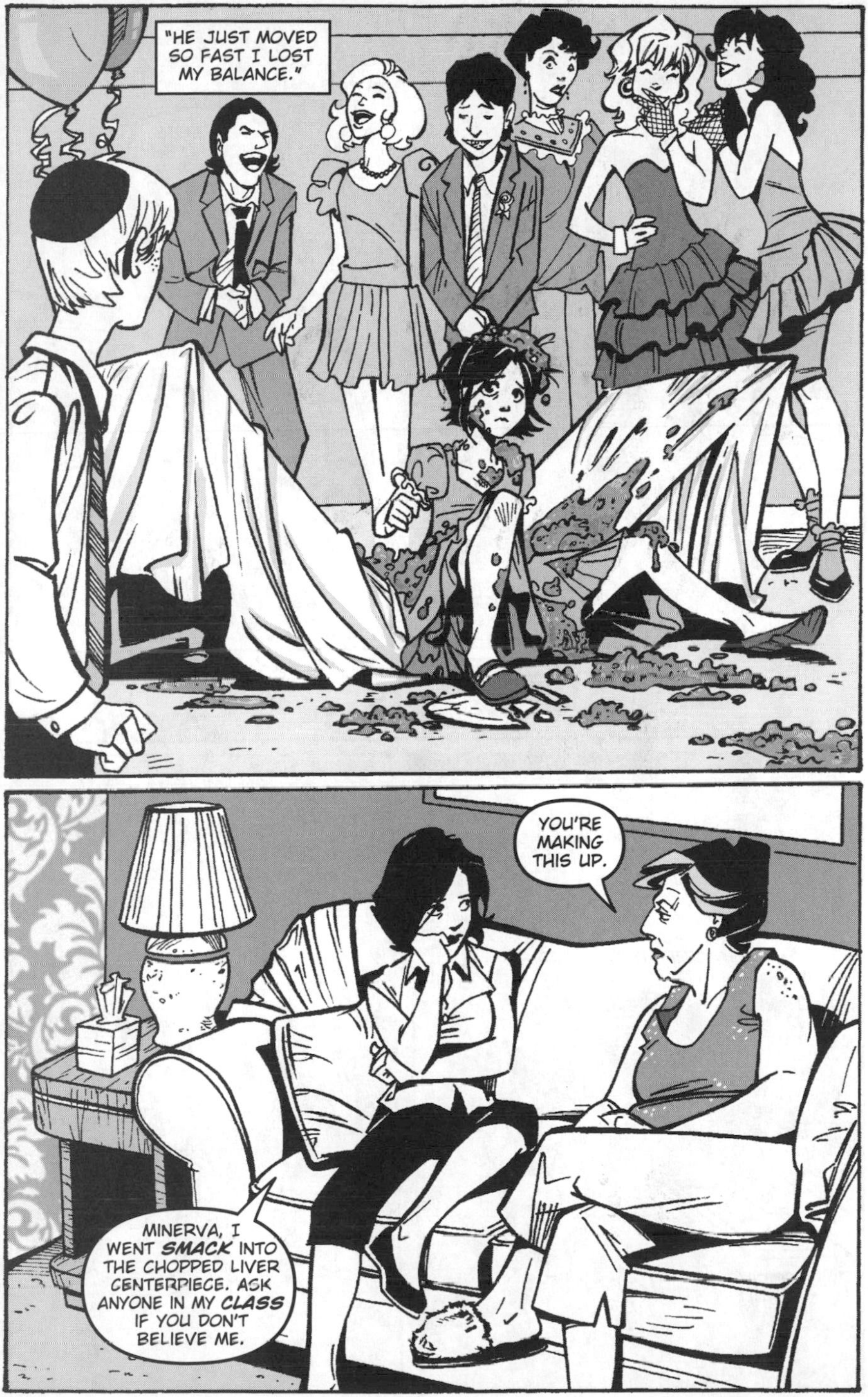
"HE JUST MOVED SO FAST I LOST MY BALANCE."
YOU'RE MAKING THIS UP.
MINERVA, I WENT SMACK INTO THE CHOPPED LIVER CENTERPIECE. ASK ANYONE IN MY CLASS IF YOU DON'T BELIEVE ME.

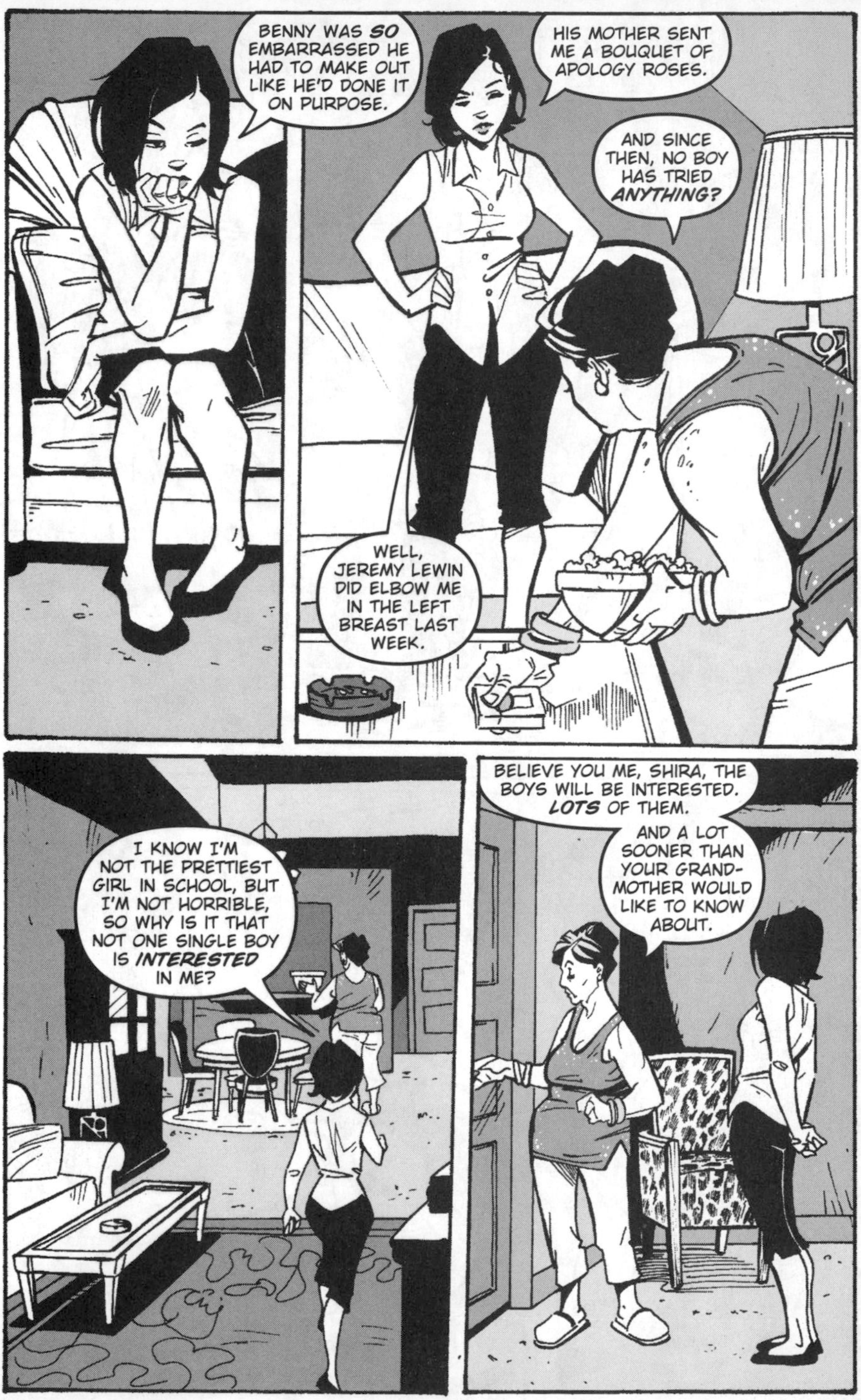
BENNY WAS SO EMBARRASSED HE HAD TO MAKE OUT LIKE HE'D DONE IT ON PURPOSE.
HIS MOTHER SENT ME A BOUQUET OF APOLOGY ROSES.
AND SINCE THEN, NO BOY HAS TRIED ANYTHING?
WELL, JEREMY LEWIN DID ELBOW ME IN THE LEFT BREAST LAST WEEK.
I KNOW I'M NOT THE PRETTIEST GIRL IN SCHOOL, BUT I'M NOT HORRIBLE, SO WHY IS IT THAT NOT ONE SINGLE BOY IS INTERESTED IN ME?
BELIEVE YOU ME, SHIRA, THE BOYS WILL BE INTERESTED. LOTS OF THEM.
AND A LOT SOONER THAN YOUR GRAND-MOTHER WOULD LIKE TO KNOW ABOUT.

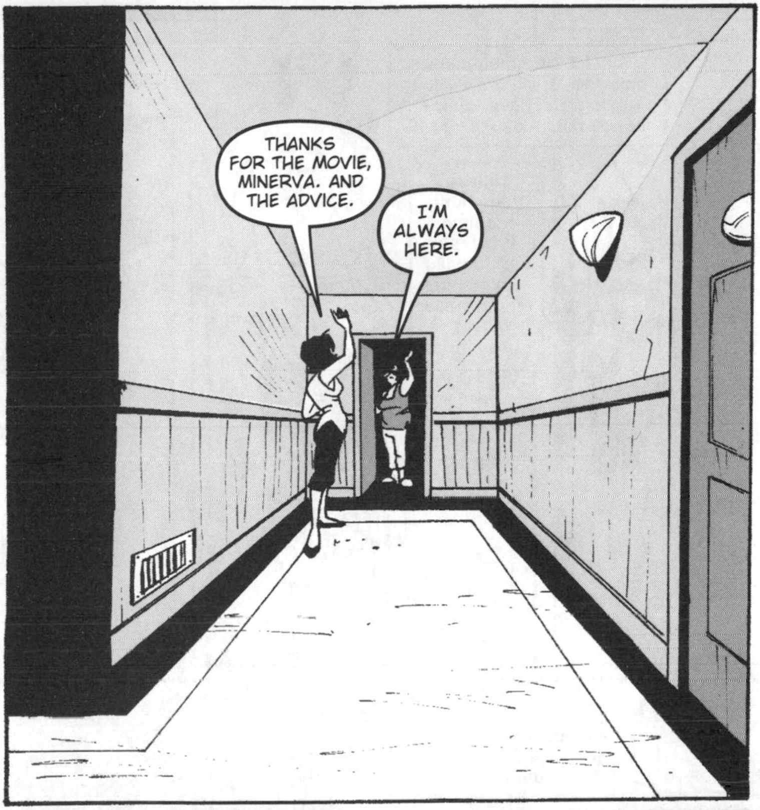
THANKS FOR THE MOVIE, MINERVA. AND THE ADVICE.
I'M ALWAYS HERE.

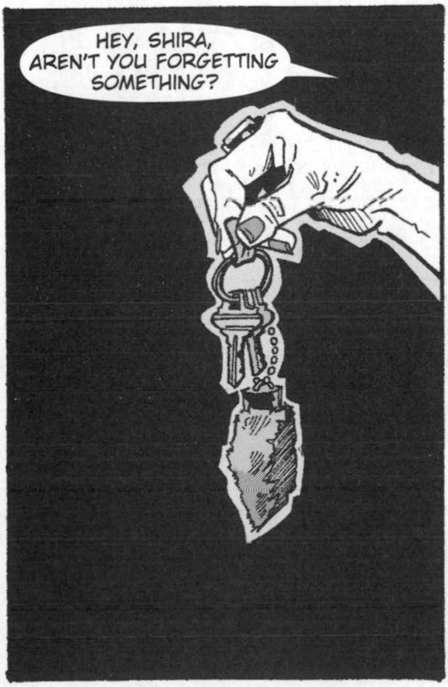
HEY, SHIRA, AREN'T YOU FORGETTING SOMETHING?

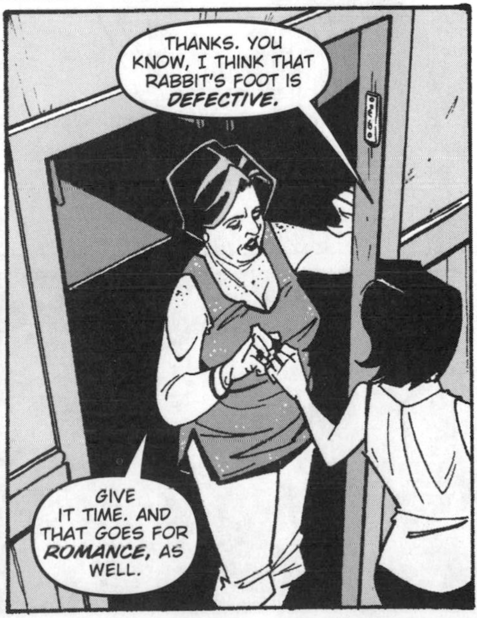
THANKS. YOU KNOW, I THINK THAT RABBIT'S FOOT IS ***DEFECTIVE.***
GIVE IT TIME. AND THAT GOES FOR ***ROMANCE,*** AS WELL.

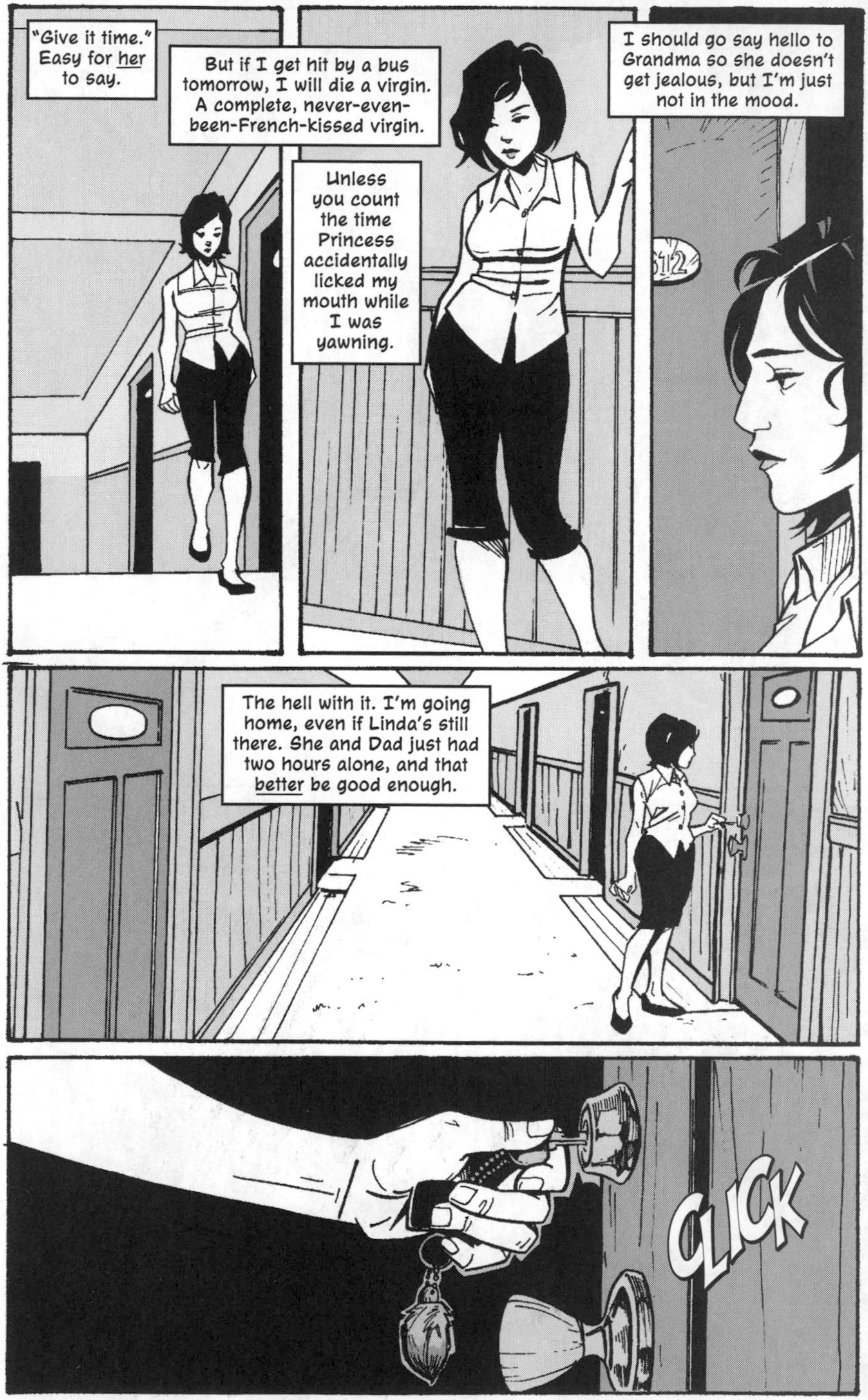
"Give it time." Easy for her to say.
But if I get hit by a bus tomorrow, I will die a virgin. A complete, never-even-been-French-kissed virgin.
Unless you count the time Princess accidentally licked my mouth while I was yawning.
I should go say hello to Grandma so she doesn't get jealous, but I'm just not in the mood.
The hell with it. I'm going home, even if Linda's still there. She and Dad just had two hours alone, and that better be good enough.
CLICK

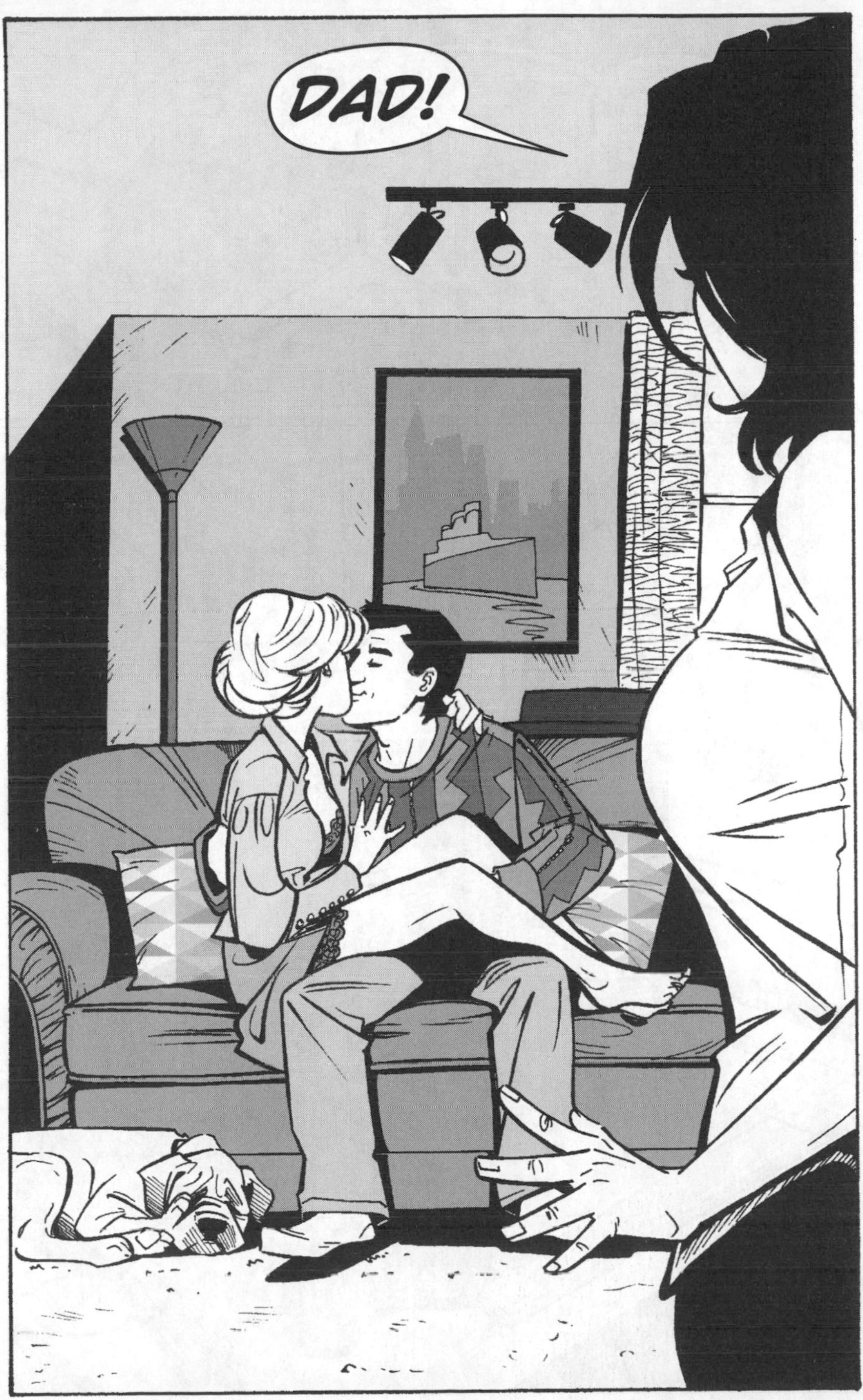
DAD!

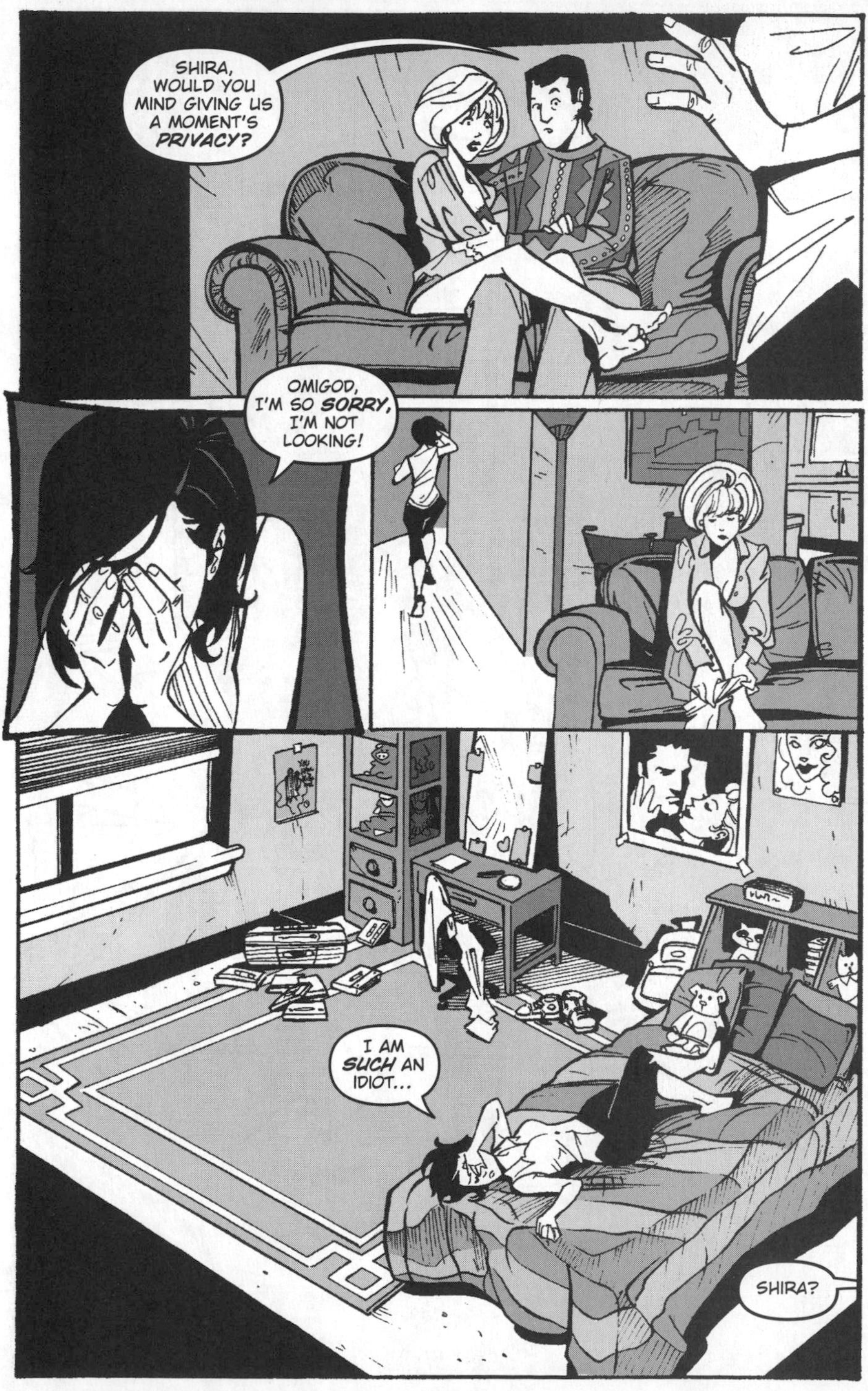
SHIRA, WOULD YOU MIND GIVING US A MOMENT'S ***PRIVACY?***
OMIGOD, I'M SO ***SORRY,*** I'M NOT LOOKING!
I AM ***SUCH*** AN IDIOT...
SHIRA?

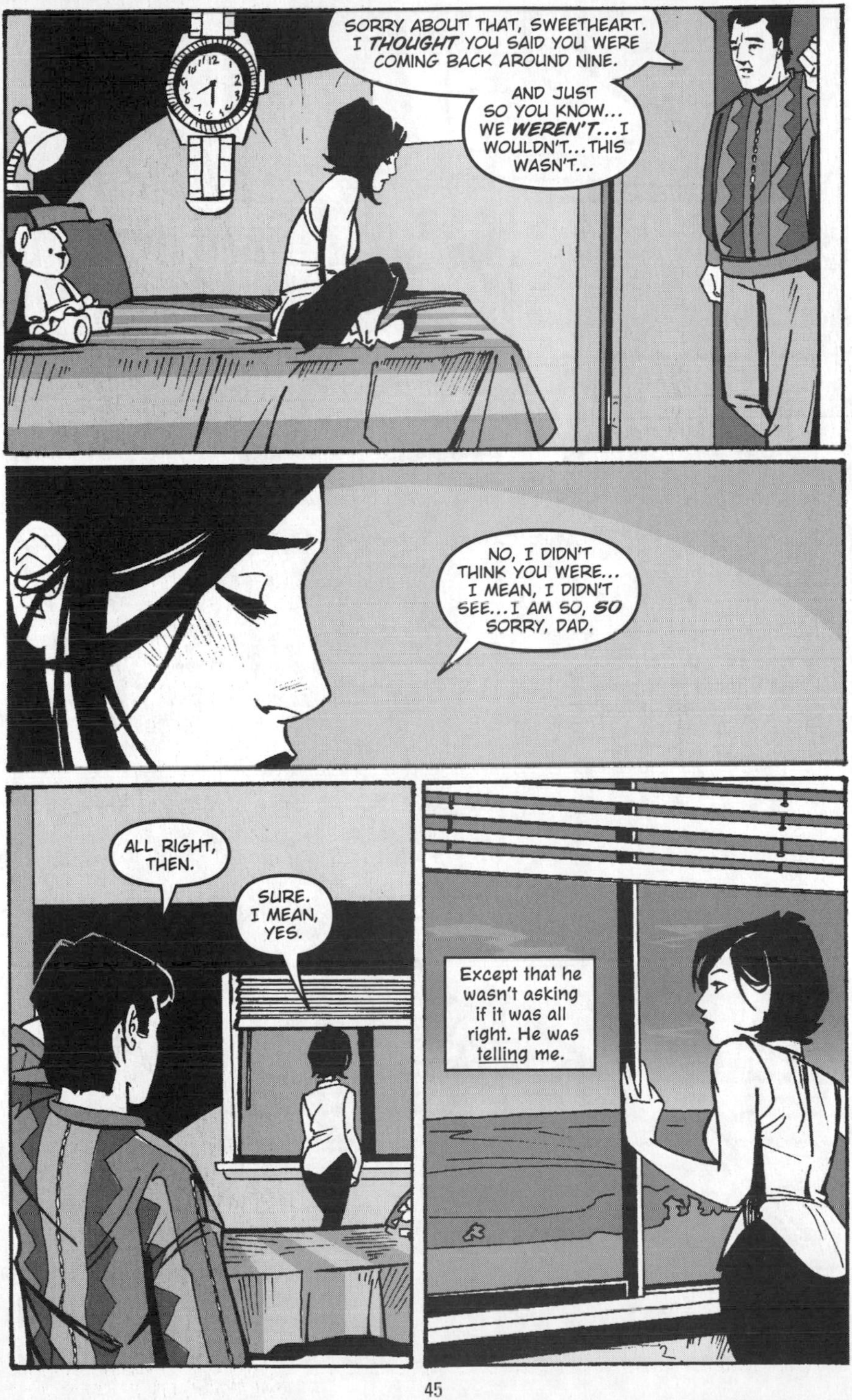
SORRY ABOUT THAT, SWEETHEART. I *THOUGHT* YOU SAID YOU WERE COMING BACK AROUND NINE.
AND JUST SO YOU KNOW... WE *WEREN'T...* I WOULDN'T...THIS WASN'T...
NO, I DIDN'T THINK YOU WERE... I MEAN, I DIDN'T SEE...I AM SO, *SO* SORRY, DAD.
ALL RIGHT, THEN.
SURE. I MEAN, YES.
Except that he wasn't asking if it was all right. He was telling me.

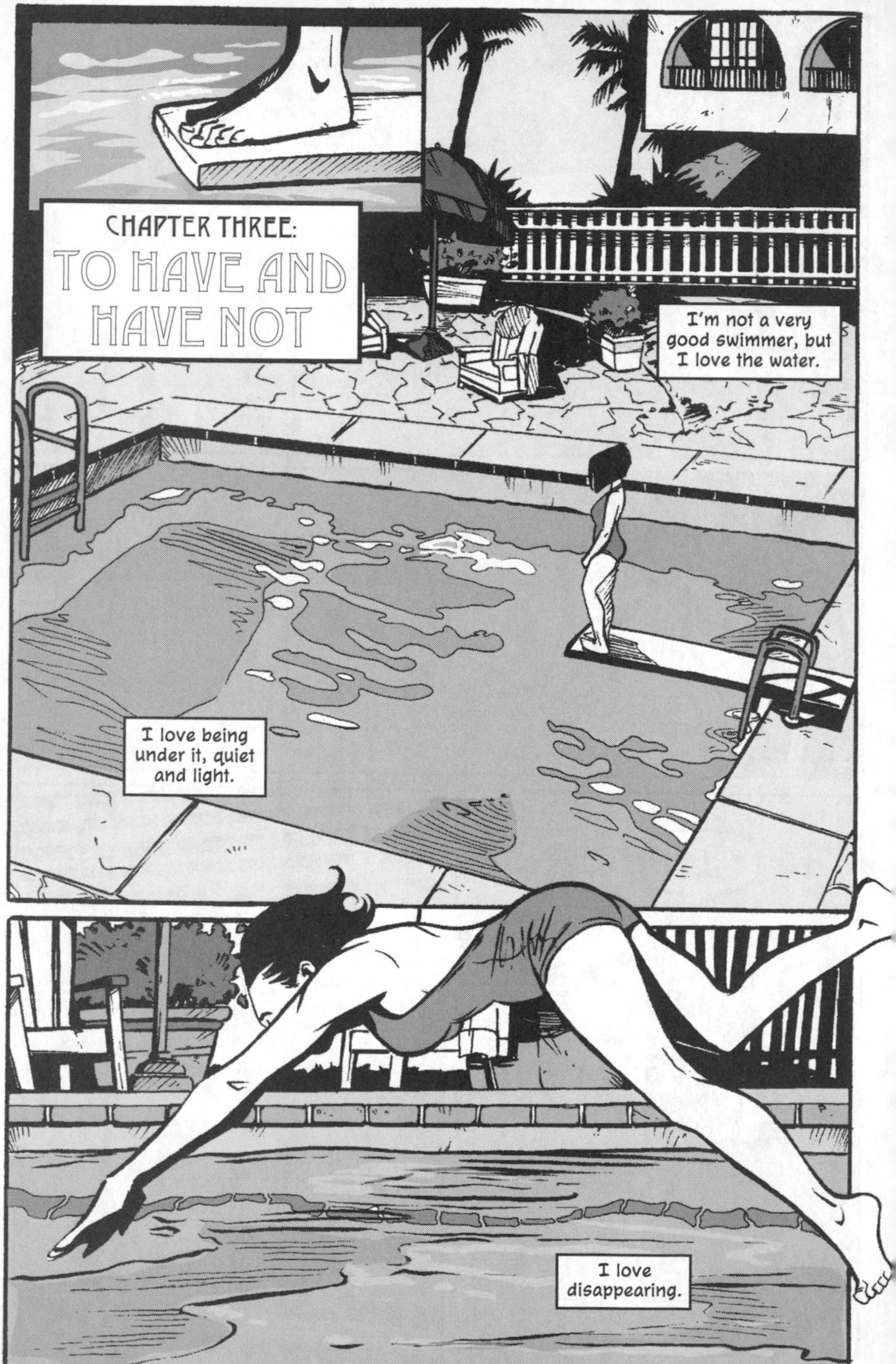
CHAPTER THREE:
TO HAVE AND HAVE NOT
I'm not a very good swimmer, but I love the water.
I love being under it, quiet and light.
I love disappearing.

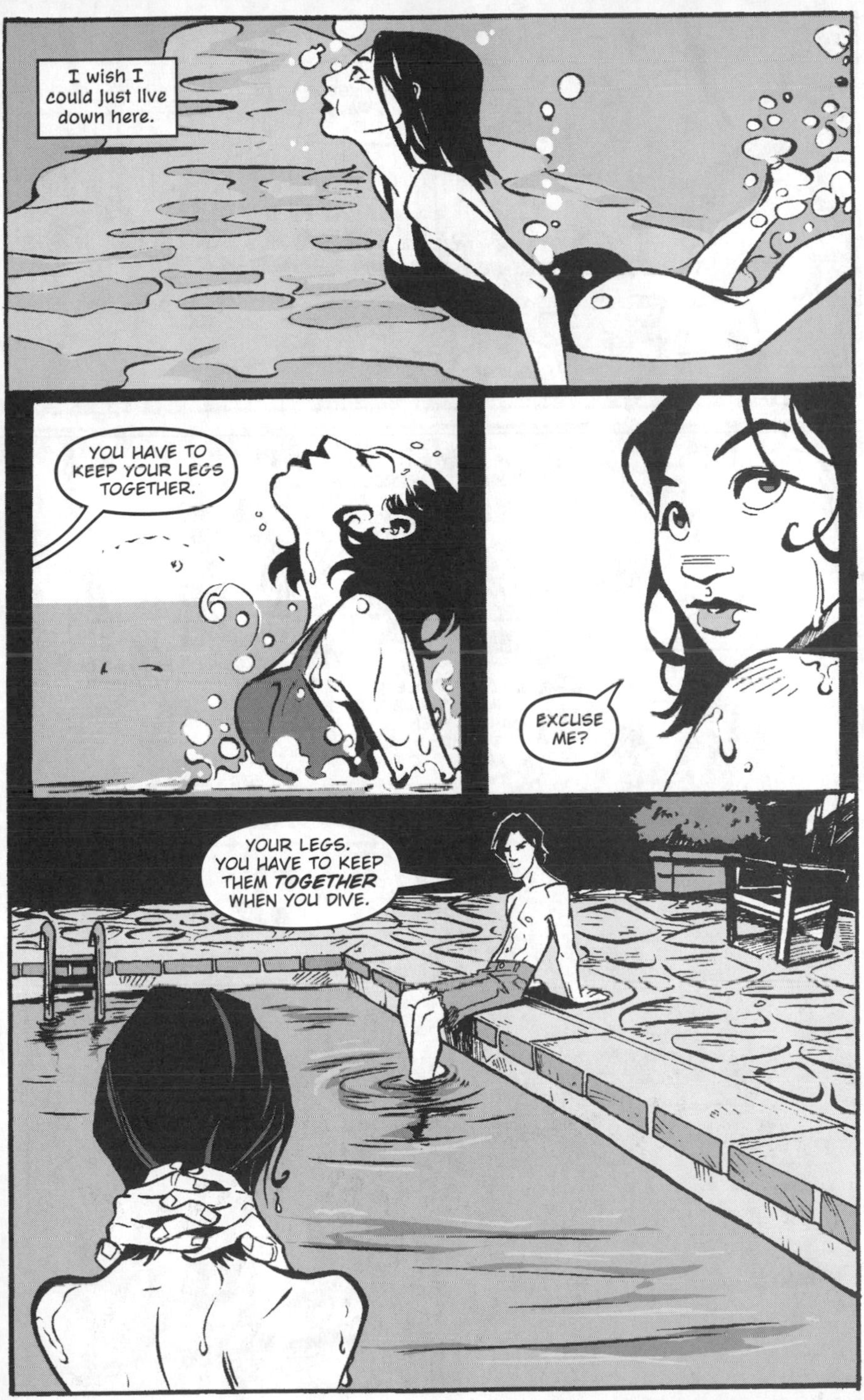
I wish I could just live down here.
YOU HAVE TO KEEP YOUR LEGS TOGETHER.
EXCUSE ME?
YOUR LEGS. YOU HAVE TO KEEP THEM *TOGETHER* WHEN YOU DIVE.

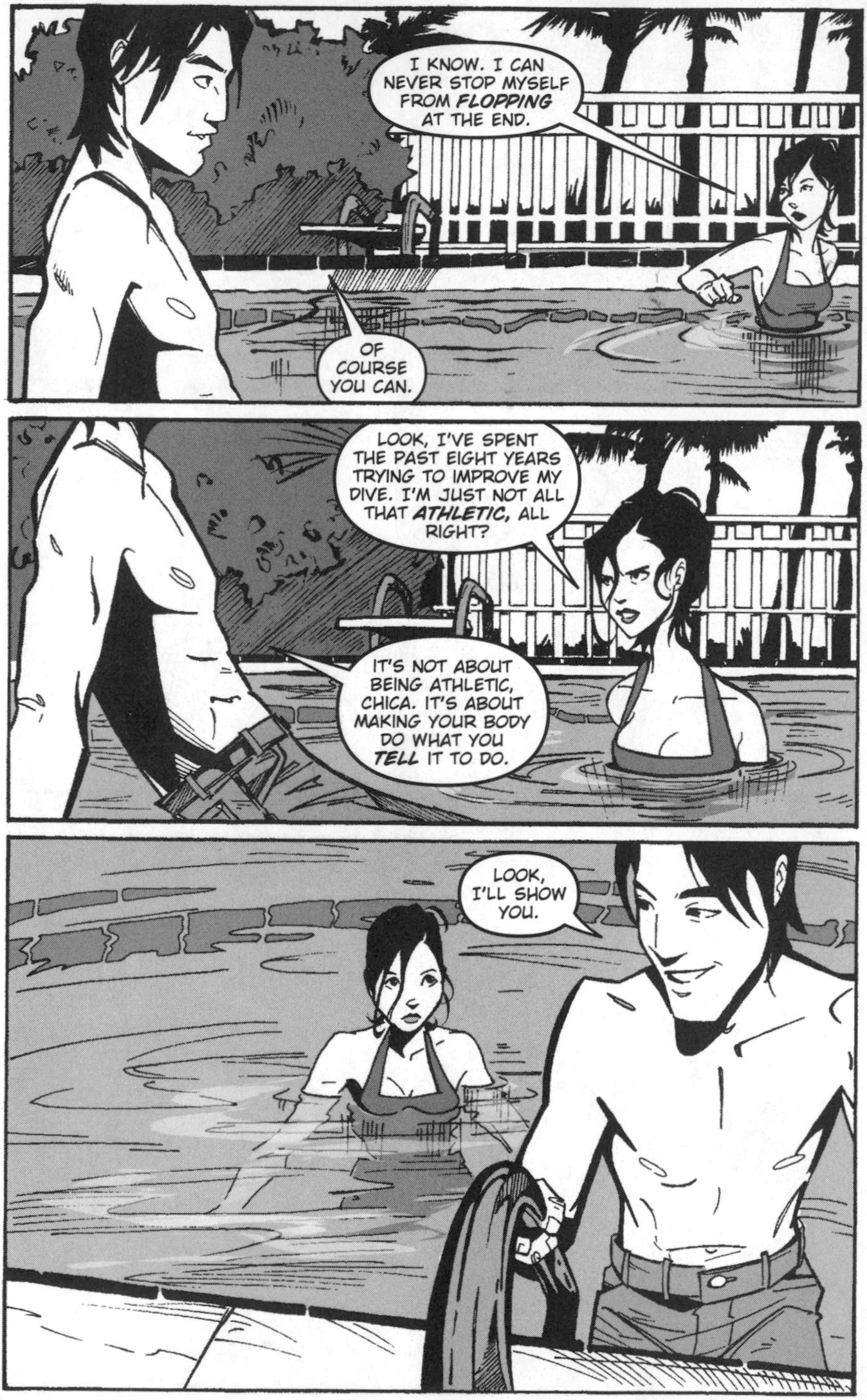
I KNOW. I CAN NEVER STOP MYSELF FROM *FLOPPING* AT THE END.
OF COURSE YOU CAN.
LOOK, I'VE SPENT THE PAST EIGHT YEARS TRYING TO IMPROVE MY DIVE. I'M JUST NOT ALL THAT *ATHLETIC*, ALL RIGHT?
IT'S NOT ABOUT BEING ATHLETIC, CHICA. IT'S ABOUT MAKING YOUR BODY DO WHAT YOU *TELL* IT TO DO.
LOOK, I'LL SHOW YOU.

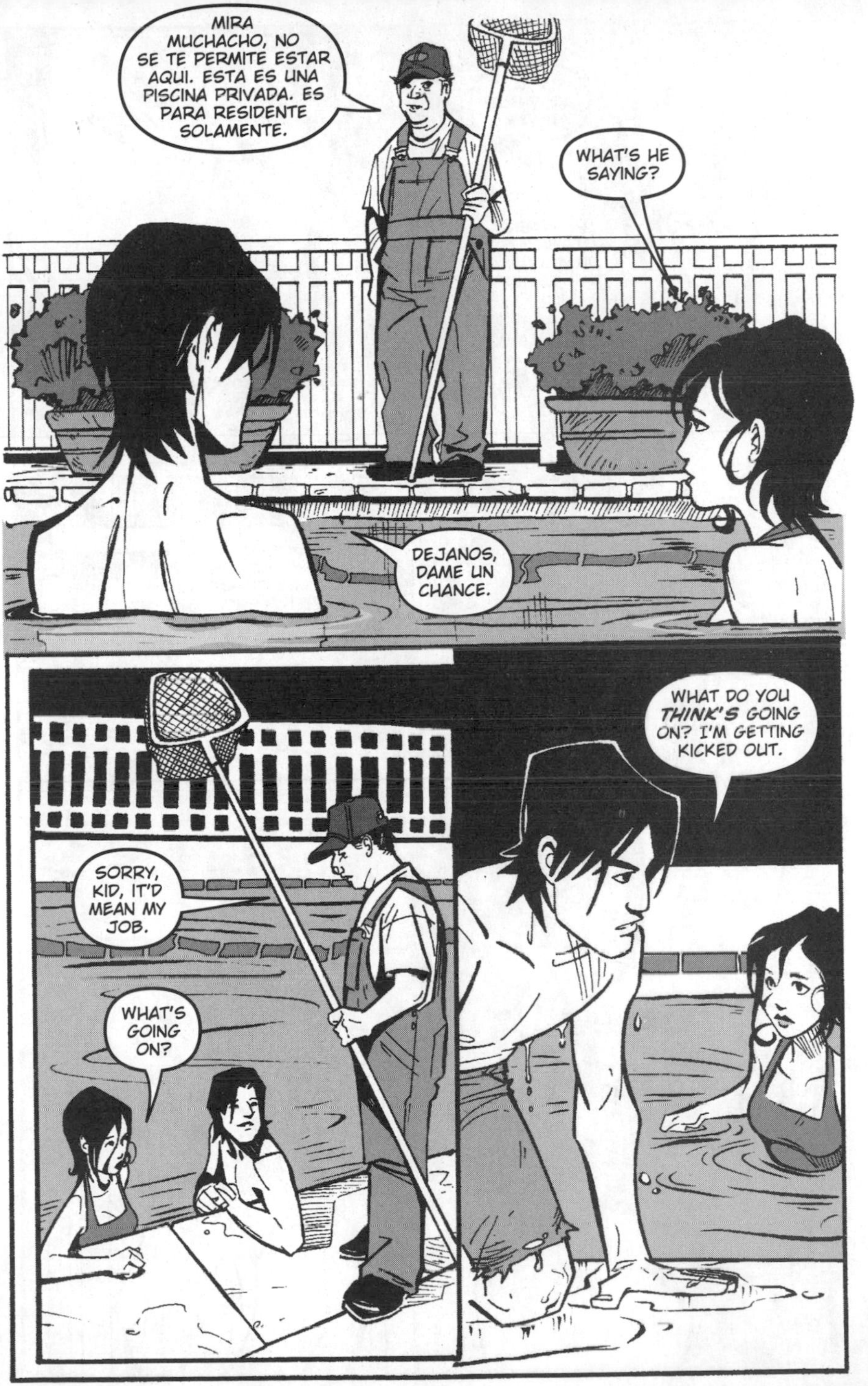
MIRA MUCHACHO, NO SE TE PERMITE ESTAR AQUI. ESTA ES UNA PISCINA PRIVADA. ES PARA RESIDENTE SOLAMENTE.
WHAT'S HE SAYING?
DEJANOS, DAME UN CHANCE.
SORRY, KID, IT'D MEAN MY JOB.
WHAT'S GOING ON?
WHAT DO YOU *THINK'S* GOING ON? I'M GETTING KICKED OUT.

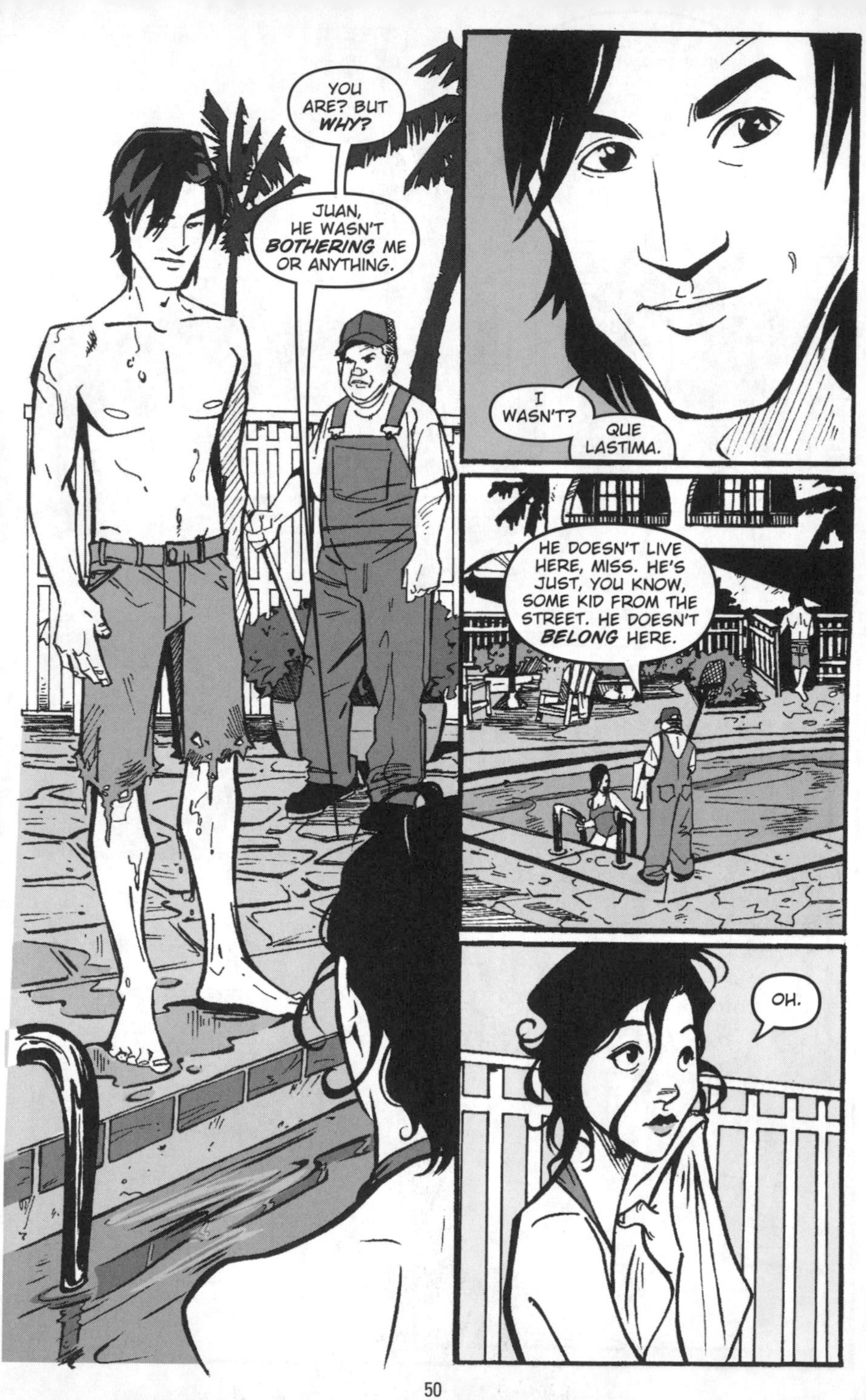
YOU ARE? BUT WHY?
JUAN, HE WASN'T BOTHERING ME OR ANYTHING.
I WASN'T?
QUE LASTIMA.
HE DOESN'T LIVE HERE, MISS. HE'S JUST, YOU KNOW, SOME KID FROM THE STREET. HE DOESN'T BELONG HERE.
OH.

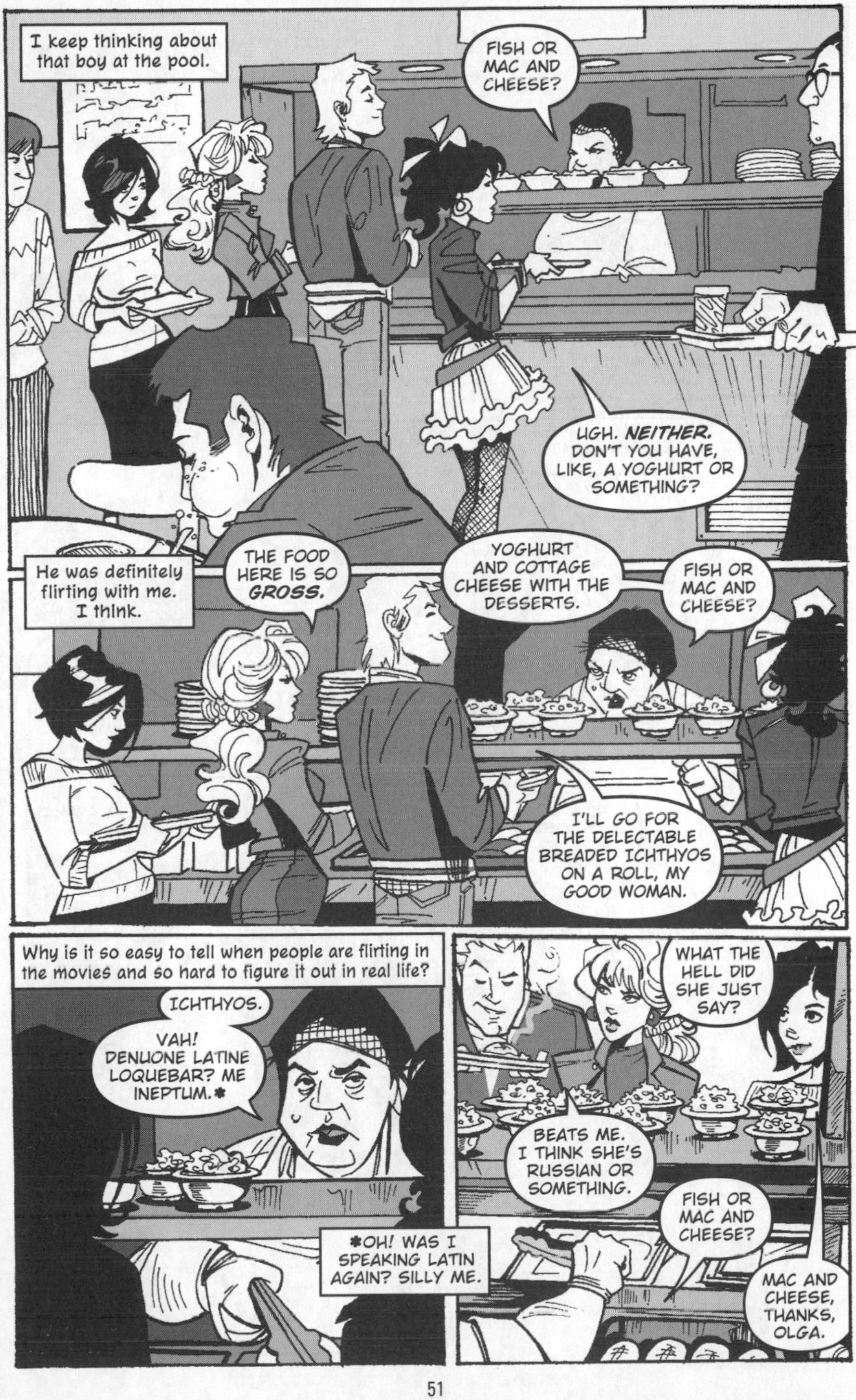
I keep thinking about that boy at the pool.
FISH OR MAC AND CHEESE?
UGH. NEITHER. DON'T YOU HAVE, LIKE, A YOGHURT OR SOMETHING?
He was definitely flirting with me. I think.
THE FOOD HERE IS SO GROSS.
YOGHURT AND COTTAGE CHEESE WITH THE DESSERTS.
FISH OR MAC AND CHEESE?
I'LL GO FOR THE DELECTABLE BREADED ICHTHYOS ON A ROLL, MY GOOD WOMAN.
Why is it so easy to tell when people are flirting in the movies and so hard to figure it out in real life?
ICHTHYOS.
VAH! DENUONE LATINE LOQUEBAR? ME INEPTUM.✽
✽OH! WAS I SPEAKING LATIN AGAIN? SILLY ME.
WHAT THE HELL DID SHE JUST SAY?
BEATS ME. I THINK SHE'S RUSSIAN OR SOMETHING.
FISH OR MAC AND CHEESE?
MAC AND CHEESE, THANKS, OLGA.

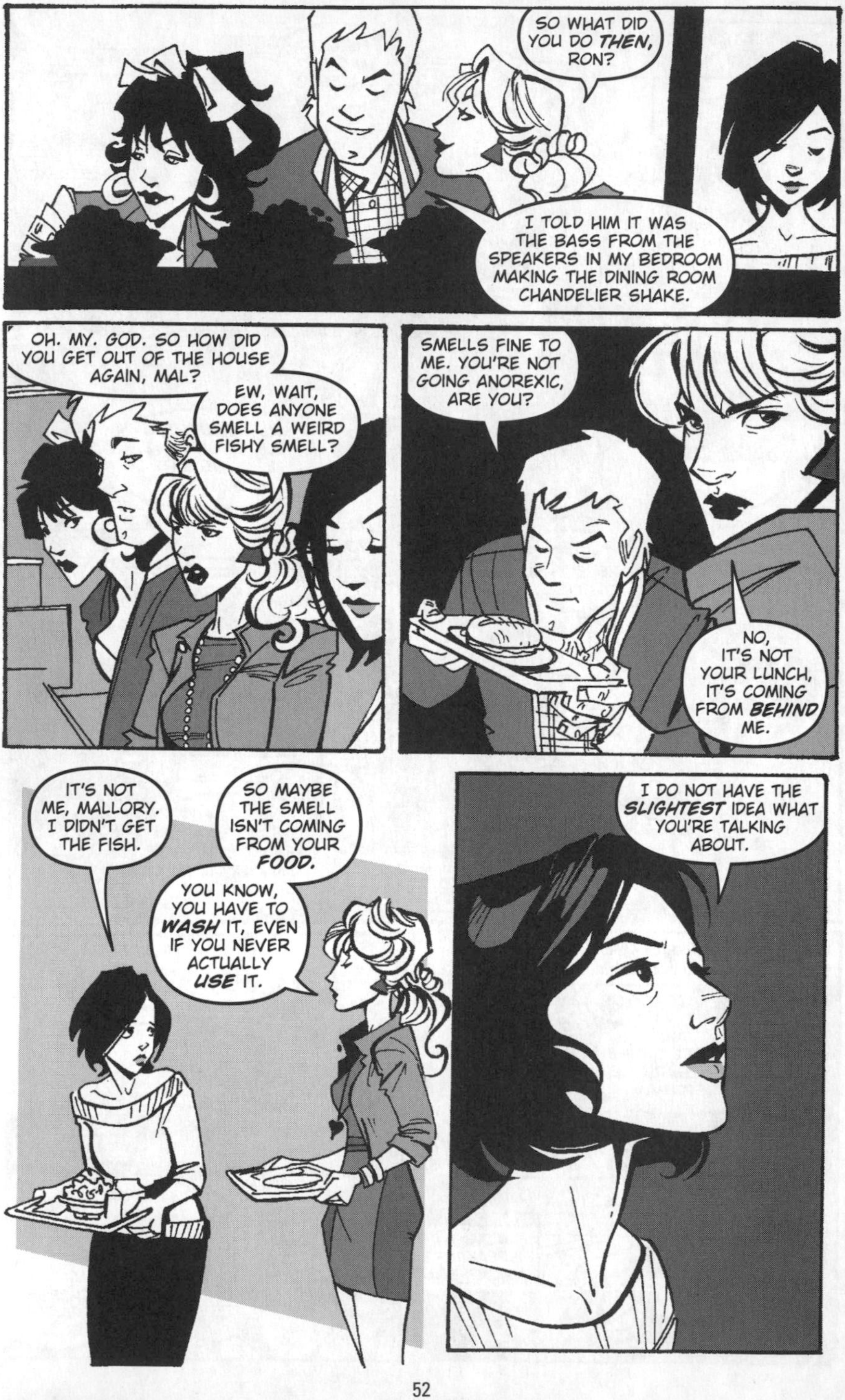
SO WHAT DID YOU DO *THEN*, RON?
I TOLD HIM IT WAS THE BASS FROM THE SPEAKERS IN MY BEDROOM MAKING THE DINING ROOM CHANDELIER SHAKE.
OH. MY. GOD. SO HOW DID YOU GET OUT OF THE HOUSE AGAIN, MAL?
EW, WAIT, DOES ANYONE SMELL A WEIRD FISHY SMELL?
SMELLS FINE TO ME. YOU'RE NOT GOING ANOREXIC, ARE YOU?
NO, IT'S NOT YOUR LUNCH, IT'S COMING FROM *BEHIND* ME.
IT'S NOT ME, MALLORY. I DIDN'T GET THE FISH.
SO MAYBE THE SMELL ISN'T COMING FROM YOUR *FOOD*.
YOU KNOW, YOU HAVE TO *WASH* IT, EVEN IF YOU NEVER ACTUALLY *USE* IT.
I DO NOT HAVE THE *SLIGHTEST* IDEA WHAT YOU'RE TALKING ABOUT.

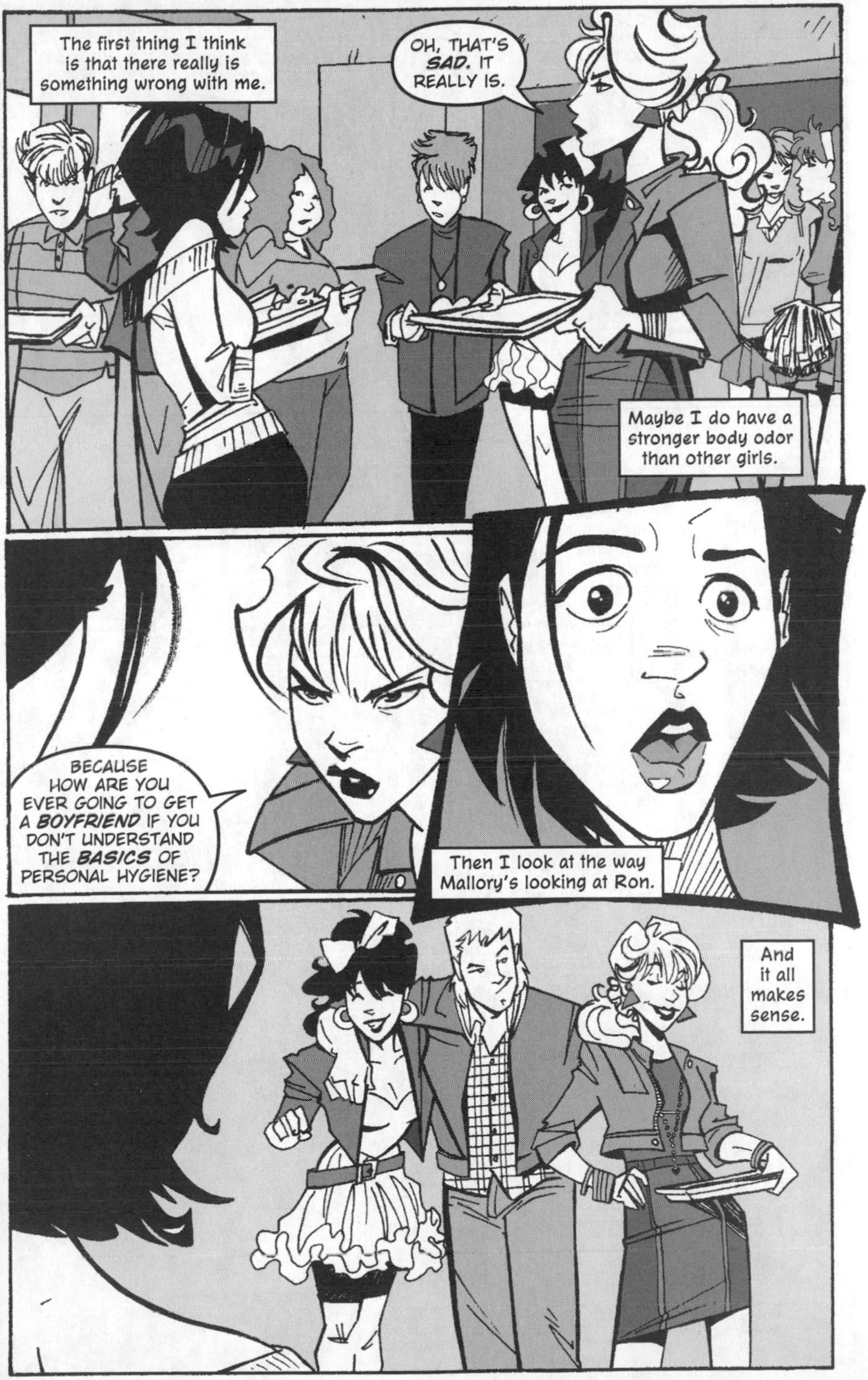

The first thing I think is that there really is something wrong with me.
OH, THAT'S *SAD.* IT REALLY IS.
Maybe I do have a stronger body odor than other girls.
BECAUSE HOW ARE YOU EVER GOING TO GET A *BOYFRIEND* IF YOU DON'T UNDERSTAND THE *BASICS* OF PERSONAL HYGIENE?
Then I look at the way Mallory's looking at Ron.
And it all makes sense.

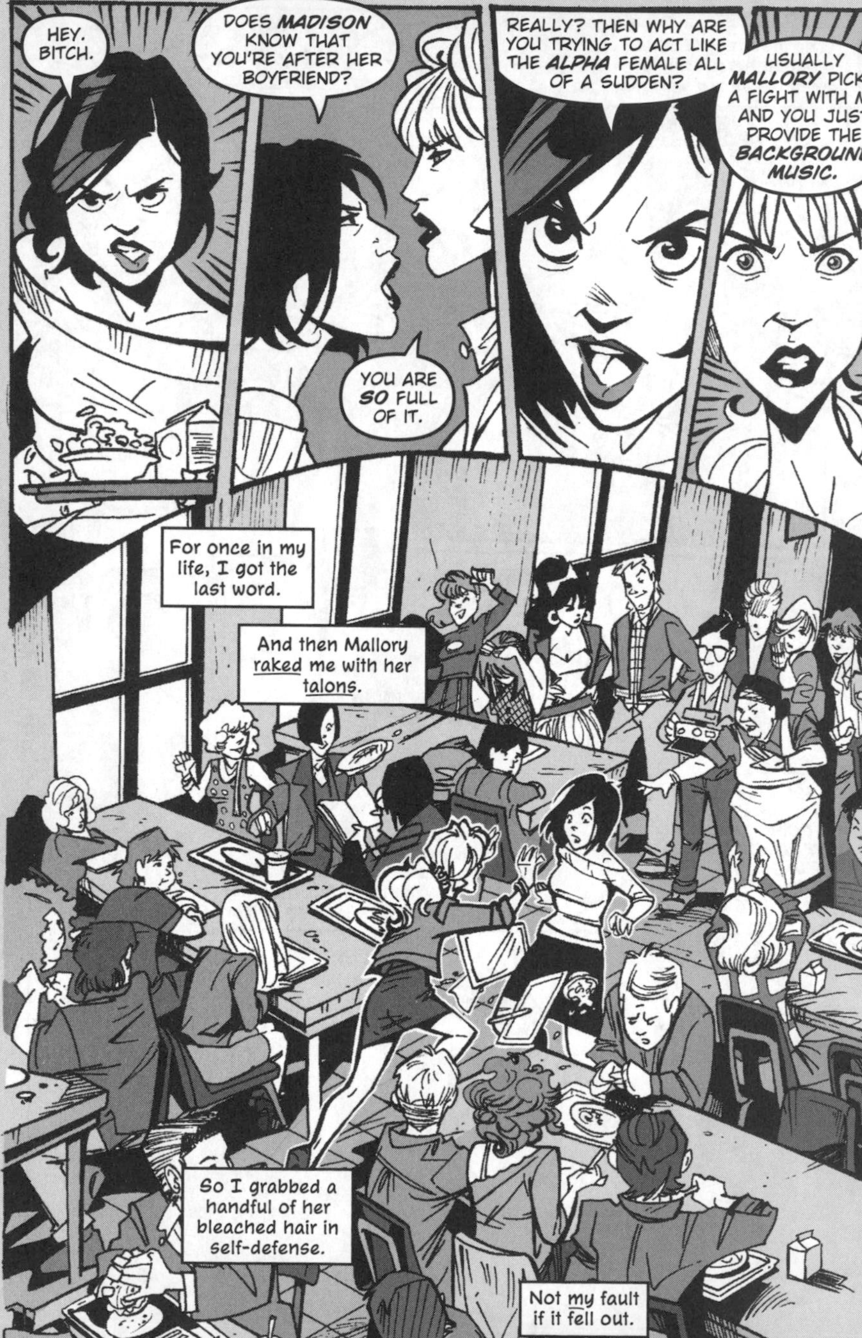
HEY. BITCH.
DOES MADISON KNOW THAT YOU'RE AFTER HER BOYFRIEND?
YOU ARE SO FULL OF IT.
REALLY? THEN WHY ARE YOU TRYING TO ACT LIKE THE ALPHA FEMALE ALL OF A SUDDEN?
USUALLY MALLORY PICKS A FIGHT WITH ME AND YOU JUST PROVIDE THE BACKGROUND MUSIC.
For once in my life, I got the last word.
And then Mallory raked me with her talons.
So I grabbed a handful of her bleached hair in self-defense.
Not my fault if it fell out.

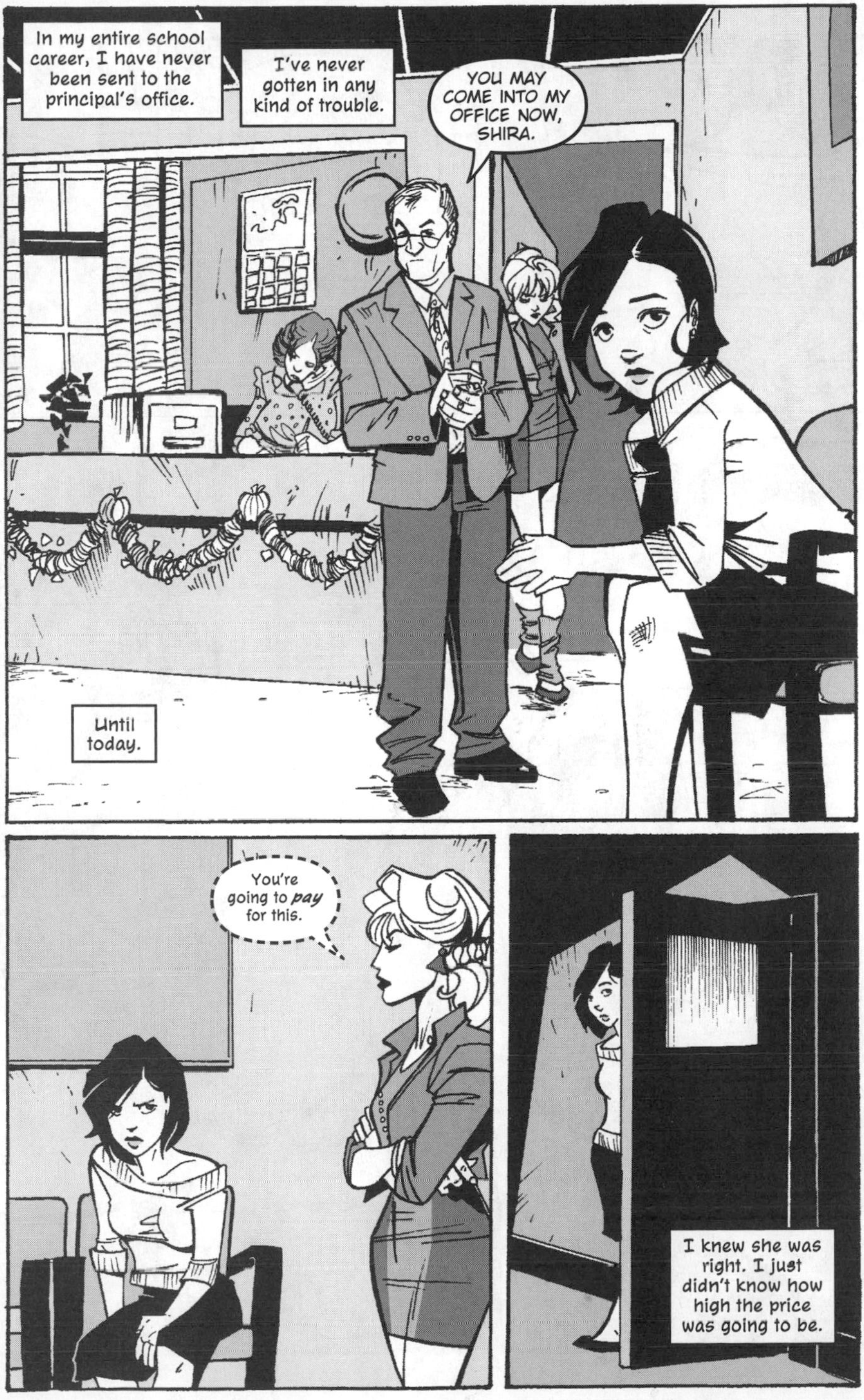
In my entire school career, I have never been sent to the principal's office.
I've never gotten in any kind of trouble.
YOU MAY COME INTO MY OFFICE NOW, SHIRA.
Until today.
You're going to *pay* for this.
I knew she was right. I just didn't know how high the price was going to be.

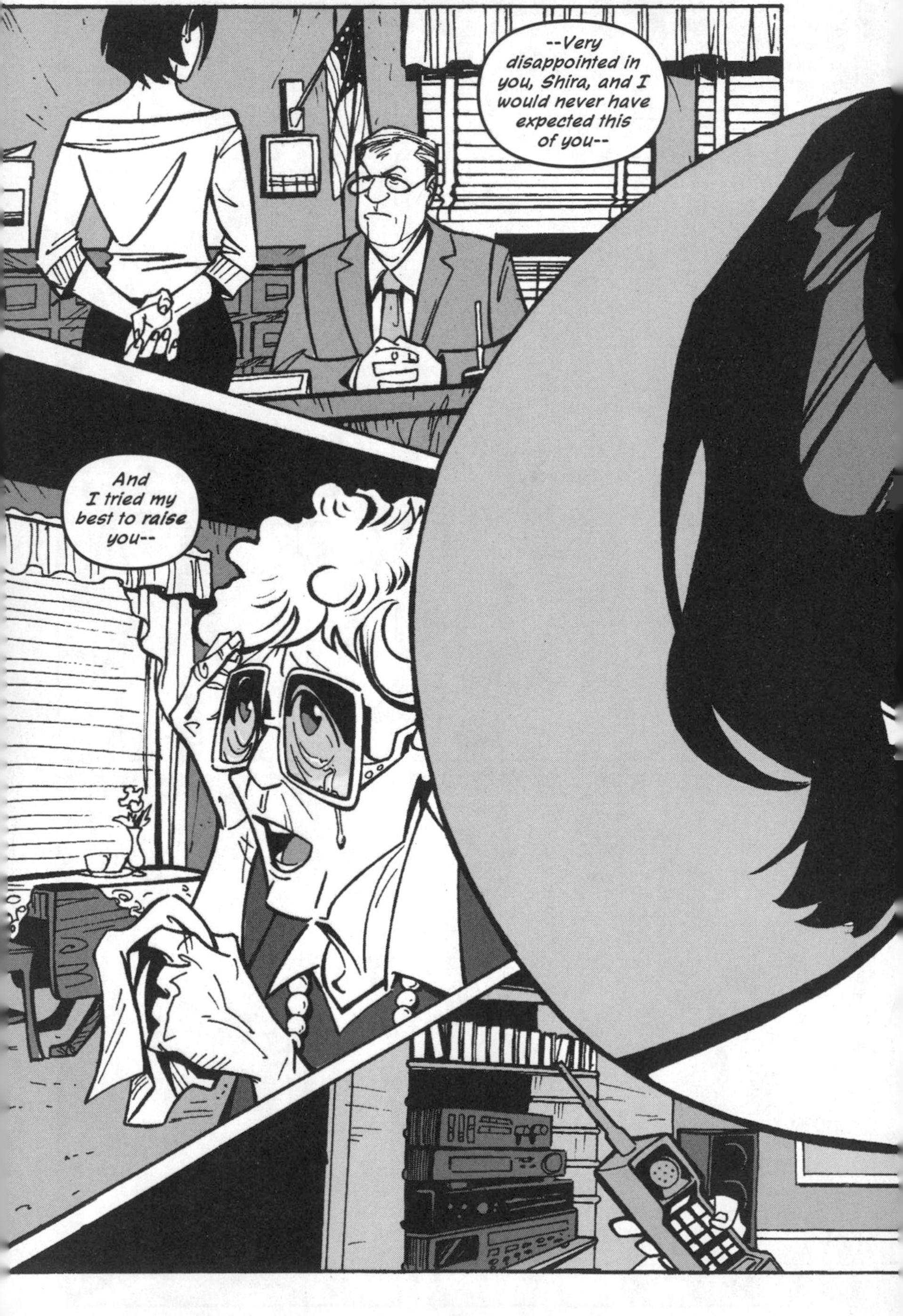
--Very disappointed in you, Shira, and I would never have expected this of you--
And I tried my best to raise you--

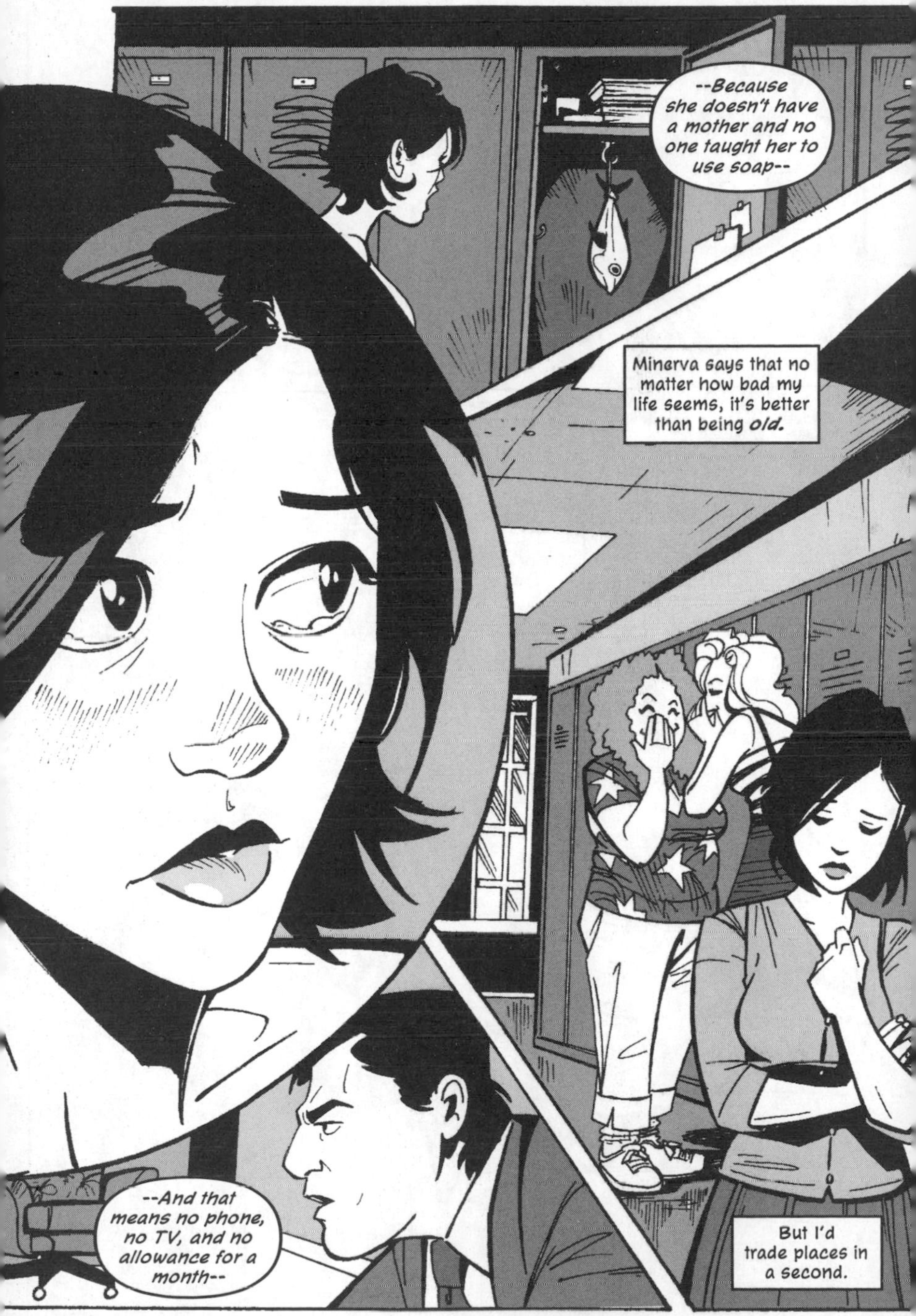
--Because she doesn't have a mother and no one taught her to use soap--
Minerva says that no matter how bad my life seems, it's better than being *old.*
--And that means no phone, no TV, and no allowance for a month--
But I'd trade places in a second.

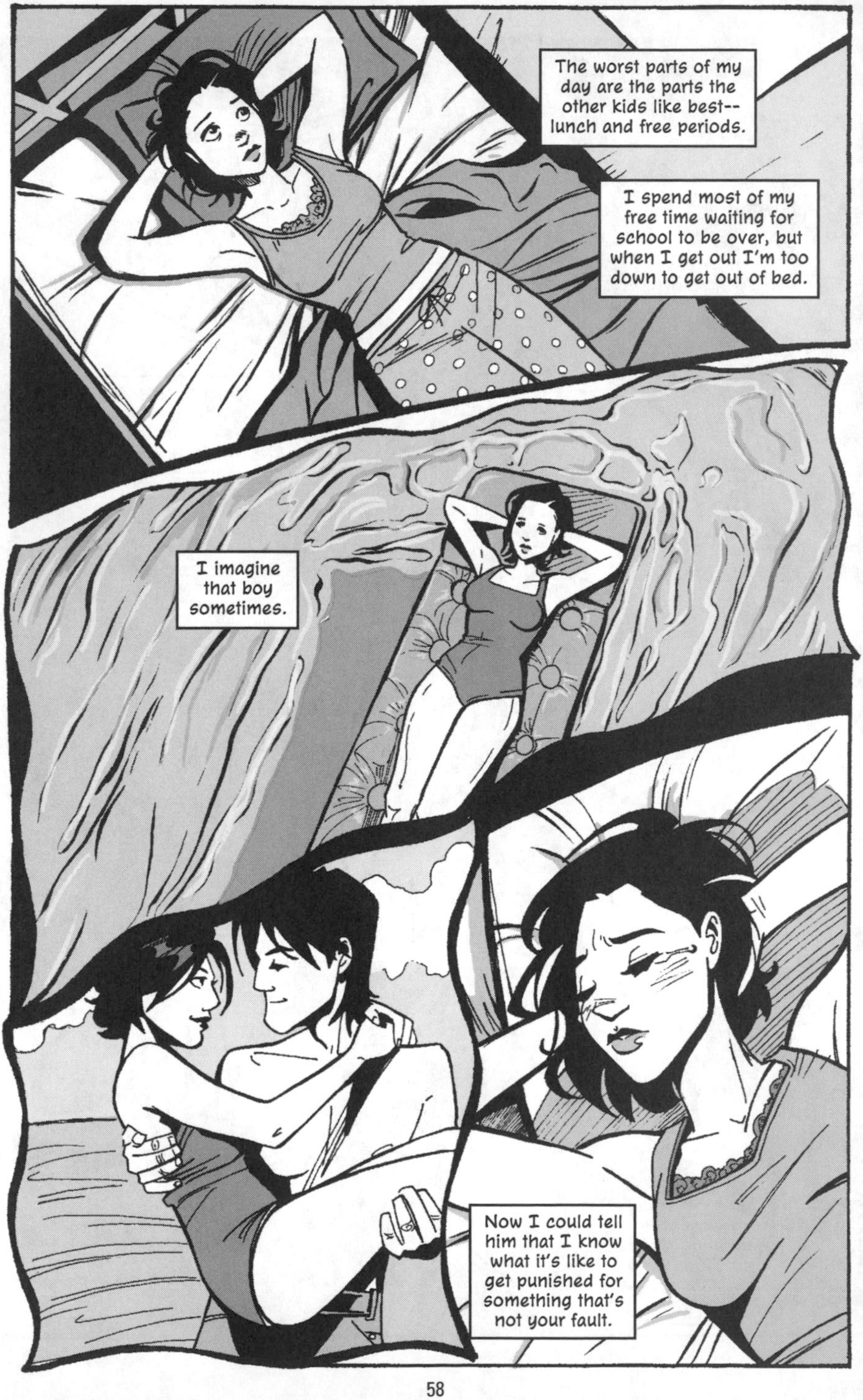
The worst parts of my day are the parts the other kids like best--lunch and free periods.
I spend most of my free time waiting for school to be over, but when I get out I'm too down to get out of bed.
I imagine that boy sometimes.
Now I could tell him that I know what it's like to get punished for something that's not your fault.

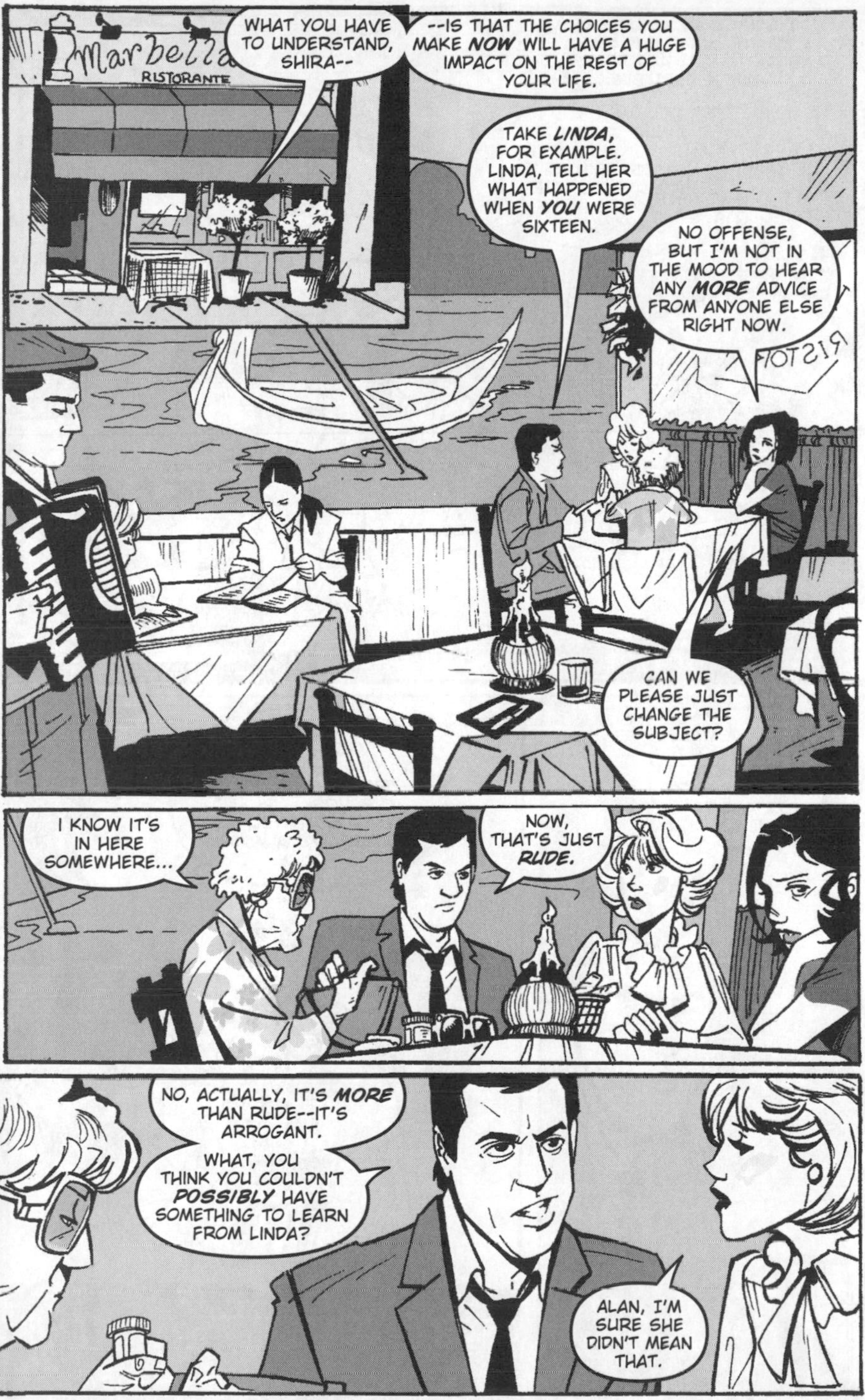
RISTORANTE
WHAT YOU HAVE TO UNDERSTAND, SHIRA--
--IS THAT THE CHOICES YOU MAKE NOW WILL HAVE A HUGE IMPACT ON THE REST OF YOUR LIFE.
TAKE LINDA, FOR EXAMPLE. LINDA, TELL HER WHAT HAPPENED WHEN YOU WERE SIXTEEN.
NO OFFENSE, BUT I'M NOT IN THE MOOD TO HEAR ANY MORE ADVICE FROM ANYONE ELSE RIGHT NOW.
CAN WE PLEASE JUST CHANGE THE SUBJECT?
I KNOW IT'S IN HERE SOMEWHERE...
NOW, THAT'S JUST RUDE.
NO, ACTUALLY, IT'S MORE THAN RUDE--IT'S ARROGANT.
WHAT, YOU THINK YOU COULDN'T POSSIBLY HAVE SOMETHING TO LEARN FROM LINDA?
ALAN, I'M SURE SHE DIDN'T MEAN THAT.

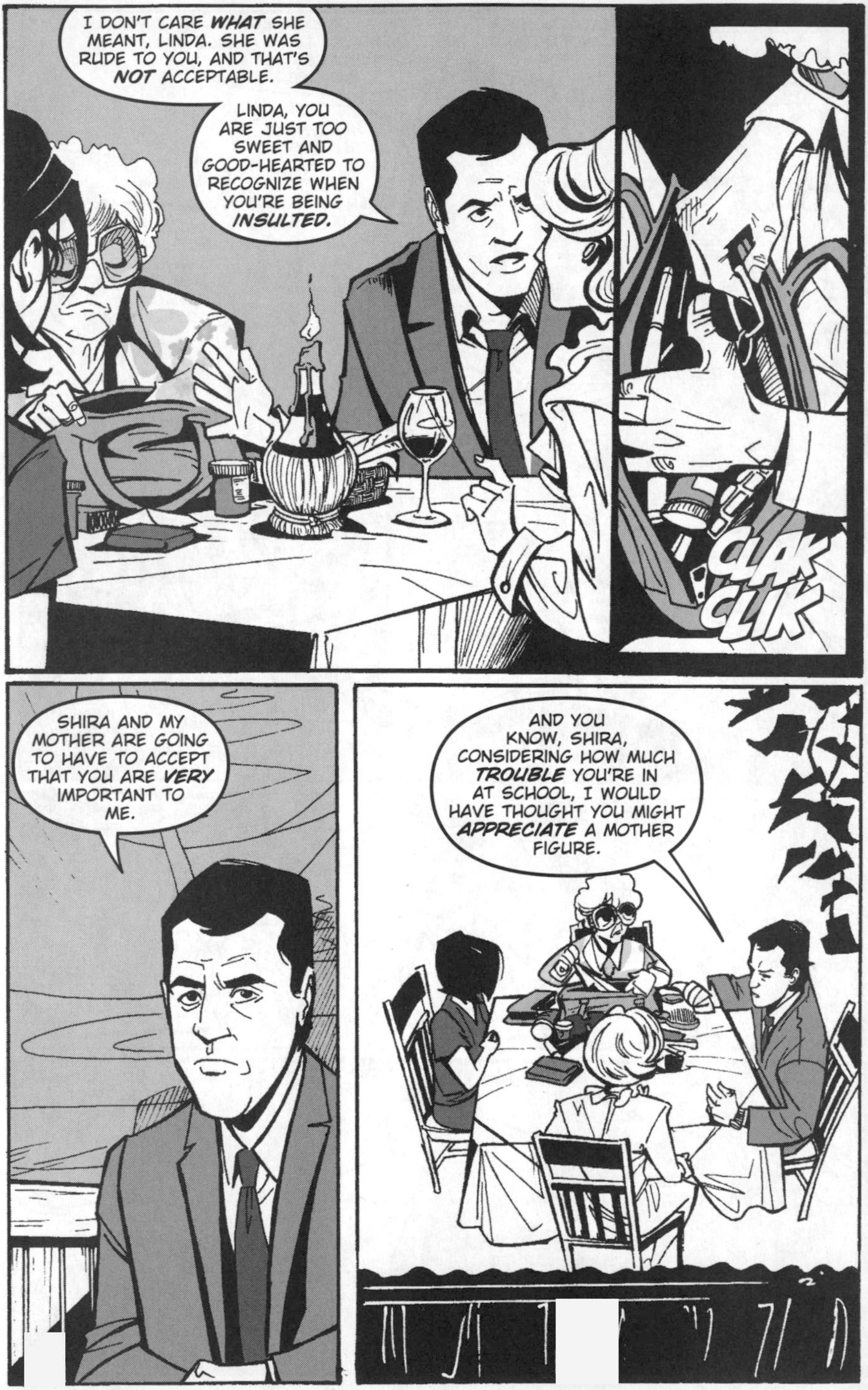
I DON'T CARE WHAT SHE MEANT, LINDA. SHE WAS RUDE TO YOU, AND THAT'S NOT ACCEPTABLE.
LINDA, YOU ARE JUST TOO SWEET AND GOOD-HEARTED TO RECOGNIZE WHEN YOU'RE BEING INSULTED.
CLAK
CLIK
SHIRA AND MY MOTHER ARE GOING TO HAVE TO ACCEPT THAT YOU ARE VERY IMPORTANT TO ME.
AND YOU KNOW, SHIRA, CONSIDERING HOW MUCH TROUBLE YOU'RE IN AT SCHOOL, I WOULD HAVE THOUGHT YOU MIGHT APPRECIATE A MOTHER FIGURE.

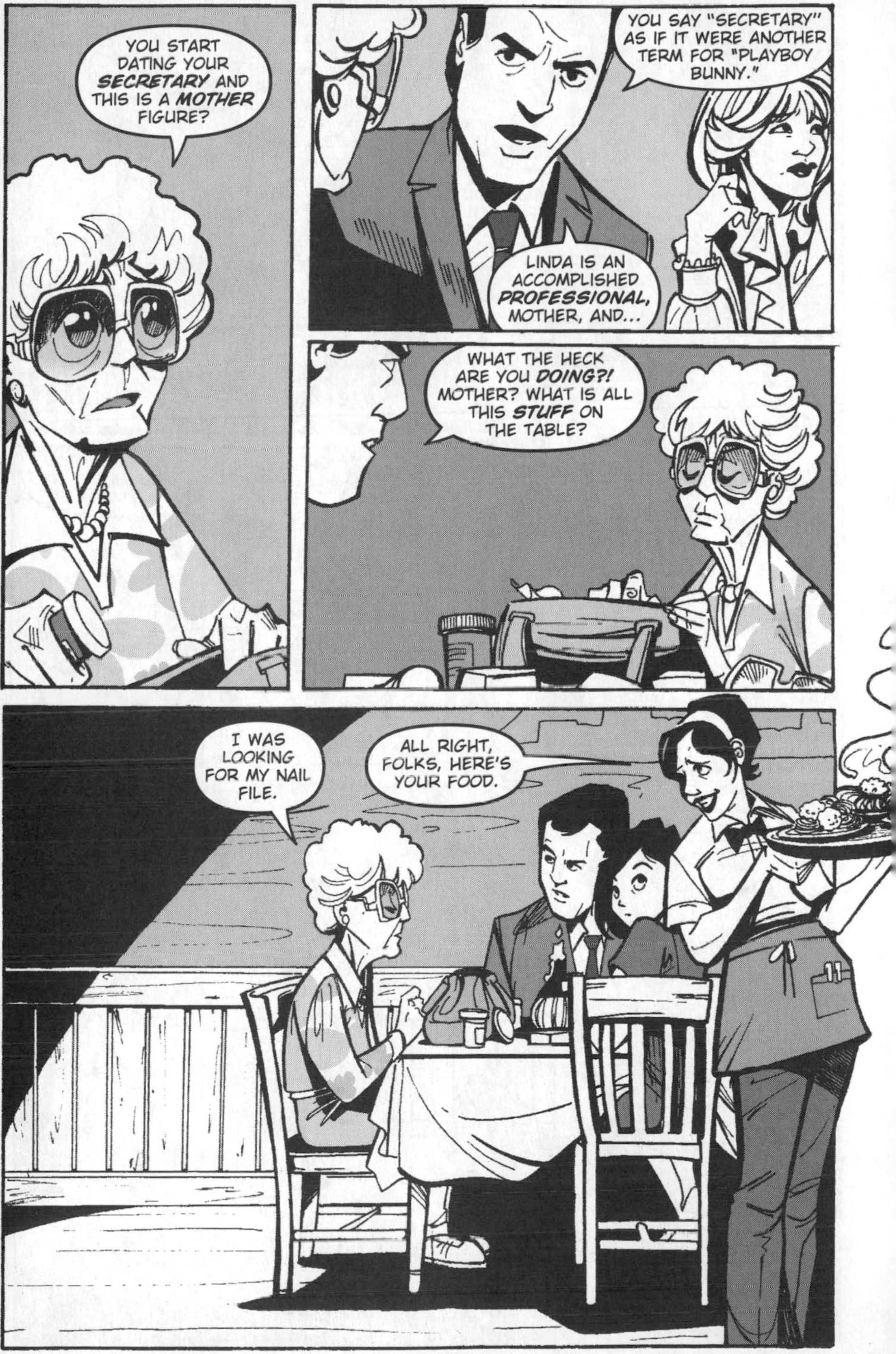

YOU START DATING YOUR SECRETARY AND THIS IS A MOTHER FIGURE?
YOU SAY "SECRETARY" AS IF IT WERE ANOTHER TERM FOR "PLAYBOY BUNNY."
LINDA IS AN ACCOMPLISHED PROFESSIONAL, MOTHER, AND...
WHAT THE HECK ARE YOU DOING?! MOTHER? WHAT IS ALL THIS STUFF ON THE TABLE?
I WAS LOOKING FOR MY NAIL FILE.
ALL RIGHT, FOLKS, HERE'S YOUR FOOD.

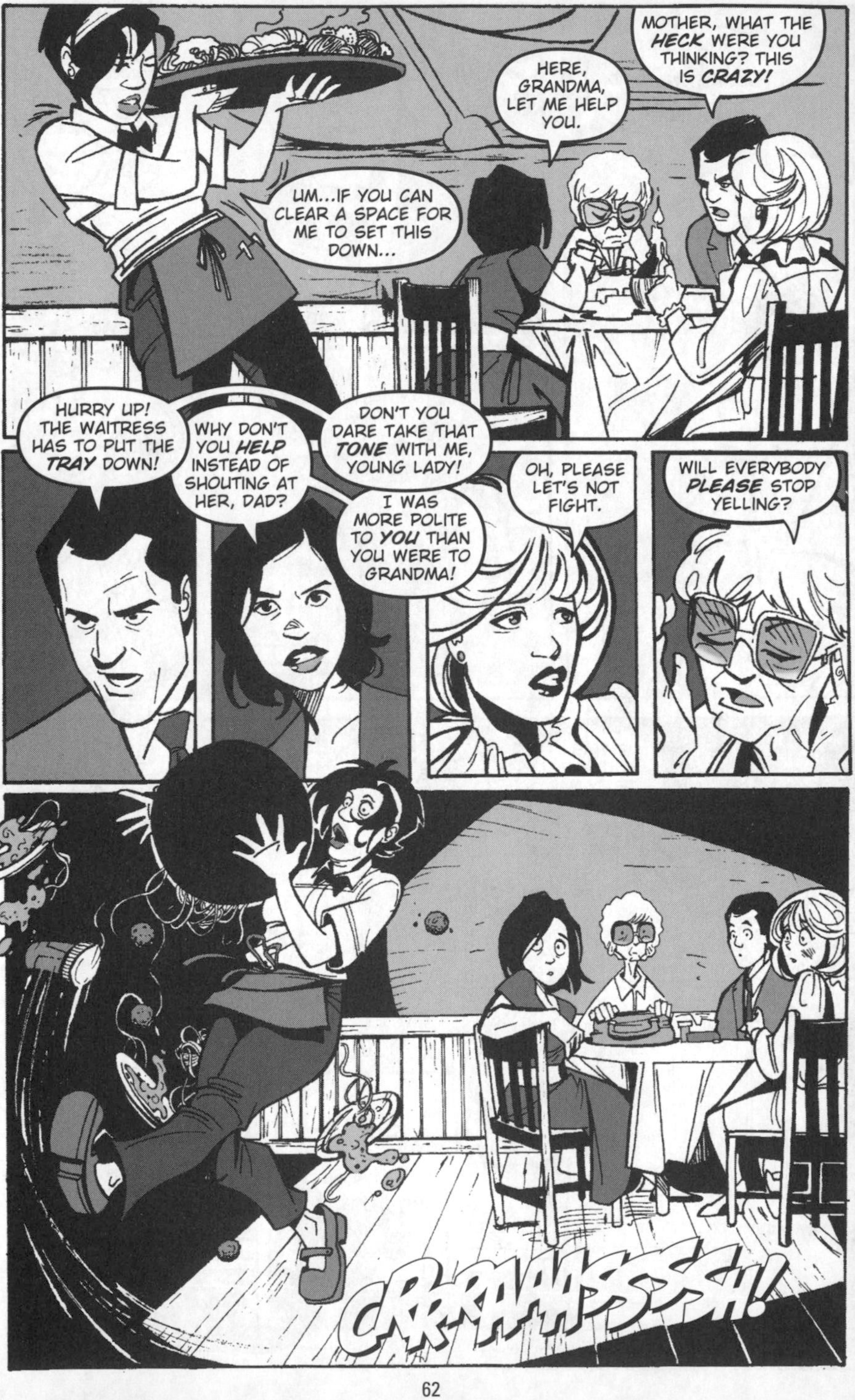
UM...IF YOU CAN CLEAR A SPACE FOR ME TO SET THIS DOWN...
HERE, GRANDMA, LET ME HELP YOU.
MOTHER, WHAT THE HECK WERE YOU THINKING? THIS IS CRAZY!
HURRY UP! THE WAITRESS HAS TO PUT THE TRAY DOWN!
WHY DON'T YOU HELP INSTEAD OF SHOUTING AT HER, DAD?
DON'T YOU DARE TAKE THAT TONE WITH ME, YOUNG LADY!
I WAS MORE POLITE TO YOU THAN YOU WERE TO GRANDMA!
OH, PLEASE LET'S NOT FIGHT.
WILL EVERYBODY PLEASE STOP YELLING?
CRRRAAASSSSH!

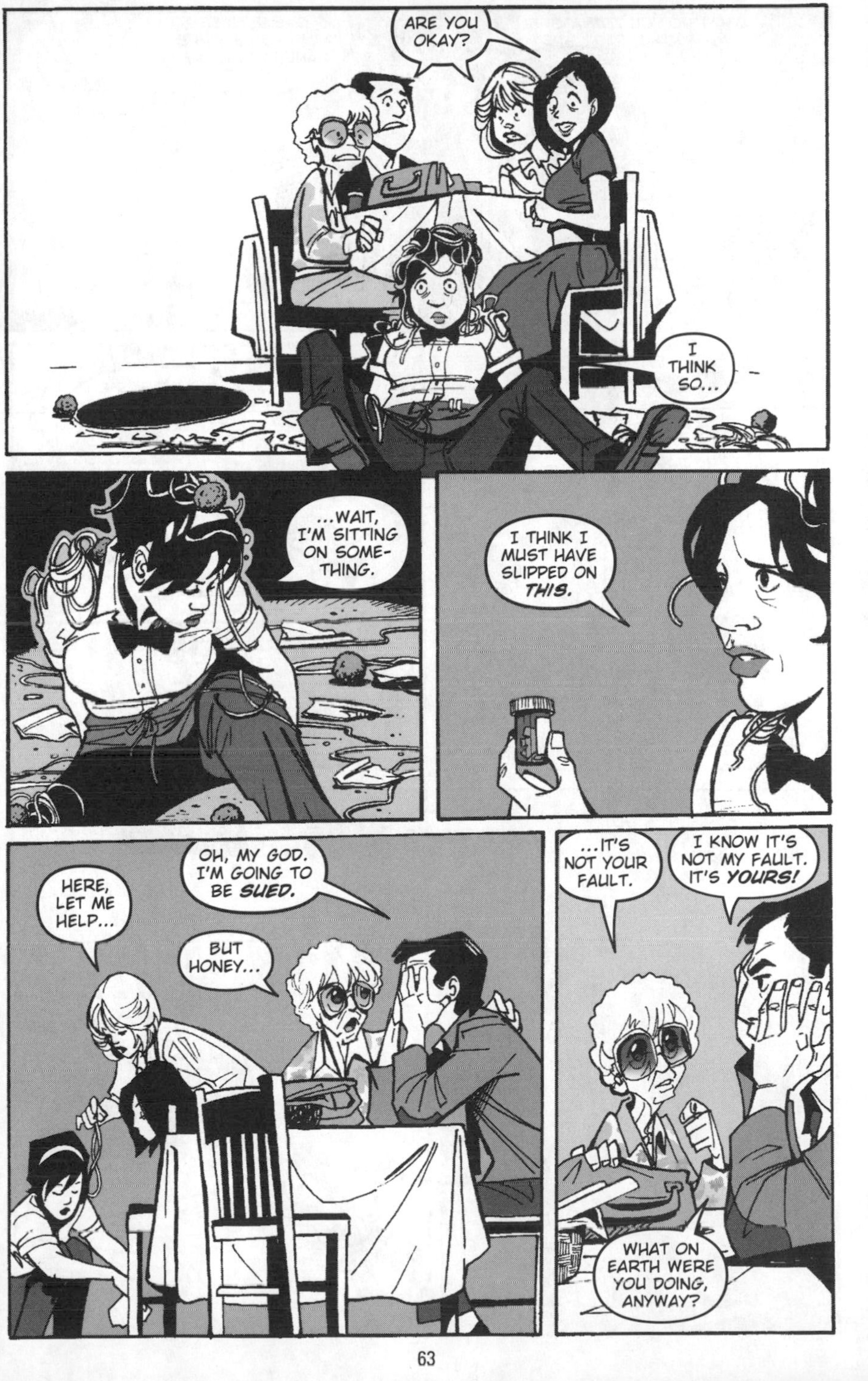
ARE YOU OKAY?
I THINK SO...
...WAIT, I'M SITTING ON SOME-THING.
I THINK I MUST HAVE SLIPPED ON *THIS.*
HERE, LET ME HELP...
OH, MY GOD. I'M GOING TO BE *SUED.*
BUT HONEY...
...IT'S NOT YOUR FAULT.
I KNOW IT'S NOT MY FAULT. IT'S *YOURS!*
WHAT ON EARTH WERE YOU DOING, ANYWAY?

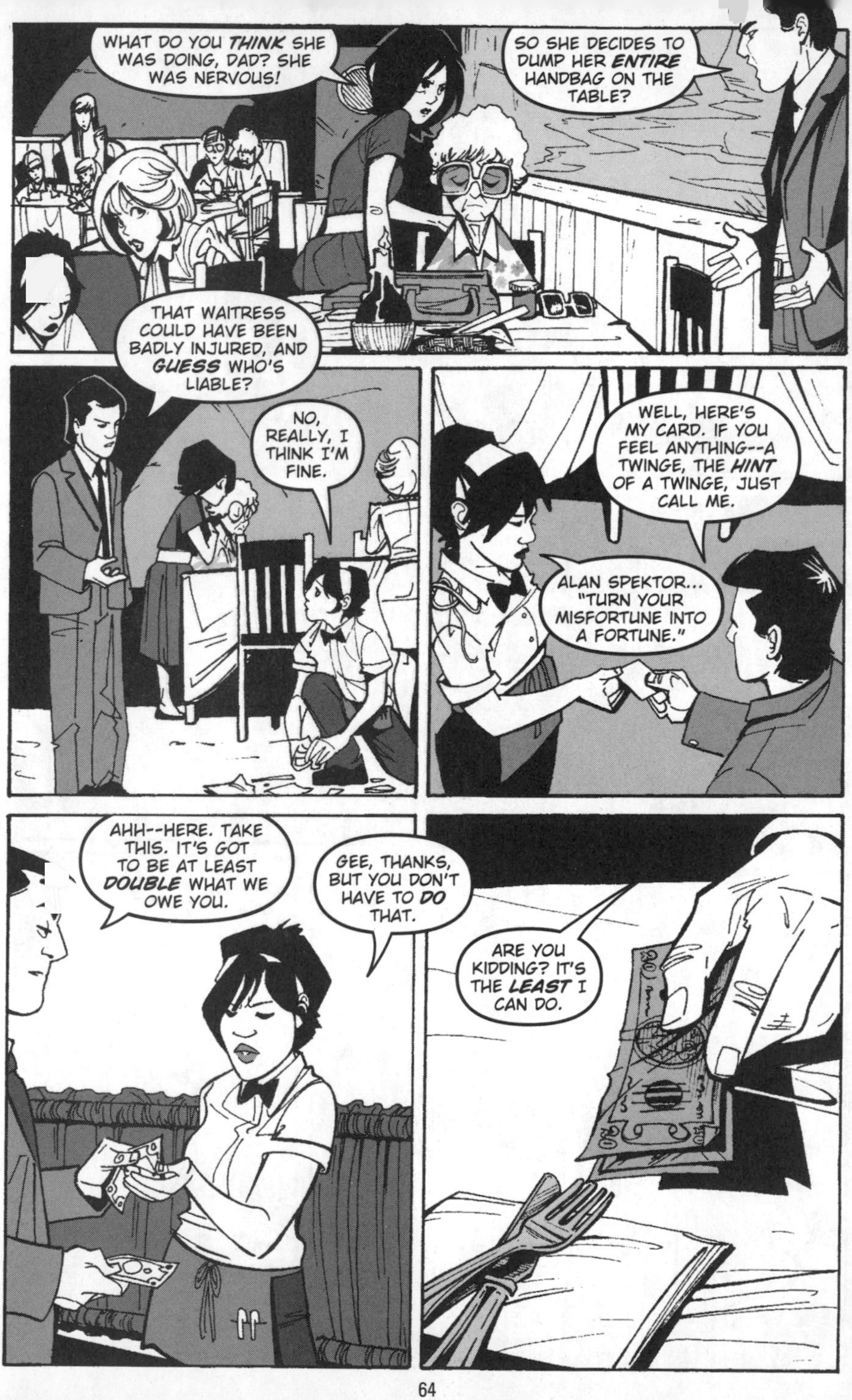
WHAT DO YOU THINK SHE WAS DOING, DAD? SHE WAS NERVOUS!
SO SHE DECIDES TO DUMP HER ENTIRE HANDBAG ON THE TABLE?
THAT WAITRESS COULD HAVE BEEN BADLY INJURED, AND GUESS WHO'S LIABLE?
NO, REALLY, I THINK I'M FINE.
WELL, HERE'S MY CARD. IF YOU FEEL ANYTHING--A TWINGE, THE HINT OF A TWINGE, JUST CALL ME.
ALAN SPEKTOR... "TURN YOUR MISFORTUNE INTO A FORTUNE."
AHH--HERE. TAKE THIS. IT'S GOT TO BE AT LEAST DOUBLE WHAT WE OWE YOU.
GEE, THANKS, BUT YOU DON'T HAVE TO DO THAT.
ARE YOU KIDDING? IT'S THE LEAST I CAN DO.

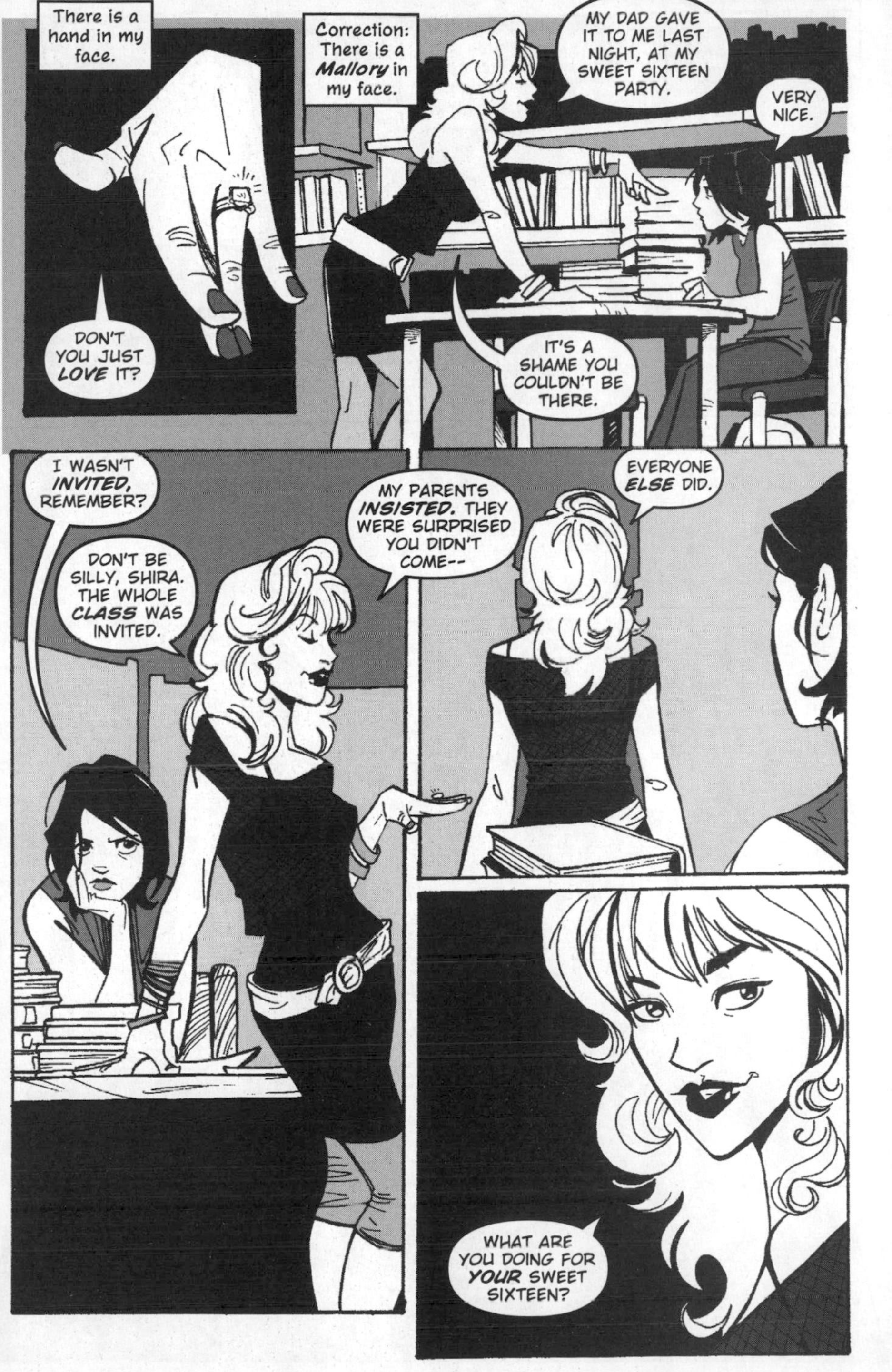
There is a hand in my face.
DON'T YOU JUST LOVE IT?
Correction: There is a Mallory in my face.
MY DAD GAVE IT TO ME LAST NIGHT, AT MY SWEET SIXTEEN PARTY.
VERY NICE.
IT'S A SHAME YOU COULDN'T BE THERE.
I WASN'T INVITED, REMEMBER?
DON'T BE SILLY, SHIRA. THE WHOLE CLASS WAS INVITED.
MY PARENTS INSISTED. THEY WERE SURPRISED YOU DIDN'T COME--
EVERYONE ELSE DID.
WHAT ARE YOU DOING FOR YOUR SWEET SIXTEEN?

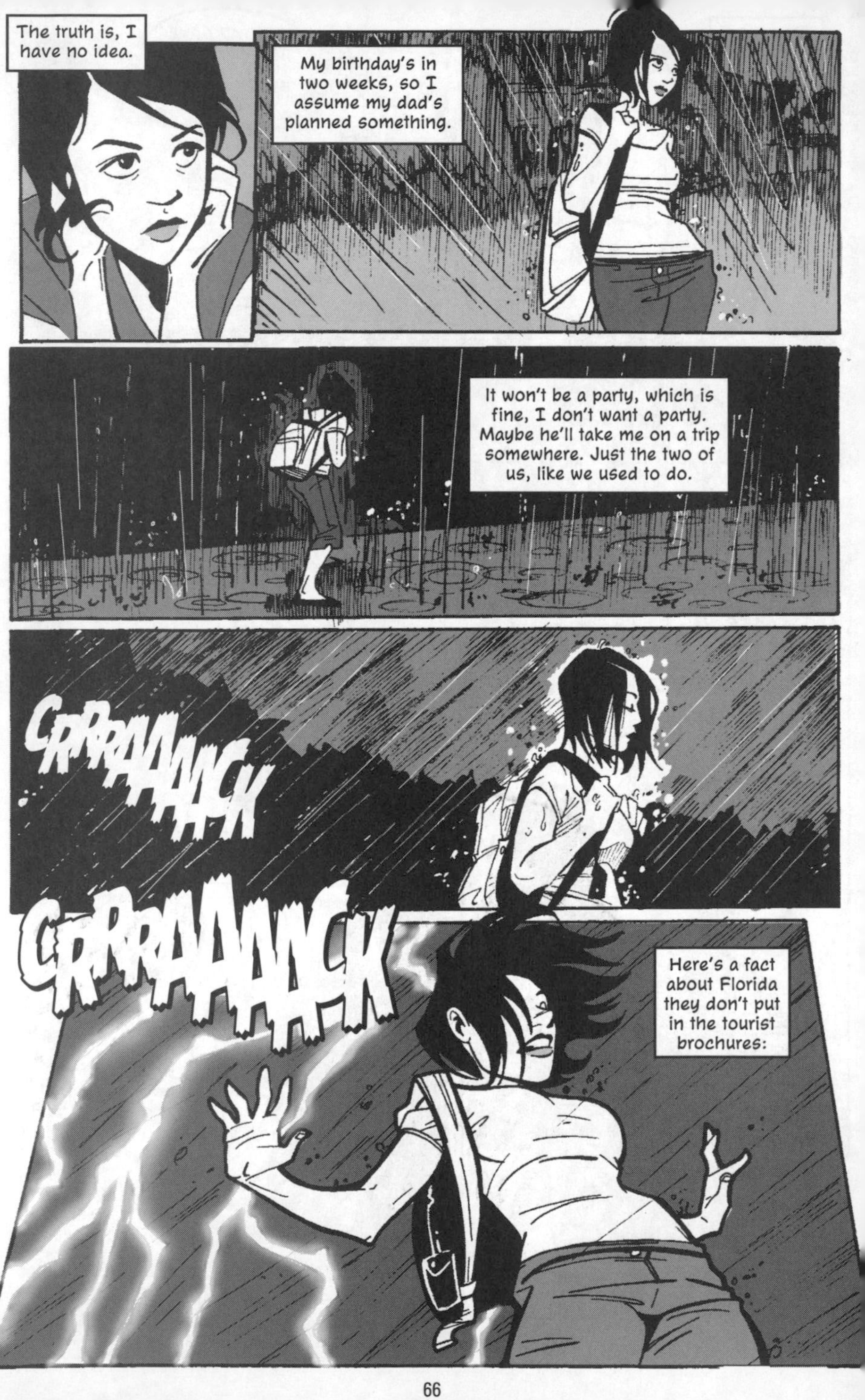
The truth is, I have no idea.
My birthday's in two weeks, so I assume my dad's planned something.
It won't be a party, which is fine, I don't want a party. Maybe he'll take me on a trip somewhere. Just the two of us, like we used to do.
CRRRAAAACK
CRRRAAAACK
Here's a fact about Florida they don't put in the tourist brochures:

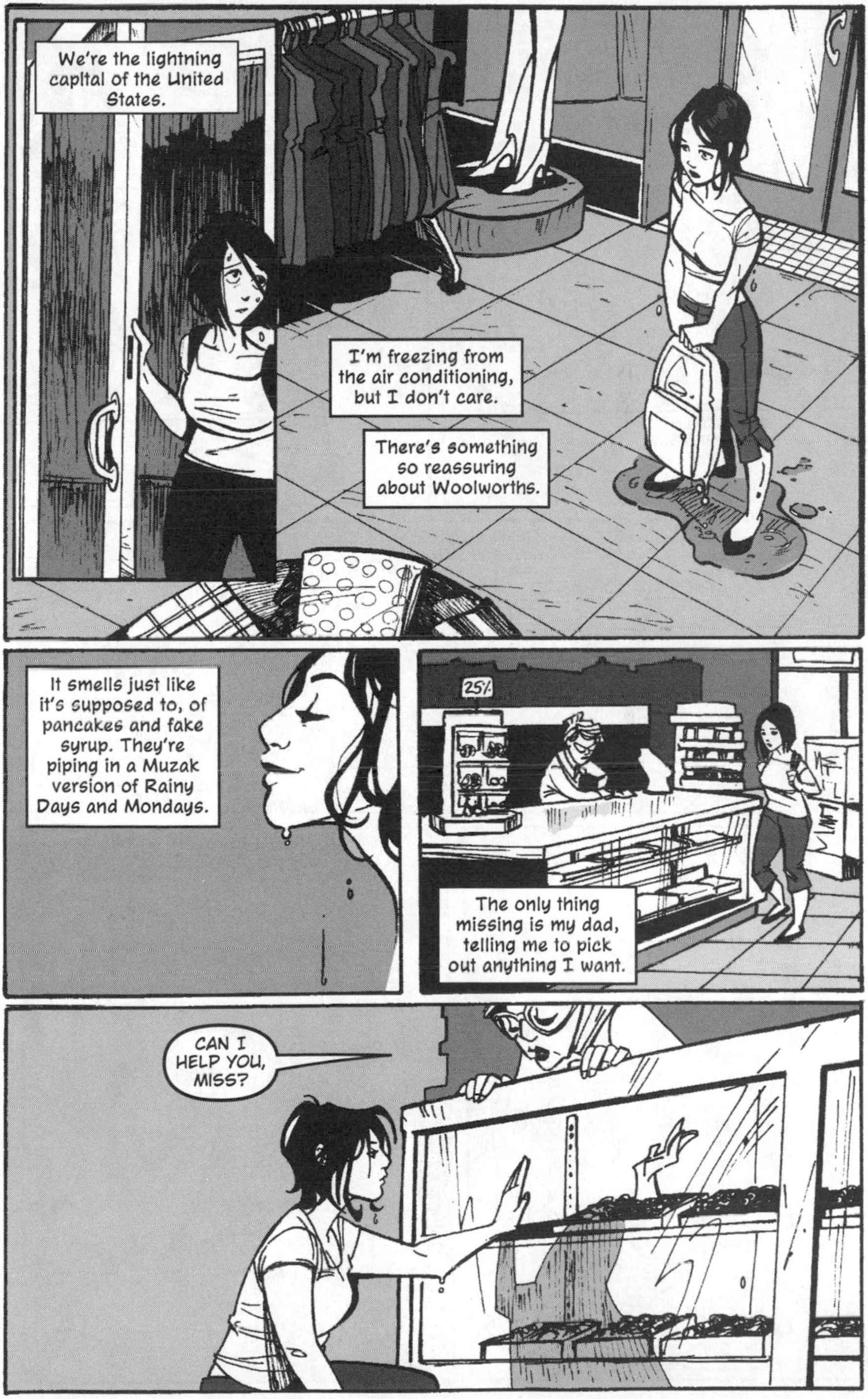
We're the lightning capital of the United States.
I'm freezing from the air conditioning, but I don't care.
There's something so reassuring about Woolworths.
It smells just like it's supposed to, of pancakes and fake syrup. They're piping in a Muzak version of Rainy Days and Mondays.
25%
The only thing missing is my dad, telling me to pick out anything I want.
CAN I HELP YOU, MISS?

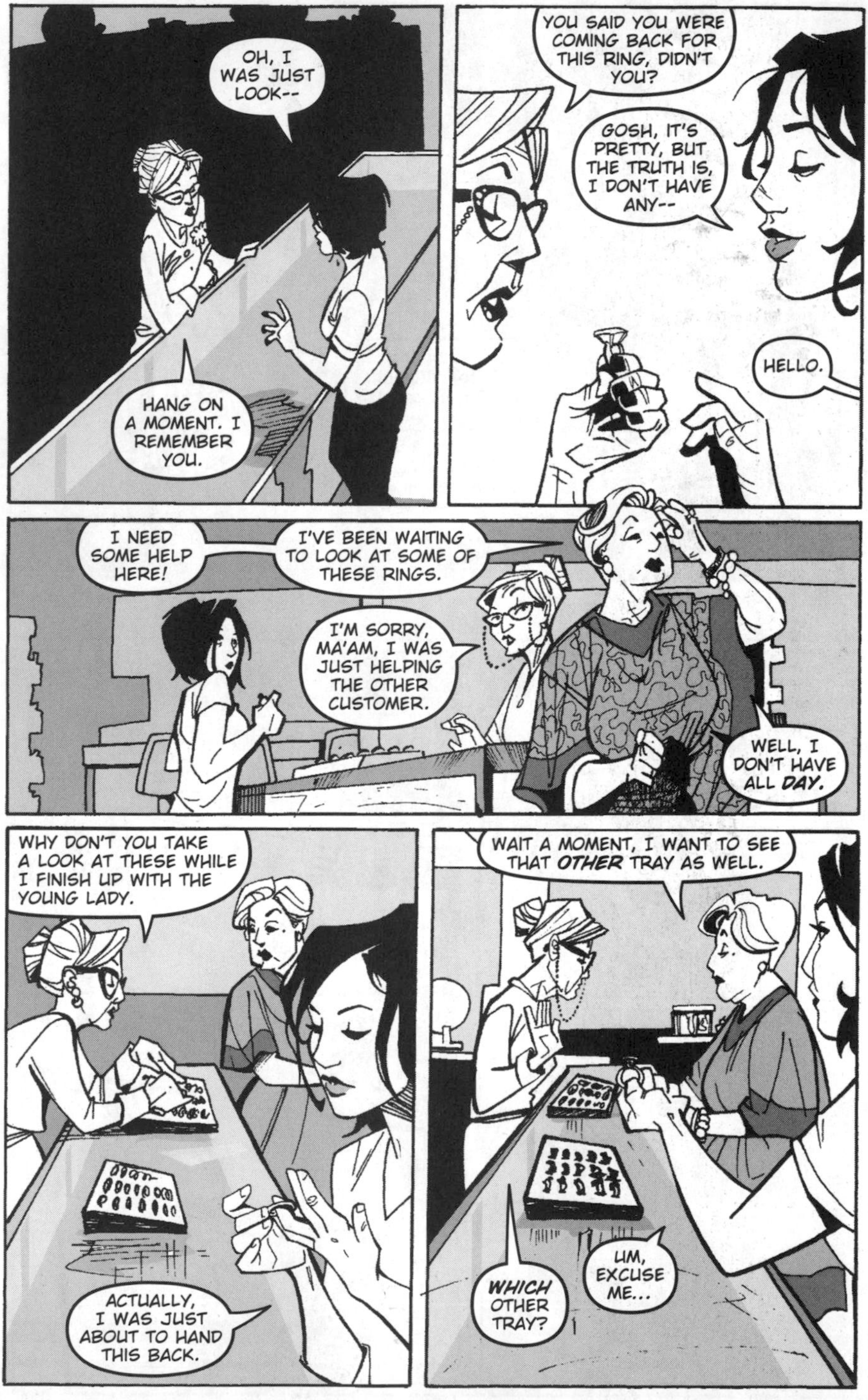
OH, I WAS JUST LOOK--
HANG ON A MOMENT. I REMEMBER YOU.
YOU SAID YOU WERE COMING BACK FOR THIS RING, DIDN'T YOU?
GOSH, IT'S PRETTY, BUT THE TRUTH IS, I DON'T HAVE ANY--
HELLO.
I NEED SOME HELP HERE!
I'VE BEEN WAITING TO LOOK AT SOME OF THESE RINGS.
I'M SORRY, MA'AM, I WAS JUST HELPING THE OTHER CUSTOMER.
WELL, I DON'T HAVE ALL DAY.
WHY DON'T YOU TAKE A LOOK AT THESE WHILE I FINISH UP WITH THE YOUNG LADY.
ACTUALLY, I WAS JUST ABOUT TO HAND THIS BACK.
WAIT A MOMENT, I WANT TO SEE THAT OTHER TRAY AS WELL.
WHICH OTHER TRAY?
UM, EXCUSE ME...

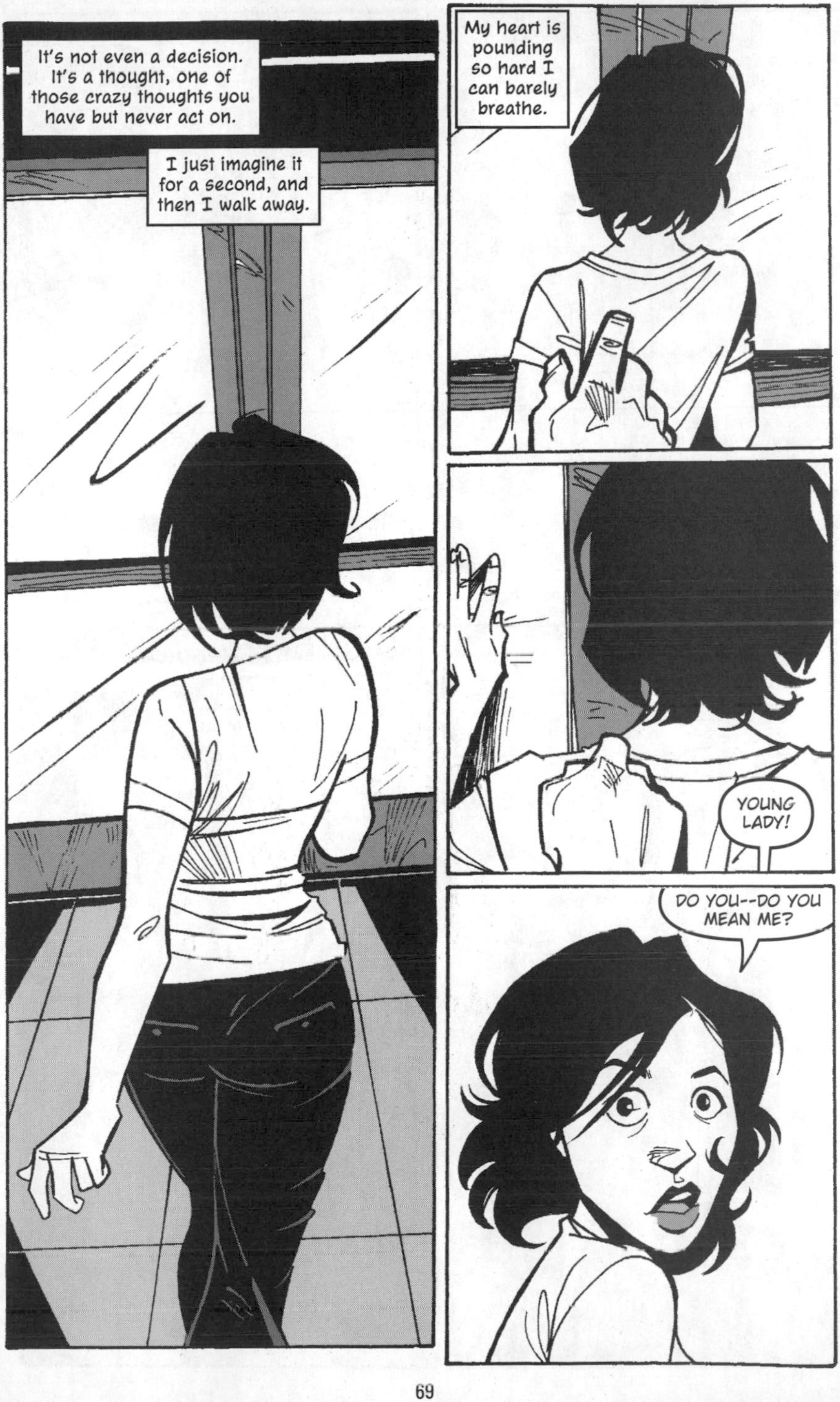
It's not even a decision. It's a thought, one of those crazy thoughts you have but never act on.
I just imagine it for a second, and then I walk away.
My heart is pounding so hard I can barely breathe.
YOUNG LADY!
DO YOU--DO YOU MEAN ME?

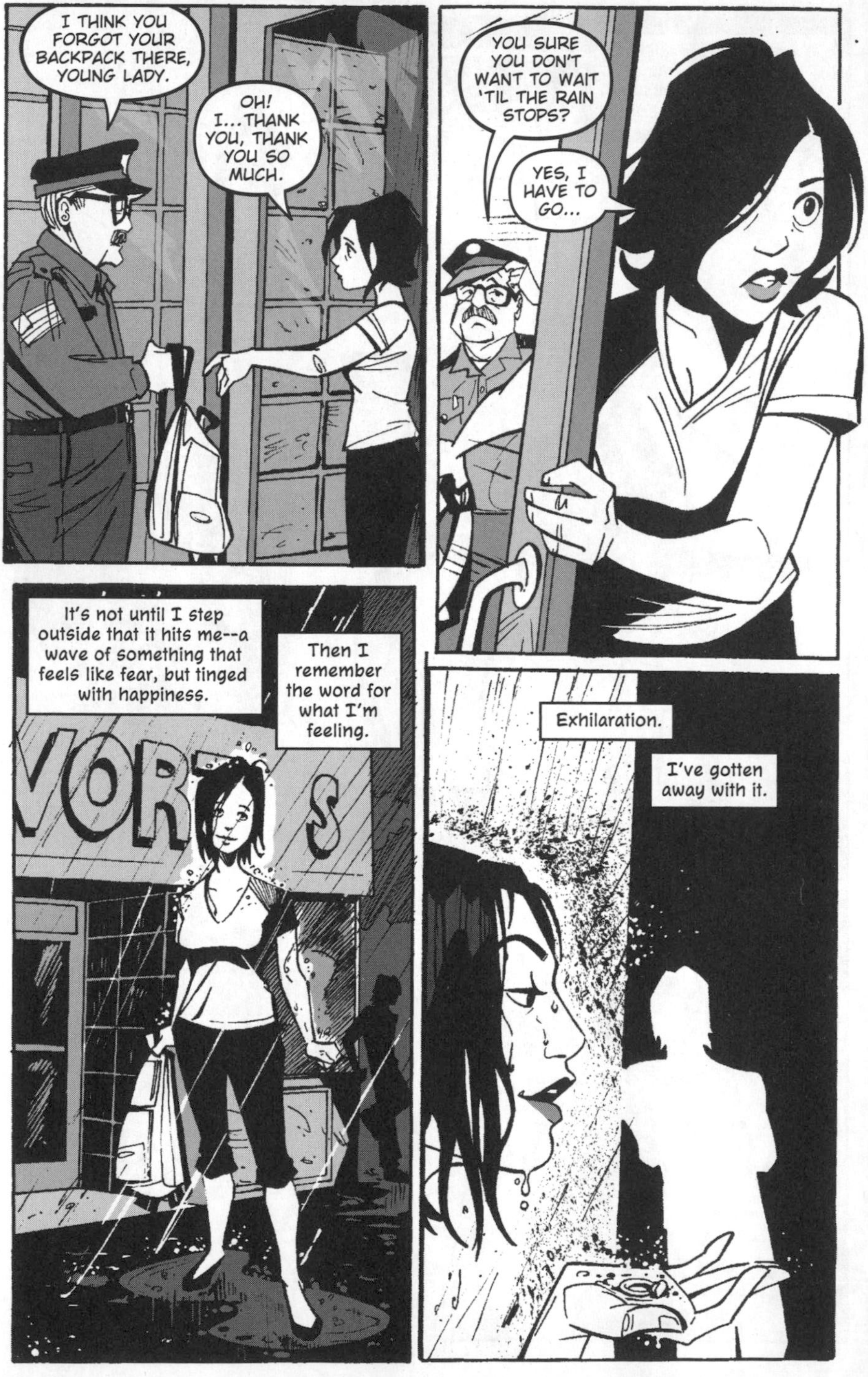
I THINK YOU FORGOT YOUR BACKPACK THERE, YOUNG LADY.
OH! I...THANK YOU, THANK YOU SO MUCH.
YOU SURE YOU DON'T WANT TO WAIT 'TIL THE RAIN STOPS?
YES, I HAVE TO GO...
It's not until I step outside that it hits me--a wave of something that feels like fear, but tinged with happiness.
Then I remember the word for what I'm feeling.
Exhilaration.
I've gotten away with it.

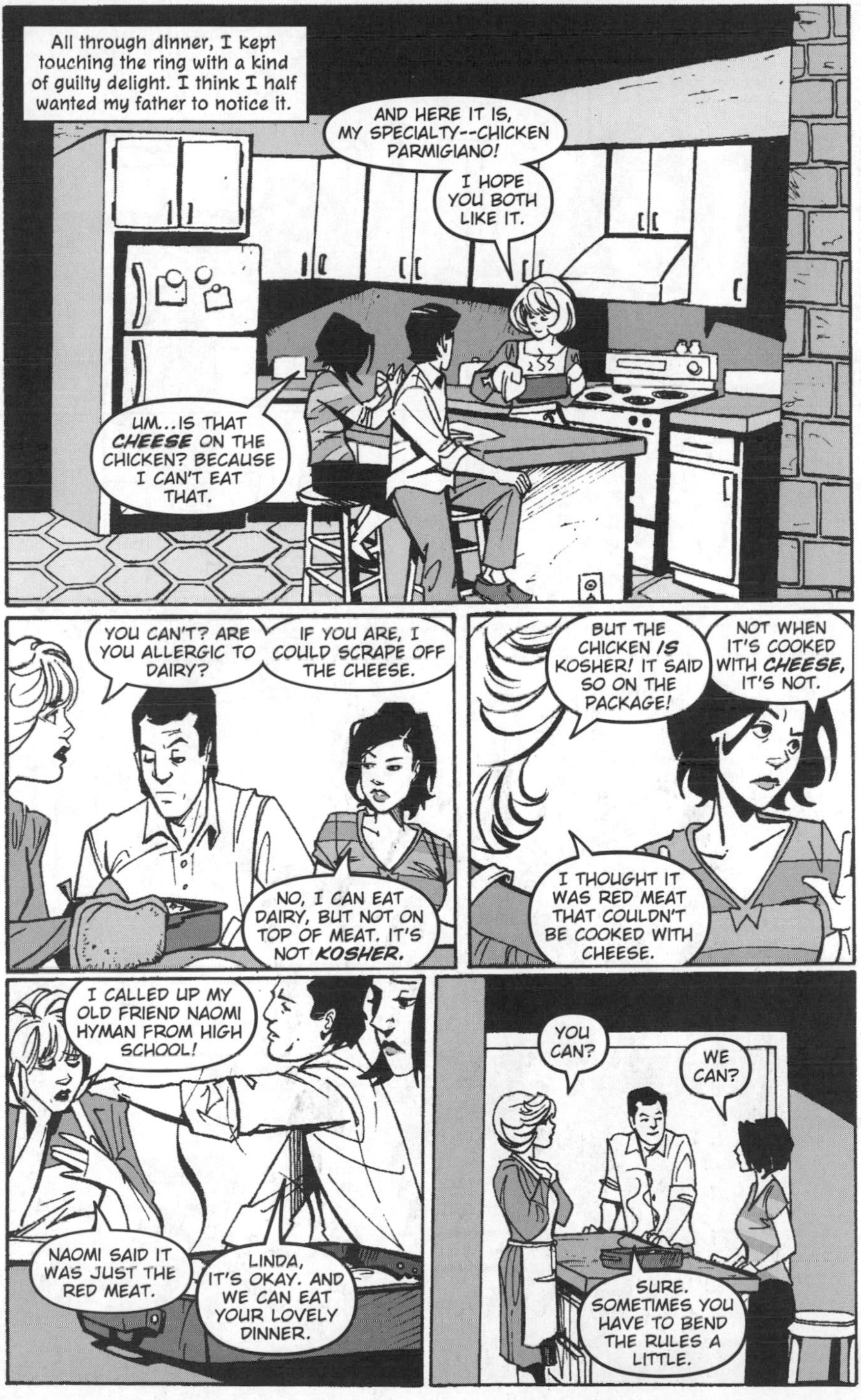
All through dinner, I kept touching the ring with a kind of guilty delight. I think I half wanted my father to notice it.
AND HERE IT IS, MY SPECIALTY--CHICKEN PARMIGIANO!
I HOPE YOU BOTH LIKE IT.
UM...IS THAT CHEESE ON THE CHICKEN? BECAUSE I CAN'T EAT THAT.
YOU CAN'T? ARE YOU ALLERGIC TO DAIRY?
IF YOU ARE, I COULD SCRAPE OFF THE CHEESE.
NO, I CAN EAT DAIRY, BUT NOT ON TOP OF MEAT. IT'S NOT KOSHER.
BUT THE CHICKEN IS KOSHER! IT SAID SO ON THE PACKAGE!
NOT WHEN IT'S COOKED WITH CHEESE, IT'S NOT.
I THOUGHT IT WAS RED MEAT THAT COULDN'T BE COOKED WITH CHEESE.
I CALLED UP MY OLD FRIEND NAOMI HYMAN FROM HIGH SCHOOL!
NAOMI SAID IT WAS JUST THE RED MEAT.
LINDA, IT'S OKAY. AND WE CAN EAT YOUR LOVELY DINNER.
YOU CAN?
WE CAN?
SURE. SOMETIMES YOU HAVE TO BEND THE RULES A LITTLE.

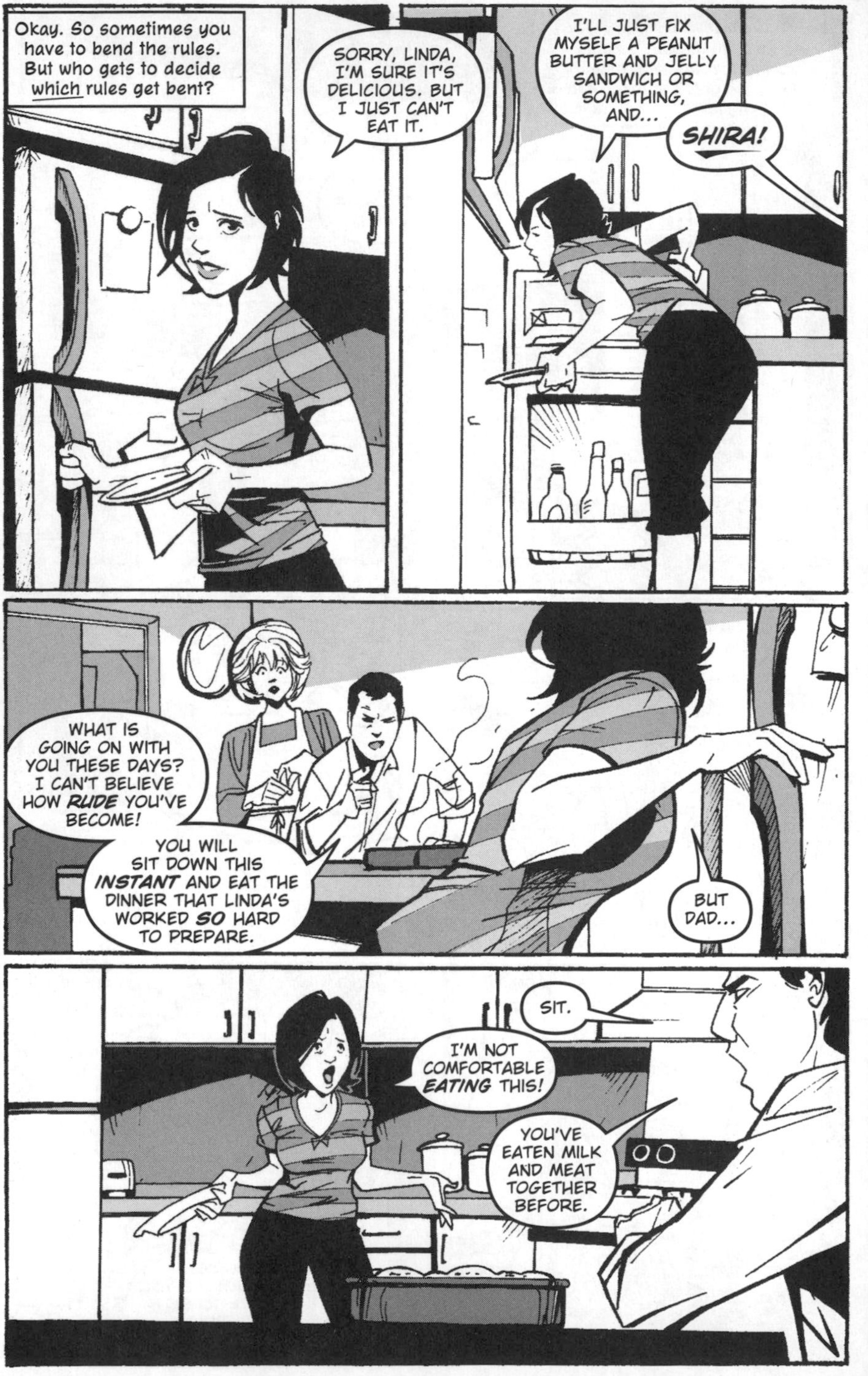
Okay. So sometimes you have to bend the rules. But who gets to decide which rules get bent?
SORRY, LINDA, I'M SURE IT'S DELICIOUS. BUT I JUST CAN'T EAT IT.
I'LL JUST FIX MYSELF A PEANUT BUTTER AND JELLY SANDWICH OR SOMETHING, AND...
SHIRA!
WHAT IS GOING ON WITH YOU THESE DAYS? I CAN'T BELIEVE HOW RUDE YOU'VE BECOME!
YOU WILL SIT DOWN THIS INSTANT AND EAT THE DINNER THAT LINDA'S WORKED SO HARD TO PREPARE.
BUT DAD...
SIT.
I'M NOT COMFORTABLE EATING THIS!
YOU'VE EATEN MILK AND MEAT TOGETHER BEFORE.

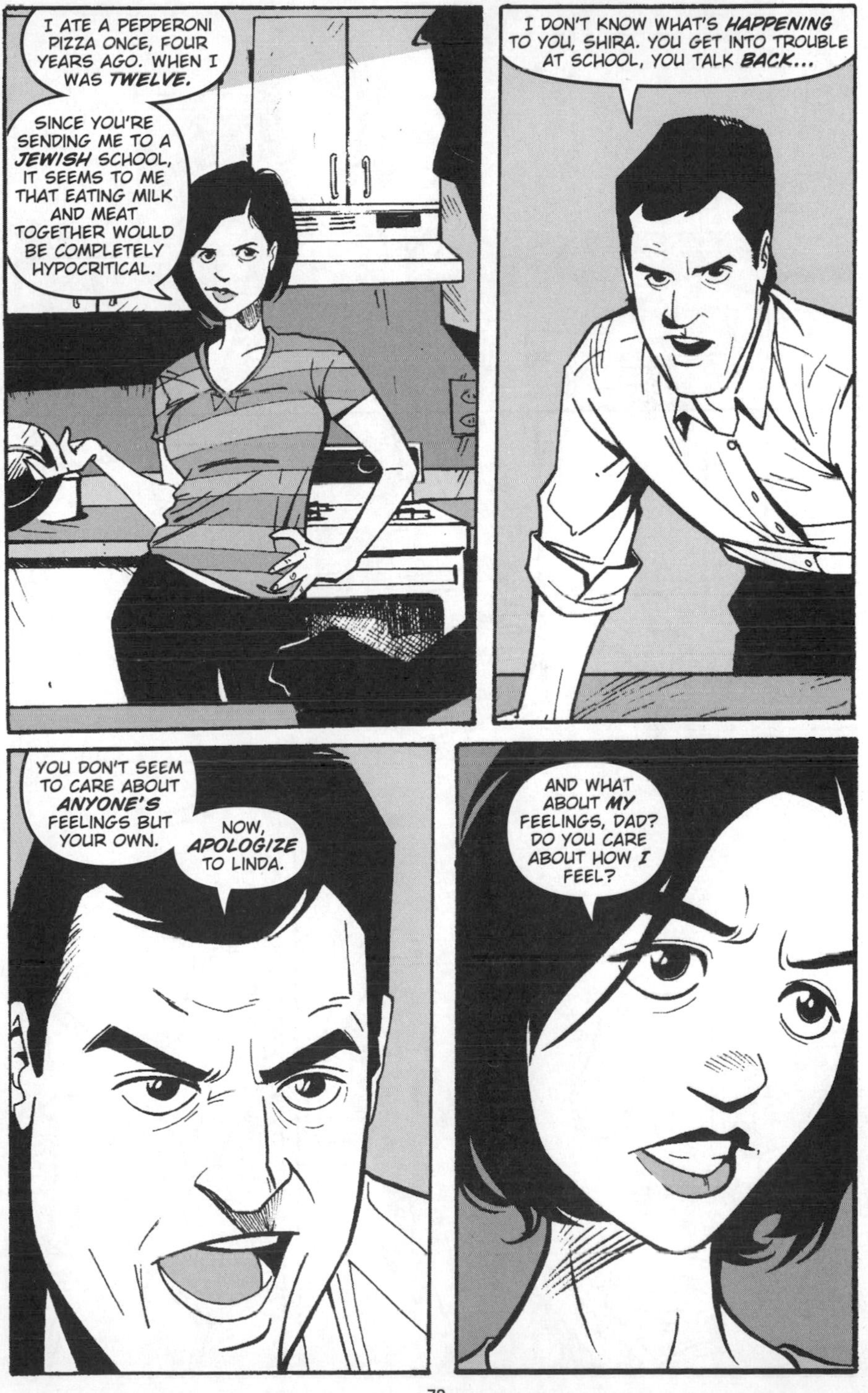
I ATE A PEPPERONI PIZZA ONCE, FOUR YEARS AGO. WHEN I WAS TWELVE.
SINCE YOU'RE SENDING ME TO A JEWISH SCHOOL, IT SEEMS TO ME THAT EATING MILK AND MEAT TOGETHER WOULD BE COMPLETELY HYPOCRITICAL.
I DON'T KNOW WHAT'S HAPPENING TO YOU, SHIRA. YOU GET INTO TROUBLE AT SCHOOL, YOU TALK BACK...
YOU DON'T SEEM TO CARE ABOUT ANYONE'S FEELINGS BUT YOUR OWN.
NOW, APOLOGIZE TO LINDA.
AND WHAT ABOUT MY FEELINGS, DAD? DO YOU CARE ABOUT HOW I FEEL?

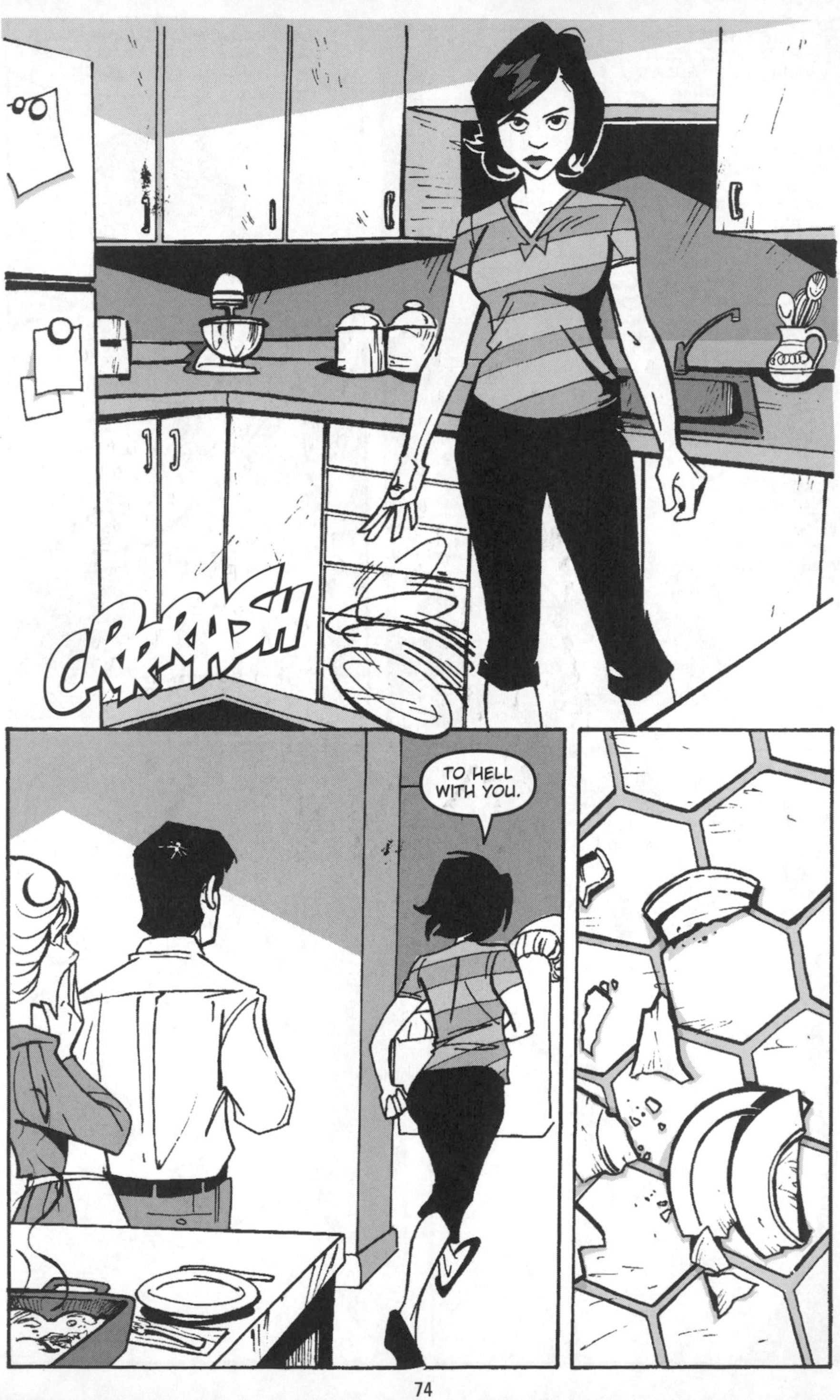
CRRRASH
TO HELL WITH YOU.

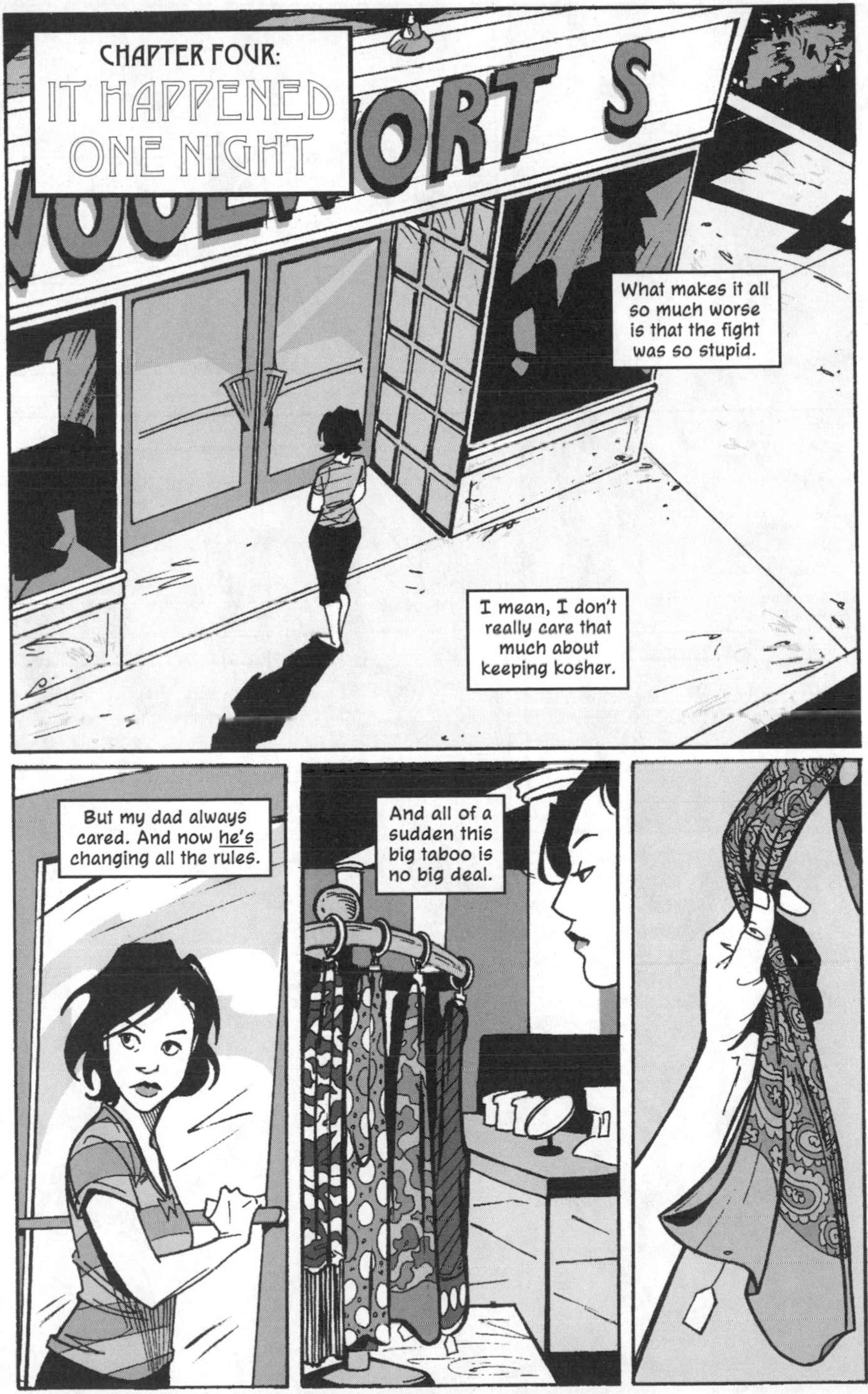
CHAPTER FOUR:
IT HAPPENED ONE NIGHT
What makes it all so much worse is that the fight was so stupid.
I mean, I don't really care that much about keeping kosher.
But my dad always cared. And now he's changing all the rules.
And all of a sudden this big taboo is no big deal.

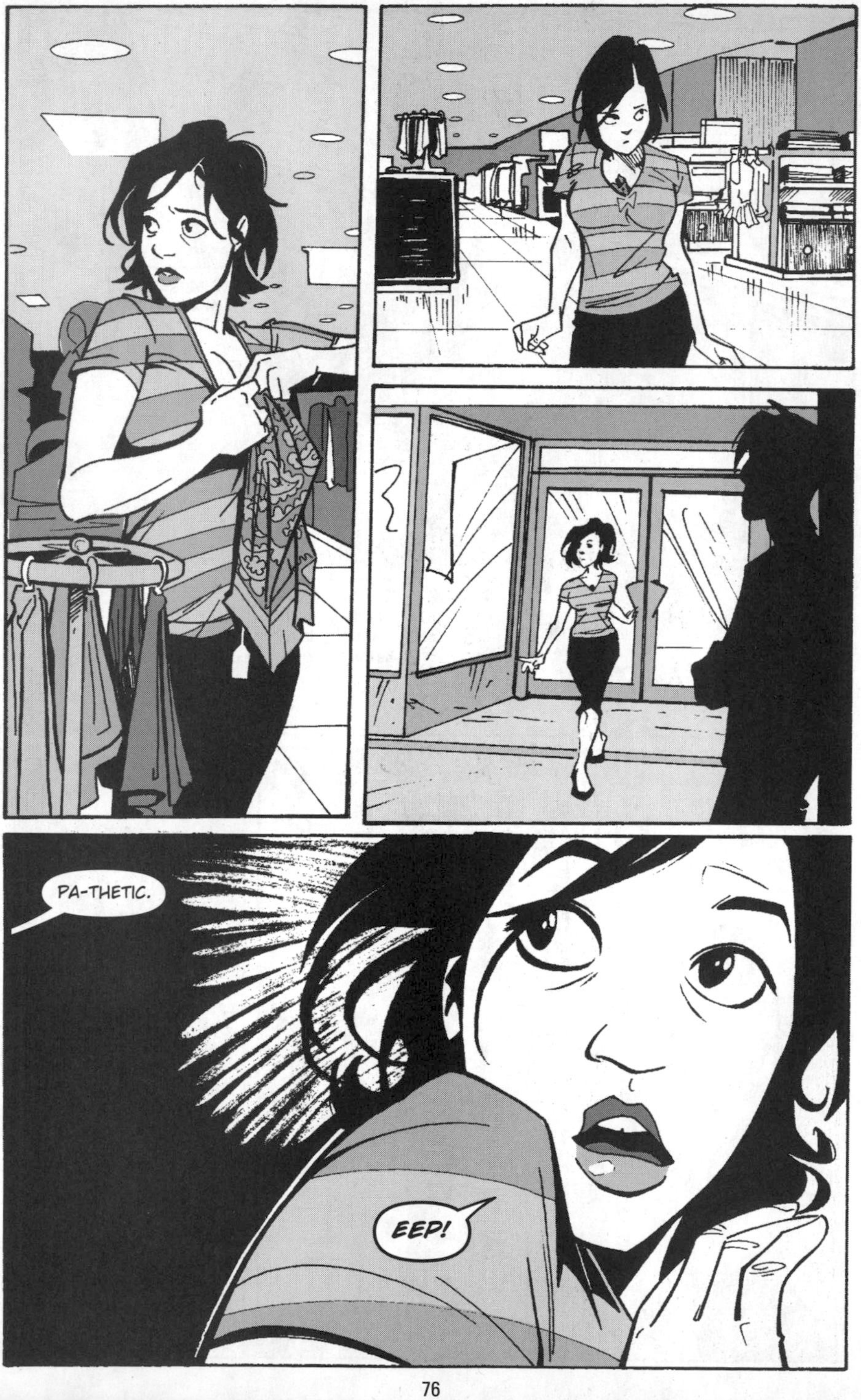
PA-THETIC.
EEP!

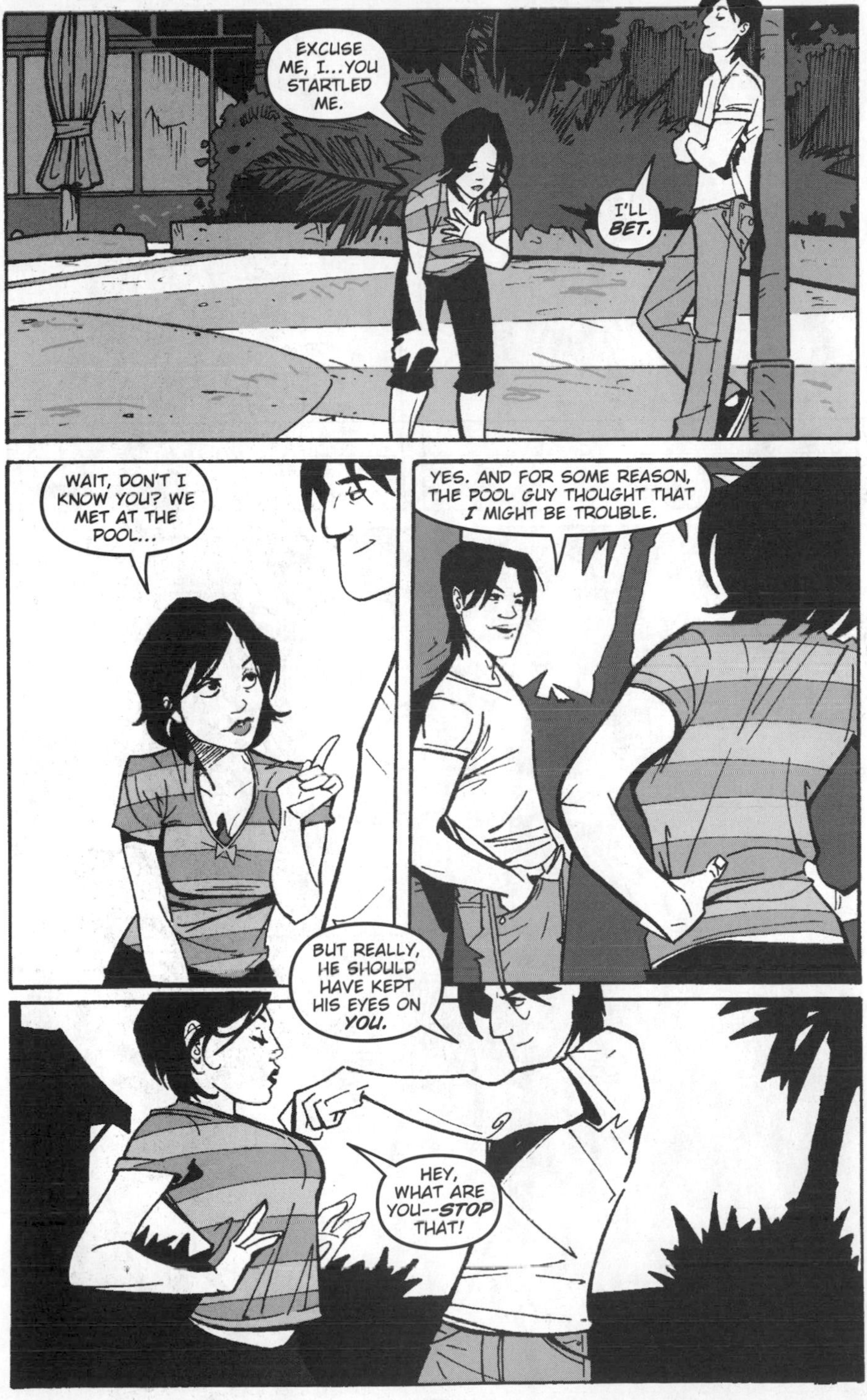
EXCUSE ME, I...YOU STARTLED ME.
I'LL *BET.*
WAIT, DON'T I KNOW YOU? WE MET AT THE POOL...
YES. AND FOR SOME REASON, THE POOL GUY THOUGHT THAT *I* MIGHT BE TROUBLE.
BUT REALLY, HE SHOULD HAVE KEPT HIS EYES ON *YOU.*
HEY, WHAT ARE YOU--*STOP* THAT!

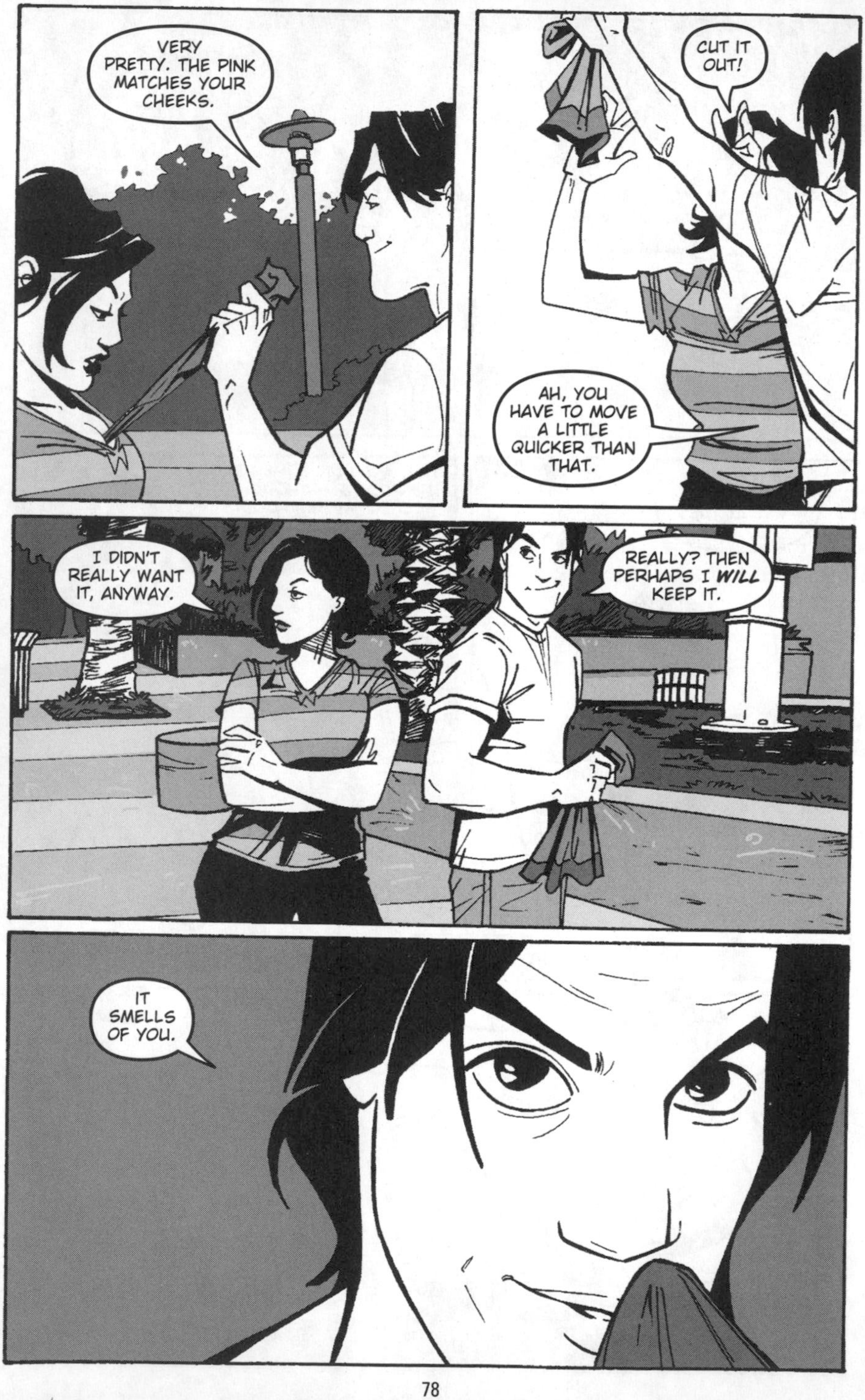
VERY PRETTY. THE PINK MATCHES YOUR CHEEKS.
CUT IT OUT!
AH, YOU HAVE TO MOVE A LITTLE QUICKER THAN THAT.
I DIDN'T REALLY WANT IT, ANYWAY.
REALLY? THEN PERHAPS I *WILL* KEEP IT.
IT SMELLS OF YOU.

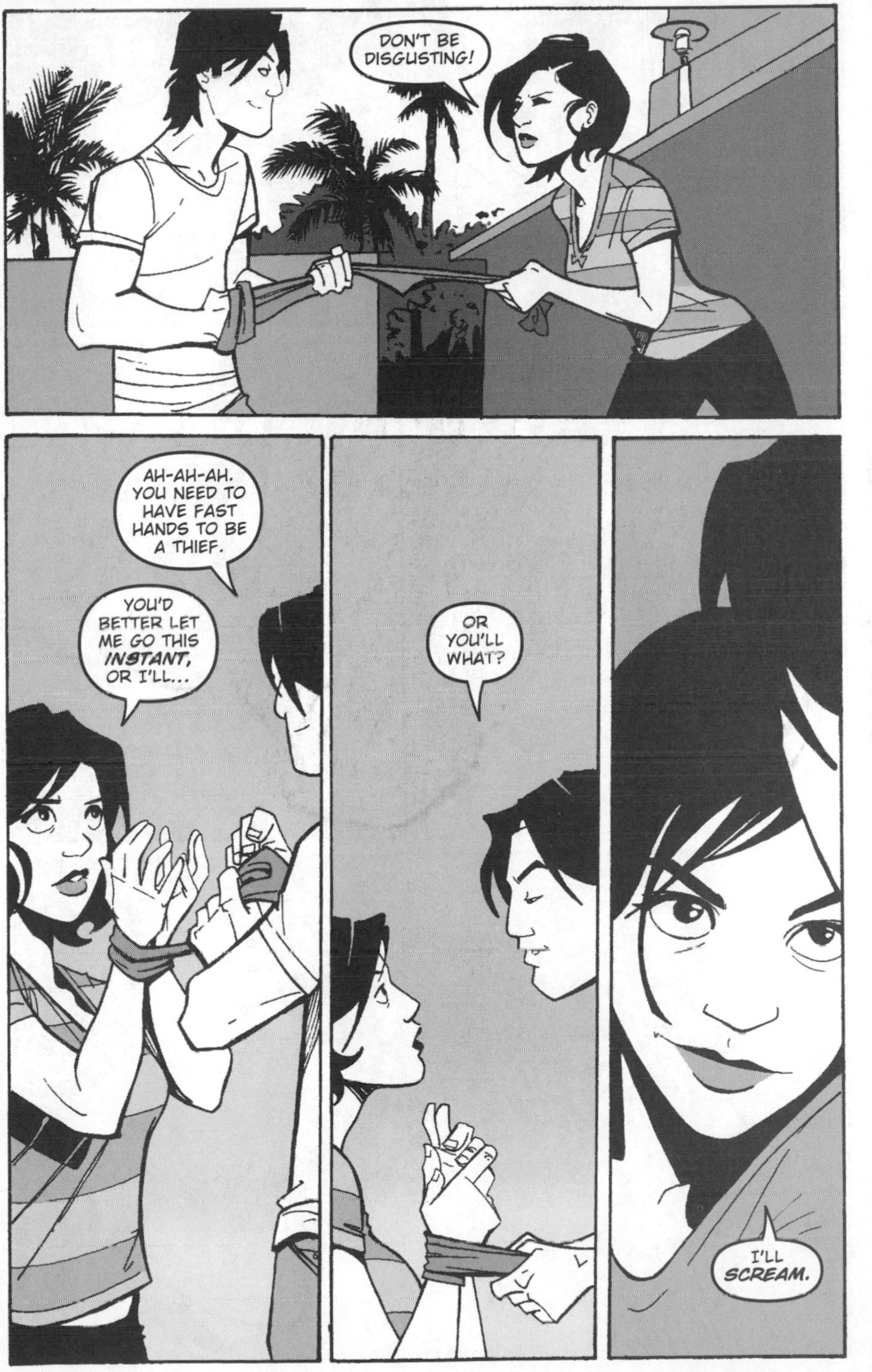
DON'T BE DISGUSTING!
AH-AH-AH. YOU NEED TO HAVE FAST HANDS TO BE A THIEF.
YOU'D BETTER LET ME GO THIS *INSTANT*, OR I'LL...
OR YOU'LL WHAT?
I'LL *SCREAM.*

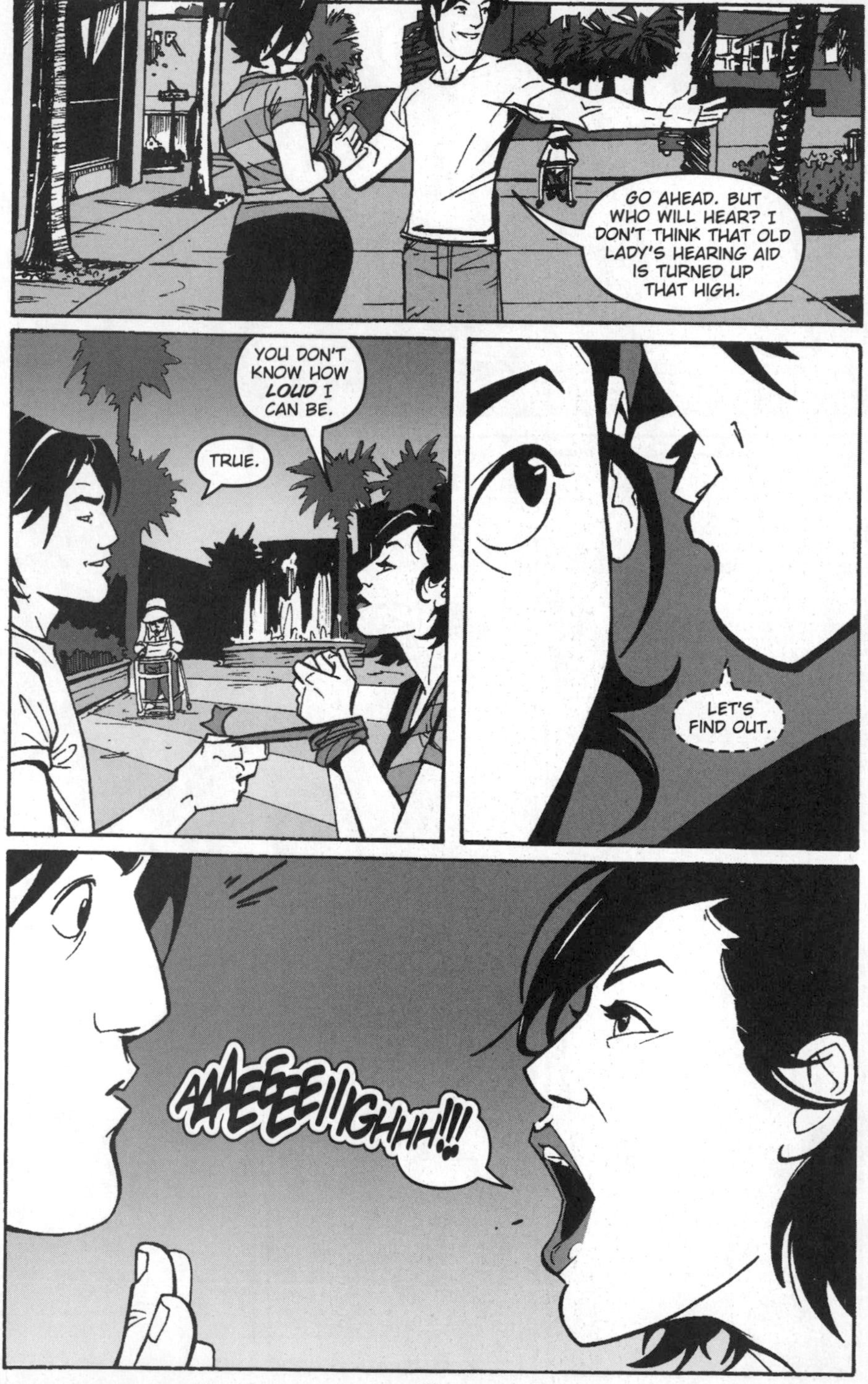
GO AHEAD. BUT WHO WILL HEAR? I DON'T THINK THAT OLD LADY'S HEARING AID IS TURNED UP THAT HIGH.
YOU DON'T KNOW HOW *LOUD* I CAN BE.
TRUE.
LET'S FIND OUT.
AAAEEEEIIIGHHH!!!

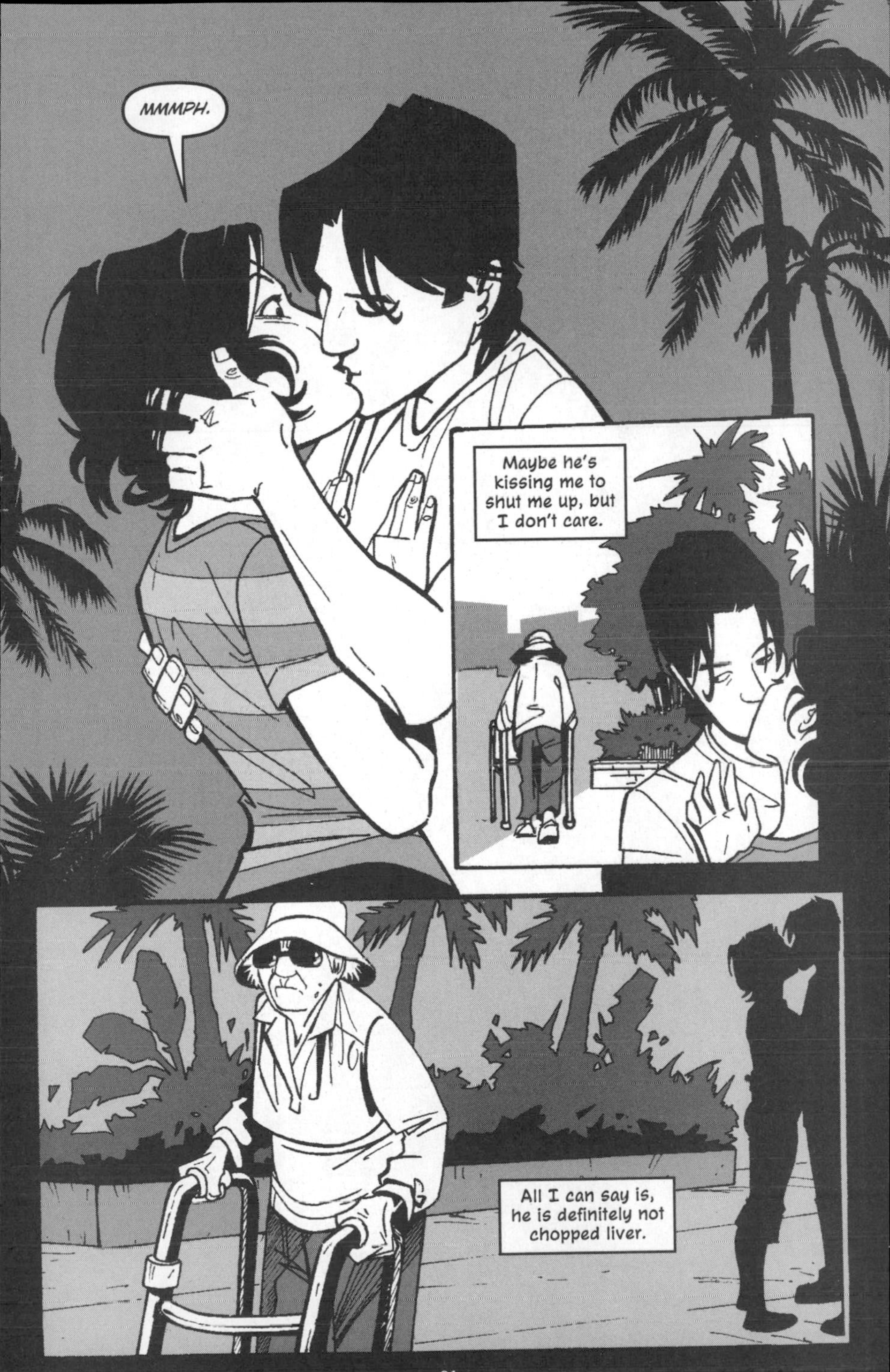
MMMPH.
Maybe he's kissing me to shut me up, but I don't care.
All I can say is, he is definitely not chopped liver.

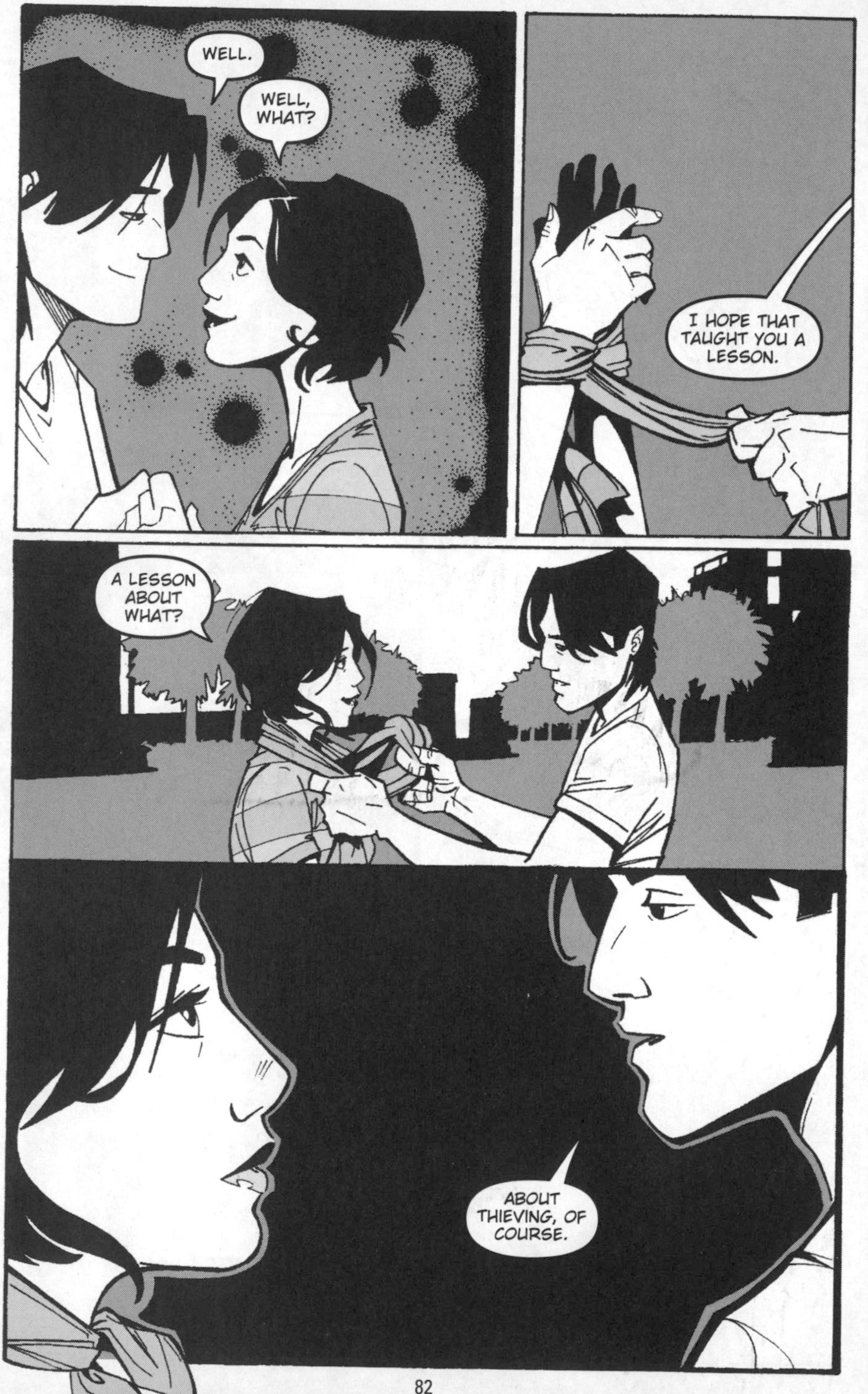
WELL.
WELL, WHAT?
I HOPE THAT TAUGHT YOU A LESSON.
A LESSON ABOUT WHAT?
ABOUT THIEVING, OF COURSE.

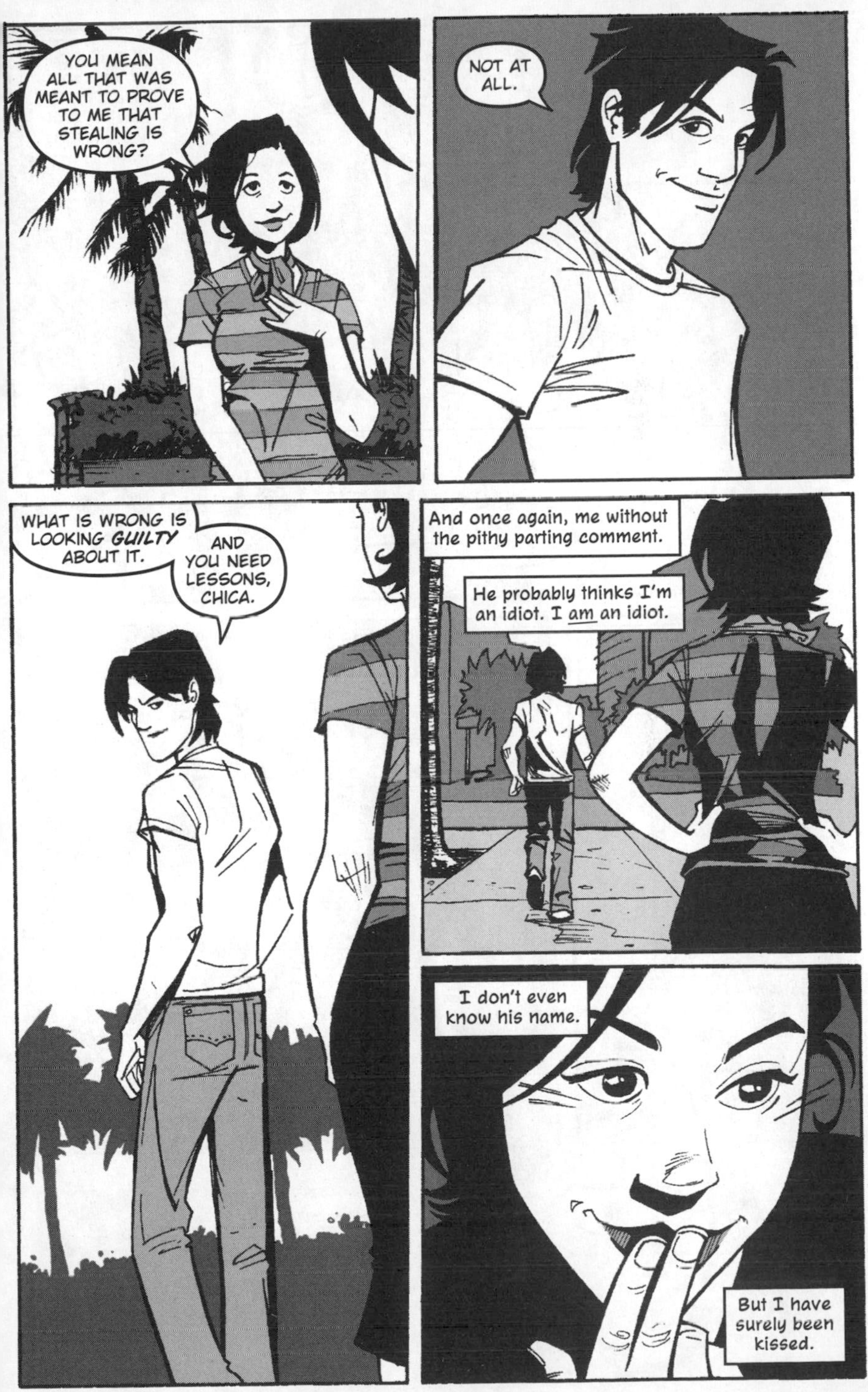
YOU MEAN ALL THAT WAS MEANT TO PROVE TO ME THAT STEALING IS WRONG?
NOT AT ALL.
WHAT IS WRONG IS LOOKING GUILTY ABOUT IT.
AND YOU NEED LESSONS, CHICA.
And once again, me without the pithy parting comment.
He probably thinks I'm an idiot. I am an idiot.
I don't even know his name.
But I have surely been kissed.

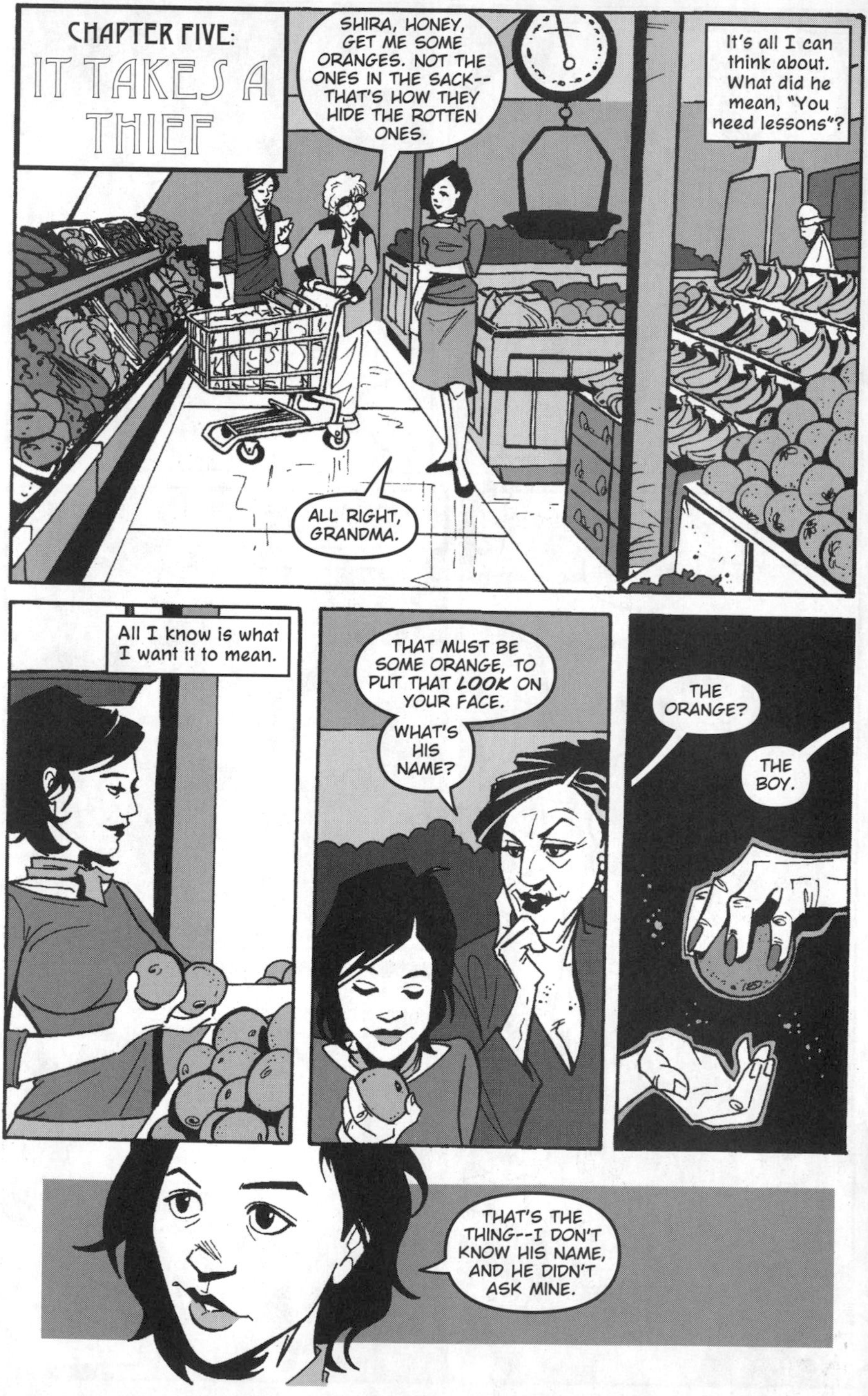
CHAPTER FIVE:
IT TAKES A THIEF
SHIRA, HONEY, GET ME SOME ORANGES. NOT THE ONES IN THE SACK-- THAT'S HOW THEY HIDE THE ROTTEN ONES.
It's all I can think about. What did he mean, "You need lessons"?
ALL RIGHT, GRANDMA.
All I know is what I want it to mean.
THAT MUST BE SOME ORANGE, TO PUT THAT *LOOK* ON YOUR FACE.
WHAT'S HIS NAME?
THE ORANGE?
THE BOY.
THAT'S THE THING--I DON'T KNOW HIS NAME, AND HE DIDN'T ASK MINE.

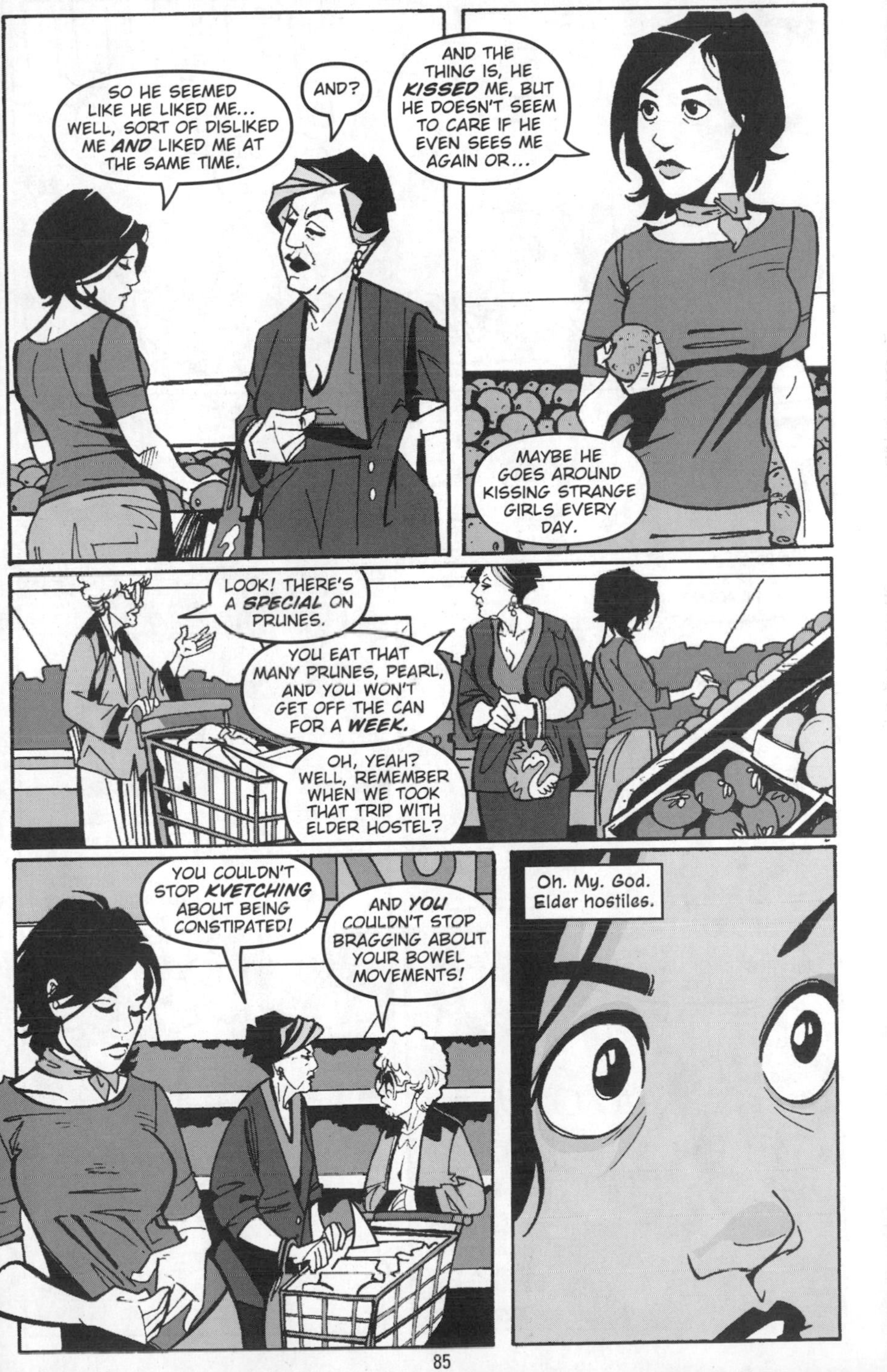
SO HE SEEMED LIKE HE LIKED ME... WELL, SORT OF DISLIKED ME AND LIKED ME AT THE SAME TIME.
AND?
AND THE THING IS, HE KISSED ME, BUT HE DOESN'T SEEM TO CARE IF HE EVEN SEES ME AGAIN OR...
MAYBE HE GOES AROUND KISSING STRANGE GIRLS EVERY DAY.
LOOK! THERE'S A SPECIAL ON PRUNES.
YOU EAT THAT MANY PRUNES, PEARL, AND YOU WON'T GET OFF THE CAN FOR A WEEK.
OH, YEAH? WELL, REMEMBER WHEN WE TOOK THAT TRIP WITH ELDER HOSTEL?
YOU COULDN'T STOP KVETCHING ABOUT BEING CONSTIPATED!
AND YOU COULDN'T STOP BRAGGING ABOUT YOUR BOWEL MOVEMENTS!
Oh. My. God. Elder hostiles.

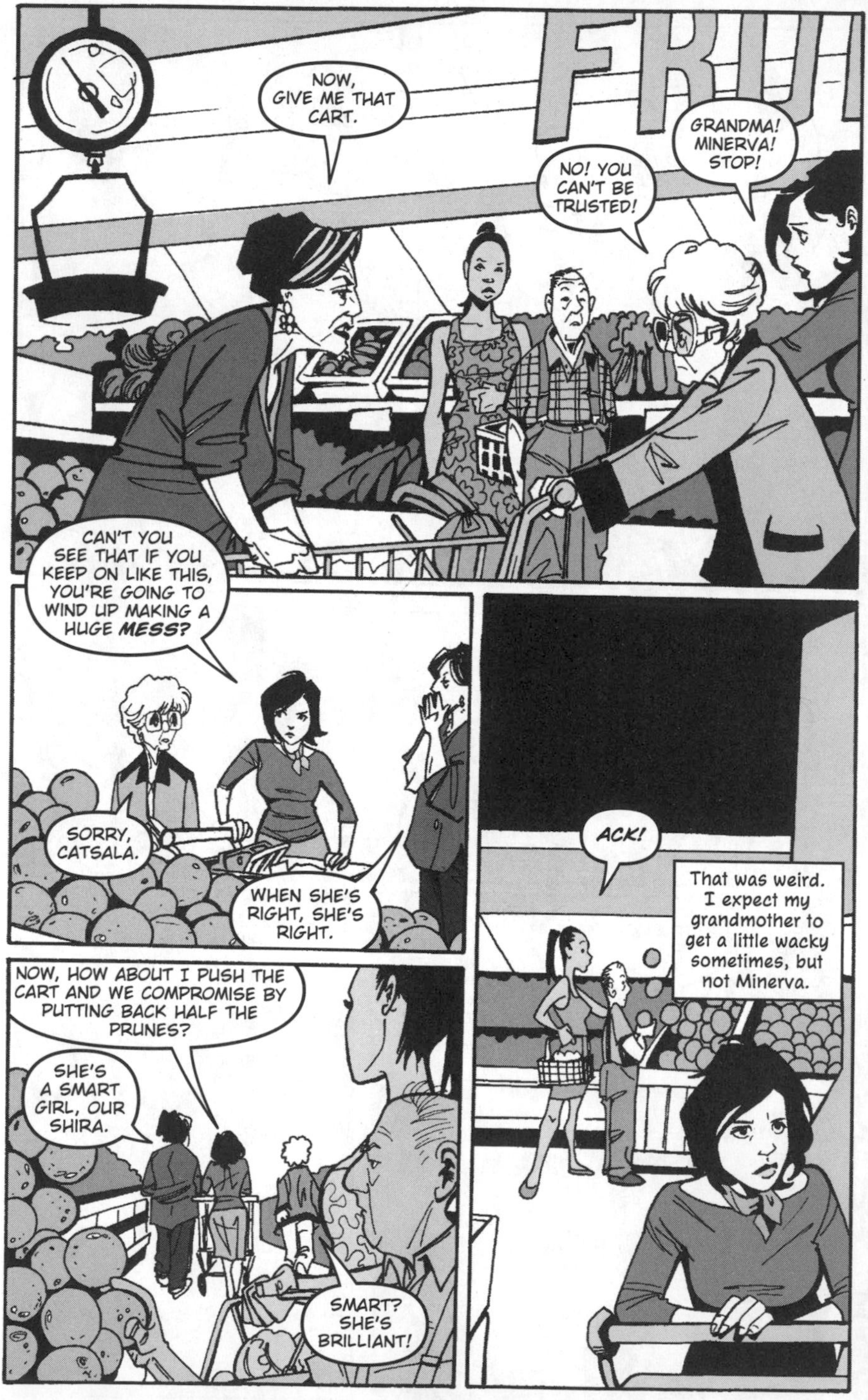
NOW, GIVE ME THAT CART.
NO! YOU CAN'T BE TRUSTED!
GRANDMA! MINERVA! STOP!
CAN'T YOU SEE THAT IF YOU KEEP ON LIKE THIS, YOU'RE GOING TO WIND UP MAKING A HUGE *MESS?*
SORRY, CATSALA.
WHEN SHE'S RIGHT, SHE'S RIGHT.
NOW, HOW ABOUT I PUSH THE CART AND WE COMPROMISE BY PUTTING BACK HALF THE PRUNES?
SHE'S A SMART GIRL, OUR SHIRA.
SMART? SHE'S BRILLIANT!
ACK!
That was weird. I expect my grandmother to get a little wacky sometimes, but not Minerva.

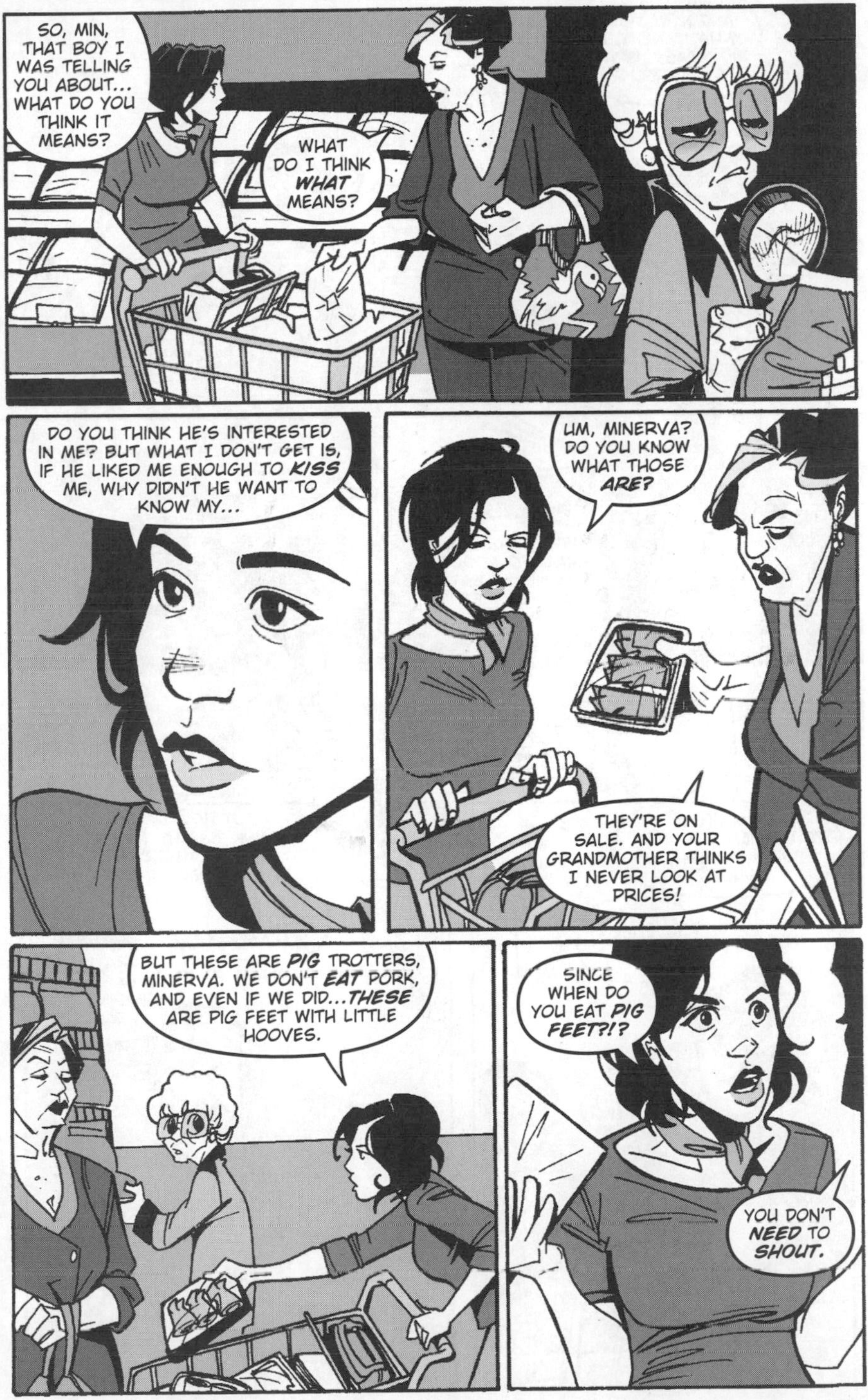
SO, MIN, THAT BOY I WAS TELLING YOU ABOUT... WHAT DO YOU THINK IT MEANS?
WHAT DO I THINK WHAT MEANS?
DO YOU THINK HE'S INTERESTED IN ME? BUT WHAT I DON'T GET IS, IF HE LIKED ME ENOUGH TO KISS ME, WHY DIDN'T HE WANT TO KNOW MY...
UM, MINERVA? DO YOU KNOW WHAT THOSE ARE?
THEY'RE ON SALE. AND YOUR GRANDMOTHER THINKS I NEVER LOOK AT PRICES!
BUT THESE ARE PIG TROTTERS, MINERVA. WE DON'T EAT PORK, AND EVEN IF WE DID...THESE ARE PIG FEET WITH LITTLE HOOVES.
SINCE WHEN DO YOU EAT PIG FEET?!?
YOU DON'T NEED TO SHOUT.

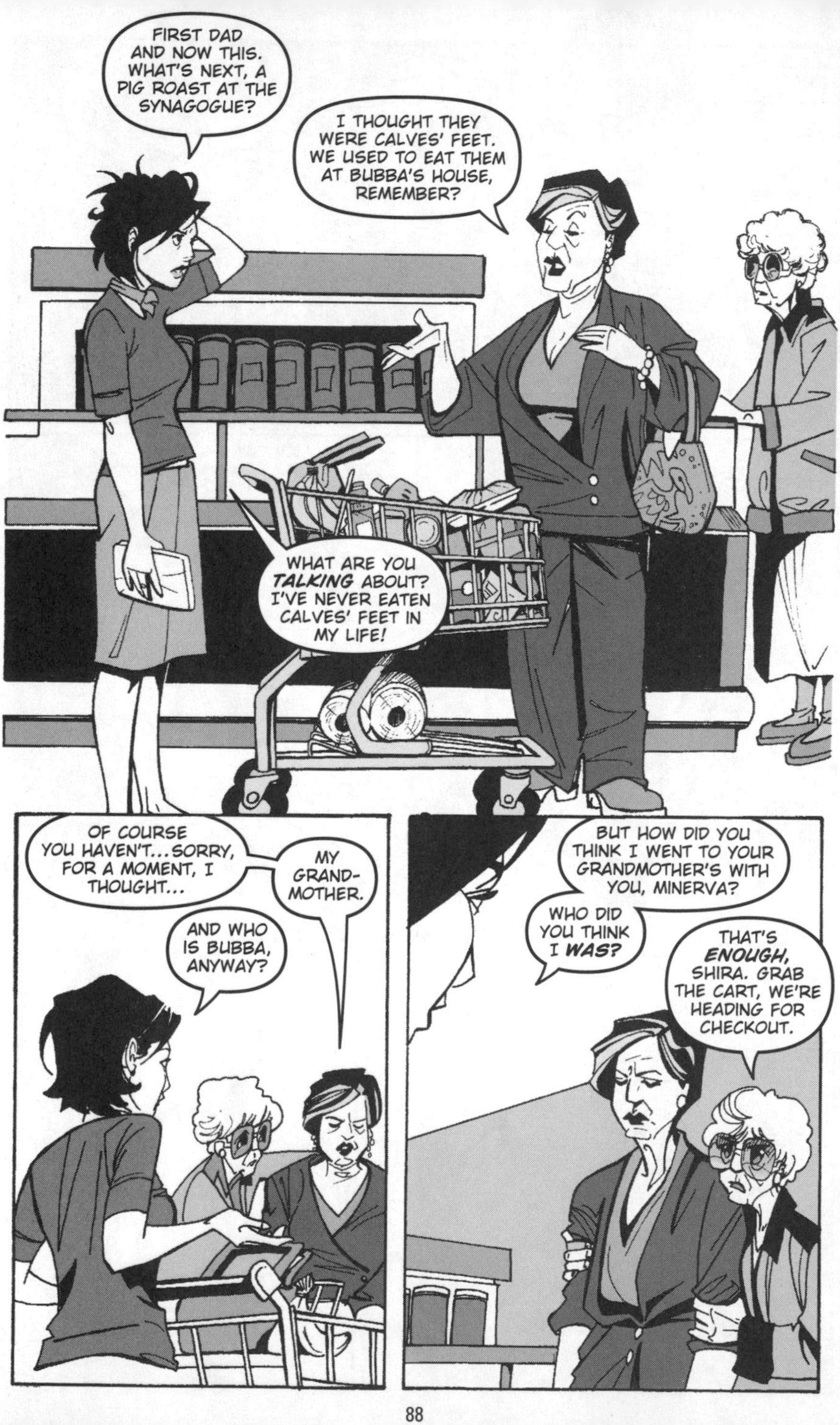
FIRST DAD AND NOW THIS. WHAT'S NEXT, A PIG ROAST AT THE SYNAGOGUE?
I THOUGHT THEY WERE CALVES' FEET. WE USED TO EAT THEM AT BUBBA'S HOUSE, REMEMBER?
WHAT ARE YOU **TALKING** ABOUT? I'VE NEVER EATEN CALVES' FEET IN MY LIFE!
OF COURSE YOU HAVEN'T... SORRY, FOR A MOMENT, I THOUGHT...
MY GRAND-MOTHER.
AND WHO IS BUBBA, ANYWAY?
BUT HOW DID YOU THINK I WENT TO YOUR GRANDMOTHER'S WITH YOU, MINERVA?
WHO DID YOU THINK I **WAS?**
THAT'S **ENOUGH,** SHIRA. GRAB THE CART, WE'RE HEADING FOR CHECKOUT.

I've heard the phrase "having a senior moment" once. A senior <u>moment</u> is forgetting the word colander or leaving the tap running in the bathroom.

Thinking that I used to hang around her grandmother's with her, <u>that's</u> a senior two-week vacation without notice.

WAIT A MINUTE, PEARL, DID YOU GET EXTRA LARGE EGGS?

WHAT DO WE NEED EXTRA LARGE FOR?

I've always thought of Minerva as my friend, but something's changed. <u>She's</u> changed.

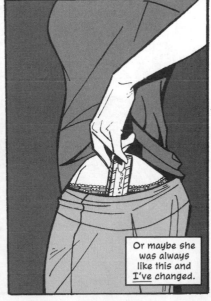

Or maybe she was always like this and <u>I've</u> changed.

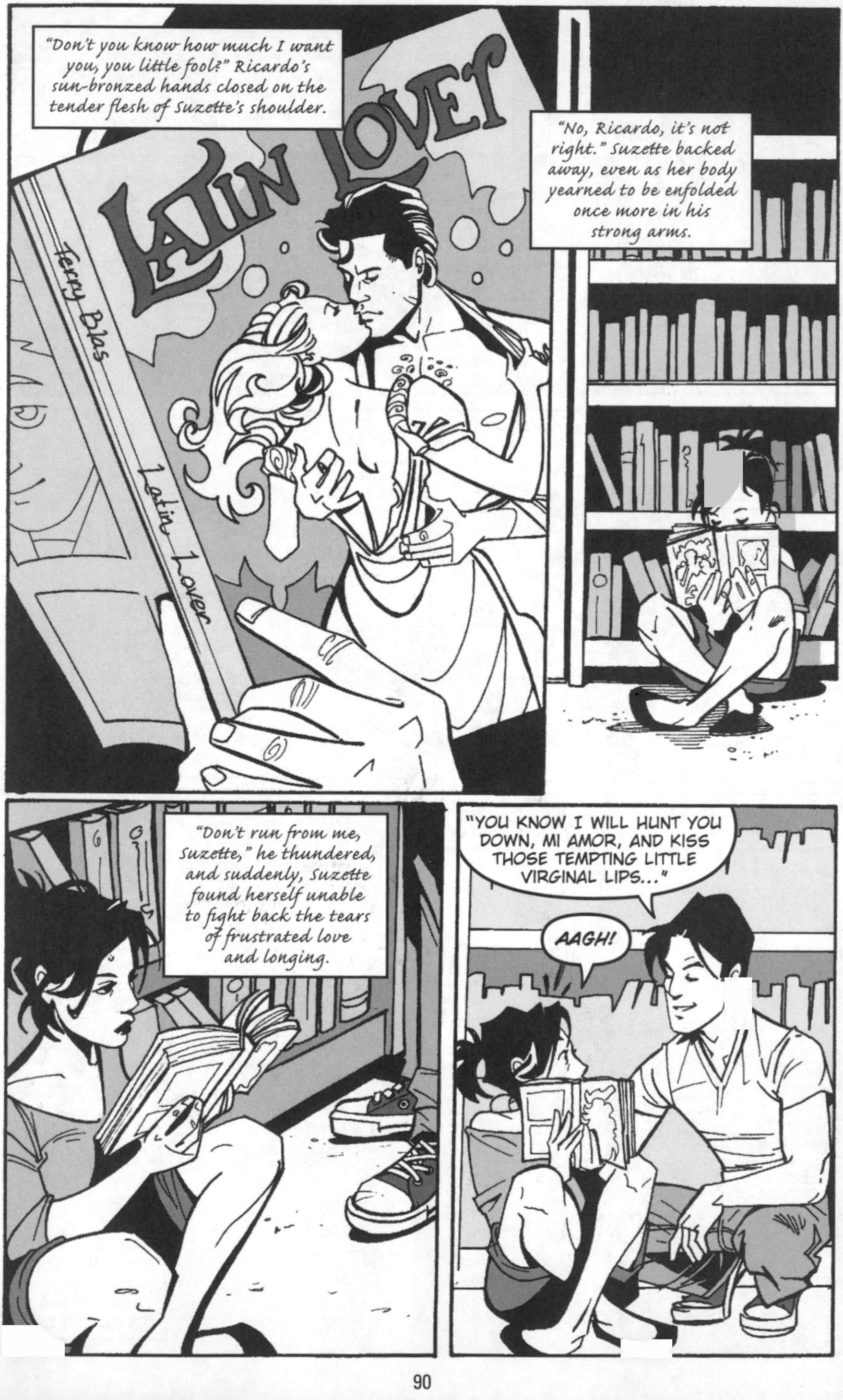
"Don't you know how much I want you, you little fool?" Ricardo's sun-bronzed hands closed on the tender flesh of Suzette's shoulder.
Latin Lover
Terry Blas
Latin Lover
"No, Ricardo, it's not right." Suzette backed away, even as her body yearned to be enfolded once more in his strong arms.
"Don't run from me, Suzette," he thundered, and suddenly, Suzette found herself unable to fight back the tears of frustrated love and longing.
"YOU KNOW I WILL HUNT YOU DOWN, MI AMOR, AND KISS THOSE TEMPTING LITTLE VIRGINAL LIPS..."
AAGH!

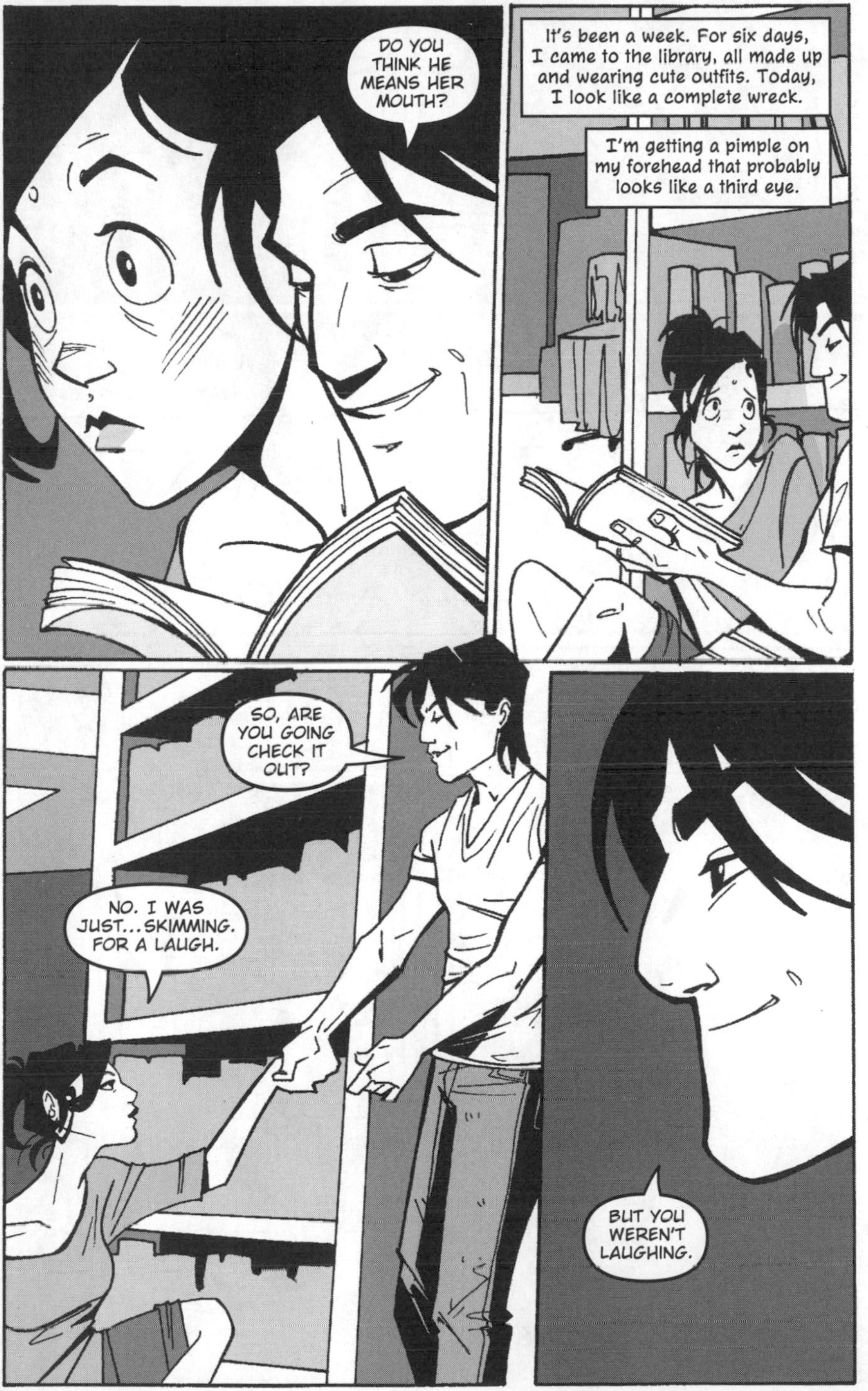
DO YOU THINK HE MEANS HER MOUTH?
It's been a week. For six days, I came to the library, all made up and wearing cute outfits. Today, I look like a complete wreck.
I'm getting a pimple on my forehead that probably looks like a third eye.
SO, ARE YOU GOING CHECK IT OUT?
NO. I WAS JUST... SKIMMING. FOR A LAUGH.
BUT YOU WEREN'T LAUGHING.

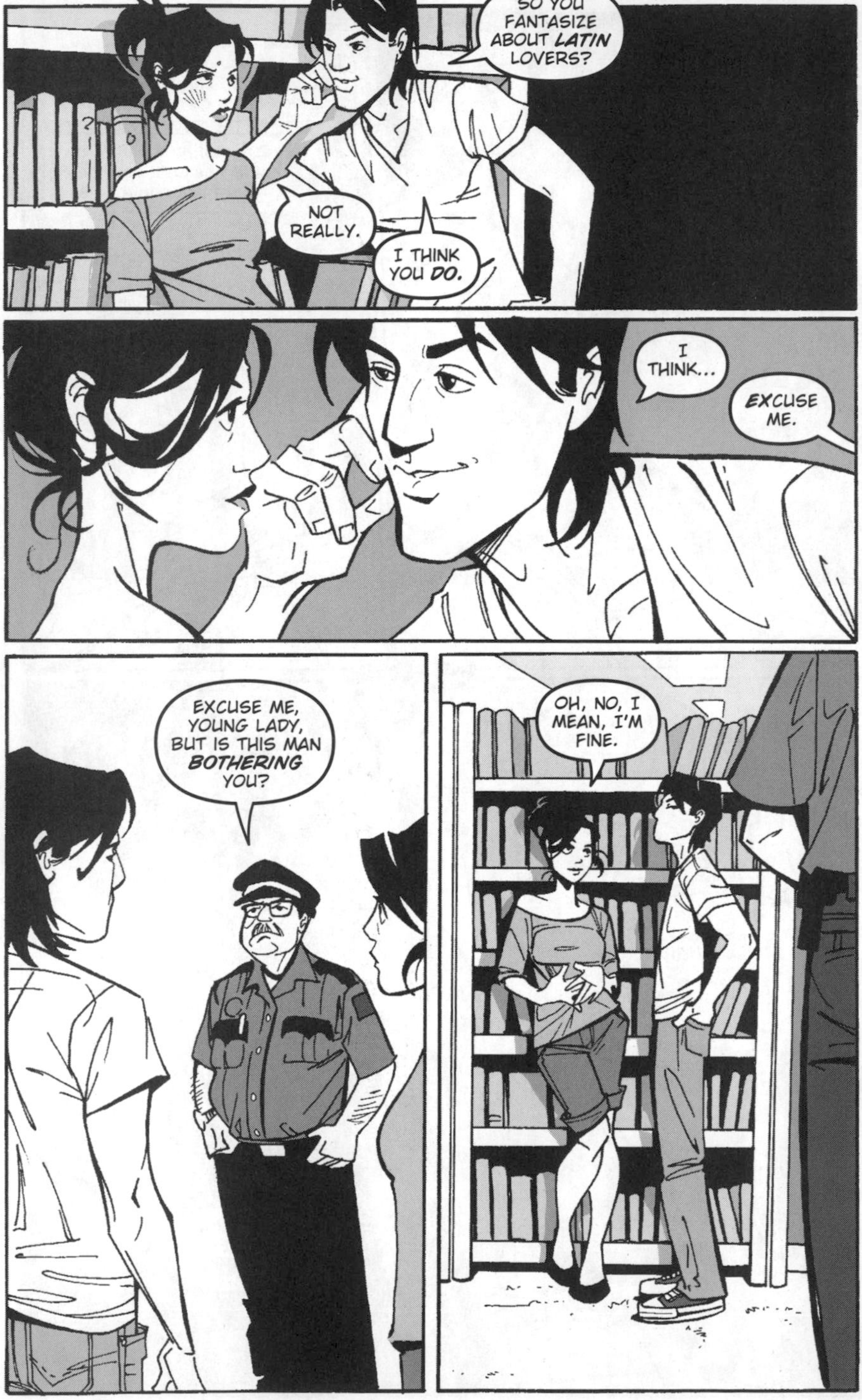
SO YOU FANTASIZE ABOUT LATIN LOVERS?
NOT REALLY.
I THINK YOU DO.
I THINK...
EXCUSE ME.
EXCUSE ME, YOUNG LADY, BUT IS THIS MAN BOTHERING YOU?
OH, NO, I MEAN, I'M FINE.

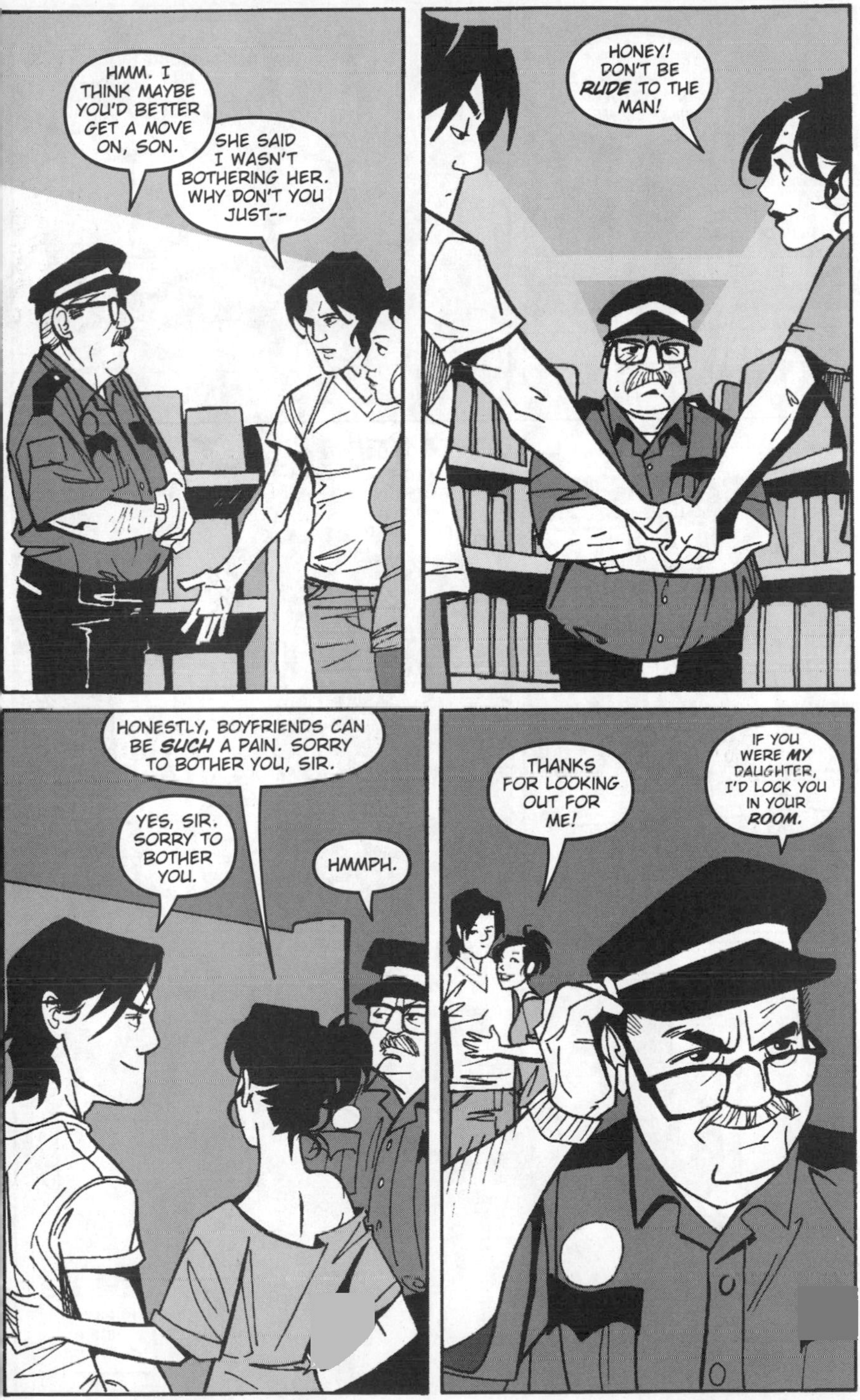
HMM. I THINK MAYBE YOU'D BETTER GET A MOVE ON, SON.
SHE SAID I WASN'T BOTHERING HER. WHY DON'T YOU JUST--
HONEY! DON'T BE RUDE TO THE MAN!
HONESTLY, BOYFRIENDS CAN BE SUCH A PAIN. SORRY TO BOTHER YOU, SIR.
YES, SIR. SORRY TO BOTHER YOU.
HMMPH.
THANKS FOR LOOKING OUT FOR ME!
IF YOU WERE MY DAUGHTER, I'D LOCK YOU IN YOUR ROOM.

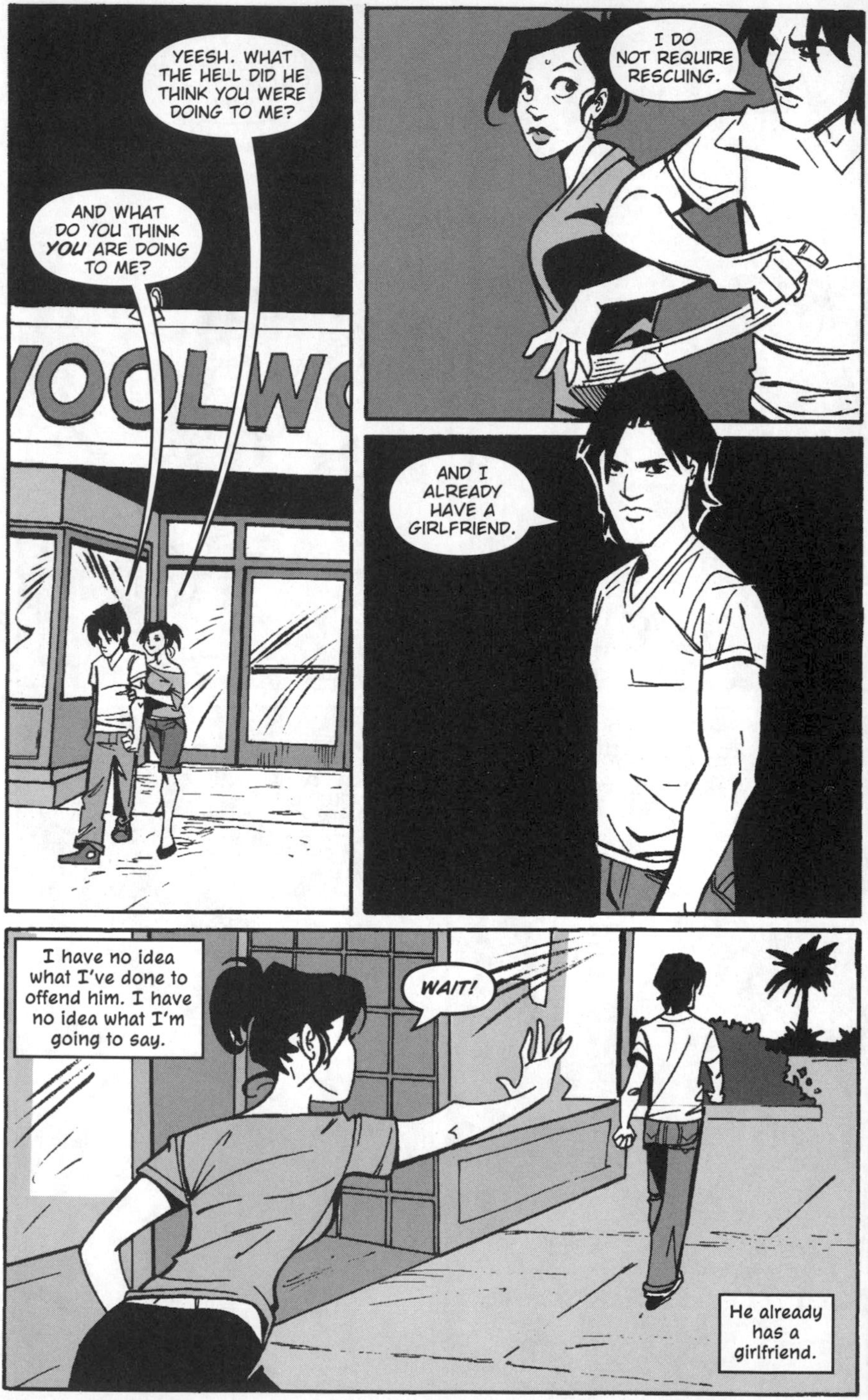
YEESH. WHAT THE HELL DID HE THINK YOU WERE DOING TO ME?
AND WHAT DO YOU THINK *YOU* ARE DOING TO ME?
VOOLWO
I DO NOT REQUIRE RESCUING.
AND I ALREADY HAVE A GIRLFRIEND.
I have no idea what I've done to offend him. I have no idea what I'm going to say.
WAIT!
He already has a girlfriend.

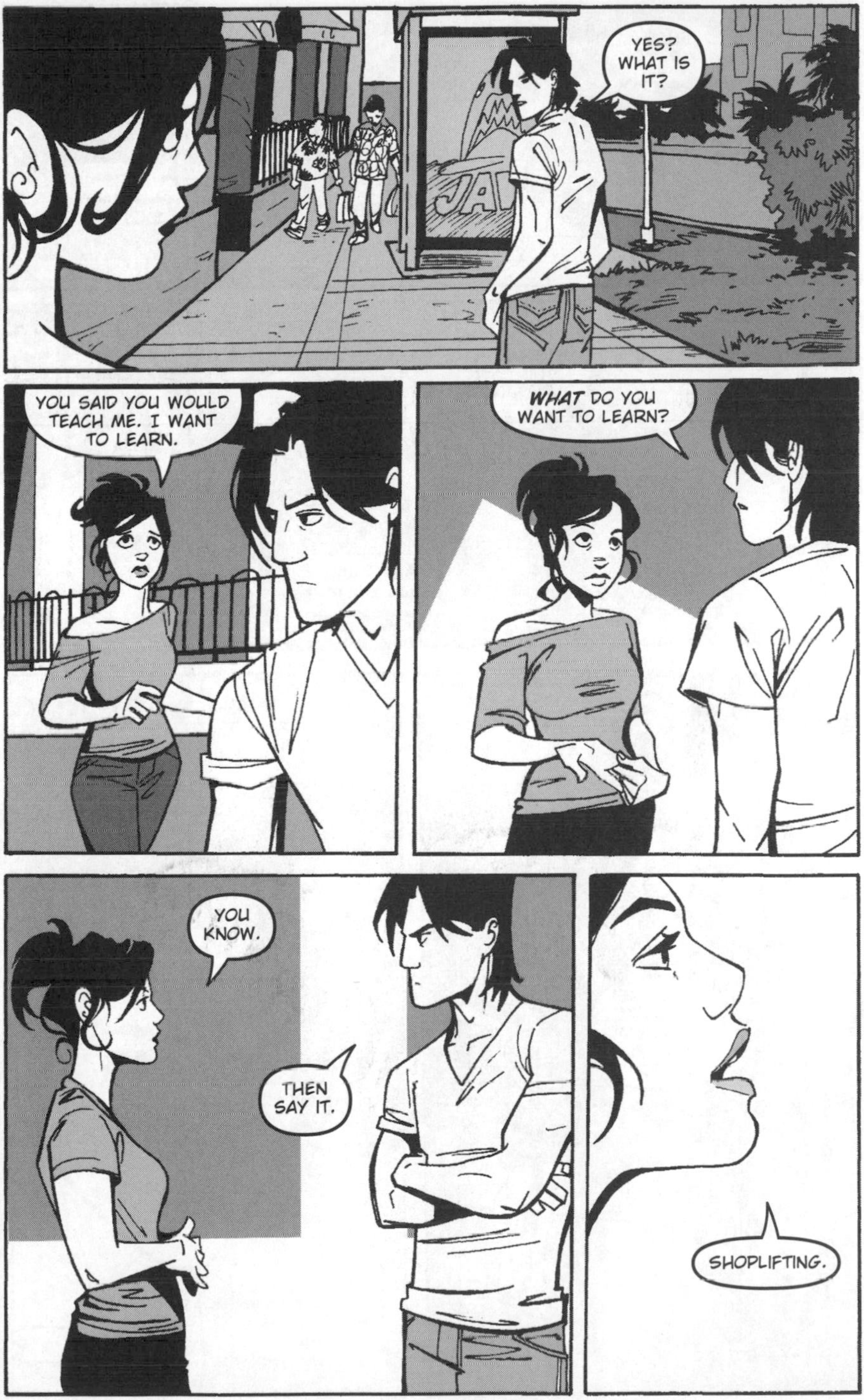
YES? WHAT IS IT?
YOU SAID YOU WOULD TEACH ME. I WANT TO LEARN.
WHAT DO YOU WANT TO LEARN?
YOU KNOW.
THEN SAY IT.
SHOPLIFTING.

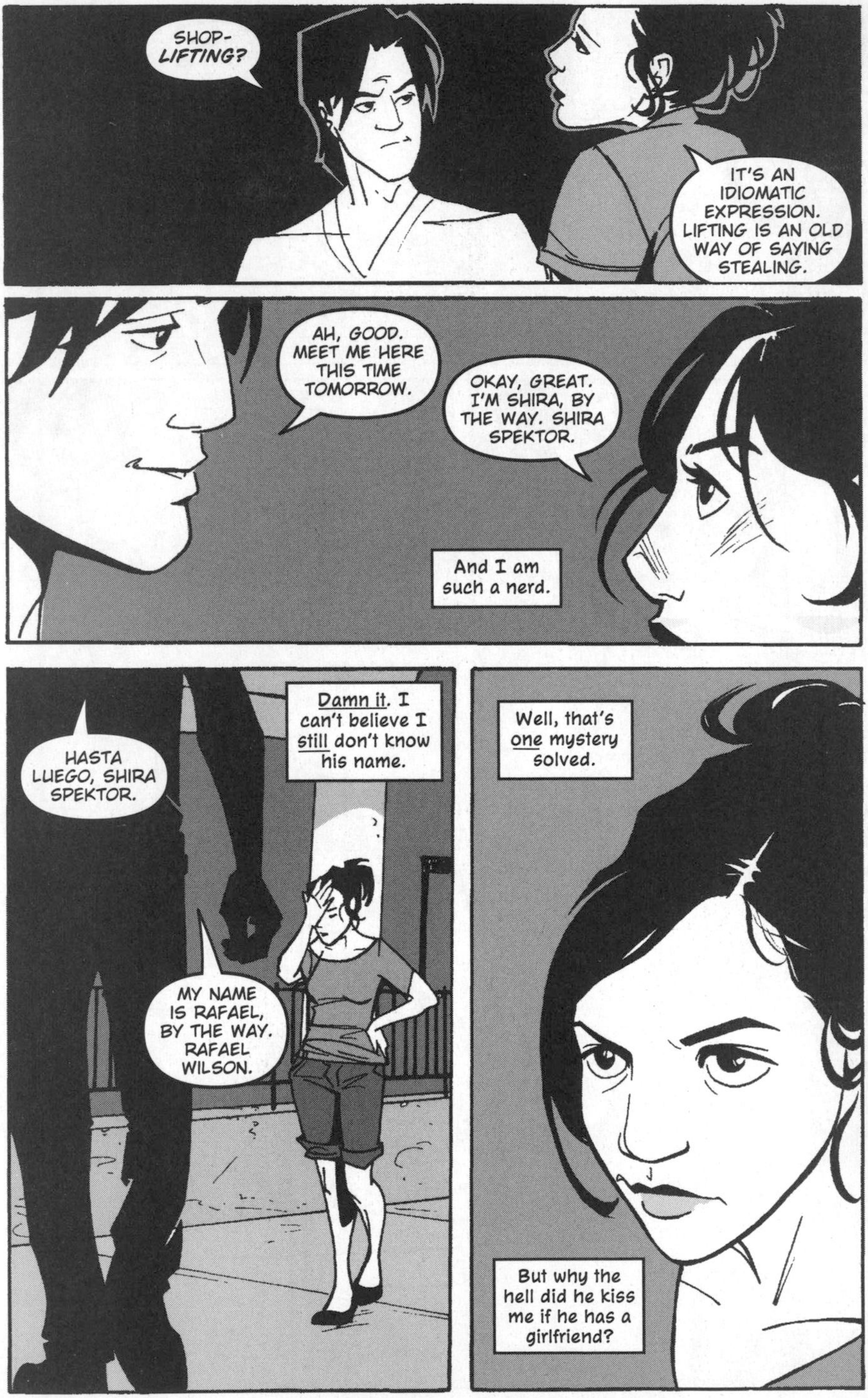
SHOP-LIFTING?
IT'S AN IDIOMATIC EXPRESSION. LIFTING IS AN OLD WAY OF SAYING STEALING.
AH, GOOD. MEET ME HERE THIS TIME TOMORROW.
OKAY, GREAT. I'M SHIRA, BY THE WAY. SHIRA SPEKTOR.
And I am such a nerd.
HASTA LUEGO, SHIRA SPEKTOR.
MY NAME IS RAFAEL, BY THE WAY. RAFAEL WILSON.
Damn it. I can't believe I still don't know his name.
Well, that's one mystery solved.
But why the hell did he kiss me if he has a girlfriend?

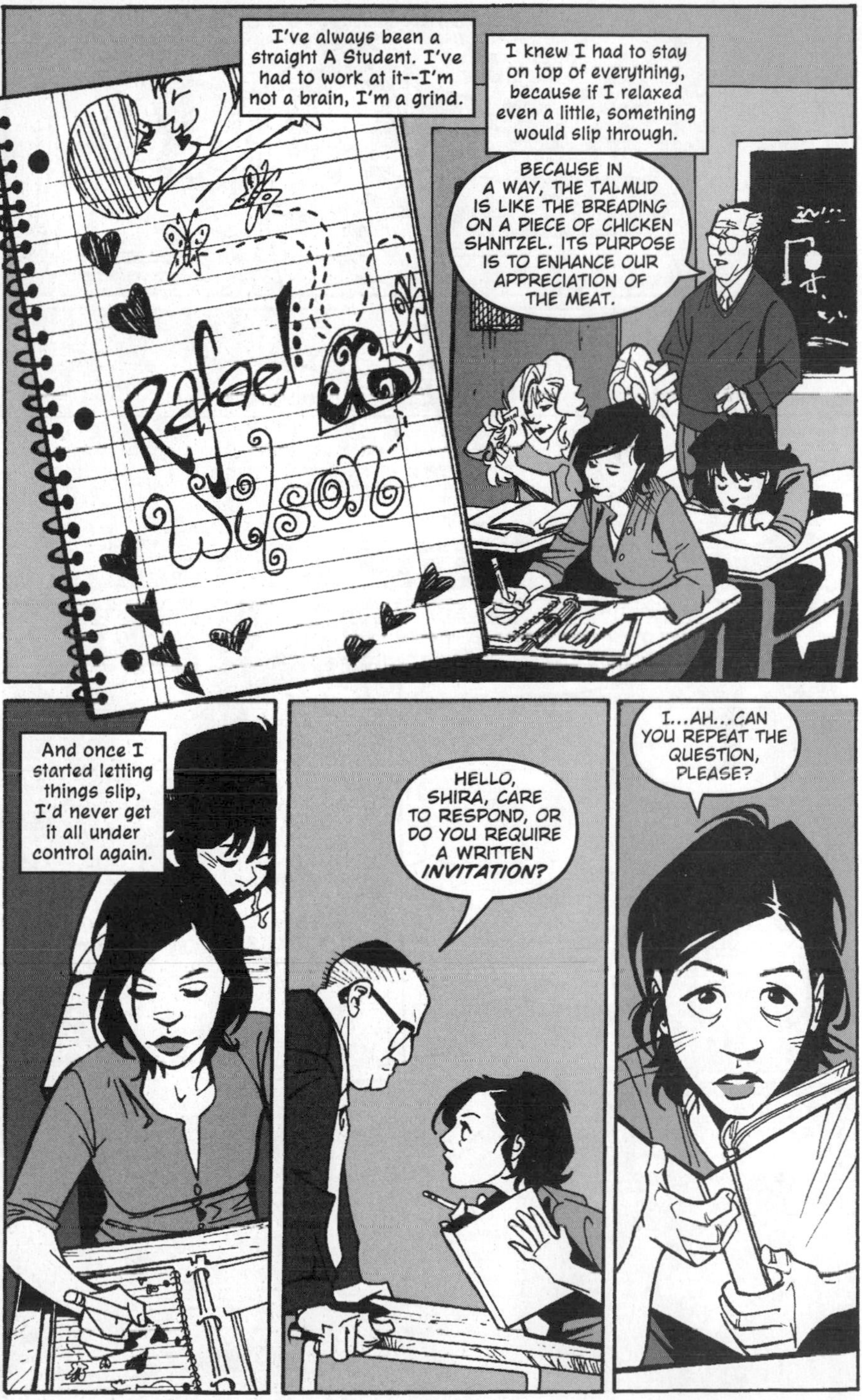
I've always been a straight A Student. I've had to work at it--I'm not a brain, I'm a grind.
I knew I had to stay on top of everything, because if I relaxed even a little, something would slip through.
BECAUSE IN A WAY, THE TALMUD IS LIKE THE BREADING ON A PIECE OF CHICKEN SHNITZEL. ITS PURPOSE IS TO ENHANCE OUR APPRECIATION OF THE MEAT.
Rafael Wilson
And once I started letting things slip, I'd never get it all under control again.
HELLO, SHIRA, CARE TO RESPOND, OR DO YOU REQUIRE A WRITTEN *INVITATION?*
I...AH...CAN YOU REPEAT THE QUESTION, PLEASE?

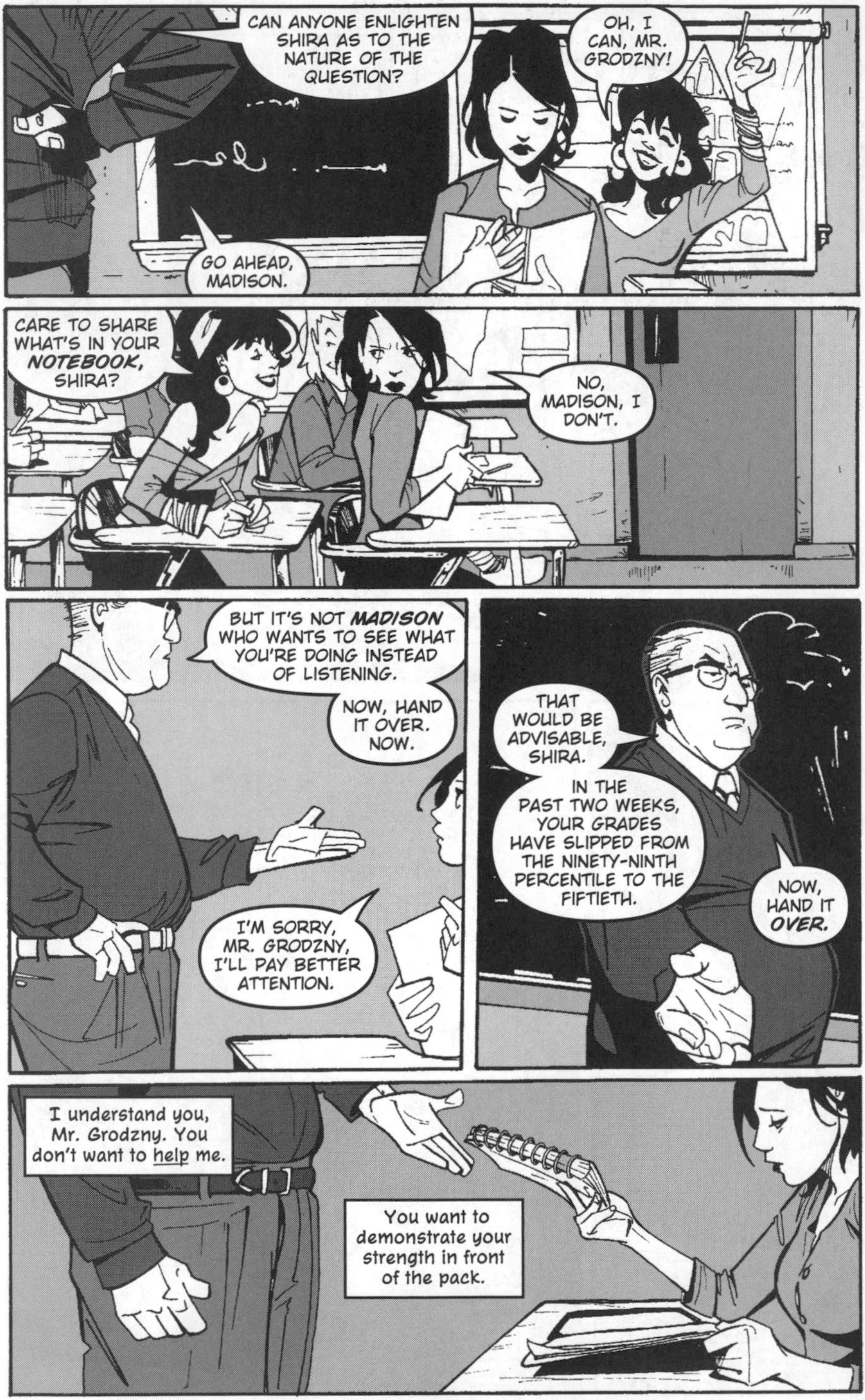
CAN ANYONE ENLIGHTEN SHIRA AS TO THE NATURE OF THE QUESTION?
OH, I CAN, MR. GRODZNY!
GO AHEAD, MADISON.
CARE TO SHARE WHAT'S IN YOUR NOTEBOOK, SHIRA?
NO, MADISON, I DON'T.
BUT IT'S NOT MADISON WHO WANTS TO SEE WHAT YOU'RE DOING INSTEAD OF LISTENING.
NOW, HAND IT OVER. NOW.
I'M SORRY, MR. GRODZNY, I'LL PAY BETTER ATTENTION.
THAT WOULD BE ADVISABLE, SHIRA.
IN THE PAST TWO WEEKS, YOUR GRADES HAVE SLIPPED FROM THE NINETY-NINTH PERCENTILE TO THE FIFTIETH.
NOW, HAND IT OVER.
I understand you, Mr. Grodzny. You don't want to help me.
You want to demonstrate your strength in front of the pack.

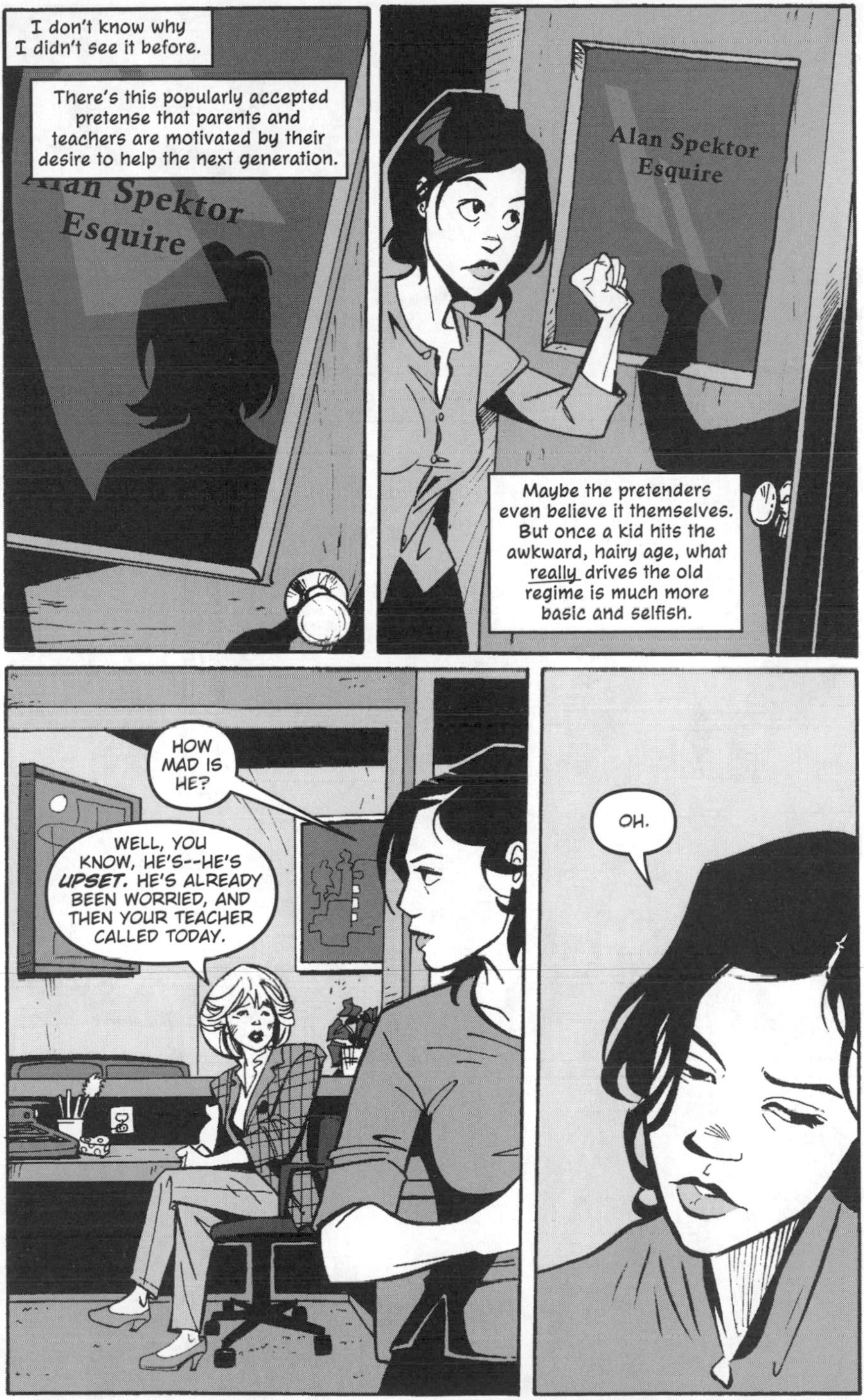
I don't know why I didn't see it before.
There's this popularly accepted pretense that parents and teachers are motivated by their desire to help the next generation.
Alan Spektor Esquire
Alan Spektor Esquire
Maybe the pretenders even believe it themselves. But once a kid hits the awkward, hairy age, what really drives the old regime is much more basic and selfish.
HOW MAD IS HE?
WELL, YOU KNOW, HE'S--HE'S *UPSET.* HE'S ALREADY BEEN WORRIED, AND THEN YOUR TEACHER CALLED TODAY.
OH.

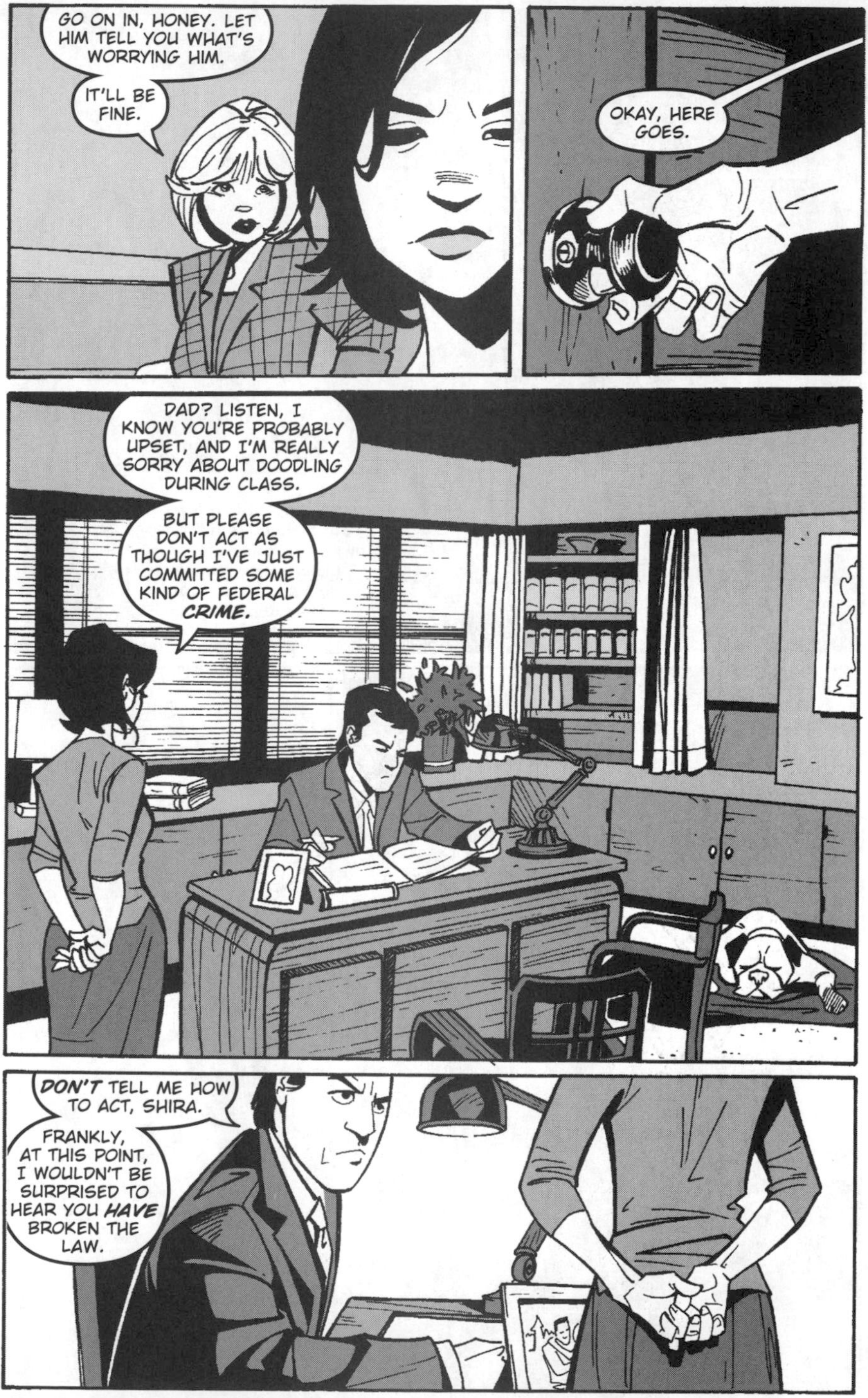
GO ON IN, HONEY. LET HIM TELL YOU WHAT'S WORRYING HIM.
IT'LL BE FINE.
OKAY, HERE GOES.
DAD? LISTEN, I KNOW YOU'RE PROBABLY UPSET, AND I'M REALLY SORRY ABOUT DOODLING DURING CLASS.
BUT PLEASE DON'T ACT AS THOUGH I'VE JUST COMMITTED SOME KIND OF FEDERAL *CRIME.*
DON'T TELL ME HOW TO ACT, SHIRA.
FRANKLY, AT THIS POINT, I WOULDN'T BE SURPRISED TO HEAR YOU *HAVE* BROKEN THE LAW.

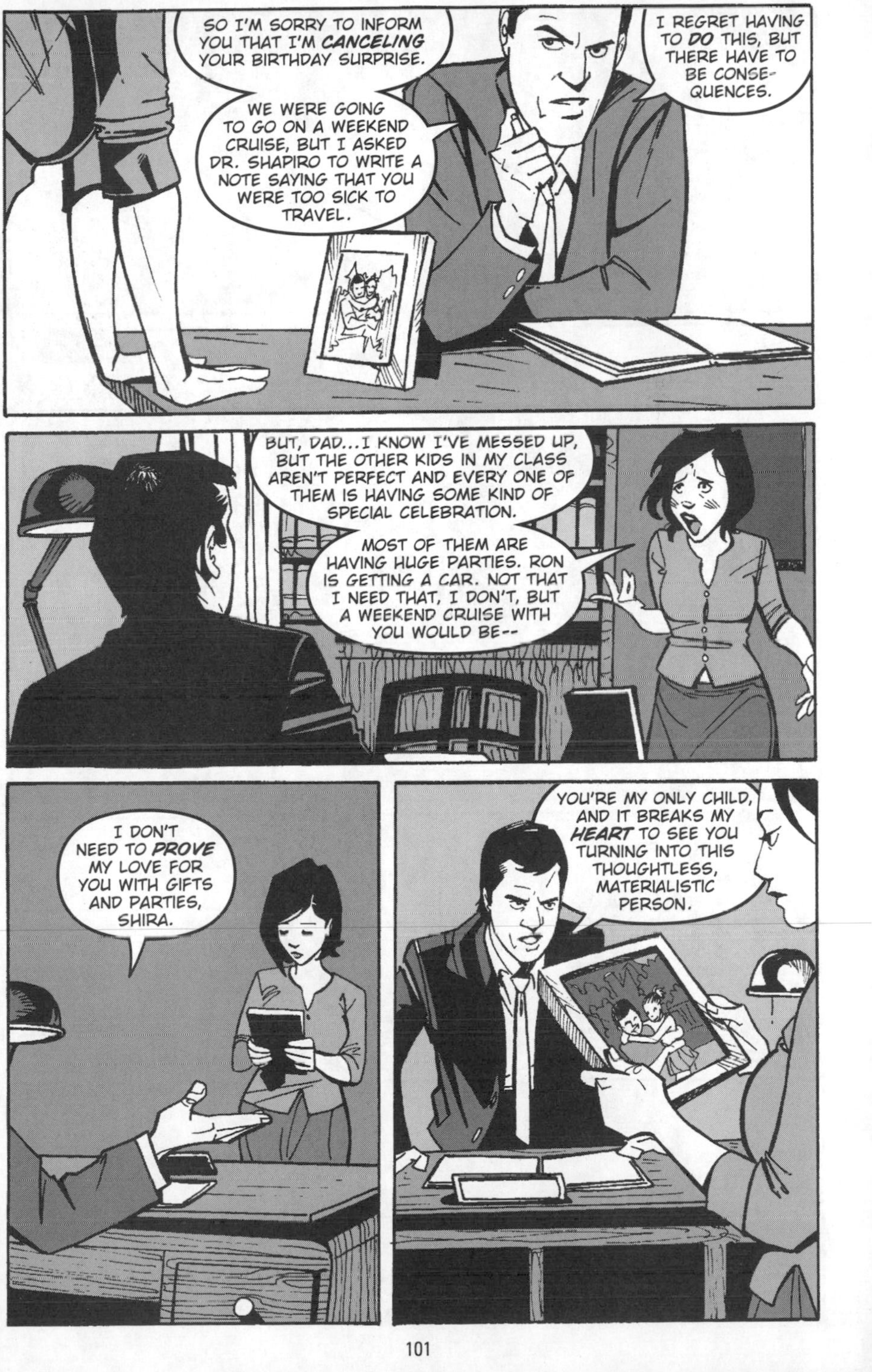
SO I'M SORRY TO INFORM YOU THAT I'M *CANCELING* YOUR BIRTHDAY SURPRISE.
WE WERE GOING TO GO ON A WEEKEND CRUISE, BUT I ASKED DR. SHAPIRO TO WRITE A NOTE SAYING THAT YOU WERE TOO SICK TO TRAVEL.
I REGRET HAVING TO *DO* THIS, BUT THERE HAVE TO BE CONSE-QUENCES.
BUT, DAD...I KNOW I'VE MESSED UP, BUT THE OTHER KIDS IN MY CLASS AREN'T PERFECT AND EVERY ONE OF THEM IS HAVING SOME KIND OF SPECIAL CELEBRATION.
MOST OF THEM ARE HAVING HUGE PARTIES. RON IS GETTING A CAR. NOT THAT I NEED THAT, I DON'T, BUT A WEEKEND CRUISE WITH YOU WOULD BE--
I DON'T NEED TO *PROVE* MY LOVE FOR YOU WITH GIFTS AND PARTIES, SHIRA.
YOU'RE MY ONLY CHILD, AND IT BREAKS MY *HEART* TO SEE YOU TURNING INTO THIS THOUGHTLESS, MATERIALISTIC PERSON.

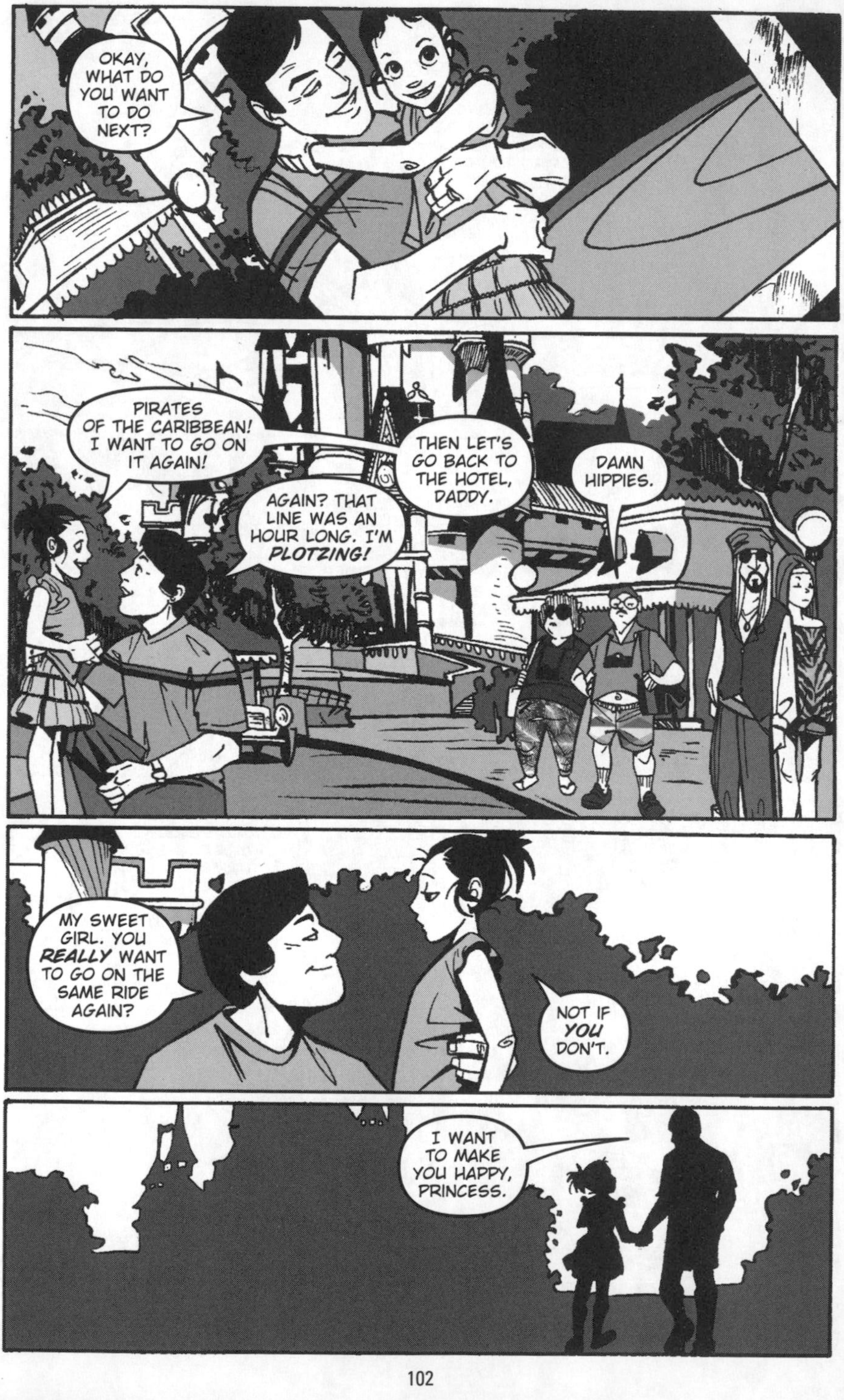
OKAY, WHAT DO YOU WANT TO DO NEXT?
PIRATES OF THE CARIBBEAN! I WANT TO GO ON IT AGAIN!
AGAIN? THAT LINE WAS AN HOUR LONG. I'M PLOTZING!
THEN LET'S GO BACK TO THE HOTEL, DADDY.
DAMN HIPPIES.
MY SWEET GIRL. YOU REALLY WANT TO GO ON THE SAME RIDE AGAIN?
NOT IF YOU DON'T.
I WANT TO MAKE YOU HAPPY, PRINCESS.

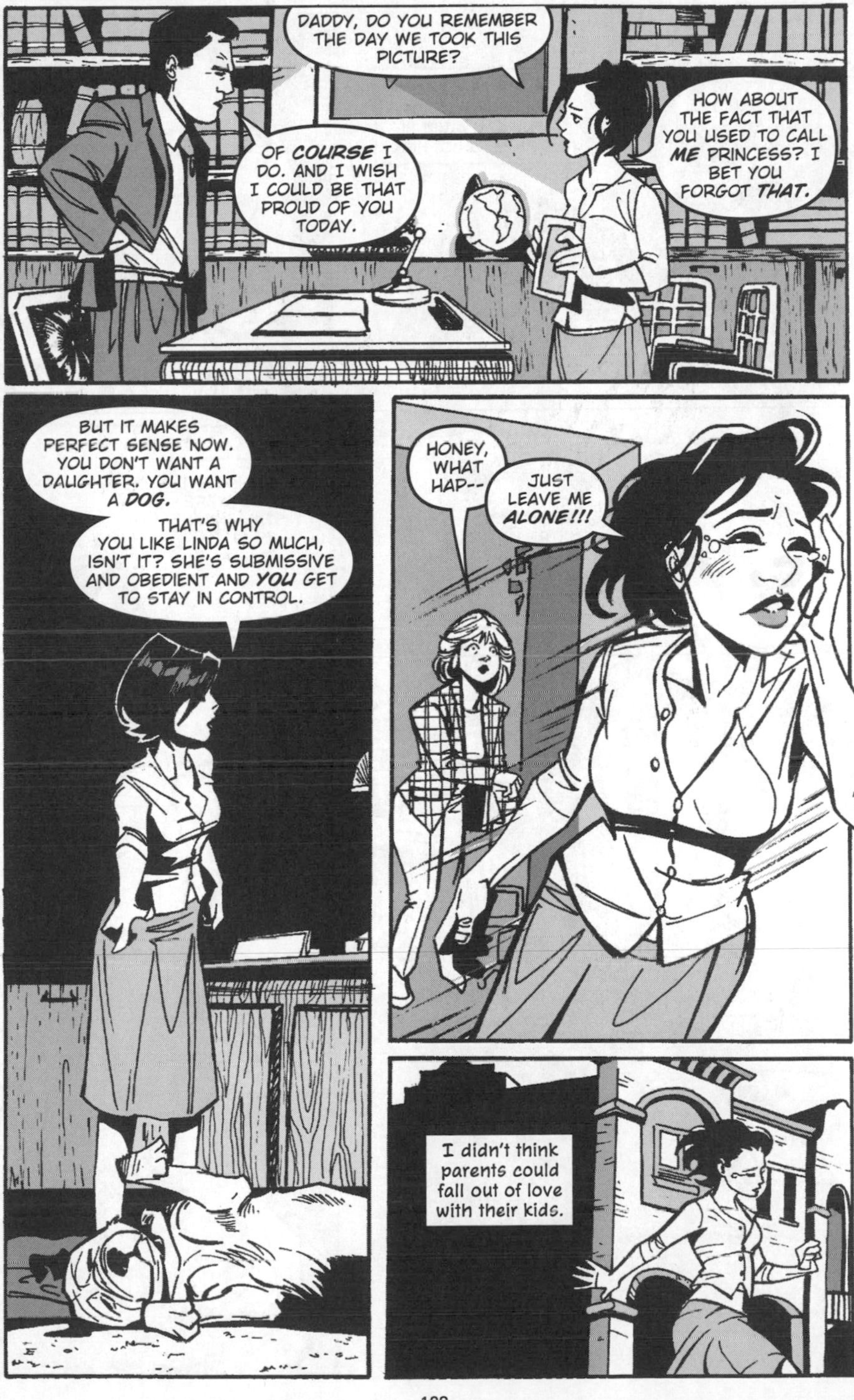

DADDY, DO YOU REMEMBER THE DAY WE TOOK THIS PICTURE?
OF COURSE I DO. AND I WISH I COULD BE THAT PROUD OF YOU TODAY.
HOW ABOUT THE FACT THAT YOU USED TO CALL ME PRINCESS? I BET YOU FORGOT THAT.
BUT IT MAKES PERFECT SENSE NOW. YOU DON'T WANT A DAUGHTER. YOU WANT A DOG.
THAT'S WHY YOU LIKE LINDA SO MUCH, ISN'T IT? SHE'S SUBMISSIVE AND OBEDIENT AND YOU GET TO STAY IN CONTROL.
HONEY, WHAT HAP--
JUST LEAVE ME ALONE!!!
I didn't think parents could fall out of love with their kids.

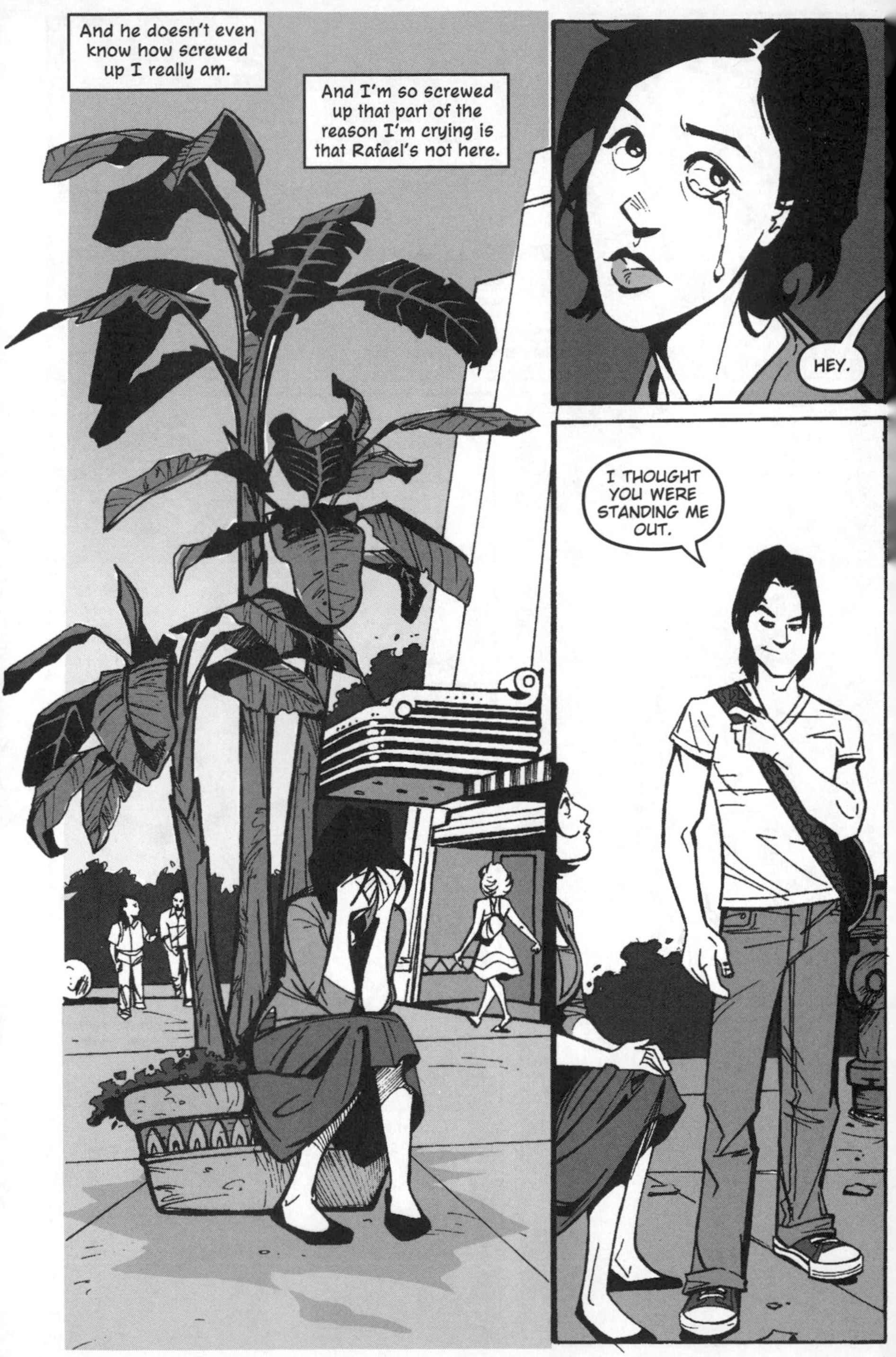
And he doesn't even know how screwed up I really am.
And I'm so screwed up that part of the reason I'm crying is that Rafael's not here.
HEY.
I THOUGHT YOU WERE STANDING ME OUT.

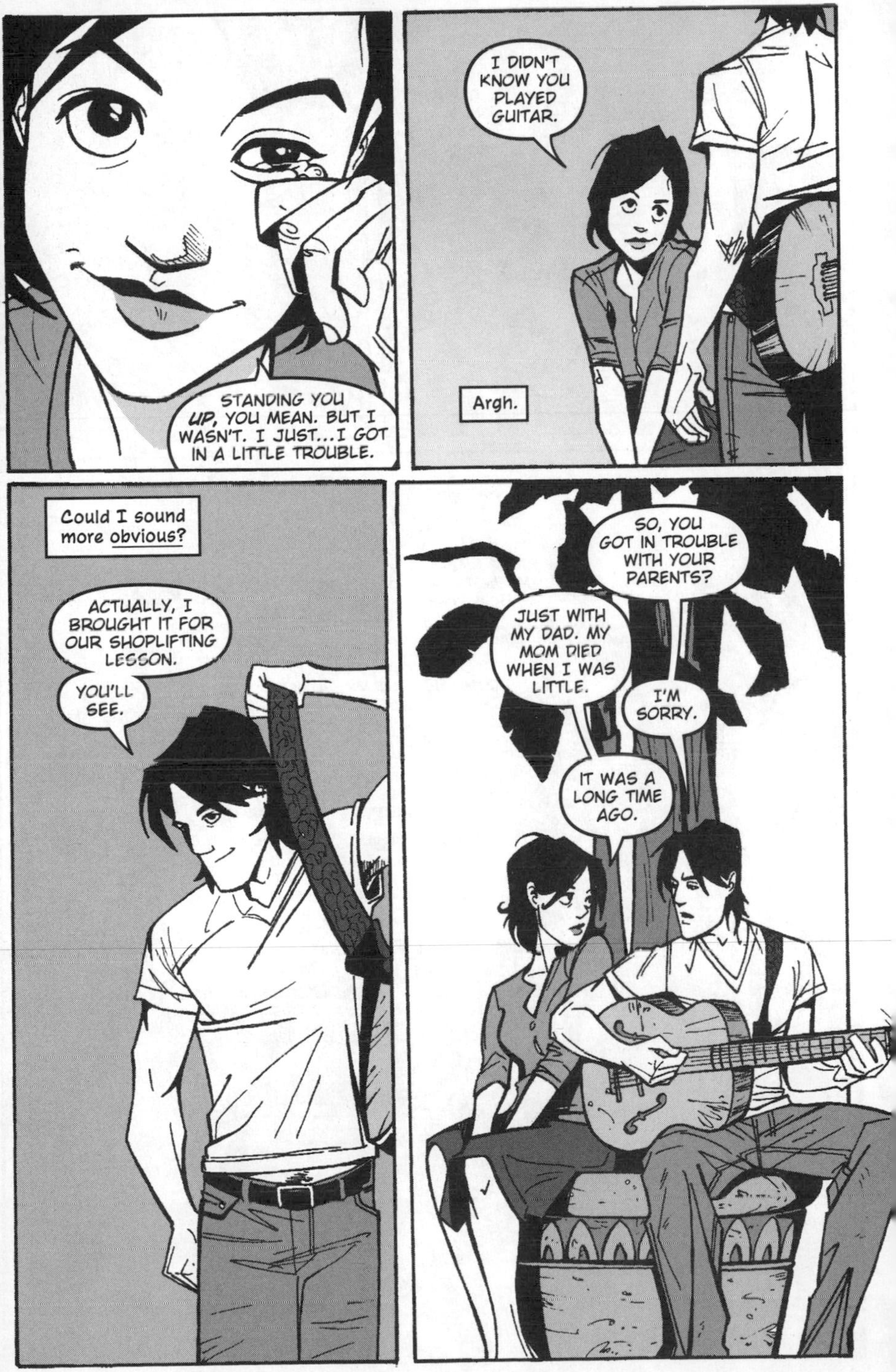
STANDING YOU *UP,* YOU MEAN. BUT I WASN'T. I JUST...I GOT IN A LITTLE TROUBLE.
I DIDN'T KNOW YOU PLAYED GUITAR.
Argh.
Could I sound more obvious?
ACTUALLY, I BROUGHT IT FOR OUR SHOPLIFTING LESSON.
YOU'LL SEE.
SO, YOU GOT IN TROUBLE WITH YOUR PARENTS?
JUST WITH MY DAD. MY MOM DIED WHEN I WAS LITTLE.
I'M SORRY.
IT WAS A LONG TIME AGO.

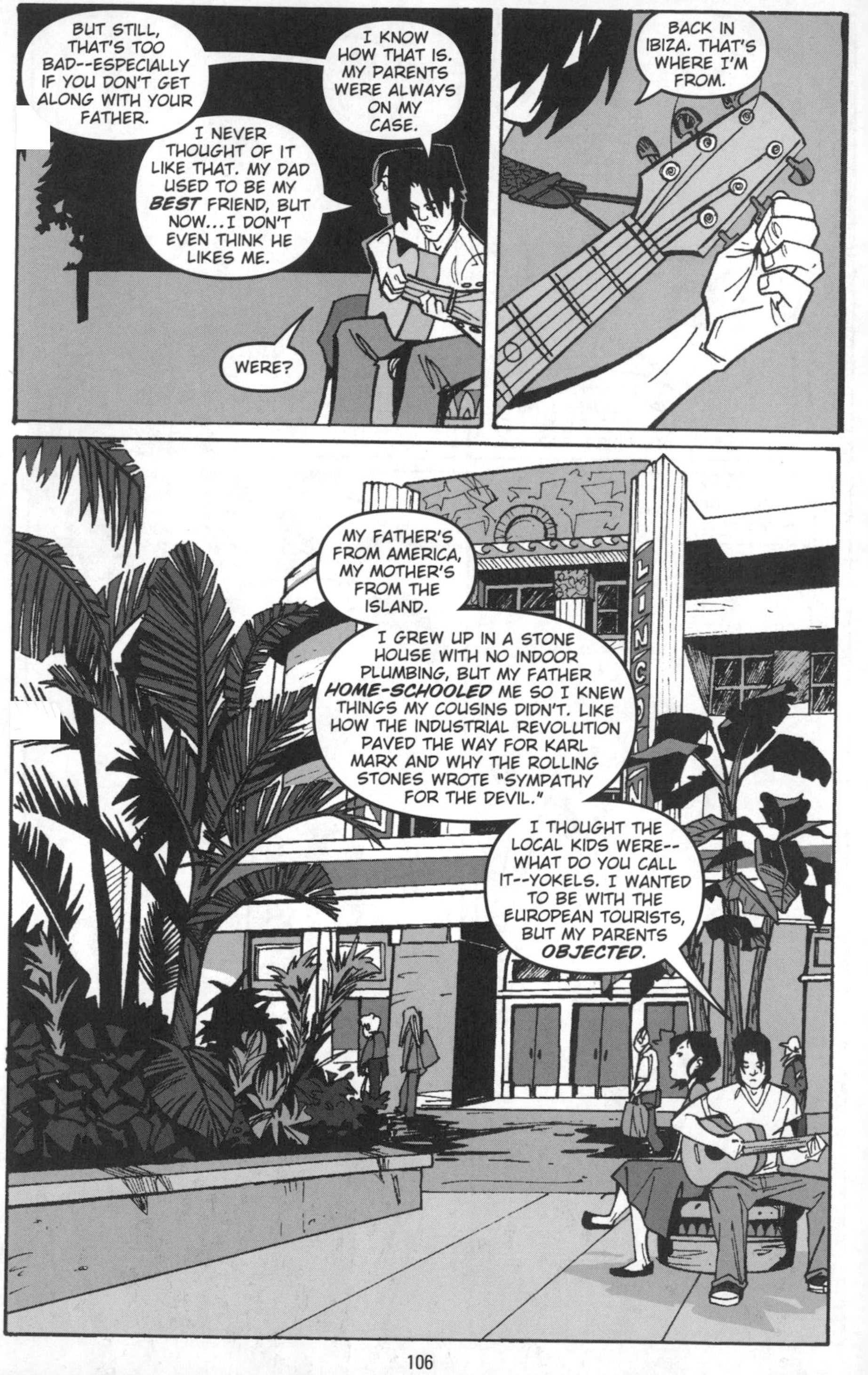
BUT STILL, THAT'S TOO BAD--ESPECIALLY IF YOU DON'T GET ALONG WITH YOUR FATHER.
I KNOW HOW THAT IS. MY PARENTS WERE ALWAYS ON MY CASE.
I NEVER THOUGHT OF IT LIKE THAT. MY DAD USED TO BE MY BEST FRIEND, BUT NOW...I DON'T EVEN THINK HE LIKES ME.
WERE?
BACK IN IBIZA. THAT'S WHERE I'M FROM.
MY FATHER'S FROM AMERICA, MY MOTHER'S FROM THE ISLAND.
I GREW UP IN A STONE HOUSE WITH NO INDOOR PLUMBING, BUT MY FATHER HOME-SCHOOLED ME SO I KNEW THINGS MY COUSINS DIDN'T. LIKE HOW THE INDUSTRIAL REVOLUTION PAVED THE WAY FOR KARL MARX AND WHY THE ROLLING STONES WROTE "SYMPATHY FOR THE DEVIL."
I THOUGHT THE LOCAL KIDS WERE--WHAT DO YOU CALL IT--YOKELS. I WANTED TO BE WITH THE EUROPEAN TOURISTS, BUT MY PARENTS OBJECTED.
LINCOLN

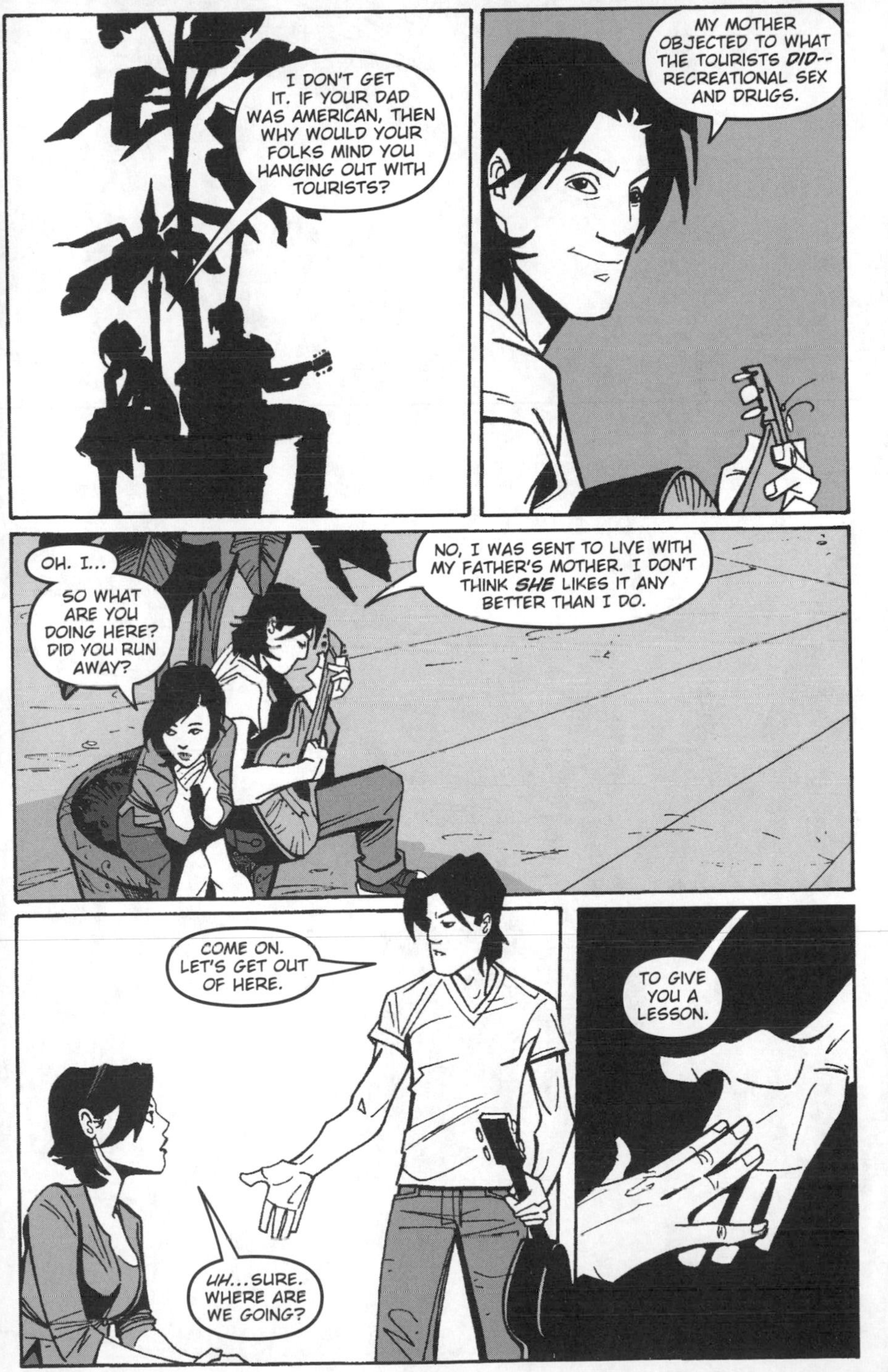
I DON'T GET IT. IF YOUR DAD WAS AMERICAN, THEN WHY WOULD YOUR FOLKS MIND YOU HANGING OUT WITH TOURISTS?
MY MOTHER OBJECTED TO WHAT THE TOURISTS *DID*-- RECREATIONAL SEX AND DRUGS.
OH. I...
SO WHAT ARE YOU DOING HERE? DID YOU RUN AWAY?
NO, I WAS SENT TO LIVE WITH MY FATHER'S MOTHER. I DON'T THINK *SHE* LIKES IT ANY BETTER THAN I DO.
COME ON. LET'S GET OUT OF HERE.
UH... SURE. WHERE ARE WE GOING?
TO GIVE YOU A LESSON.

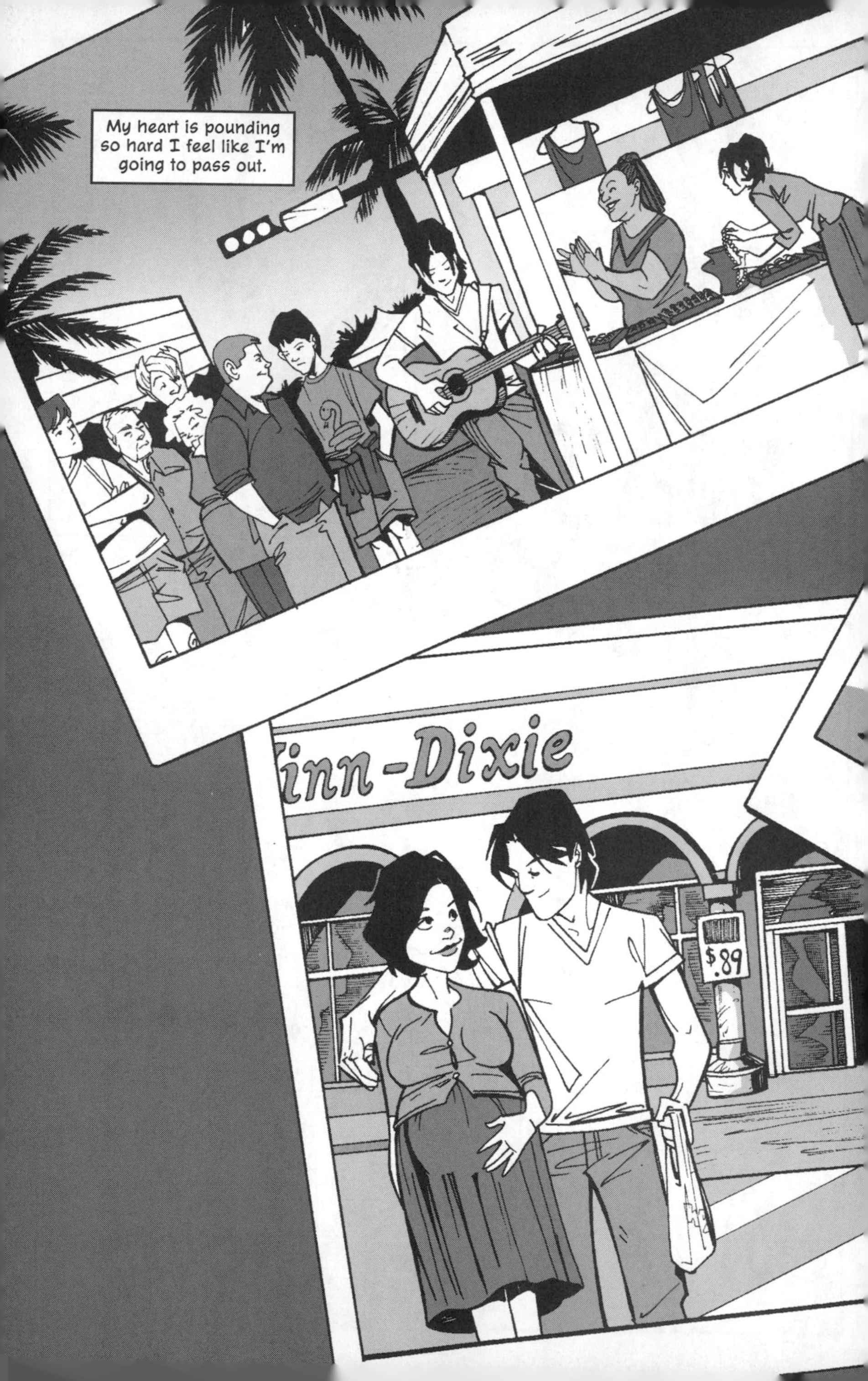
My heart is pounding so hard I feel like I'm going to pass out.
inn-Dixie
$.89

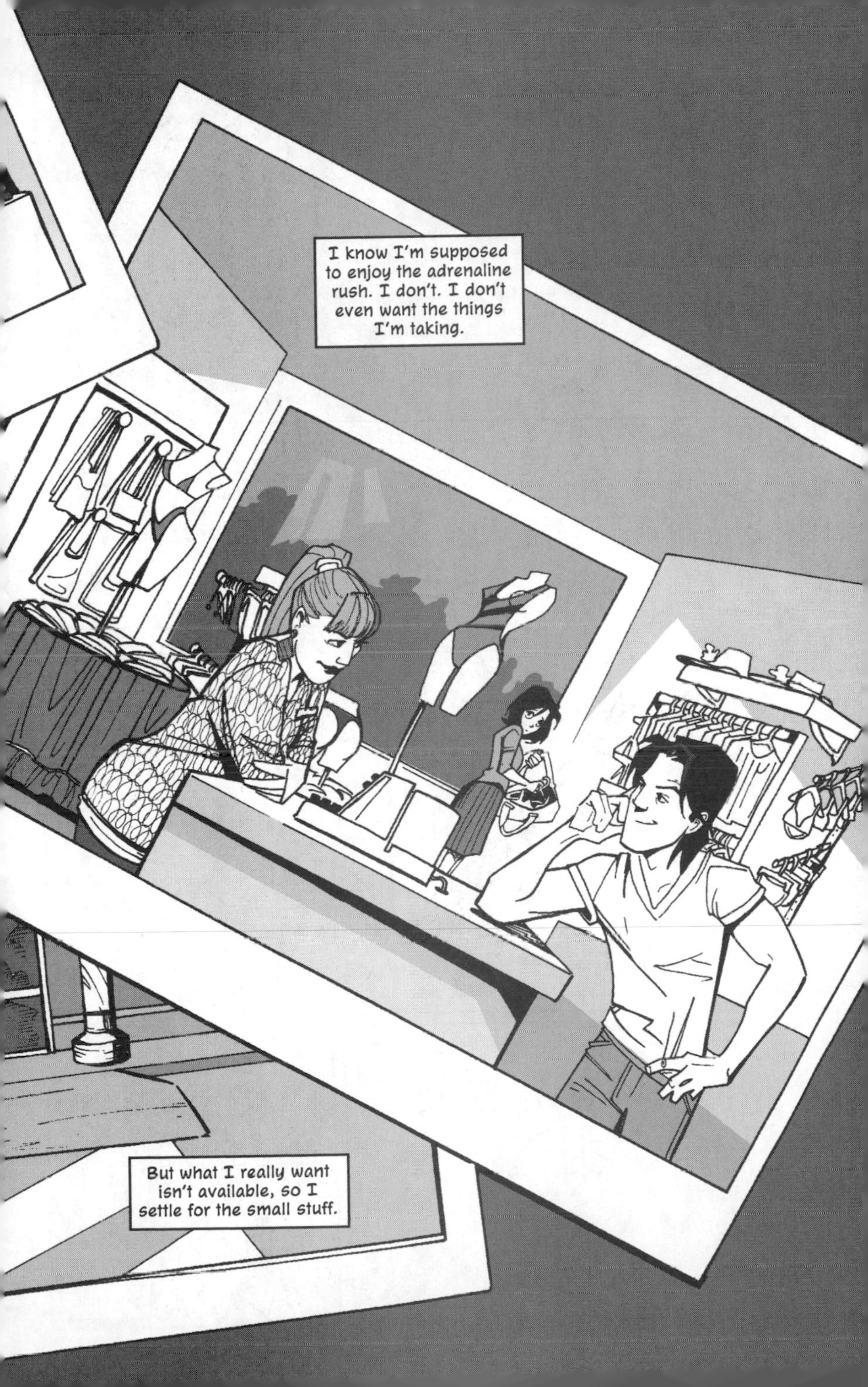
I know I'm supposed to enjoy the adrenaline rush. I don't. I don't even want the things I'm taking.
But what I really want isn't available, so I settle for the small stuff.

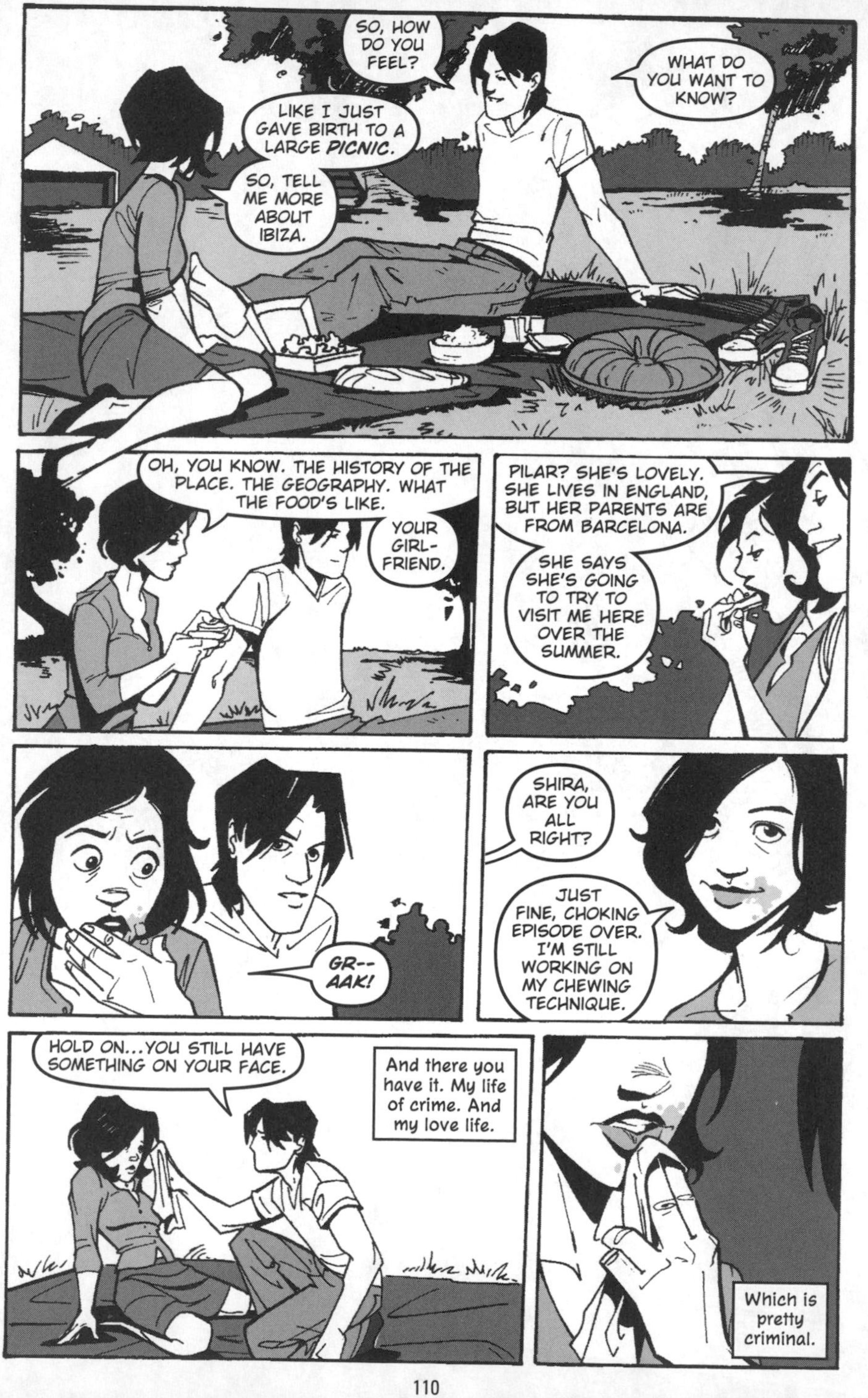
SO, HOW DO YOU FEEL?
LIKE I JUST GAVE BIRTH TO A LARGE *PICNIC*.
SO, TELL ME MORE ABOUT IBIZA.
WHAT DO YOU WANT TO KNOW?
OH, YOU KNOW. THE HISTORY OF THE PLACE. THE GEOGRAPHY. WHAT THE FOOD'S LIKE.
YOUR GIRL-FRIEND.
PILAR? SHE'S LOVELY. SHE LIVES IN ENGLAND, BUT HER PARENTS ARE FROM BARCELONA.
SHE SAYS SHE'S GOING TO TRY TO VISIT ME HERE OVER THE SUMMER.
GR-- AAK!
SHIRA, ARE YOU ALL RIGHT?
JUST FINE, CHOKING EPISODE OVER. I'M STILL WORKING ON MY CHEWING TECHNIQUE.
HOLD ON...YOU STILL HAVE SOMETHING ON YOUR FACE.
And there you have it. My life of crime. And my love life.
Which is pretty criminal.

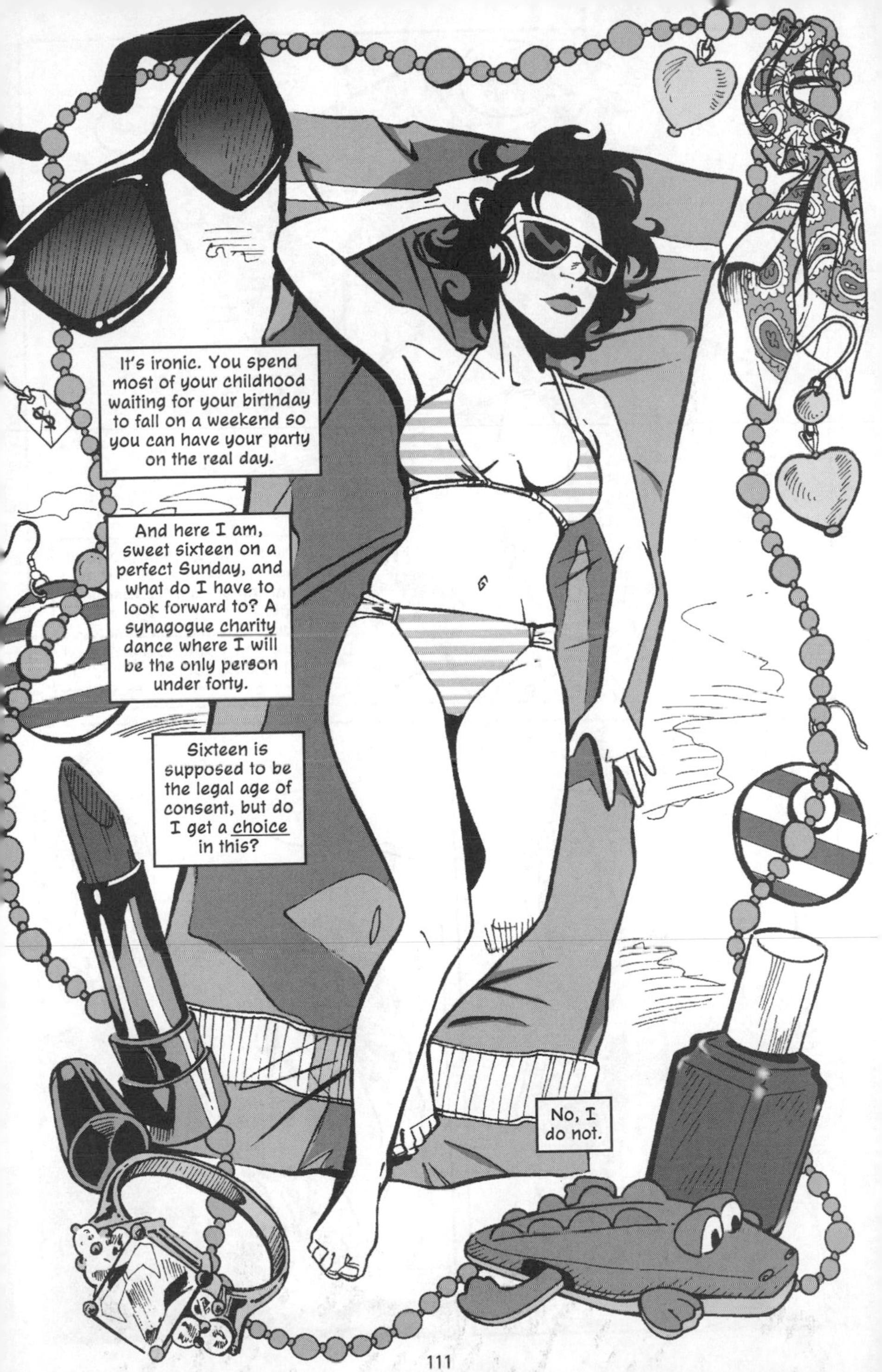
It's ironic. You spend most of your childhood waiting for your birthday to fall on a weekend so you can have your party on the real day.
And here I am, sweet sixteen on a perfect Sunday, and what do I have to look forward to? A synagogue charity dance where I will be the only person under forty.
Sixteen is supposed to be the legal age of consent, but do I get a choice in this?
No, I do not.

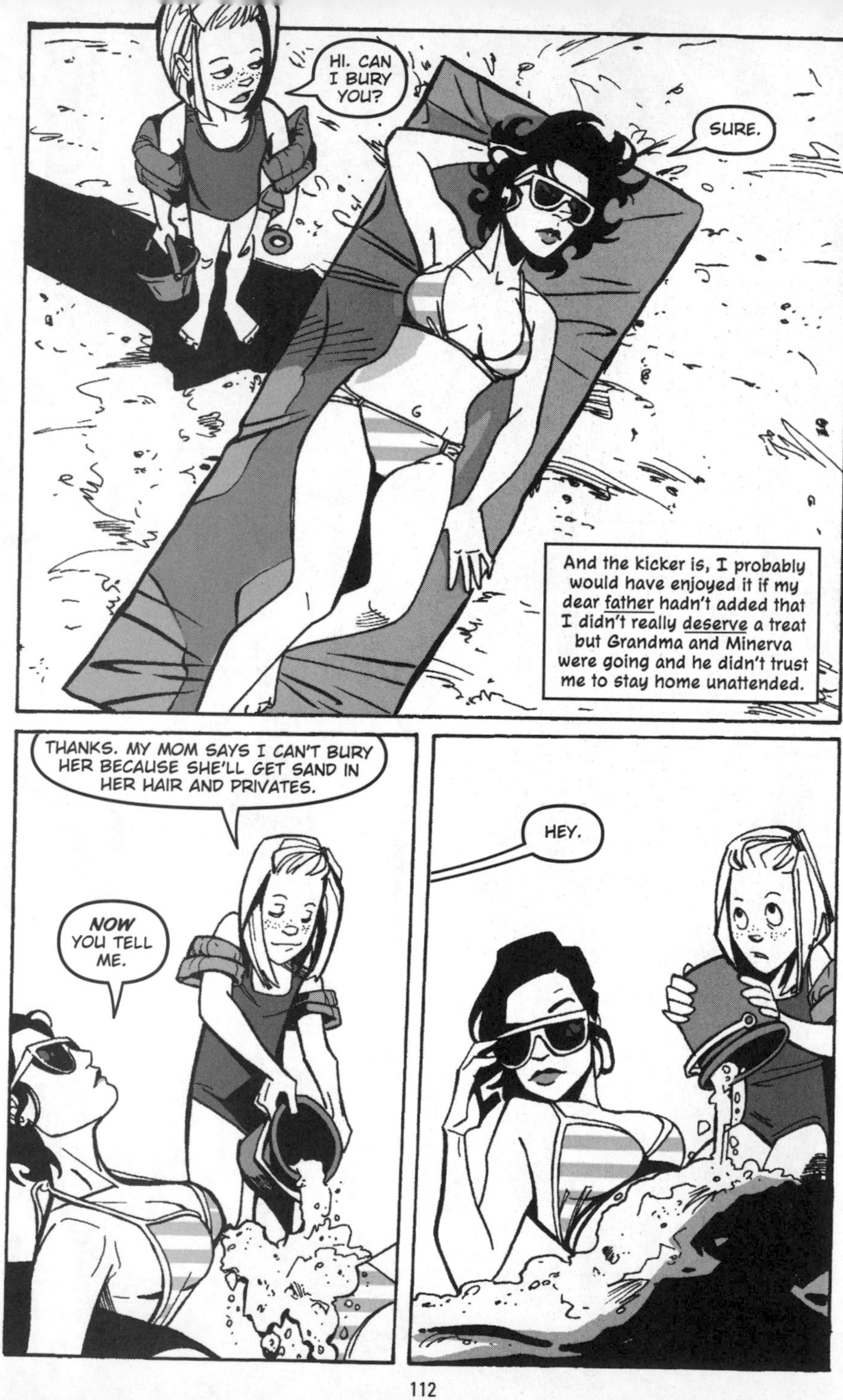
HI. CAN I BURY YOU?
SURE.
And the kicker is, I probably would have enjoyed it if my dear father hadn't added that I didn't really deserve a treat but Grandma and Minerva were going and he didn't trust me to stay home unattended.
THANKS. MY MOM SAYS I CAN'T BURY HER BECAUSE SHE'LL GET SAND IN HER HAIR AND PRIVATES.
NOW YOU TELL ME.
HEY.

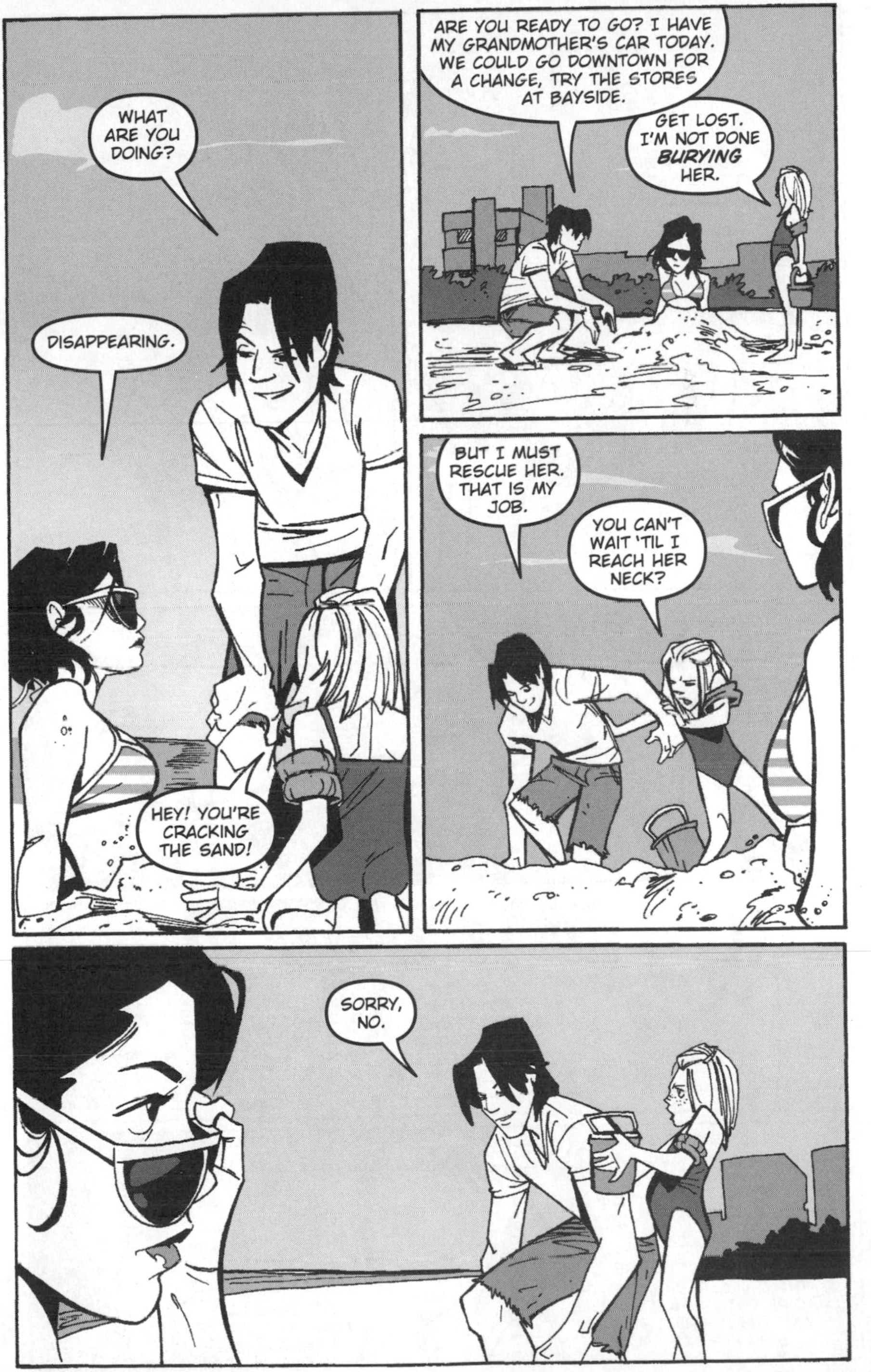
WHAT ARE YOU DOING?
DISAPPEARING.
HEY! YOU'RE CRACKING THE SAND!
ARE YOU READY TO GO? I HAVE MY GRANDMOTHER'S CAR TODAY. WE COULD GO DOWNTOWN FOR A CHANGE, TRY THE STORES AT BAYSIDE.
GET LOST. I'M NOT DONE BURYING HER.
BUT I MUST RESCUE HER. THAT IS MY JOB.
YOU CAN'T WAIT 'TIL I REACH HER NECK?
SORRY, NO.

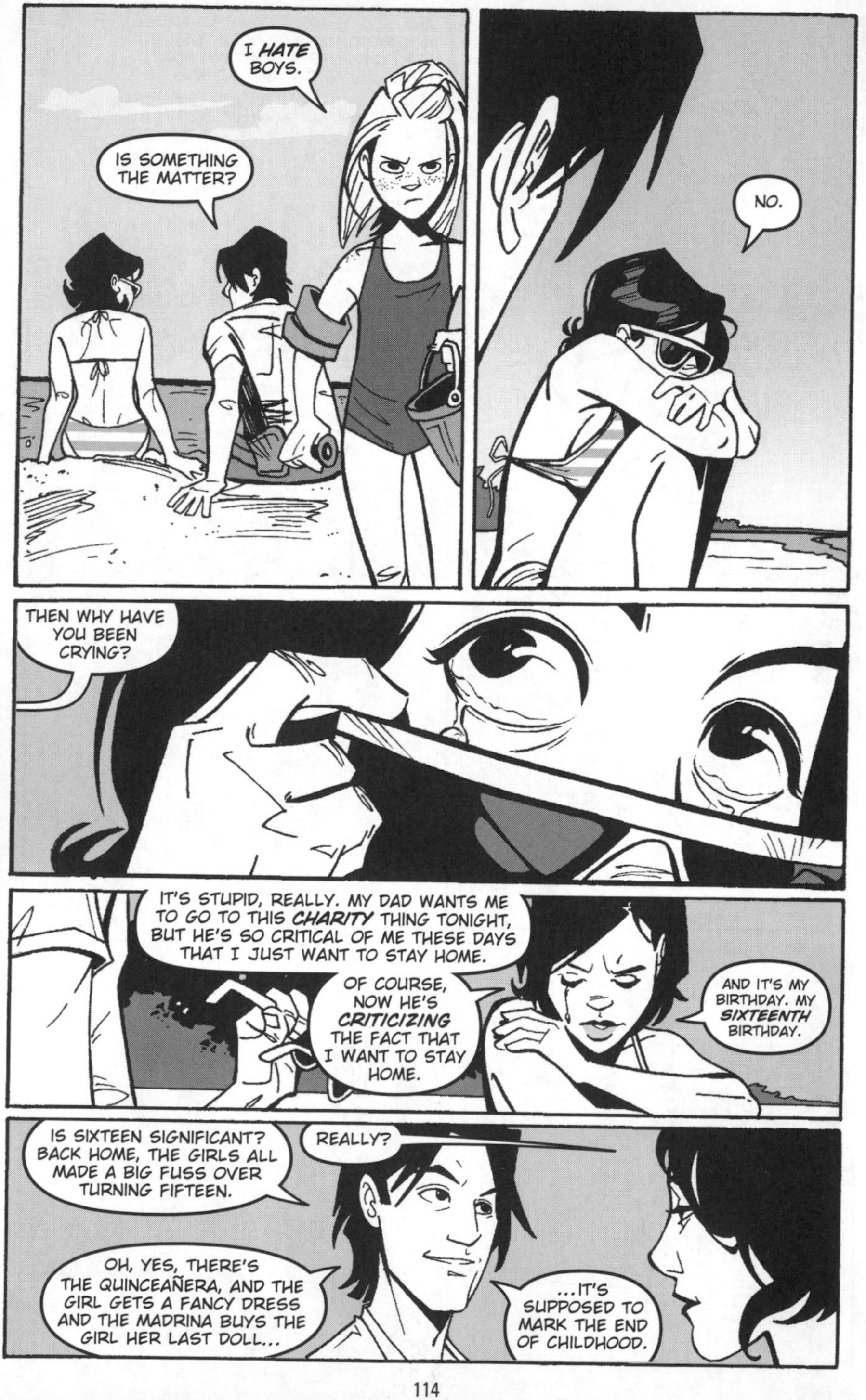
I HATE BOYS.
IS SOMETHING THE MATTER?
NO.
THEN WHY HAVE YOU BEEN CRYING?
IT'S STUPID, REALLY. MY DAD WANTS ME TO GO TO THIS CHARITY THING TONIGHT, BUT HE'S SO CRITICAL OF ME THESE DAYS THAT I JUST WANT TO STAY HOME.
OF COURSE, NOW HE'S CRITICIZING THE FACT THAT I WANT TO STAY HOME.
AND IT'S MY BIRTHDAY. MY SIXTEENTH BIRTHDAY.
IS SIXTEEN SIGNIFICANT? BACK HOME, THE GIRLS ALL MADE A BIG FUSS OVER TURNING FIFTEEN.
REALLY?
OH, YES, THERE'S THE QUINCEAÑERA, AND THE GIRL GETS A FANCY DRESS AND THE MADRINA BUYS THE GIRL HER LAST DOLL...
...IT'S SUPPOSED TO MARK THE END OF CHILDHOOD.

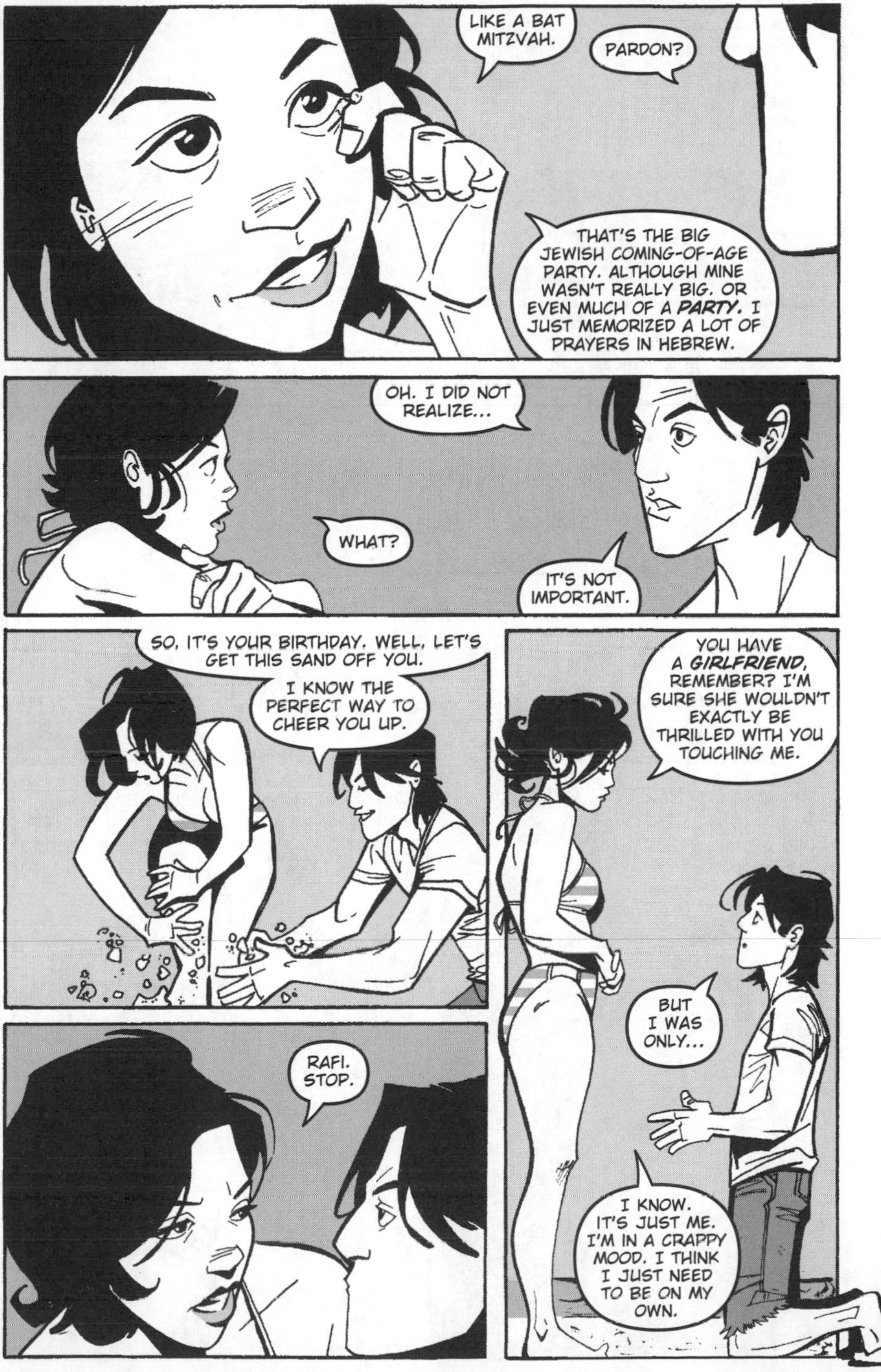
LIKE A BAT MITZVAH.
PARDON?
THAT'S THE BIG JEWISH COMING-OF-AGE PARTY. ALTHOUGH MINE WASN'T REALLY BIG. OR EVEN MUCH OF A PARTY. I JUST MEMORIZED A LOT OF PRAYERS IN HEBREW.
OH. I DID NOT REALIZE...
WHAT?
IT'S NOT IMPORTANT.
SO, IT'S YOUR BIRTHDAY. WELL, LET'S GET THIS SAND OFF YOU.
I KNOW THE PERFECT WAY TO CHEER YOU UP.
RAFI. STOP.
YOU HAVE A GIRLFRIEND, REMEMBER? I'M SURE SHE WOULDN'T EXACTLY BE THRILLED WITH YOU TOUCHING ME.
BUT I WAS ONLY...
I KNOW. IT'S JUST ME. I'M IN A CRAPPY MOOD. I THINK I JUST NEED TO BE ON MY OWN.

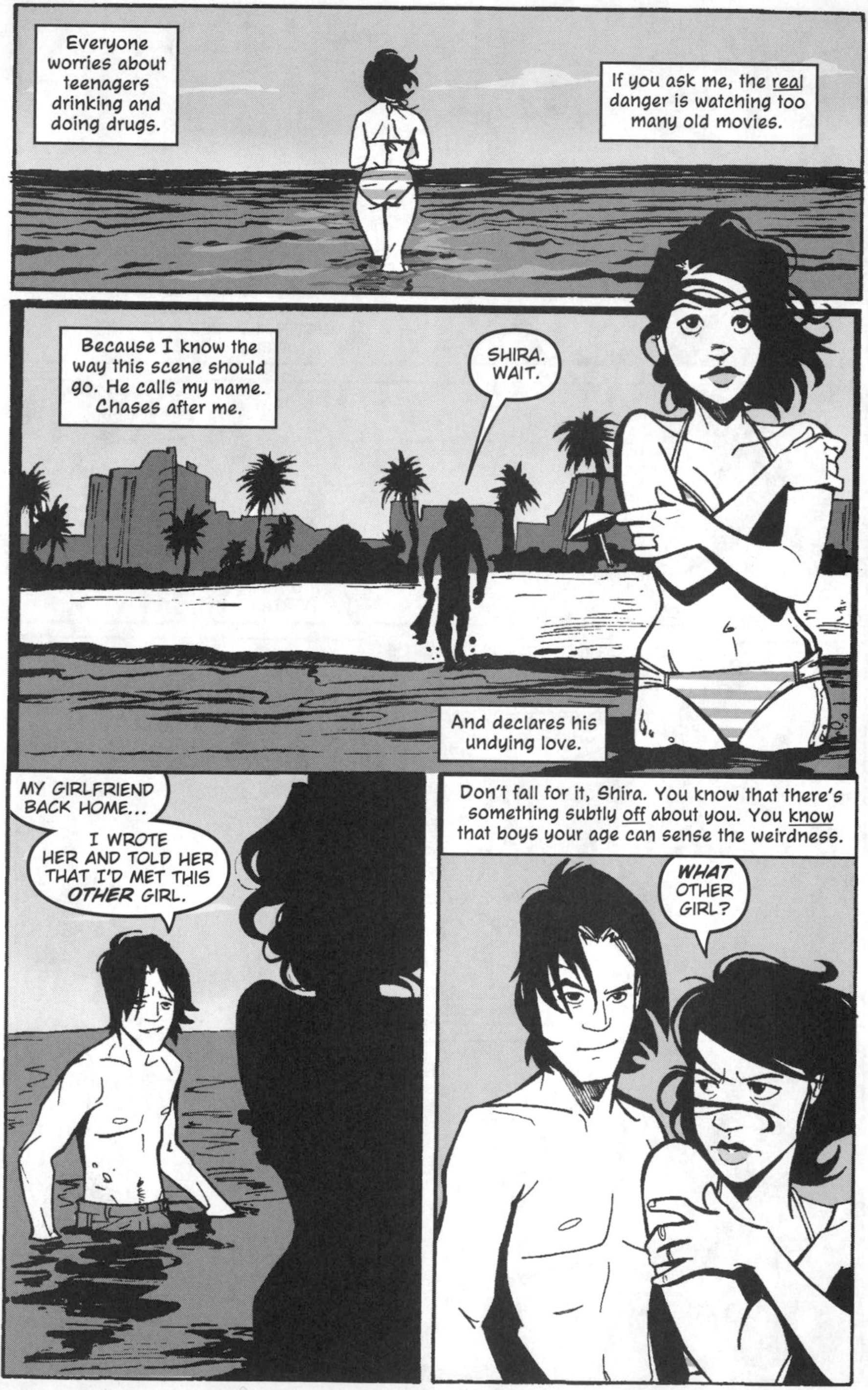
Everyone worries about teenagers drinking and doing drugs.
If you ask me, the real danger is watching too many old movies.
Because I know the way this scene should go. He calls my name. Chases after me.
SHIRA. WAIT.
And declares his undying love.
MY GIRLFRIEND BACK HOME...
I WROTE HER AND TOLD HER THAT I'D MET THIS OTHER GIRL.
Don't fall for it, Shira. You know that there's something subtly off about you. You know that boys your age can sense the weirdness.
WHAT OTHER GIRL?

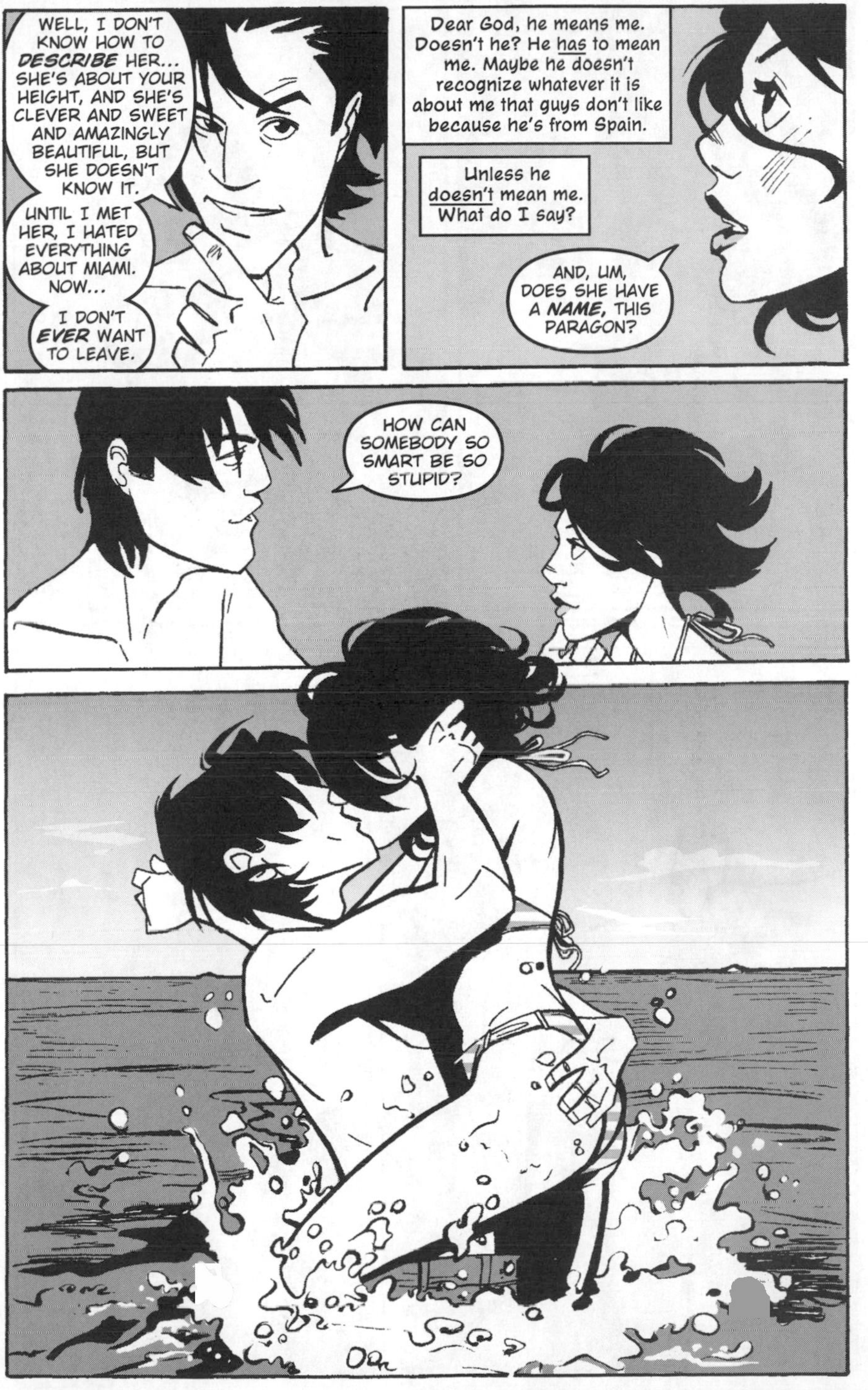
WELL, I DON'T KNOW HOW TO DESCRIBE HER... SHE'S ABOUT YOUR HEIGHT, AND SHE'S CLEVER AND SWEET AND AMAZINGLY BEAUTIFUL, BUT SHE DOESN'T KNOW IT.
UNTIL I MET HER, I HATED EVERYTHING ABOUT MIAMI. NOW...
I DON'T EVER WANT TO LEAVE.
Dear God, he means me. Doesn't he? He has to mean me. Maybe he doesn't recognize whatever it is about me that guys don't like because he's from Spain.
Unless he doesn't mean me. What do I say?
AND, UM, DOES SHE HAVE A NAME, THIS PARAGON?
HOW CAN SOMEBODY SO SMART BE SO STUPID?

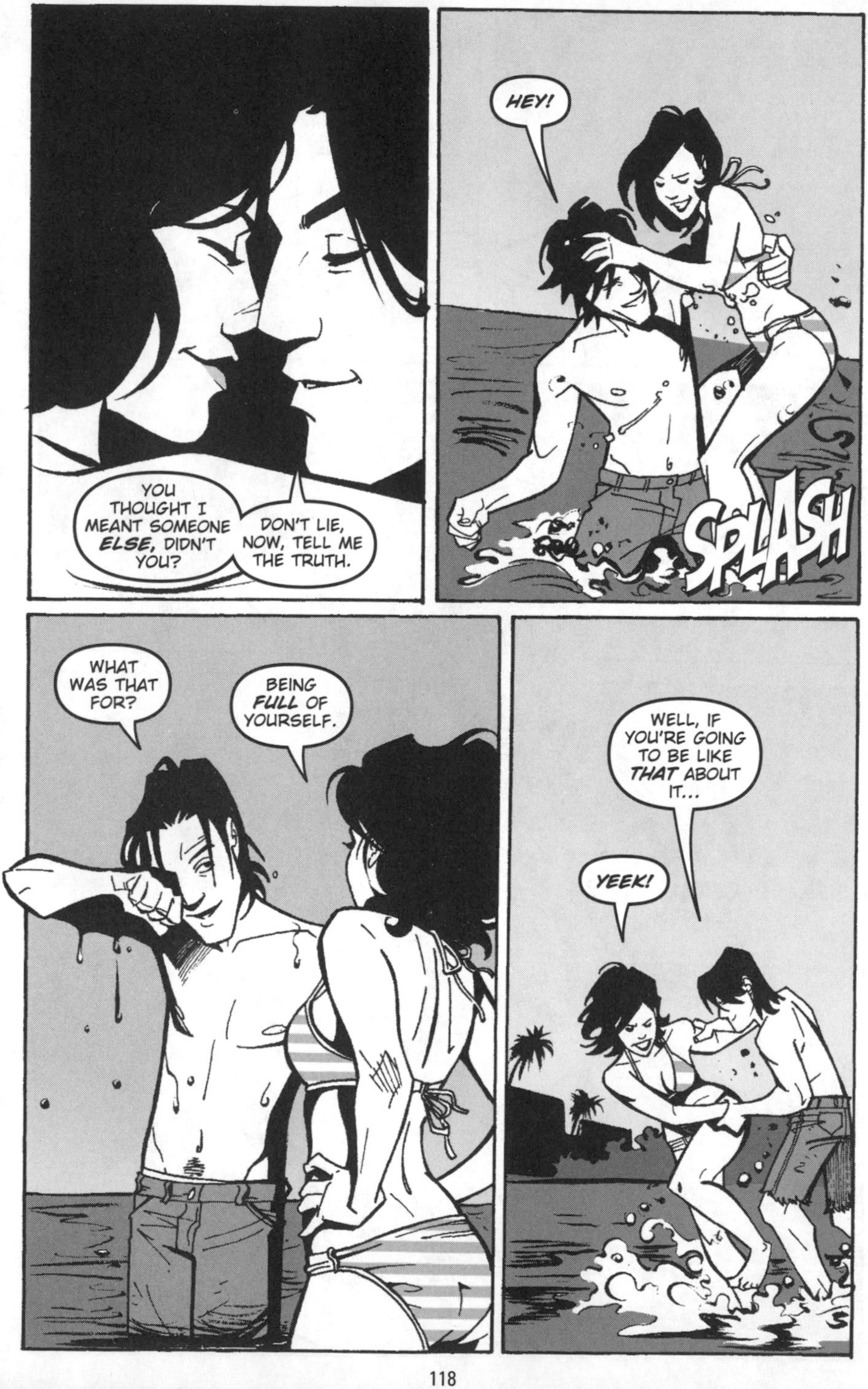
YOU THOUGHT I MEANT SOMEONE *ELSE,* DIDN'T YOU?
DON'T LIE, NOW, TELL ME THE TRUTH.
HEY!
SPLASH
WHAT WAS THAT FOR?
BEING *FULL* OF YOURSELF.
WELL, IF YOU'RE GOING TO BE LIKE *THAT* ABOUT IT...
YEEK!

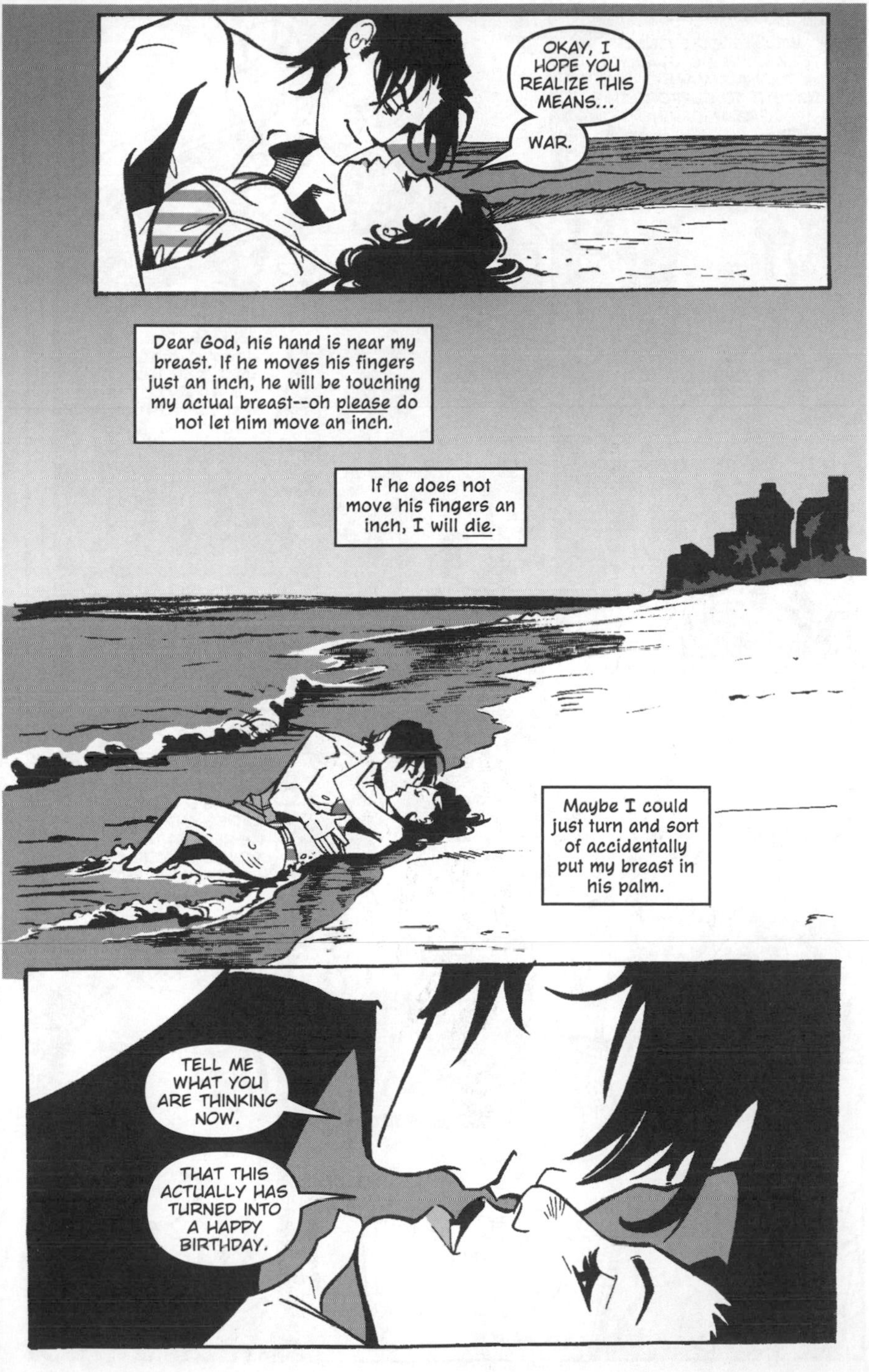
OKAY, I HOPE YOU REALIZE THIS MEANS...
WAR.
Dear God, his hand is near my breast. If he moves his fingers just an inch, he will be touching my actual breast--oh please do not let him move an inch.
If he does not move his fingers an inch, I will die.
Maybe I could just turn and sort of accidentally put my breast in his palm.
TELL ME WHAT YOU ARE THINKING NOW.
THAT THIS ACTUALLY HAS TURNED INTO A HAPPY BIRTHDAY.

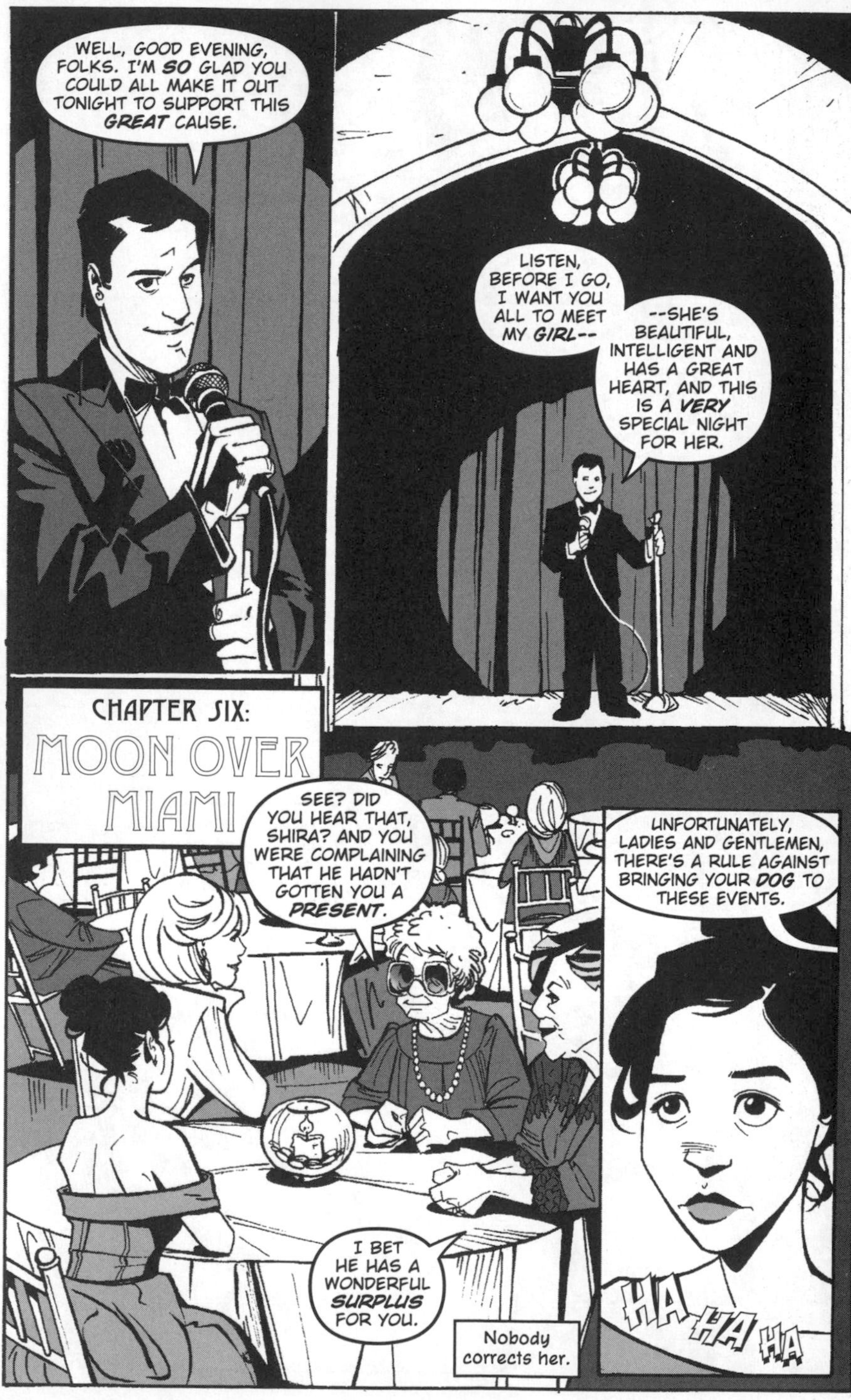
WELL, GOOD EVENING, FOLKS. I'M SO GLAD YOU COULD ALL MAKE IT OUT TONIGHT TO SUPPORT THIS GREAT CAUSE.
LISTEN, BEFORE I GO, I WANT YOU ALL TO MEET MY GIRL--
--SHE'S BEAUTIFUL, INTELLIGENT AND HAS A GREAT HEART, AND THIS IS A VERY SPECIAL NIGHT FOR HER.
CHAPTER SIX:
MOON OVER MIAMI
SEE? DID YOU HEAR THAT, SHIRA? AND YOU WERE COMPLAINING THAT HE HADN'T GOTTEN YOU A PRESENT.
I BET HE HAS A WONDERFUL SURPLUS FOR YOU.
Nobody corrects her.
UNFORTUNATELY, LADIES AND GENTLEMEN, THERE'S A RULE AGAINST BRINGING YOUR DOG TO THESE EVENTS.
HA HA HA

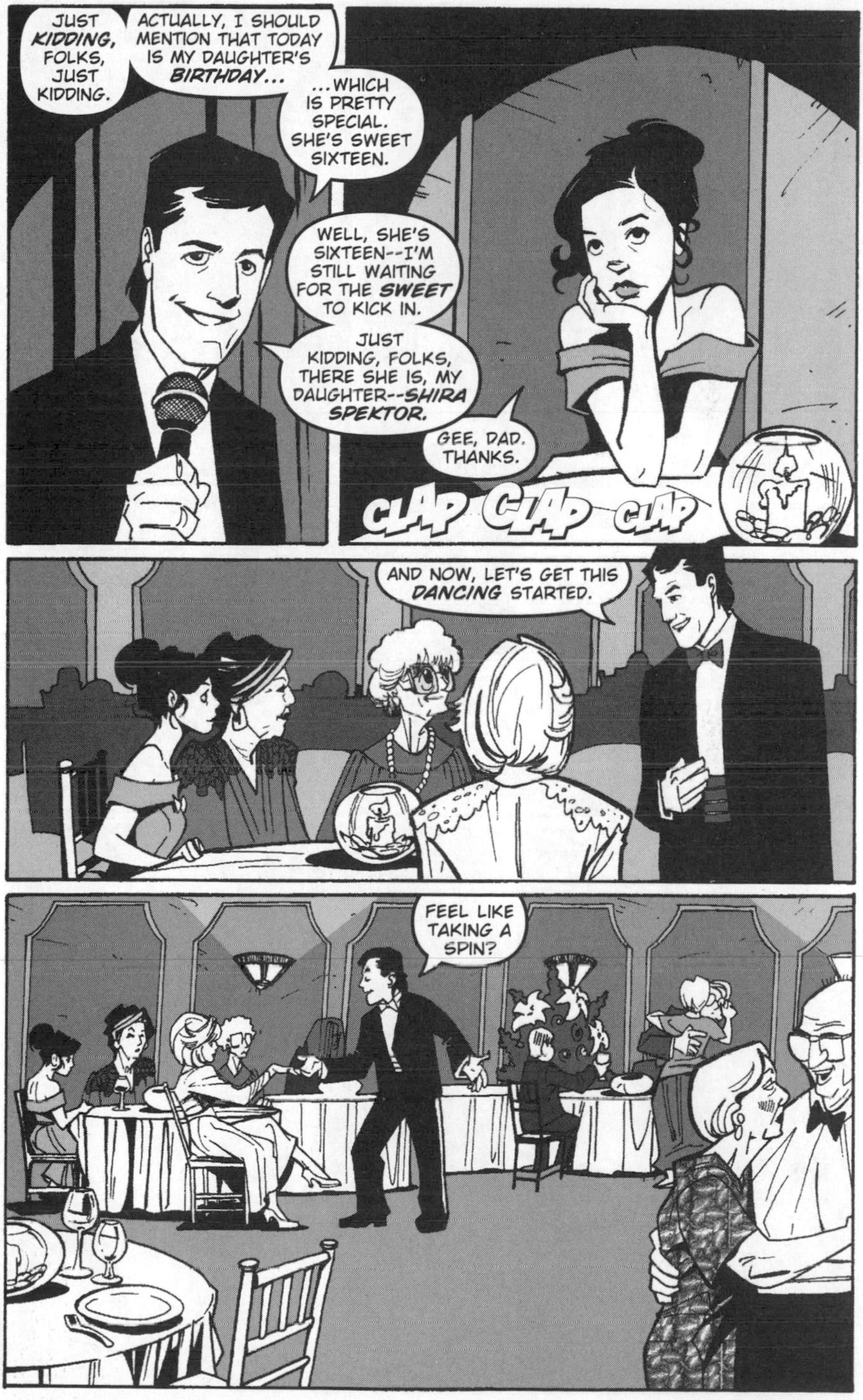
JUST KIDDING, FOLKS, JUST KIDDING.
ACTUALLY, I SHOULD MENTION THAT TODAY IS MY DAUGHTER'S BIRTHDAY...
...WHICH IS PRETTY SPECIAL. SHE'S SWEET SIXTEEN.
WELL, SHE'S SIXTEEN--I'M STILL WAITING FOR THE SWEET TO KICK IN.
JUST KIDDING, FOLKS, THERE SHE IS, MY DAUGHTER--SHIRA SPEKTOR.
GEE, DAD. THANKS.
CLAP CLAP CLAP
AND NOW, LET'S GET THIS DANCING STARTED.
FEEL LIKE TAKING A SPIN?

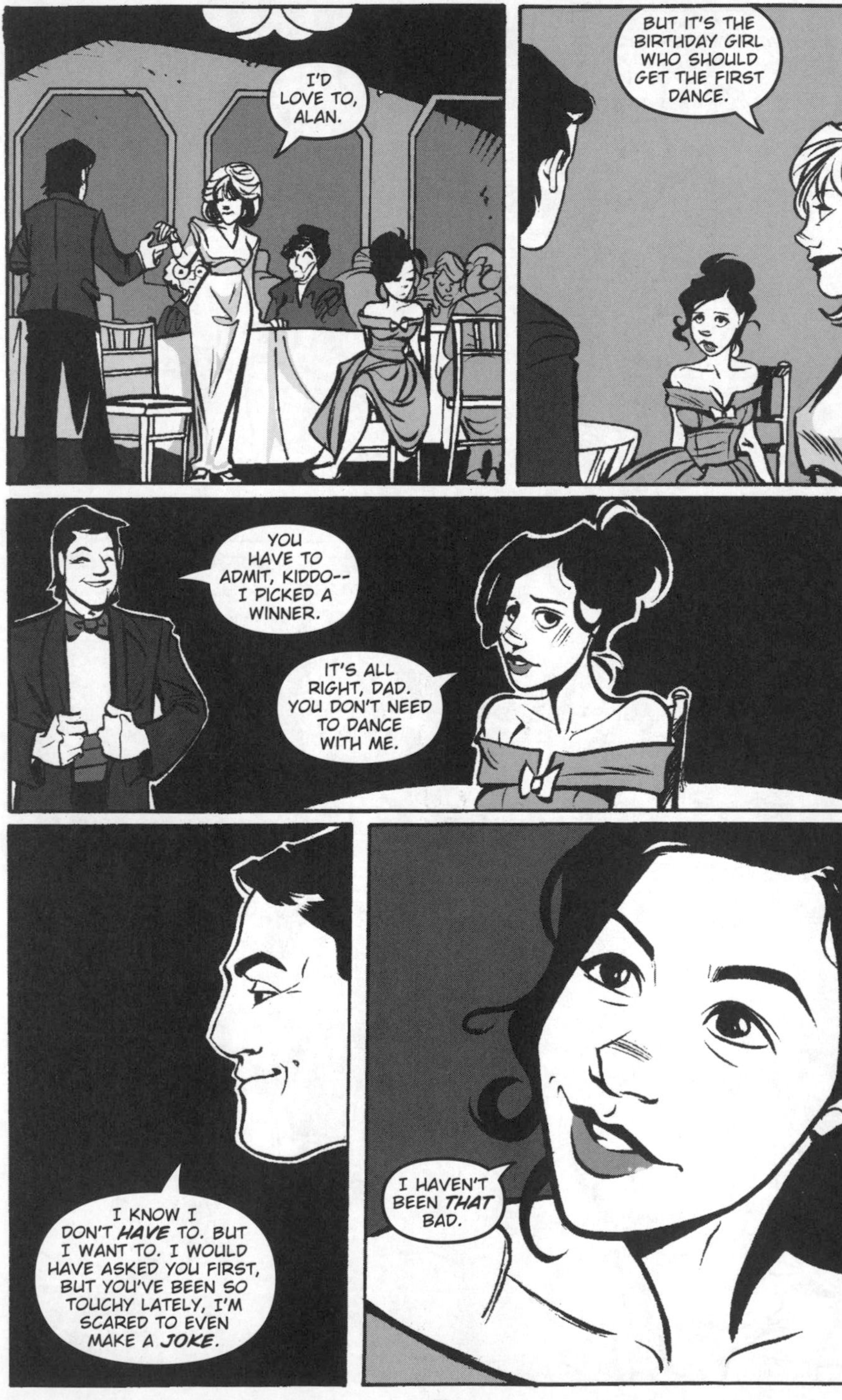
I'D LOVE TO, ALAN.
BUT IT'S THE BIRTHDAY GIRL WHO SHOULD GET THE FIRST DANCE.
YOU HAVE TO ADMIT, KIDDO-- I PICKED A WINNER.
IT'S ALL RIGHT, DAD. YOU DON'T NEED TO DANCE WITH ME.
I KNOW I DON'T *HAVE* TO. BUT I WANT TO. I WOULD HAVE ASKED YOU FIRST, BUT YOU'VE BEEN SO TOUCHY LATELY, I'M SCARED TO EVEN MAKE A *JOKE*.
I HAVEN'T BEEN *THAT* BAD.

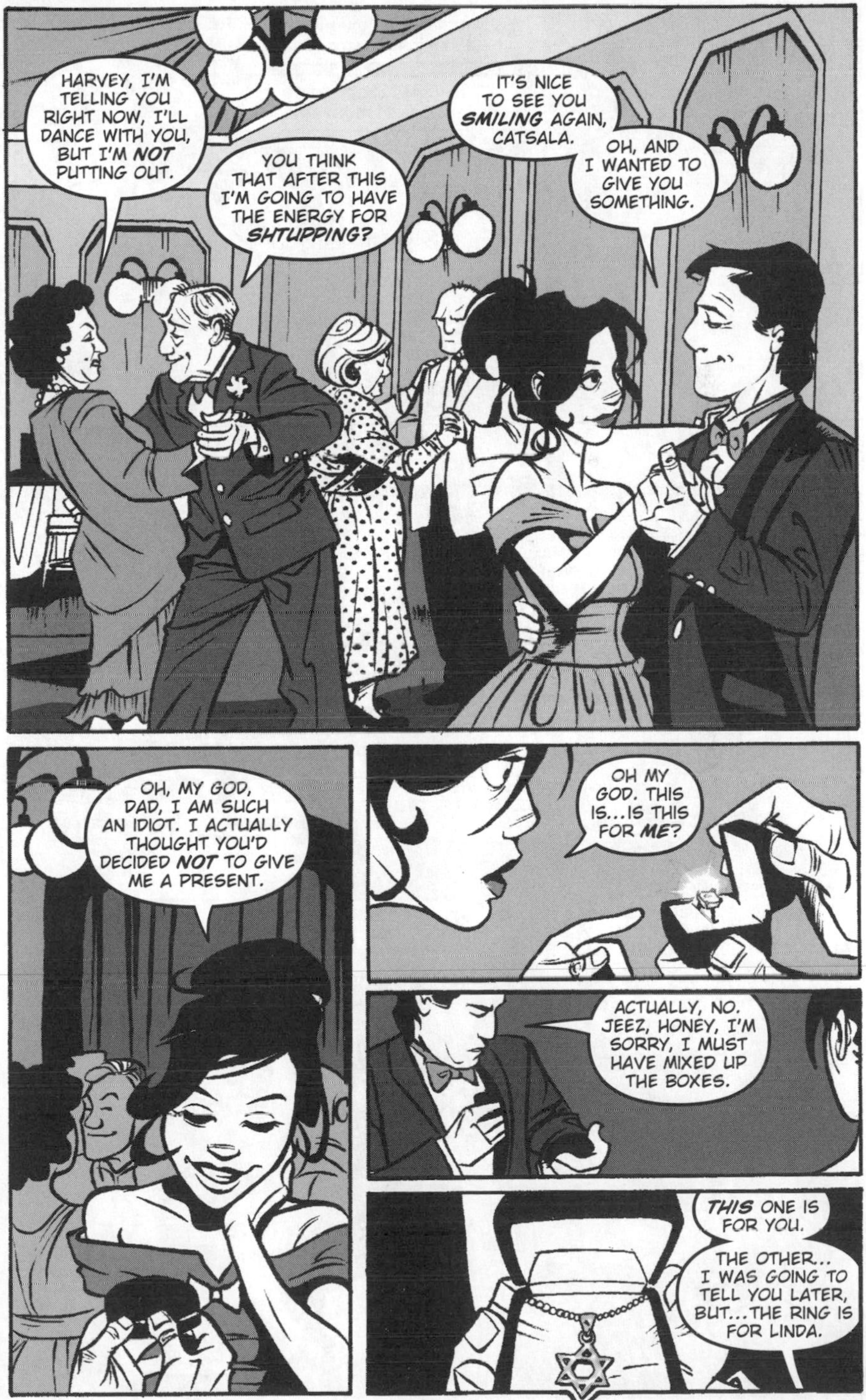
HARVEY, I'M TELLING YOU RIGHT NOW, I'LL DANCE WITH YOU, BUT I'M ***NOT*** PUTTING OUT.
YOU THINK THAT AFTER THIS I'M GOING TO HAVE THE ENERGY FOR ***SHTUPPING?***
IT'S NICE TO SEE YOU ***SMILING*** AGAIN, CATSALA.
OH, AND I WANTED TO GIVE YOU SOMETHING.
OH, MY GOD, DAD, I AM SUCH AN IDIOT. I ACTUALLY THOUGHT YOU'D DECIDED ***NOT*** TO GIVE ME A PRESENT.
OH MY GOD. THIS IS...IS THIS FOR ***ME?***
ACTUALLY, NO. JEEZ, HONEY, I'M SORRY, I MUST HAVE MIXED UP THE BOXES.
THIS ONE IS FOR YOU.
THE OTHER... I WAS GOING TO TELL YOU LATER, BUT...THE RING IS FOR LINDA.

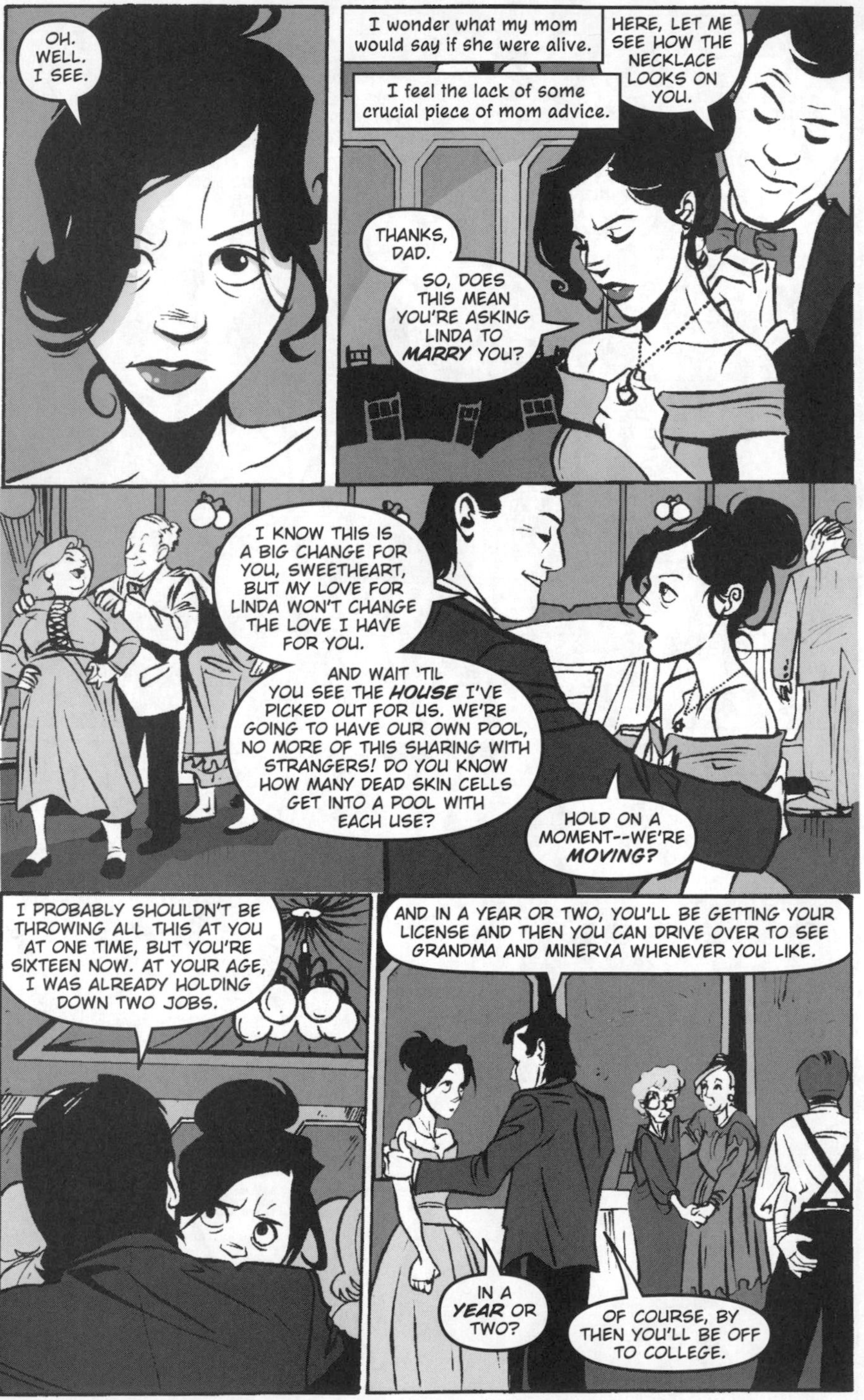
OH. WELL. I SEE.
I wonder what my mom would say if she were alive.
I feel the lack of some crucial piece of mom advice.
HERE, LET ME SEE HOW THE NECKLACE LOOKS ON YOU.
THANKS, DAD.
SO, DOES THIS MEAN YOU'RE ASKING LINDA TO MARRY YOU?
I KNOW THIS IS A BIG CHANGE FOR YOU, SWEETHEART, BUT MY LOVE FOR LINDA WON'T CHANGE THE LOVE I HAVE FOR YOU.
AND WAIT 'TIL YOU SEE THE HOUSE I'VE PICKED OUT FOR US. WE'RE GOING TO HAVE OUR OWN POOL, NO MORE OF THIS SHARING WITH STRANGERS! DO YOU KNOW HOW MANY DEAD SKIN CELLS GET INTO A POOL WITH EACH USE?
HOLD ON A MOMENT--WE'RE MOVING?
I PROBABLY SHOULDN'T BE THROWING ALL THIS AT YOU AT ONE TIME, BUT YOU'RE SIXTEEN NOW. AT YOUR AGE, I WAS ALREADY HOLDING DOWN TWO JOBS.
AND IN A YEAR OR TWO, YOU'LL BE GETTING YOUR LICENSE AND THEN YOU CAN DRIVE OVER TO SEE GRANDMA AND MINERVA WHENEVER YOU LIKE.
IN A YEAR OR TWO?
OF COURSE, BY THEN YOU'LL BE OFF TO COLLEGE.

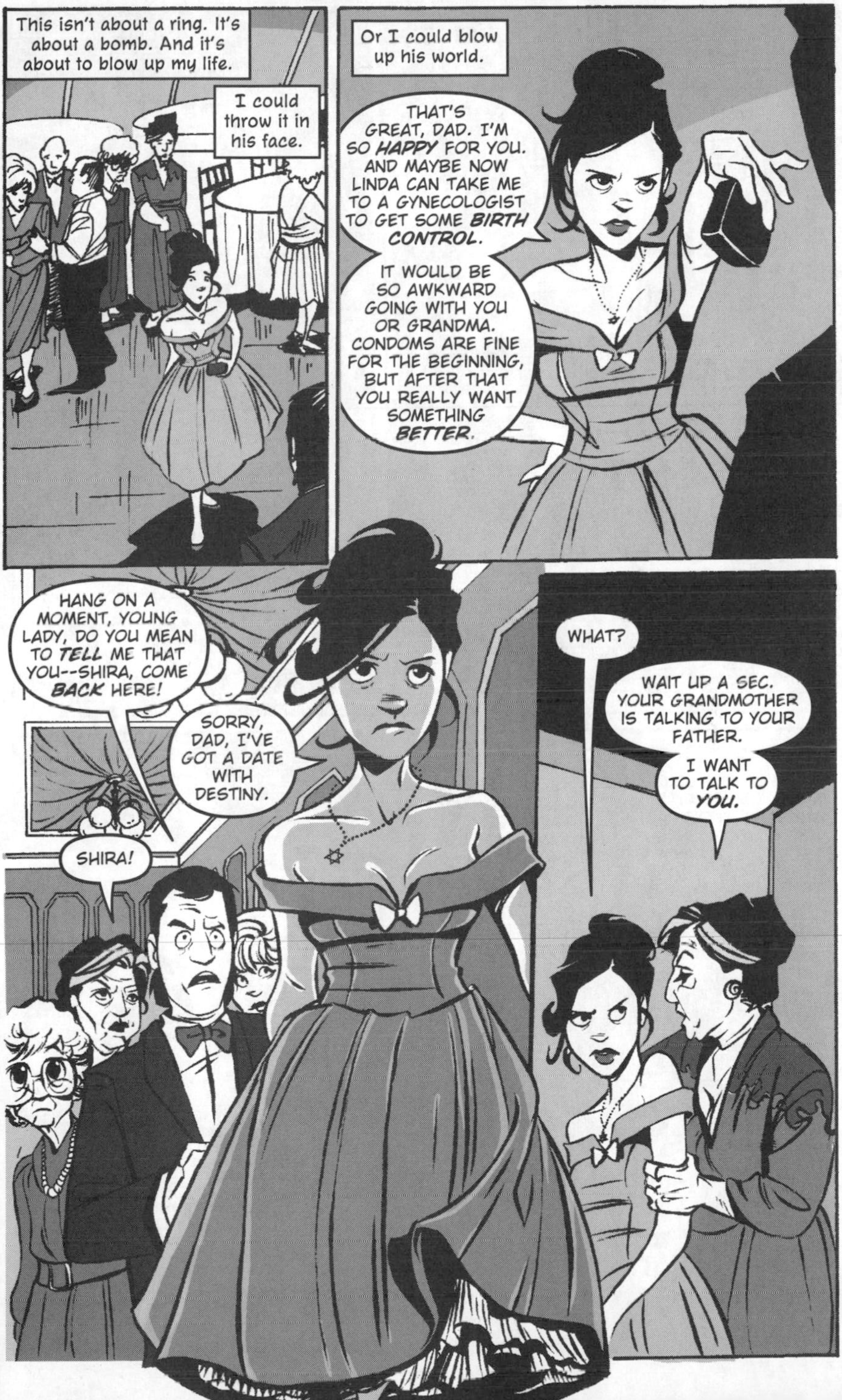
This isn't about a ring. It's about a bomb. And it's about to blow up my life.
I could throw it in his face.
Or I could blow up his world.
THAT'S GREAT, DAD. I'M SO HAPPY FOR YOU. AND MAYBE NOW LINDA CAN TAKE ME TO A GYNECOLOGIST TO GET SOME BIRTH CONTROL.
IT WOULD BE SO AWKWARD GOING WITH YOU OR GRANDMA. CONDOMS ARE FINE FOR THE BEGINNING, BUT AFTER THAT YOU REALLY WANT SOMETHING BETTER.
HANG ON A MOMENT, YOUNG LADY, DO YOU MEAN TO TELL ME THAT YOU--SHIRA, COME BACK HERE!
SORRY, DAD, I'VE GOT A DATE WITH DESTINY.
SHIRA!
WHAT?
WAIT UP A SEC. YOUR GRANDMOTHER IS TALKING TO YOUR FATHER.
I WANT TO TALK TO YOU.

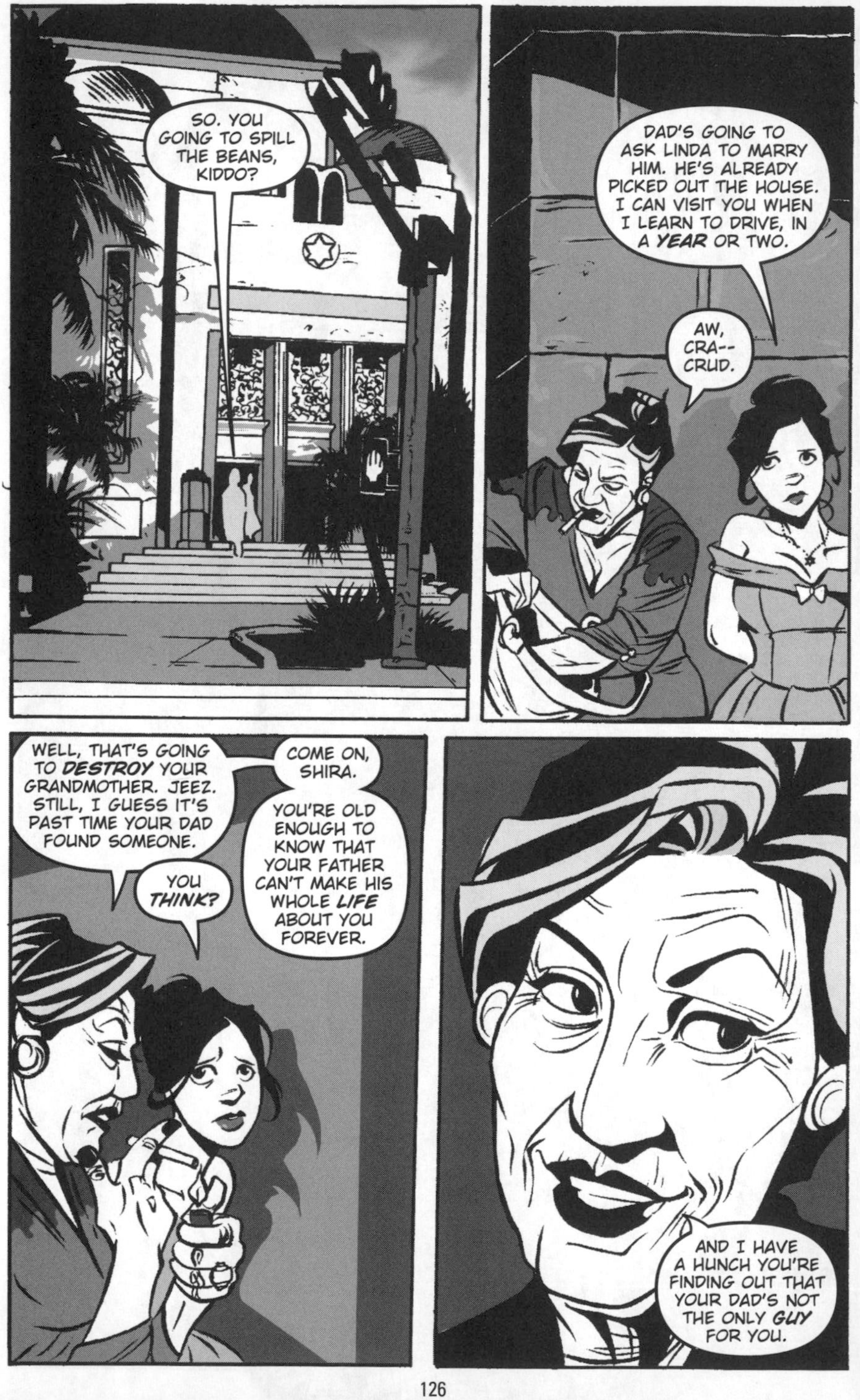
SO. YOU GOING TO SPILL THE BEANS, KIDDO?
DAD'S GOING TO ASK LINDA TO MARRY HIM. HE'S ALREADY PICKED OUT THE HOUSE. I CAN VISIT YOU WHEN I LEARN TO DRIVE, IN A ***YEAR*** OR TWO.
AW, CRA-- CRUD.
WELL, THAT'S GOING TO ***DESTROY*** YOUR GRANDMOTHER. JEEZ. STILL, I GUESS IT'S PAST TIME YOUR DAD FOUND SOMEONE.
YOU ***THINK?***
COME ON, SHIRA.
YOU'RE OLD ENOUGH TO KNOW THAT YOUR FATHER CAN'T MAKE HIS WHOLE ***LIFE*** ABOUT YOU FOREVER.
AND I HAVE A HUNCH YOU'RE FINDING OUT THAT YOUR DAD'S NOT THE ONLY ***GUY*** FOR YOU.

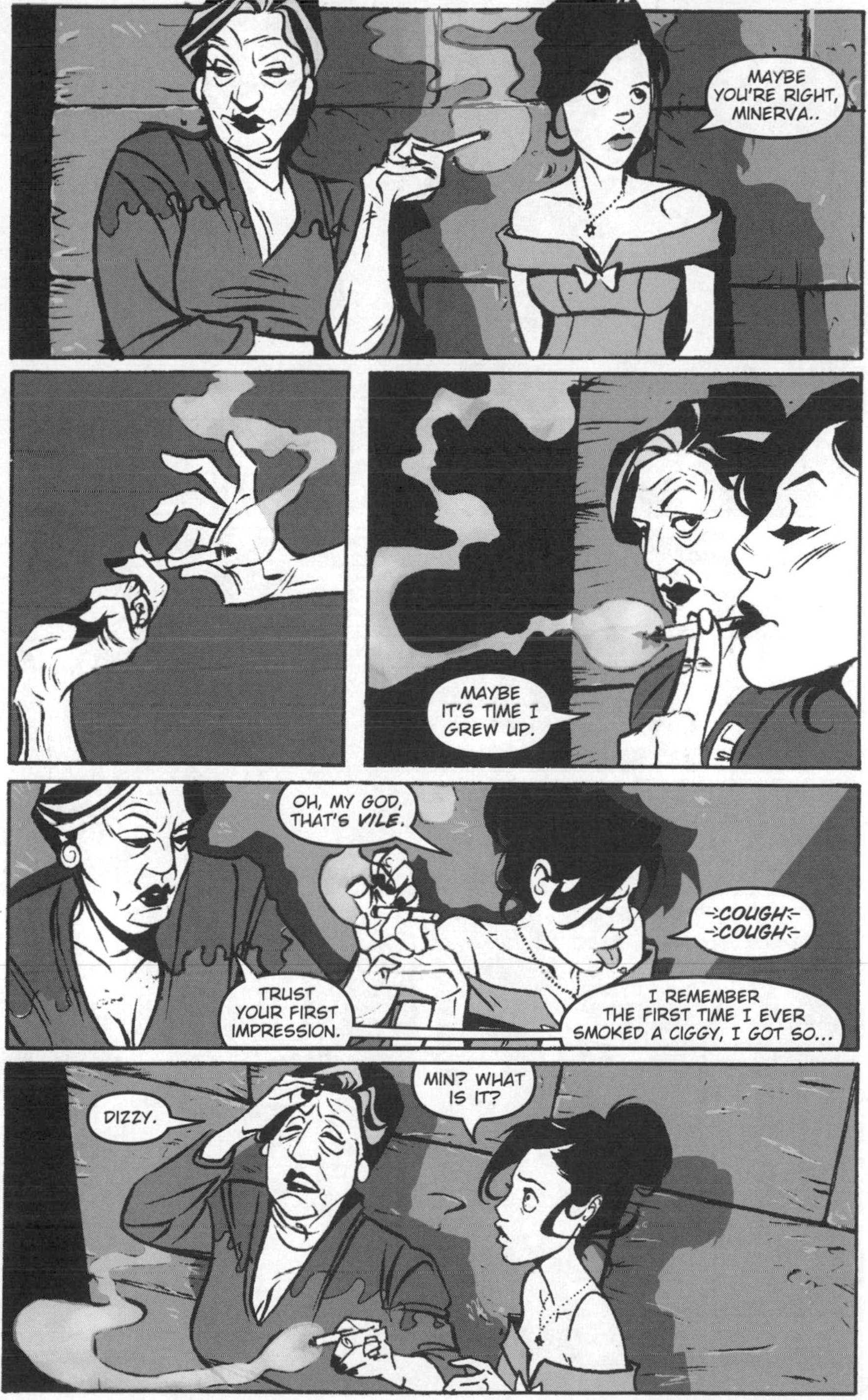
MAYBE YOU'RE RIGHT, MINERVA..
MAYBE IT'S TIME I GREW UP.
OH, MY GOD, THAT'S *VILE*.
-COUGH- -COUGH-
TRUST YOUR FIRST IMPRESSION.
I REMEMBER THE FIRST TIME I EVER SMOKED A CIGGY, I GOT SO...
DIZZY.
MIN? WHAT IS IT?

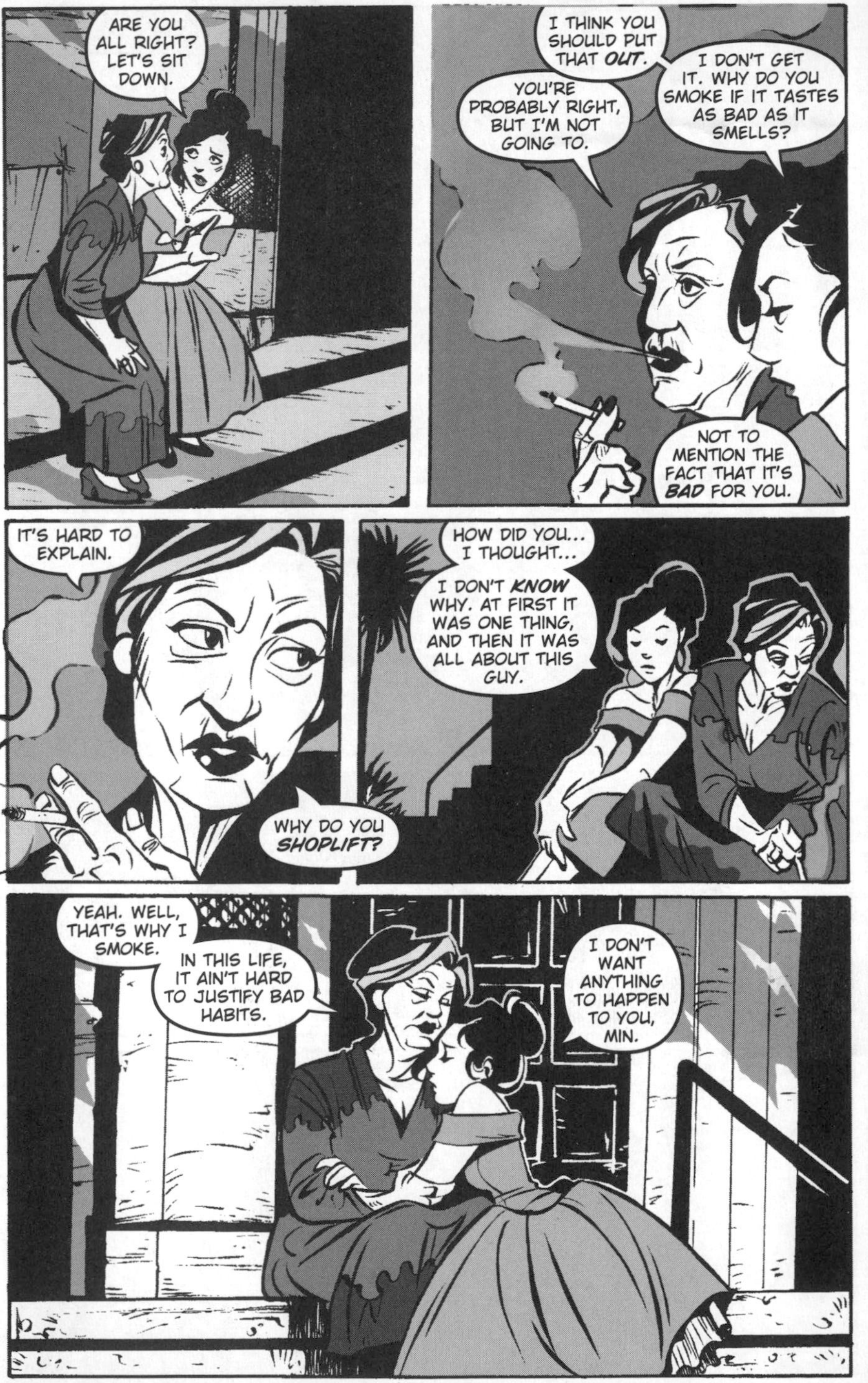
ARE YOU ALL RIGHT? LET'S SIT DOWN.
I THINK YOU SHOULD PUT THAT OUT.
YOU'RE PROBABLY RIGHT, BUT I'M NOT GOING TO.
I DON'T GET IT. WHY DO YOU SMOKE IF IT TASTES AS BAD AS IT SMELLS?
NOT TO MENTION THE FACT THAT IT'S BAD FOR YOU.
IT'S HARD TO EXPLAIN.
WHY DO YOU SHOPLIFT?
HOW DID YOU... I THOUGHT...
I DON'T KNOW WHY. AT FIRST IT WAS ONE THING, AND THEN IT WAS ALL ABOUT THIS GUY.
YEAH. WELL, THAT'S WHY I SMOKE.
IN THIS LIFE, IT AIN'T HARD TO JUSTIFY BAD HABITS.
I DON'T WANT ANYTHING TO HAPPEN TO YOU, MIN.

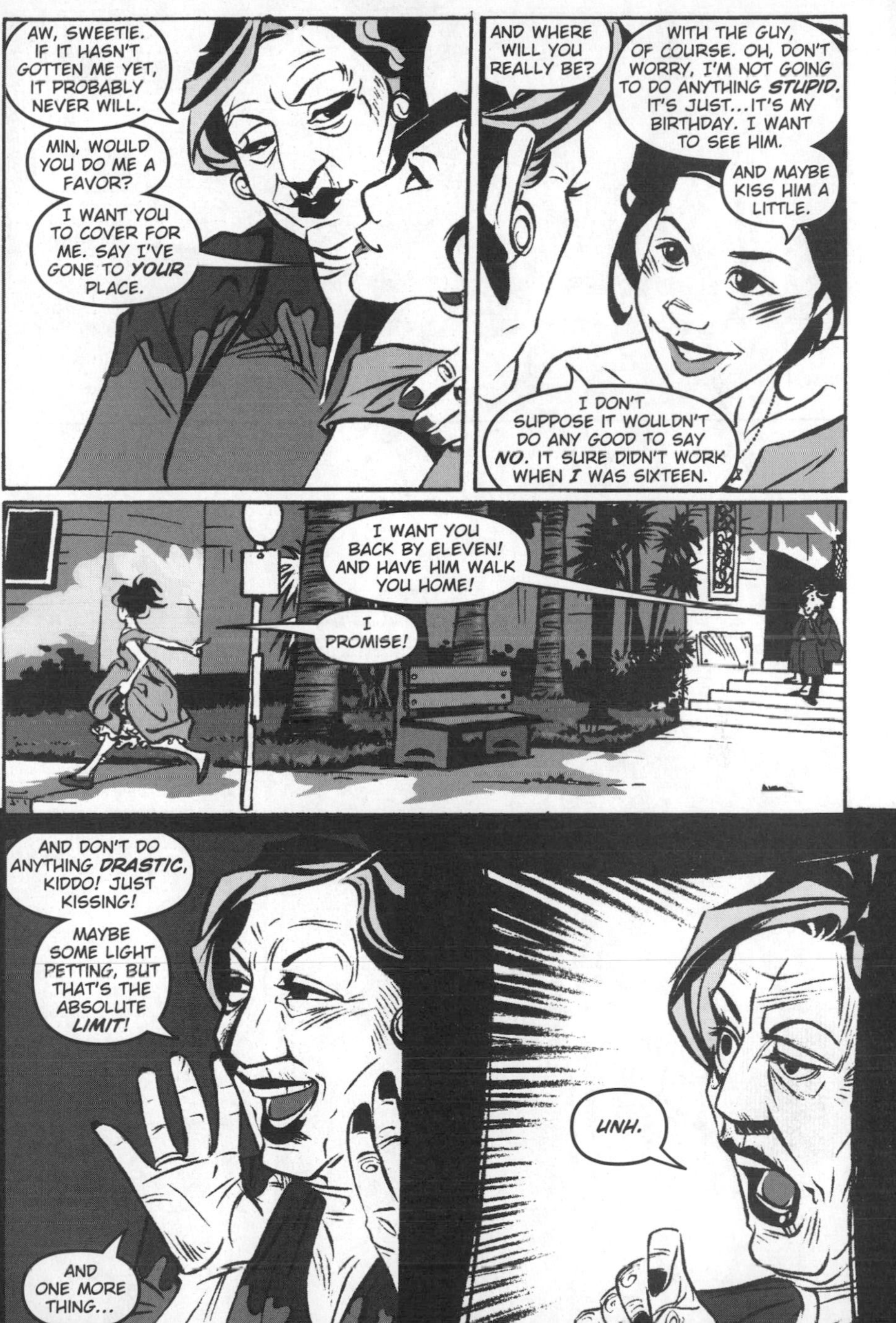
AW, SWEETIE. IF IT HASN'T GOTTEN ME YET, IT PROBABLY NEVER WILL.
MIN, WOULD YOU DO ME A FAVOR?
I WANT YOU TO COVER FOR ME. SAY I'VE GONE TO *YOUR* PLACE.
AND WHERE WILL YOU REALLY BE?
WITH THE GUY, OF COURSE. OH, DON'T WORRY, I'M NOT GOING TO DO ANYTHING *STUPID.* IT'S JUST...IT'S MY BIRTHDAY. I WANT TO SEE HIM.
AND MAYBE KISS HIM A LITTLE.
I DON'T SUPPOSE IT WOULDN'T DO ANY GOOD TO SAY *NO.* IT SURE DIDN'T WORK WHEN *I* WAS SIXTEEN.
I WANT YOU BACK BY ELEVEN! AND HAVE HIM WALK YOU HOME!
I PROMISE!
AND DON'T DO ANYTHING *DRASTIC,* KIDDO! JUST KISSING!
MAYBE SOME LIGHT PETTING, BUT THAT'S THE ABSOLUTE *LIMIT!*
AND ONE MORE THING...
UNH.

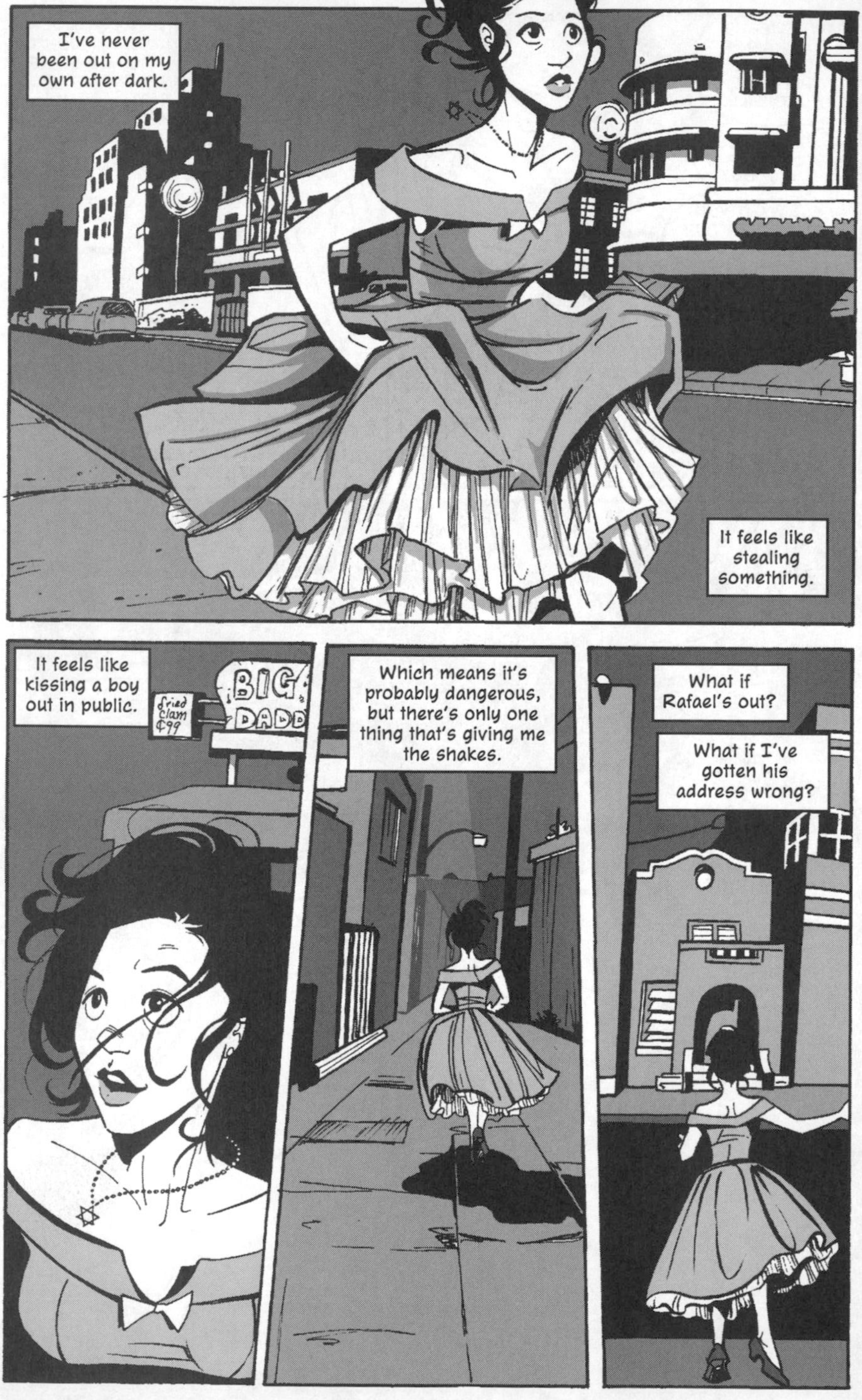
I've never been out on my own after dark.
It feels like stealing something.
It feels like kissing a boy out in public.
BIG
DADD
fried clam ¢99
Which means it's probably dangerous, but there's only one thing that's giving me the shakes.
What if Rafael's out?
What if I've gotten his address wrong?

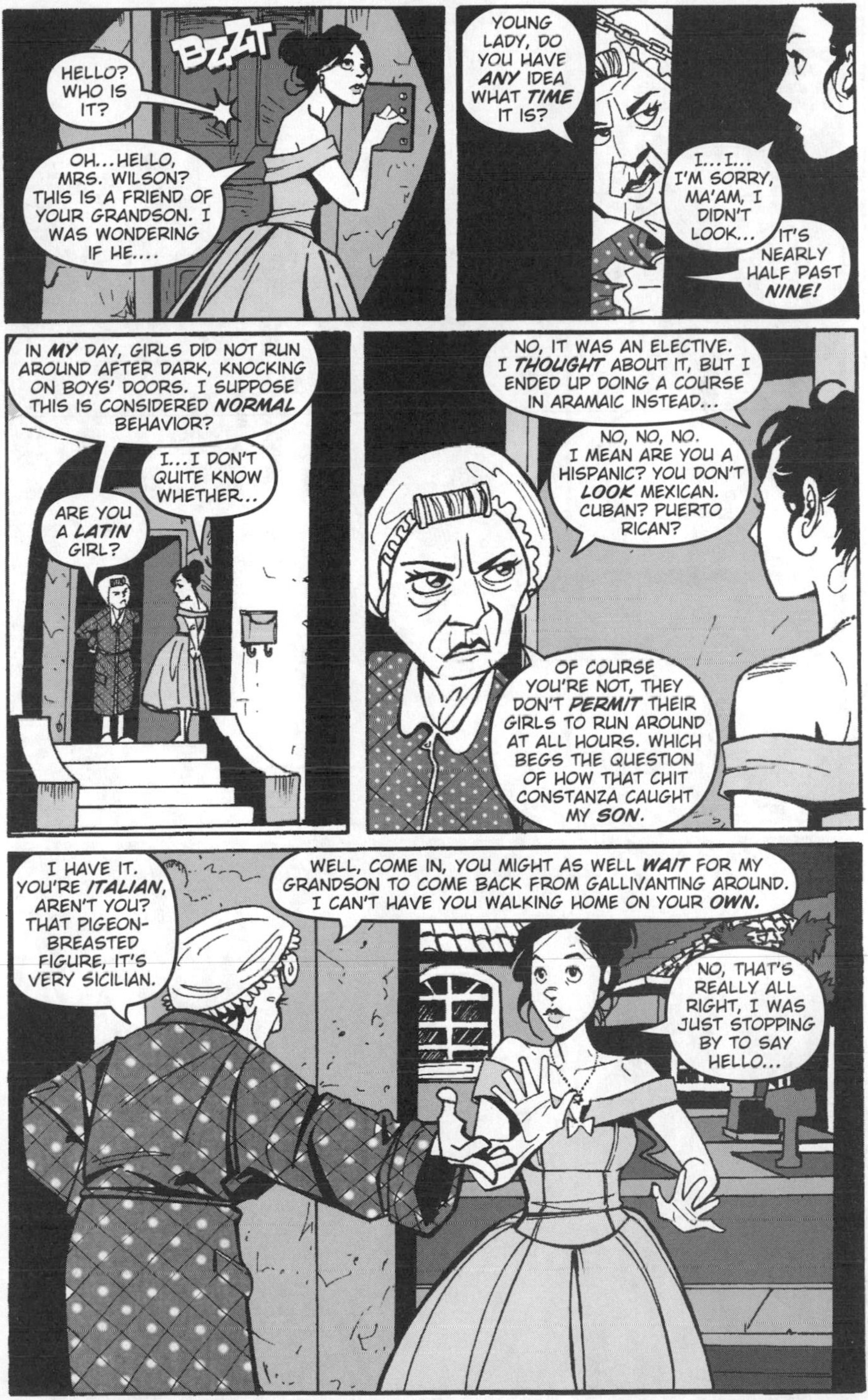
BZZZT
HELLO? WHO IS IT?
OH...HELLO, MRS. WILSON? THIS IS A FRIEND OF YOUR GRANDSON. I WAS WONDERING IF HE....
YOUNG LADY, DO YOU HAVE ANY IDEA WHAT TIME IT IS?
I...I... I'M SORRY, MA'AM, I DIDN'T LOOK...
IT'S NEARLY HALF PAST NINE!
IN MY DAY, GIRLS DID NOT RUN AROUND AFTER DARK, KNOCKING ON BOYS' DOORS. I SUPPOSE THIS IS CONSIDERED NORMAL BEHAVIOR?
I...I DON'T QUITE KNOW WHETHER...
ARE YOU A LATIN GIRL?
NO, IT WAS AN ELECTIVE. I THOUGHT ABOUT IT, BUT I ENDED UP DOING A COURSE IN ARAMAIC INSTEAD...
NO, NO, NO. I MEAN ARE YOU A HISPANIC? YOU DON'T LOOK MEXICAN. CUBAN? PUERTO RICAN?
OF COURSE YOU'RE NOT, THEY DON'T PERMIT THEIR GIRLS TO RUN AROUND AT ALL HOURS. WHICH BEGS THE QUESTION OF HOW THAT CHIT CONSTANZA CAUGHT MY SON.
I HAVE IT. YOU'RE ITALIAN, AREN'T YOU? THAT PIGEON-BREASTED FIGURE, IT'S VERY SICILIAN.
WELL, COME IN, YOU MIGHT AS WELL WAIT FOR MY GRANDSON TO COME BACK FROM GALLIVANTING AROUND. I CAN'T HAVE YOU WALKING HOME ON YOUR OWN.
NO, THAT'S REALLY ALL RIGHT, I WAS JUST STOPPING BY TO SAY HELLO...

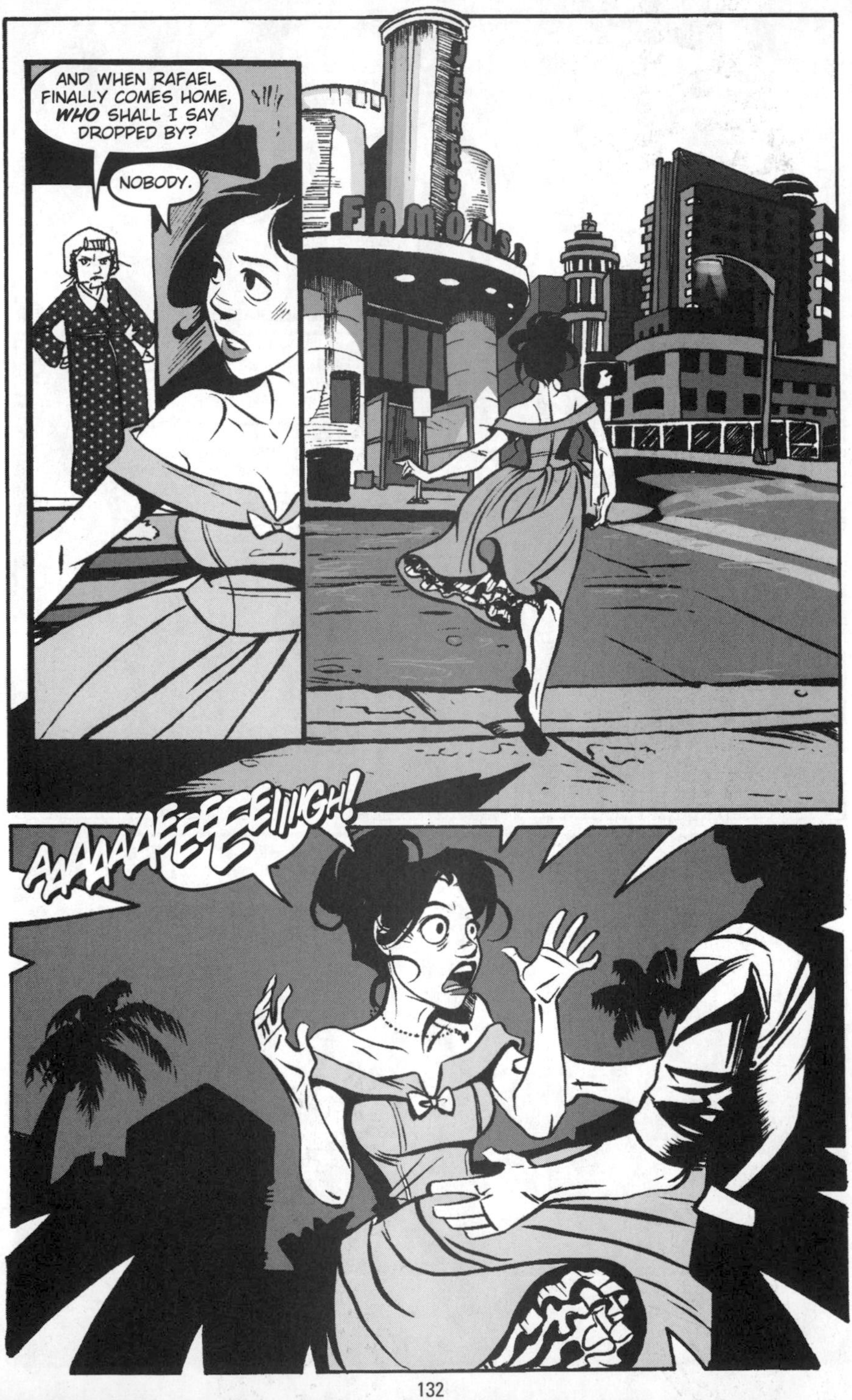
AND WHEN RAFAEL FINALLY COMES HOME, WHO SHALL I SAY DROPPED BY?
NOBODY.
FAMOUS
AAAAAEEEEEIIIIGH!

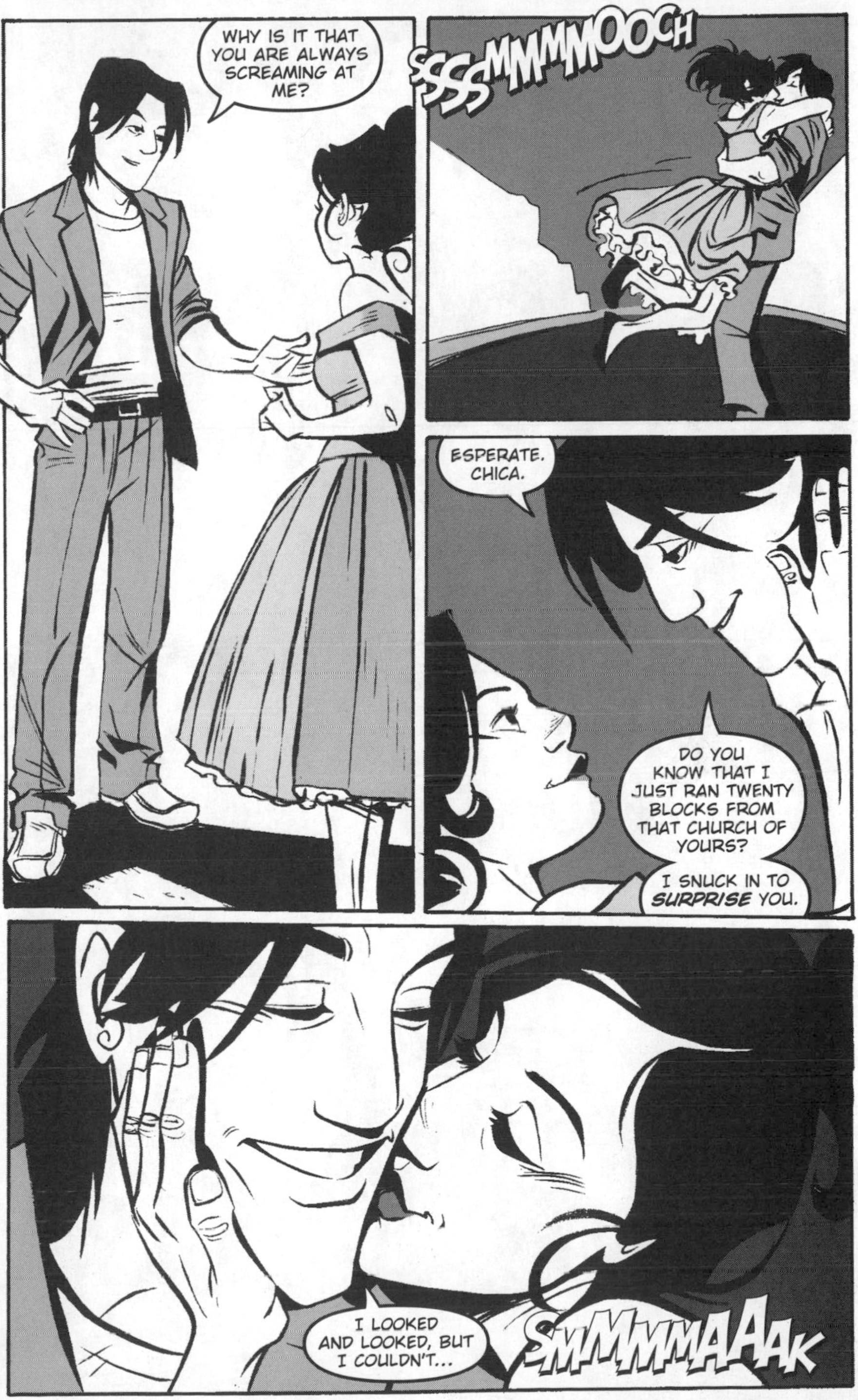
WHY IS IT THAT YOU ARE ALWAYS SCREAMING AT ME?
SSSSMMMMMOOCH
ESPERATE. CHICA.
DO YOU KNOW THAT I JUST RAN TWENTY BLOCKS FROM THAT CHURCH OF YOURS?
I SNUCK IN TO *SURPRISE* YOU.
I LOOKED AND LOOKED, BUT I COULDN'T...
SMMMMMAAAAK

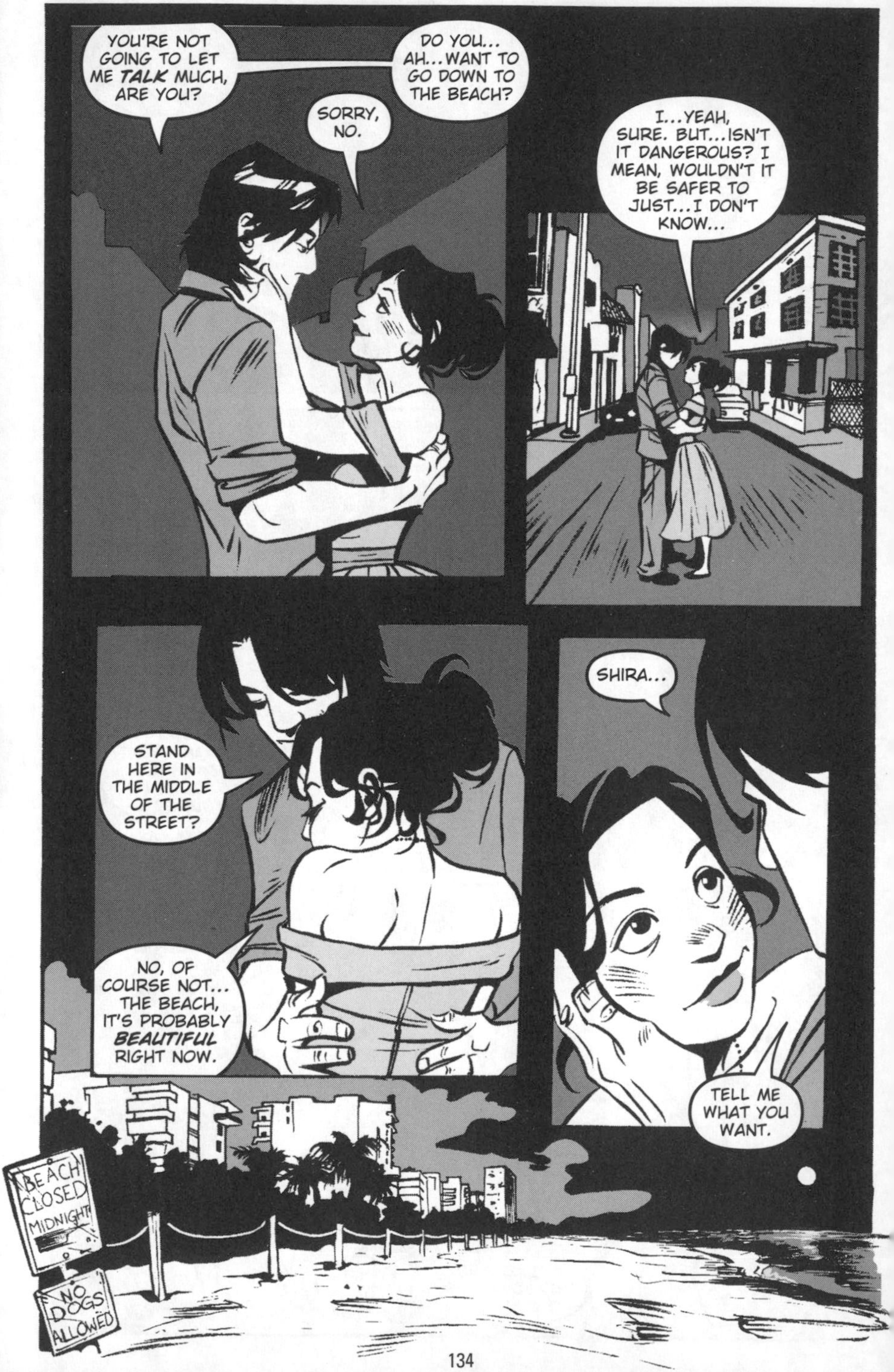
YOU'RE NOT GOING TO LET ME TALK MUCH, ARE YOU?
SORRY, NO.
DO YOU... AH...WANT TO GO DOWN TO THE BEACH?
I...YEAH, SURE. BUT...ISN'T IT DANGEROUS? I MEAN, WOULDN'T IT BE SAFER TO JUST...I DON'T KNOW...
STAND HERE IN THE MIDDLE OF THE STREET?
NO, OF COURSE NOT... THE BEACH, IT'S PROBABLY BEAUTIFUL RIGHT NOW.
SHIRA...
TELL ME WHAT YOU WANT.
BEACH CLOSED MIDNIGHT
NO DOGS ALLOWED

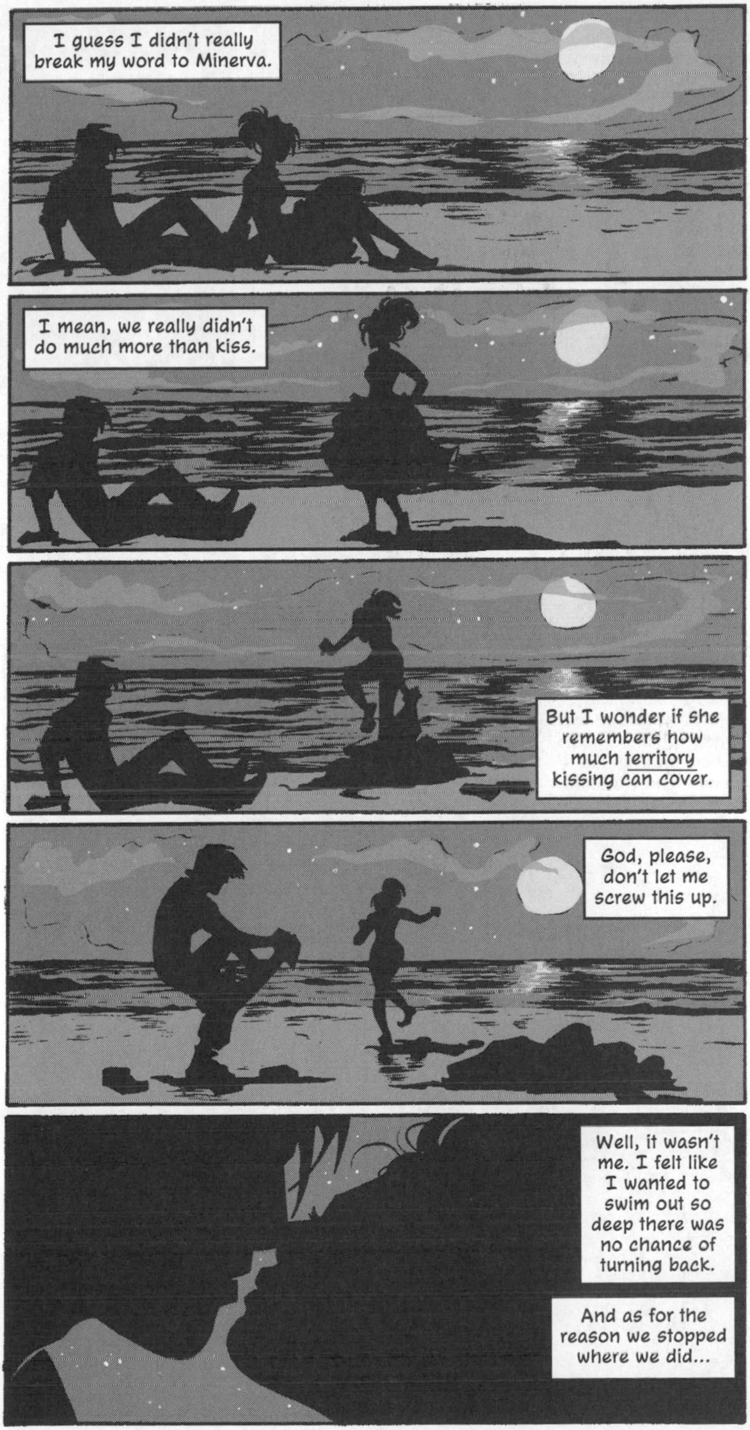
I guess I didn't really break my word to Minerva.
I mean, we really didn't do much more than kiss.
But I wonder if she remembers how much territory kissing can cover.
God, please, don't let me screw this up.
Well, it wasn't me. I felt like I wanted to swim out so deep there was no chance of turning back.
And as for the reason we stopped where we did...

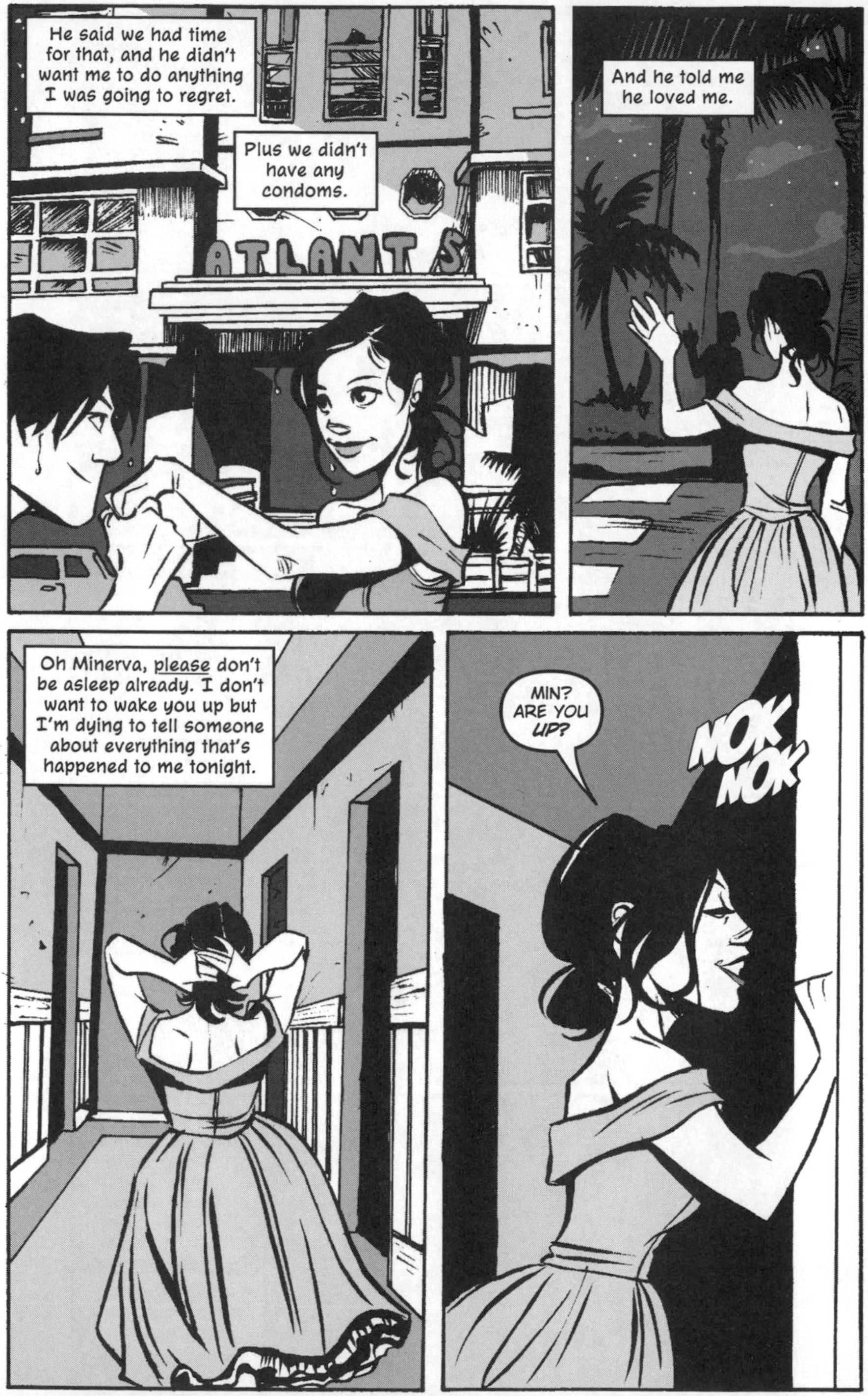
He said we had time for that, and he didn't want me to do anything I was going to regret.
Plus we didn't have any condoms.
ATLANT S
And he told me he loved me.
Oh Minerva, please don't be asleep already. I don't want to wake you up but I'm dying to tell someone about everything that's happened to me tonight.
MIN? ARE YOU *UP?*
NOK NOK

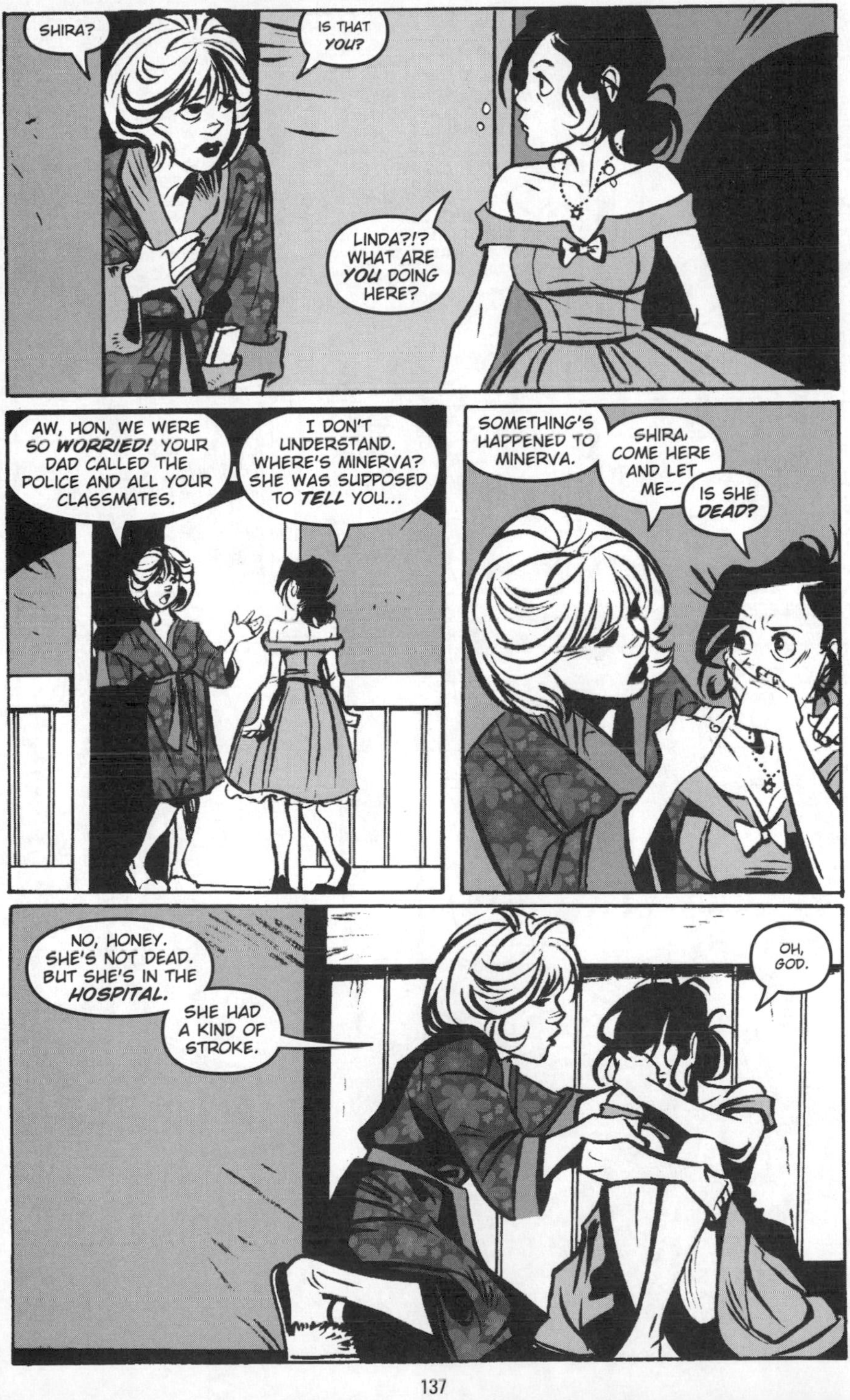
SHIRA?
IS THAT YOU?
LINDA?!? WHAT ARE YOU DOING HERE?
AW, HON, WE WERE SO WORRIED! YOUR DAD CALLED THE POLICE AND ALL YOUR CLASSMATES.
I DON'T UNDERSTAND. WHERE'S MINERVA? SHE WAS SUPPOSED TO TELL YOU...
SOMETHING'S HAPPENED TO MINERVA.
SHIRA, COME HERE AND LET ME--
IS SHE DEAD?
NO, HONEY. SHE'S NOT DEAD. BUT SHE'S IN THE HOSPITAL.
SHE HAD A KIND OF STROKE.
OH, GOD.

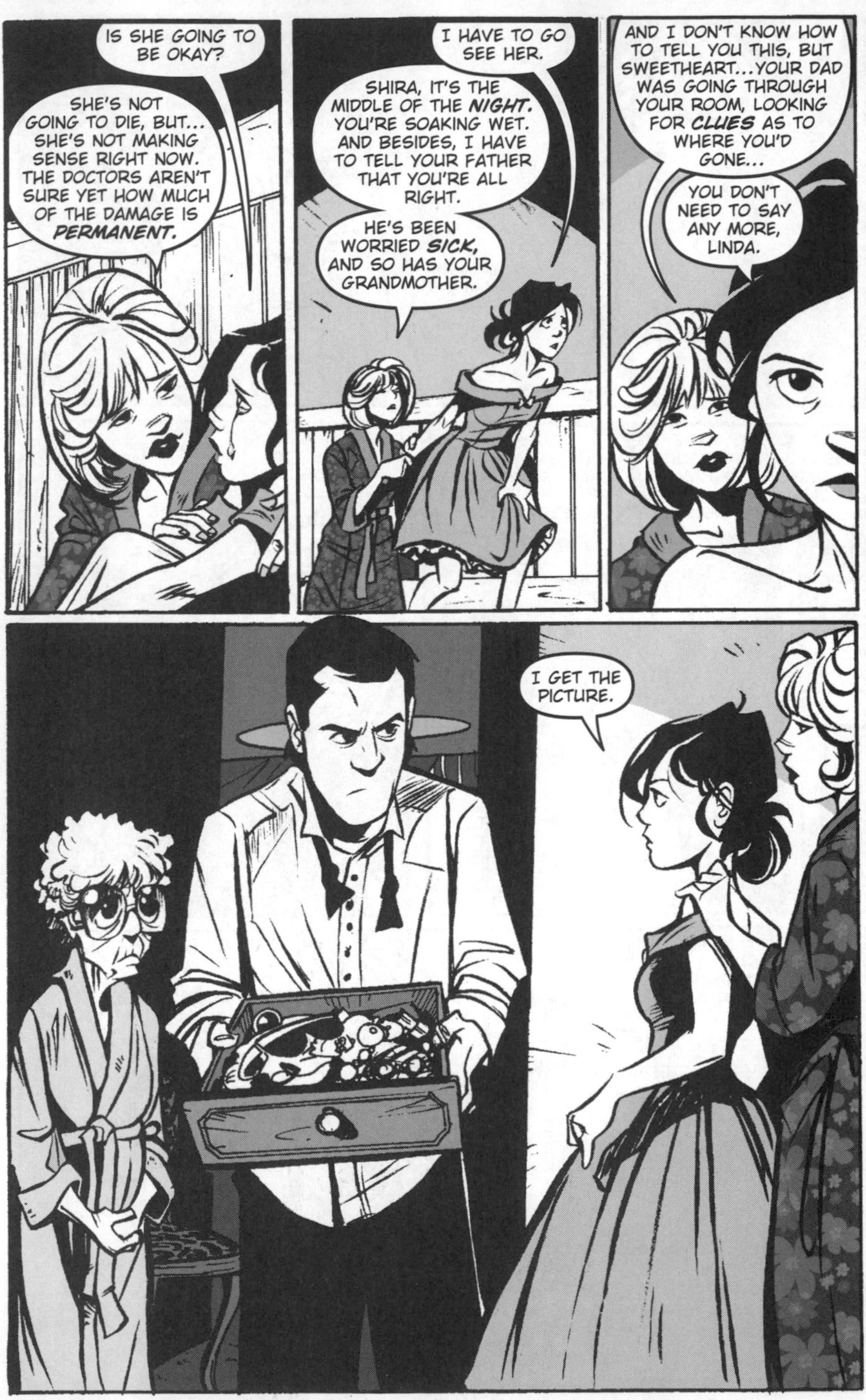
IS SHE GOING TO BE OKAY?
SHE'S NOT GOING TO DIE, BUT... SHE'S NOT MAKING SENSE RIGHT NOW. THE DOCTORS AREN'T SURE YET HOW MUCH OF THE DAMAGE IS PERMANENT.
I HAVE TO GO SEE HER.
SHIRA, IT'S THE MIDDLE OF THE NIGHT. YOU'RE SOAKING WET. AND BESIDES, I HAVE TO TELL YOUR FATHER THAT YOU'RE ALL RIGHT.
HE'S BEEN WORRIED SICK, AND SO HAS YOUR GRANDMOTHER.
AND I DON'T KNOW HOW TO TELL YOU THIS, BUT SWEETHEART...YOUR DAD WAS GOING THROUGH YOUR ROOM, LOOKING FOR CLUES AS TO WHERE YOU'D GONE...
YOU DON'T NEED TO SAY ANY MORE, LINDA.
I GET THE PICTURE.

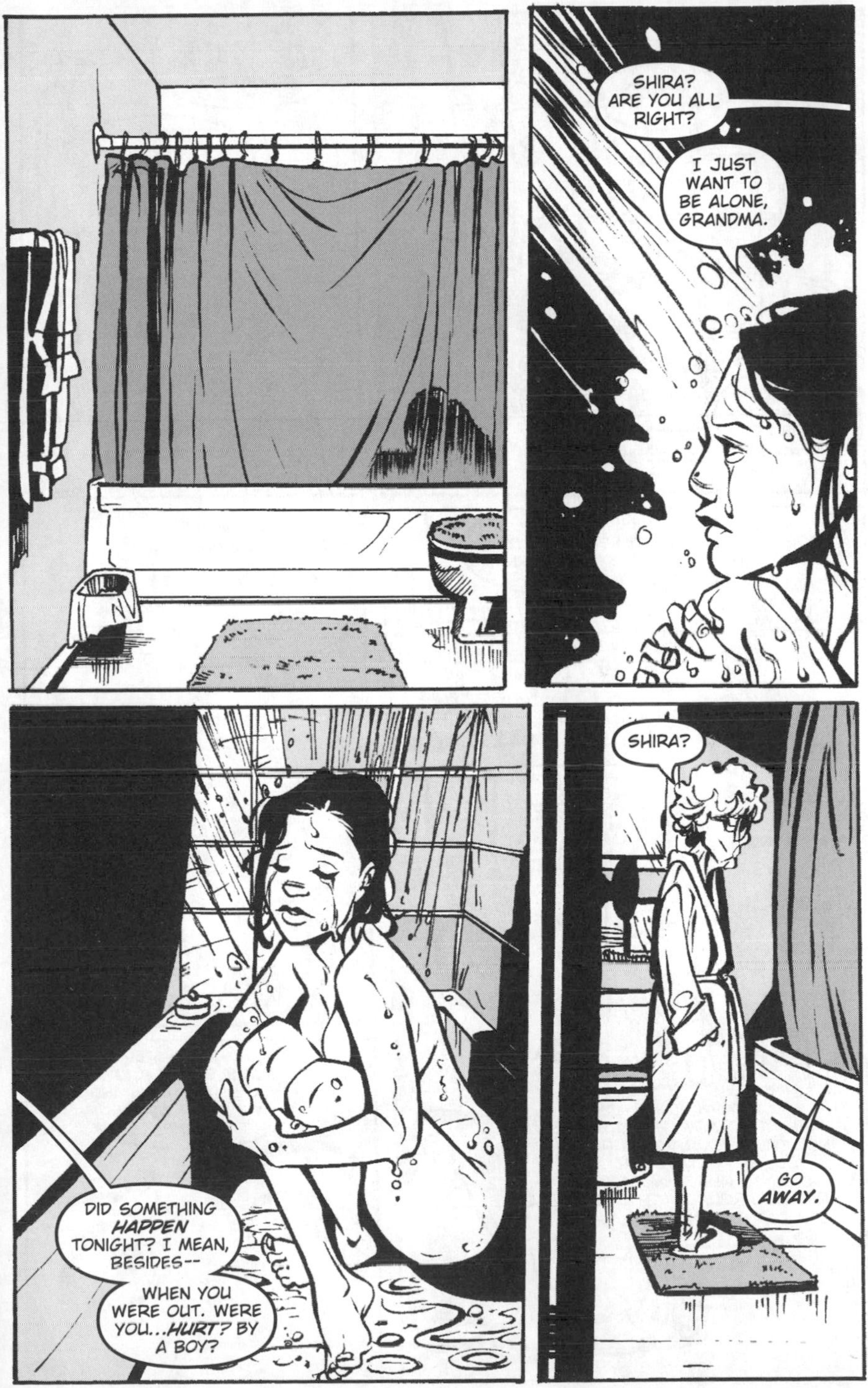
SHIRA? ARE YOU ALL RIGHT?
I JUST WANT TO BE ALONE, GRANDMA.
DID SOMETHING HAPPEN TONIGHT? I MEAN, BESIDES--
WHEN YOU WERE OUT. WERE YOU...HURT? BY A BOY?
SHIRA?
GO AWAY.

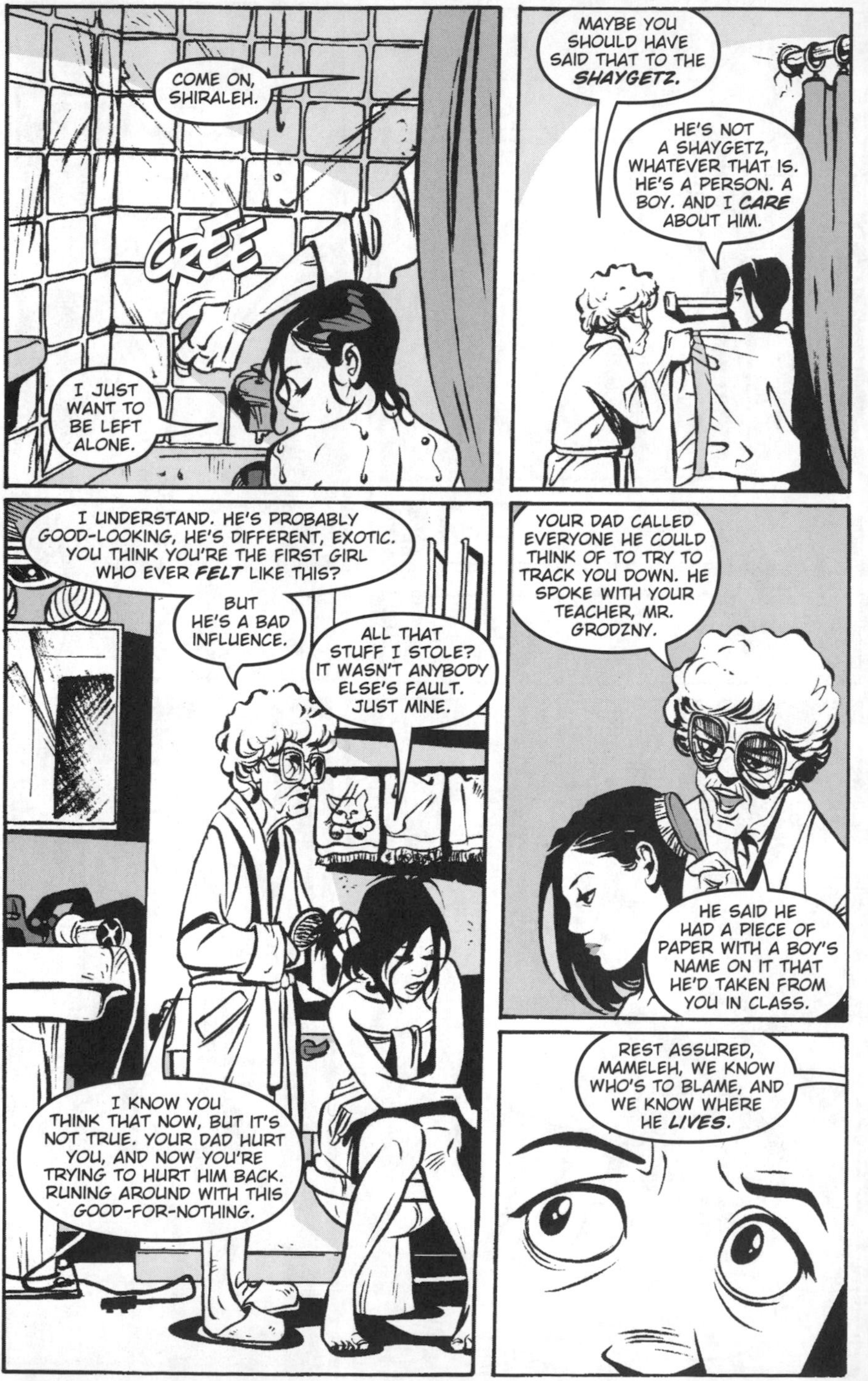
COME ON, SHIRALEH.
CREE
I JUST WANT TO BE LEFT ALONE.
MAYBE YOU SHOULD HAVE SAID THAT TO THE SHAYGETZ.
HE'S NOT A SHAYGETZ, WHATEVER THAT IS. HE'S A PERSON. A BOY. AND I CARE ABOUT HIM.
I UNDERSTAND. HE'S PROBABLY GOOD-LOOKING, HE'S DIFFERENT, EXOTIC. YOU THINK YOU'RE THE FIRST GIRL WHO EVER FELT LIKE THIS?
BUT HE'S A BAD INFLUENCE.
ALL THAT STUFF I STOLE? IT WASN'T ANYBODY ELSE'S FAULT. JUST MINE.
I KNOW YOU THINK THAT NOW, BUT IT'S NOT TRUE. YOUR DAD HURT YOU, AND NOW YOU'RE TRYING TO HURT HIM BACK. RUNING AROUND WITH THIS GOOD-FOR-NOTHING.
YOUR DAD CALLED EVERYONE HE COULD THINK OF TO TRY TO TRACK YOU DOWN. HE SPOKE WITH YOUR TEACHER, MR. GRODZNY.
HE SAID HE HAD A PIECE OF PAPER WITH A BOY'S NAME ON IT THAT HE'D TAKEN FROM YOU IN CLASS.
REST ASSURED, MAMELEH, WE KNOW WHO'S TO BLAME, AND WE KNOW WHERE HE LIVES.

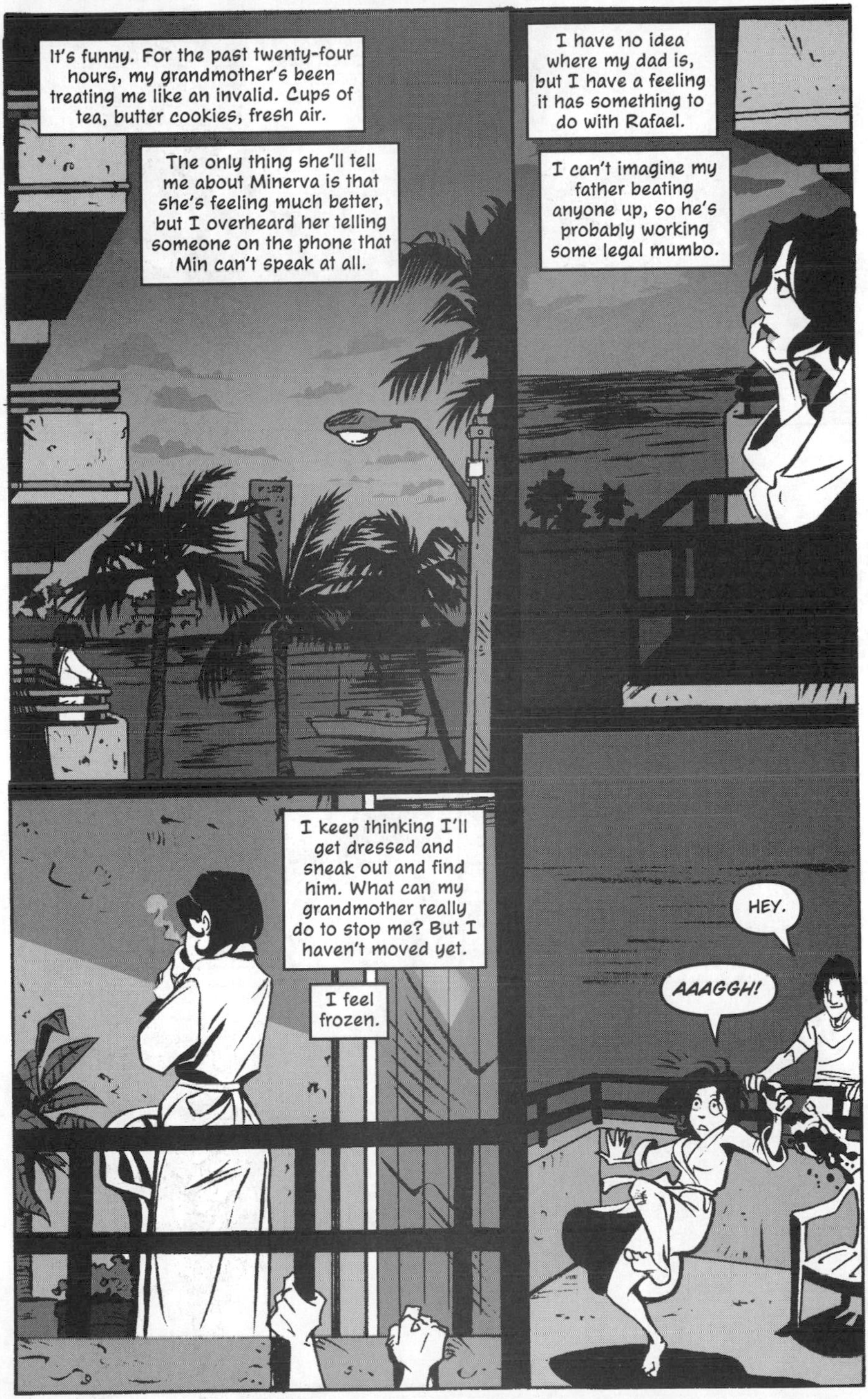
It's funny. For the past twenty-four hours, my grandmother's been treating me like an invalid. Cups of tea, butter cookies, fresh air.
The only thing she'll tell me about Minerva is that she's feeling much better, but I overheard her telling someone on the phone that Min can't speak at all.
I have no idea where my dad is, but I have a feeling it has something to do with Rafael.
I can't imagine my father beating anyone up, so he's probably working some legal mumbo.
I keep thinking I'll get dressed and sneak out and find him. What can my grandmother really do to stop me? But I haven't moved yet.
I feel frozen.
HEY.
AAAGGH!

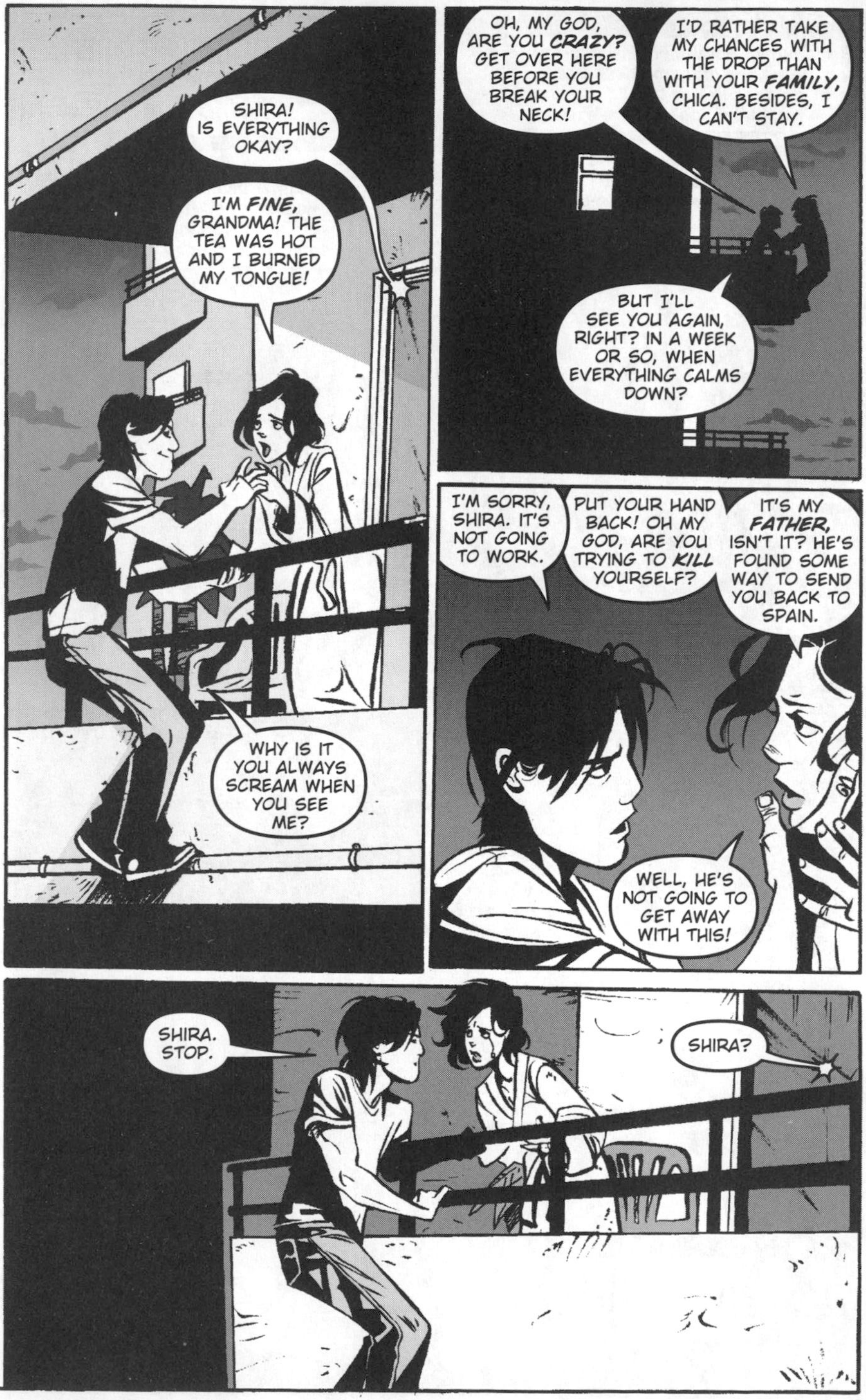
SHIRA! IS EVERYTHING OKAY?
I'M FINE, GRANDMA! THE TEA WAS HOT AND I BURNED MY TONGUE!
WHY IS IT YOU ALWAYS SCREAM WHEN YOU SEE ME?
OH, MY GOD, ARE YOU CRAZY? GET OVER HERE BEFORE YOU BREAK YOUR NECK!
I'D RATHER TAKE MY CHANCES WITH THE DROP THAN WITH YOUR FAMILY, CHICA. BESIDES, I CAN'T STAY.
BUT I'LL SEE YOU AGAIN, RIGHT? IN A WEEK OR SO, WHEN EVERYTHING CALMS DOWN?
I'M SORRY, SHIRA. IT'S NOT GOING TO WORK.
PUT YOUR HAND BACK! OH MY GOD, ARE YOU TRYING TO KILL YOURSELF?
IT'S MY FATHER, ISN'T IT? HE'S FOUND SOME WAY TO SEND YOU BACK TO SPAIN.
WELL, HE'S NOT GOING TO GET AWAY WITH THIS!
SHIRA. STOP.
SHIRA?

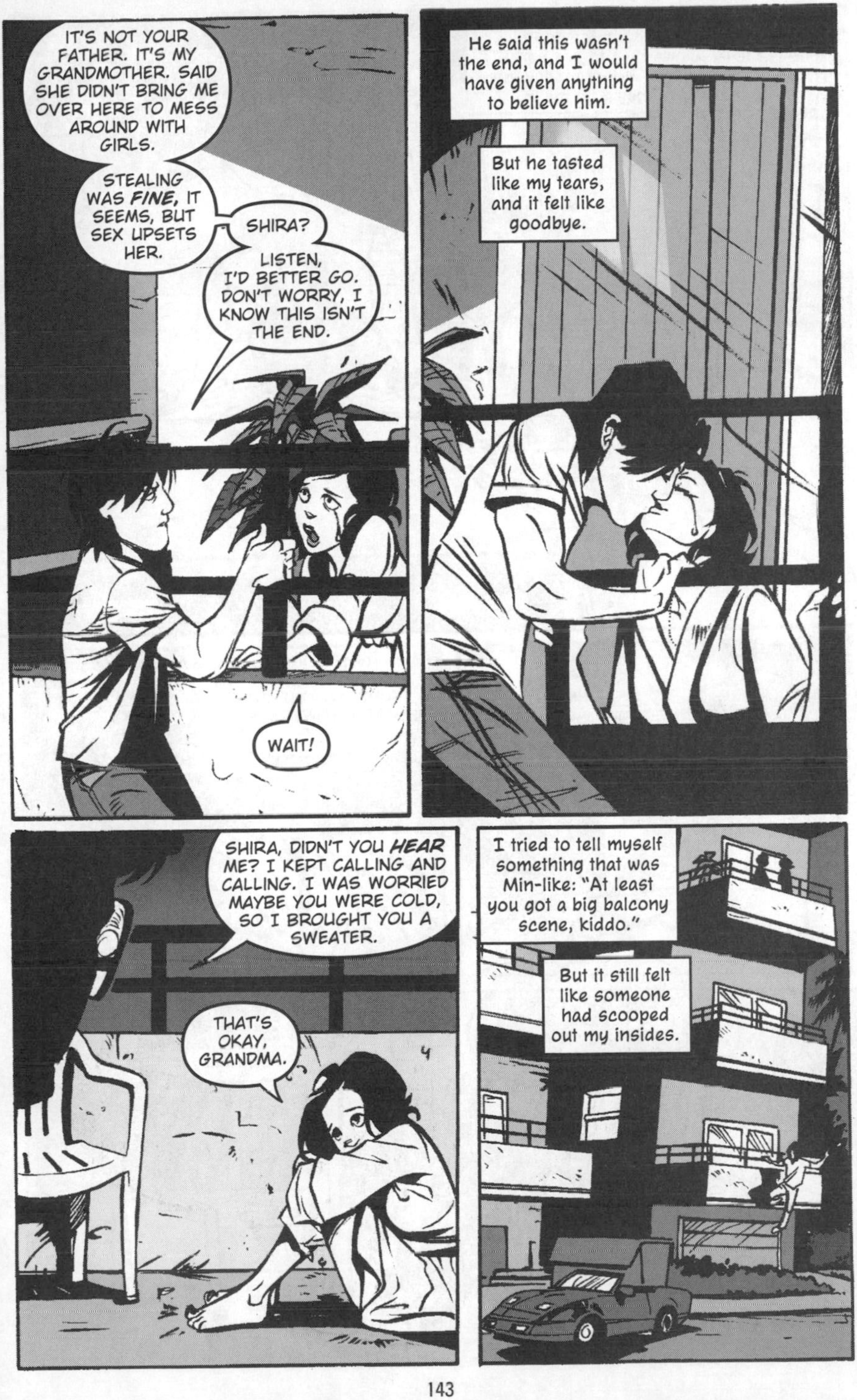
IT'S NOT YOUR FATHER. IT'S MY GRANDMOTHER. SAID SHE DIDN'T BRING ME OVER HERE TO MESS AROUND WITH GIRLS.
STEALING WAS *FINE,* IT SEEMS, BUT SEX UPSETS HER.
SHIRA?
LISTEN, I'D BETTER GO. DON'T WORRY, I KNOW THIS ISN'T THE END.
WAIT!
He said this wasn't the end, and I would have given anything to believe him.
But he tasted like my tears, and it felt like goodbye.
SHIRA, DIDN'T YOU ***HEAR*** ME? I KEPT CALLING AND CALLING. I WAS WORRIED MAYBE YOU WERE COLD, SO I BROUGHT YOU A SWEATER.
THAT'S OKAY, GRANDMA.
I tried to tell myself something that was Min-like: "At least you got a big balcony scene, kiddo."
But it still felt like someone had scooped out my insides.

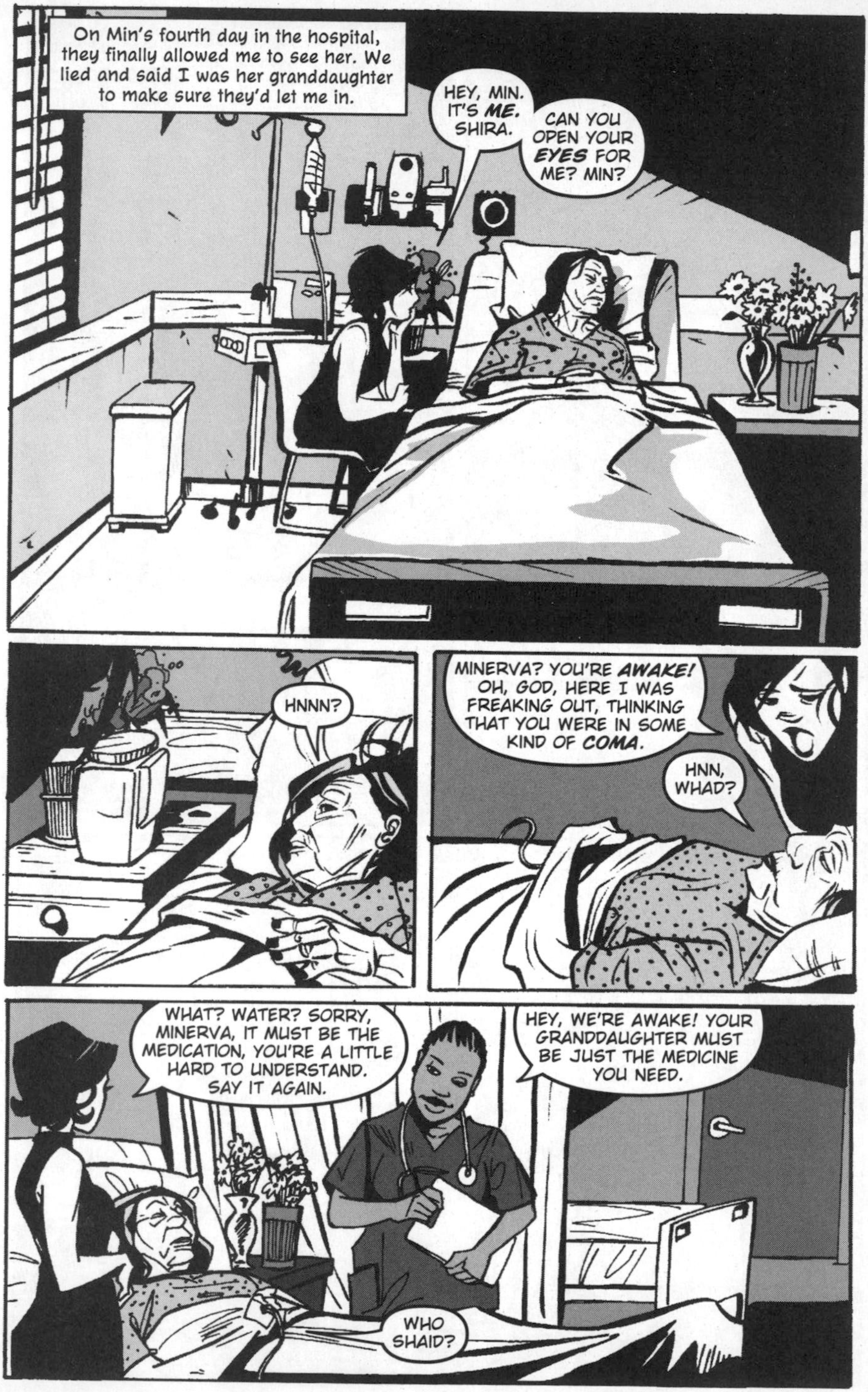
On Min's fourth day in the hospital, they finally allowed me to see her. We lied and said I was her granddaughter to make sure they'd let me in.
HEY, MIN. IT'S ME. SHIRA.
CAN YOU OPEN YOUR EYES FOR ME? MIN?
HNNN?
MINERVA? YOU'RE AWAKE! OH, GOD, HERE I WAS FREAKING OUT, THINKING THAT YOU WERE IN SOME KIND OF COMA.
HNN, WHAD?
WHAT? WATER? SORRY, MINERVA, IT MUST BE THE MEDICATION, YOU'RE A LITTLE HARD TO UNDERSTAND. SAY IT AGAIN.
HEY, WE'RE AWAKE! YOUR GRANDDAUGHTER MUST BE JUST THE MEDICINE YOU NEED.
WHO SHAID?

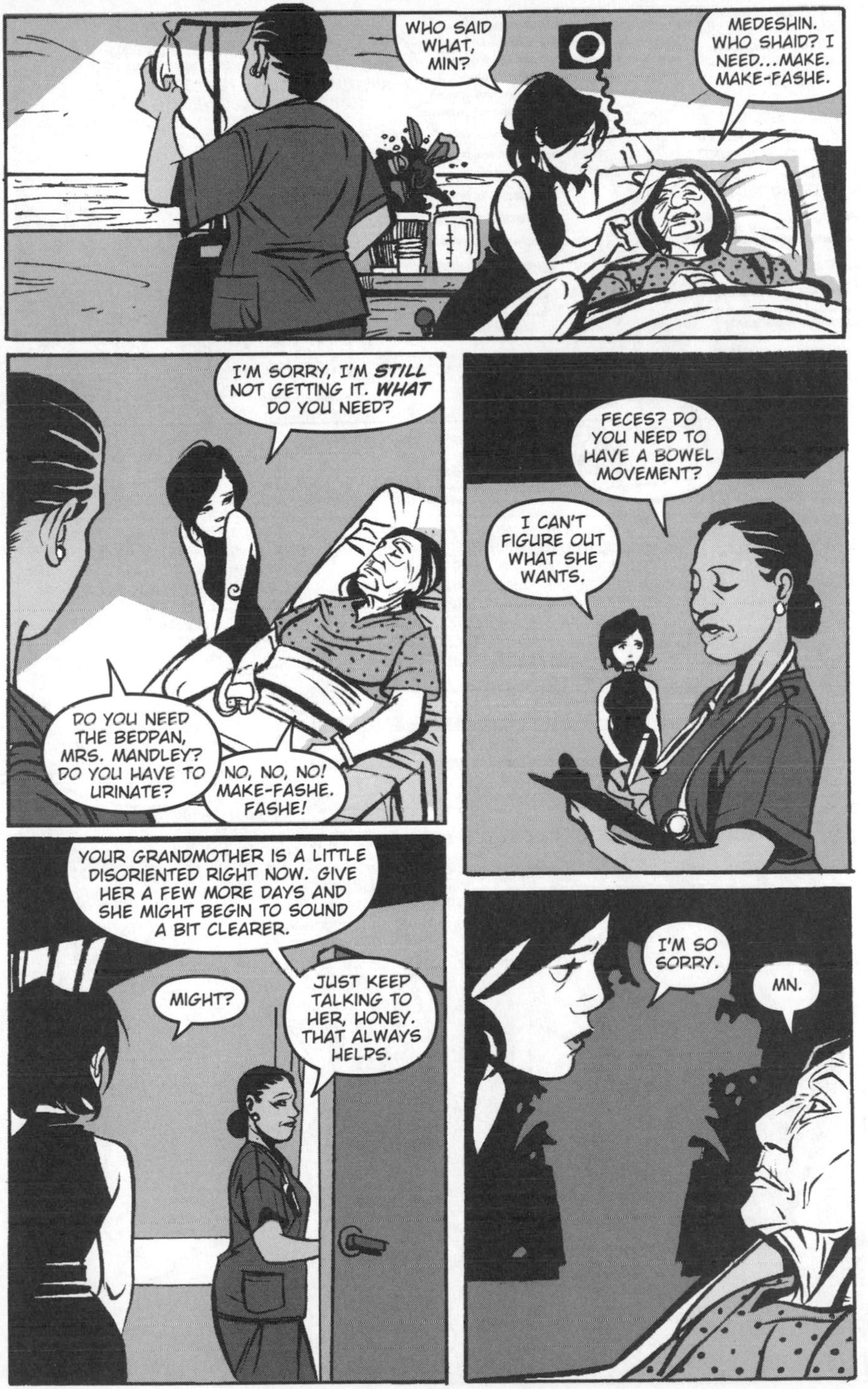

WHO SAID WHAT, MIN?
MEDESHIN. WHO SHAID? I NEED...MAKE. MAKE-FASHE.
I'M SORRY, I'M STILL NOT GETTING IT. WHAT DO YOU NEED?
DO YOU NEED THE BEDPAN, MRS. MANDLEY? DO YOU HAVE TO URINATE?
NO, NO, NO! MAKE-FASHE. FASHE!
FECES? DO YOU NEED TO HAVE A BOWEL MOVEMENT?
I CAN'T FIGURE OUT WHAT SHE WANTS.
YOUR GRANDMOTHER IS A LITTLE DISORIENTED RIGHT NOW. GIVE HER A FEW MORE DAYS AND SHE MIGHT BEGIN TO SOUND A BIT CLEARER.
MIGHT?
JUST KEEP TALKING TO HER, HONEY. THAT ALWAYS HELPS.
I'M SO SORRY.
MN.

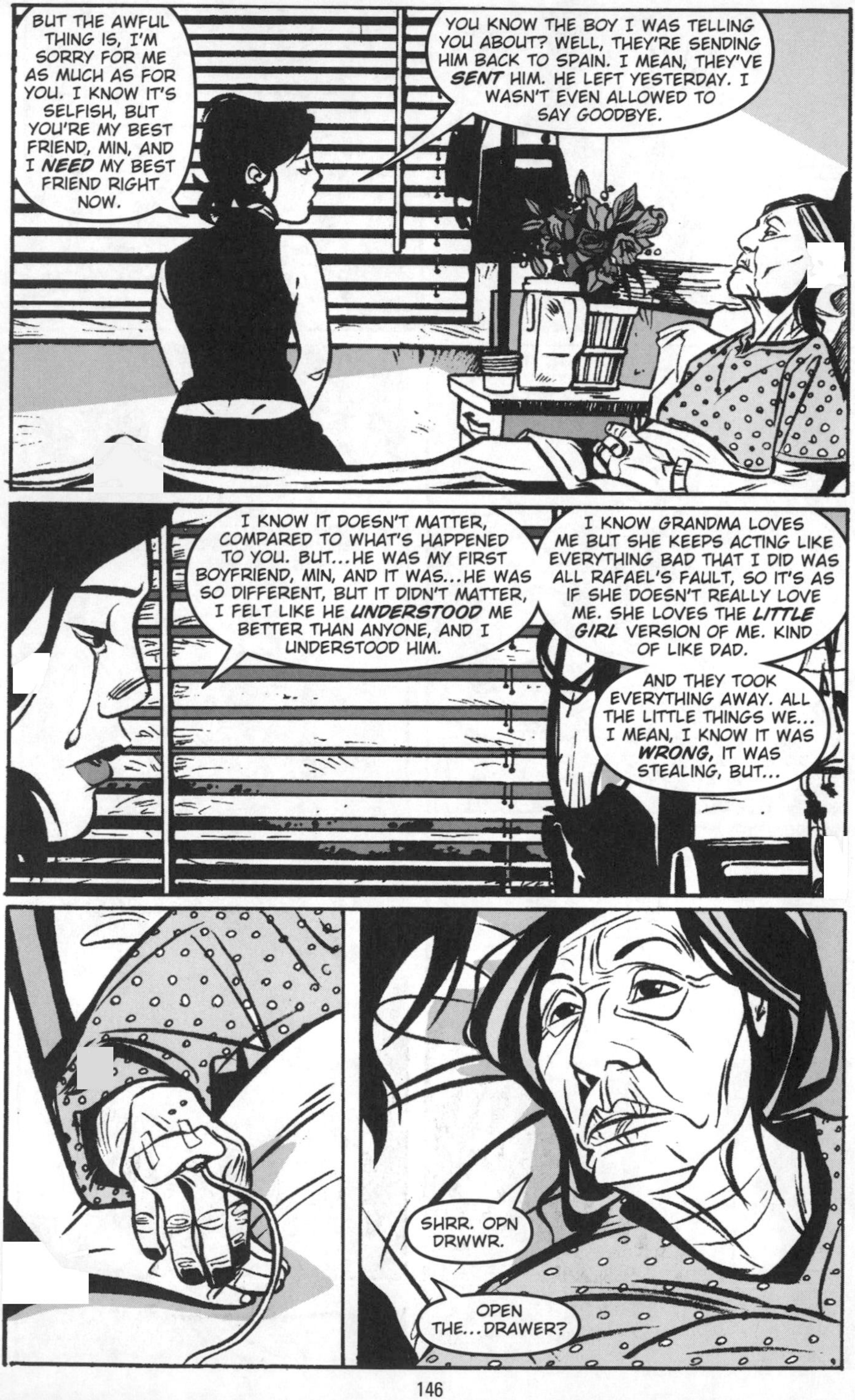
BUT THE AWFUL THING IS, I'M SORRY FOR ME AS MUCH AS FOR YOU. I KNOW IT'S SELFISH, BUT YOU'RE MY BEST FRIEND, MIN, AND I *NEED* MY BEST FRIEND RIGHT NOW.
YOU KNOW THE BOY I WAS TELLING YOU ABOUT? WELL, THEY'RE SENDING HIM BACK TO SPAIN. I MEAN, THEY'VE *SENT* HIM. HE LEFT YESTERDAY. I WASN'T EVEN ALLOWED TO SAY GOODBYE.
I KNOW IT DOESN'T MATTER, COMPARED TO WHAT'S HAPPENED TO YOU. BUT...HE WAS MY FIRST BOYFRIEND, MIN, AND IT WAS...HE WAS SO DIFFERENT, BUT IT DIDN'T MATTER, I FELT LIKE HE *UNDERSTOOD* ME BETTER THAN ANYONE, AND I UNDERSTOOD HIM.
I KNOW GRANDMA LOVES ME BUT SHE KEEPS ACTING LIKE EVERYTHING BAD THAT I DID WAS ALL RAFAEL'S FAULT, SO IT'S AS IF SHE DOESN'T REALLY LOVE ME. SHE LOVES THE *LITTLE GIRL* VERSION OF ME. KIND OF LIKE DAD.
AND THEY TOOK EVERYTHING AWAY. ALL THE LITTLE THINGS WE... I MEAN, I KNOW IT WAS *WRONG,* IT WAS STEALING, BUT...
SHRR. OPN DRWWR.
OPEN THE...DRAWER?

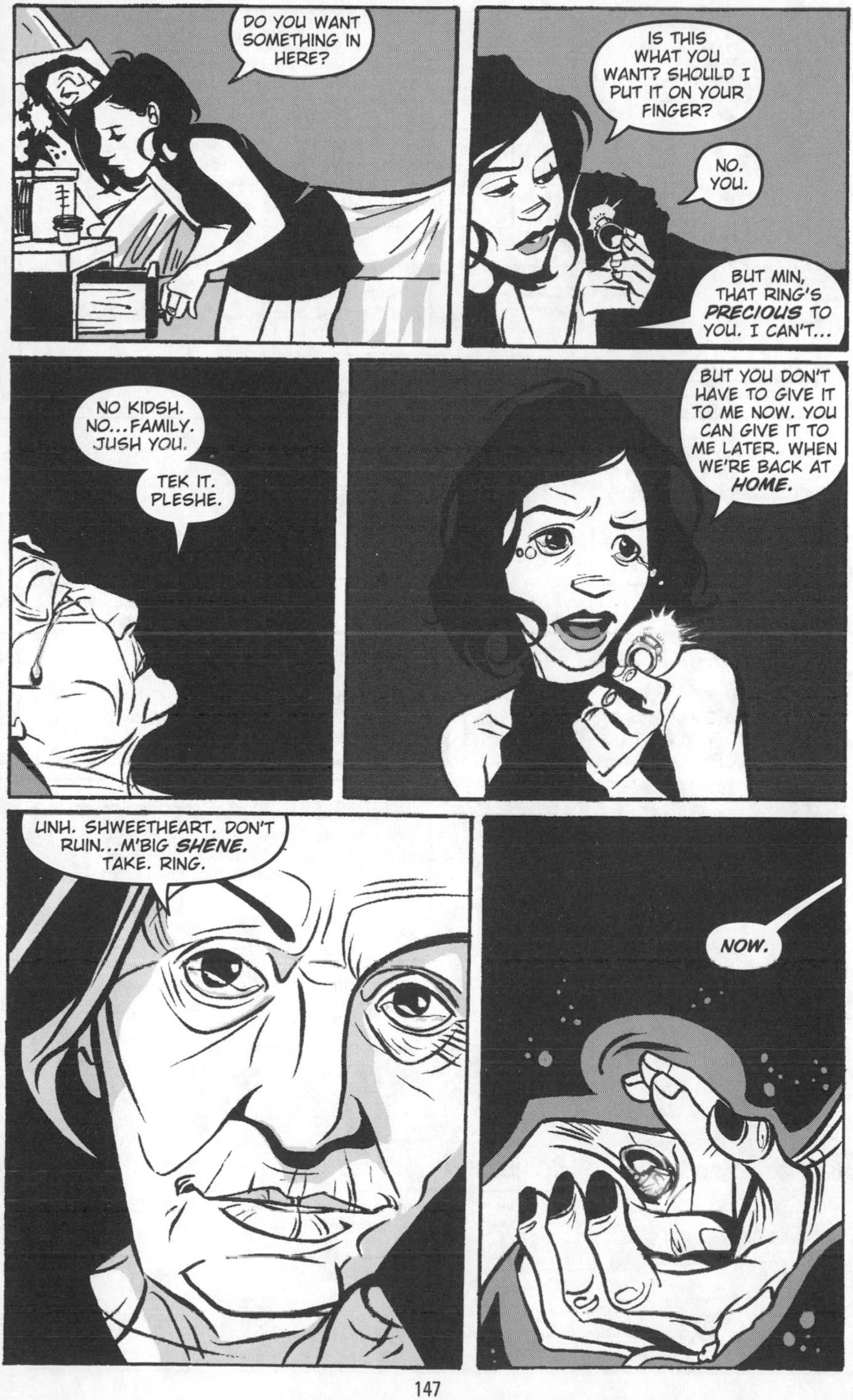
DO YOU WANT SOMETHING IN HERE?
IS THIS WHAT YOU WANT? SHOULD I PUT IT ON YOUR FINGER?
NO. YOU.
BUT MIN, THAT RING'S *PRECIOUS* TO YOU. I CAN'T...
NO KIDSH. NO...FAMILY. JUSH YOU.
TEK IT. PLESHE.
BUT YOU DON'T HAVE TO GIVE IT TO ME NOW. YOU CAN GIVE IT TO ME LATER. WHEN WE'RE BACK AT *HOME.*
UNH. SHWEETHEART. DON'T RUIN...M'BIG *SHENE.* TAKE. RING.
NOW.

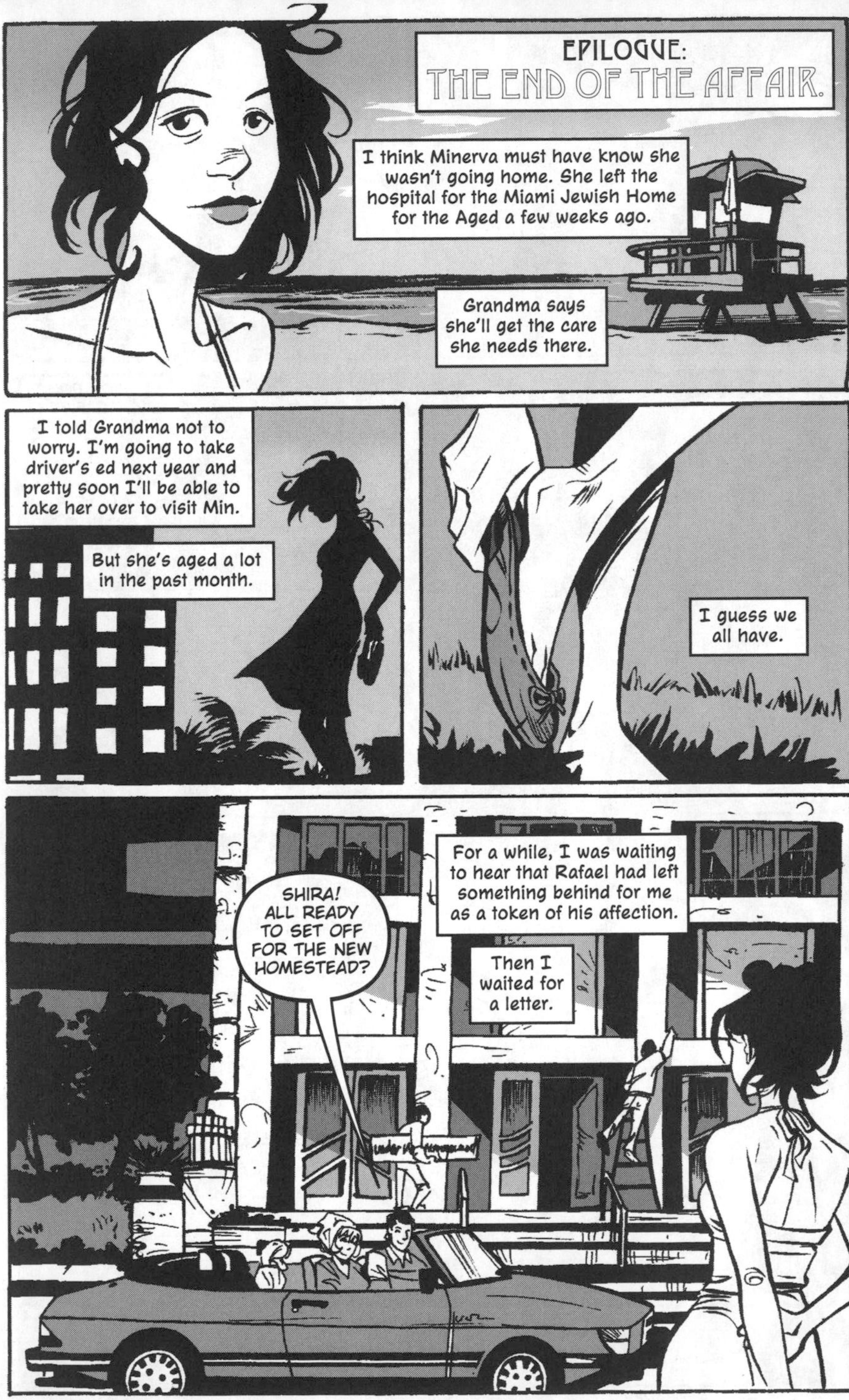
EPILOGUE:
THE END OF THE AFFAIR.
I think Minerva must have know she wasn't going home. She left the hospital for the Miami Jewish Home for the Aged a few weeks ago.
Grandma says she'll get the care she needs there.
I told Grandma not to worry. I'm going to take driver's ed next year and pretty soon I'll be able to take her over to visit Min.
But she's aged a lot in the past month.
I guess we all have.
For a while, I was waiting to hear that Rafael had left something behind for me as a token of his affection.
SHIRA! ALL READY TO SET OFF FOR THE NEW HOMESTEAD?
Then I waited for a letter.

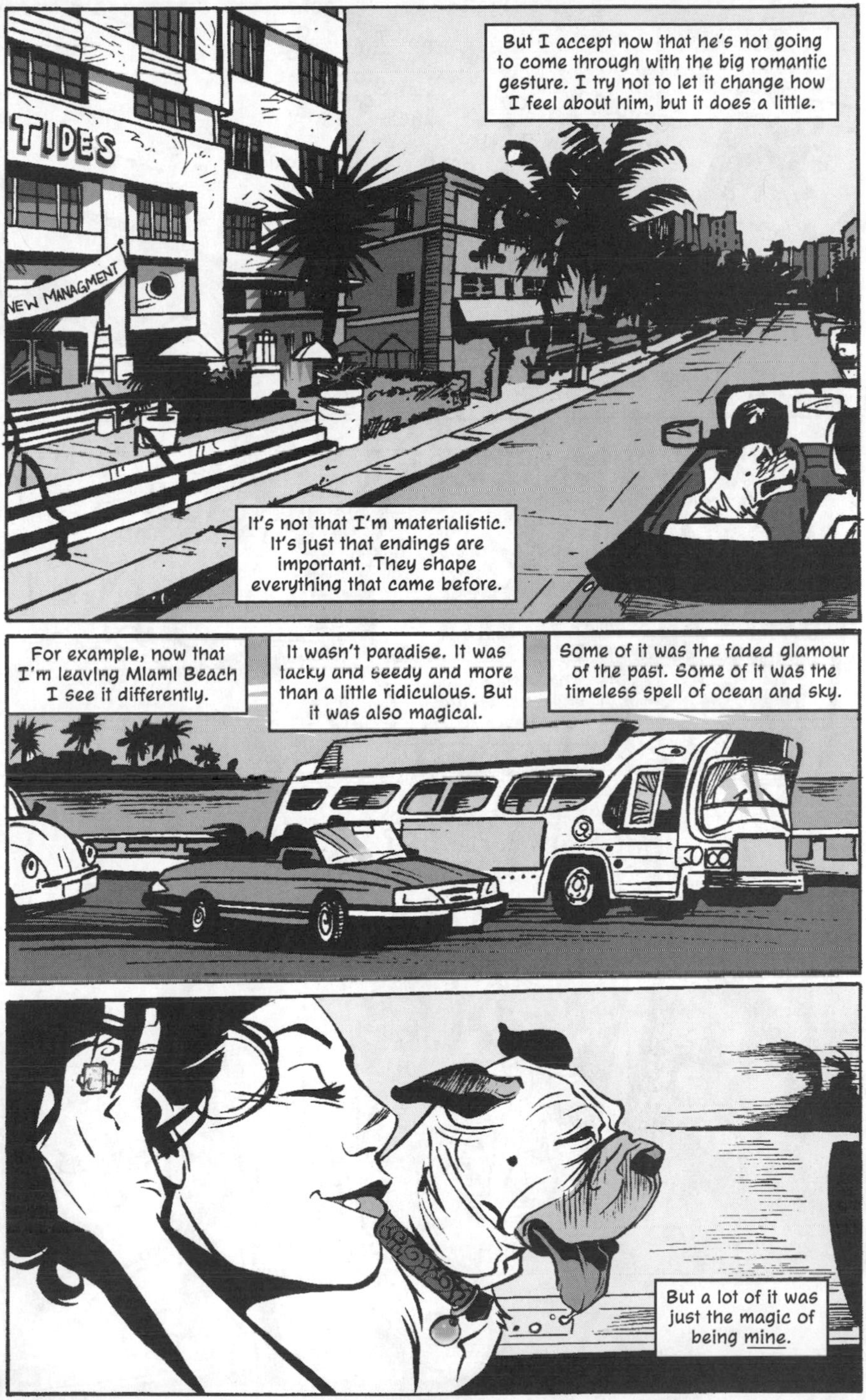
But I accept now that he's not going to come through with the big romantic gesture. I try not to let it change how I feel about him, but it does a little.
TIDES
NEW MANAGMENT
It's not that I'm materialistic. It's just that endings are important. They shape everything that came before.
For example, now that I'm leaving Miami Beach I see it differently.
It wasn't paradise. It was tacky and seedy and more than a little ridiculous. But it was also magical.
Some of it was the faded glamour of the past. Some of it was the timeless spell of ocean and sky.
But a lot of it was just the magic of being mine.

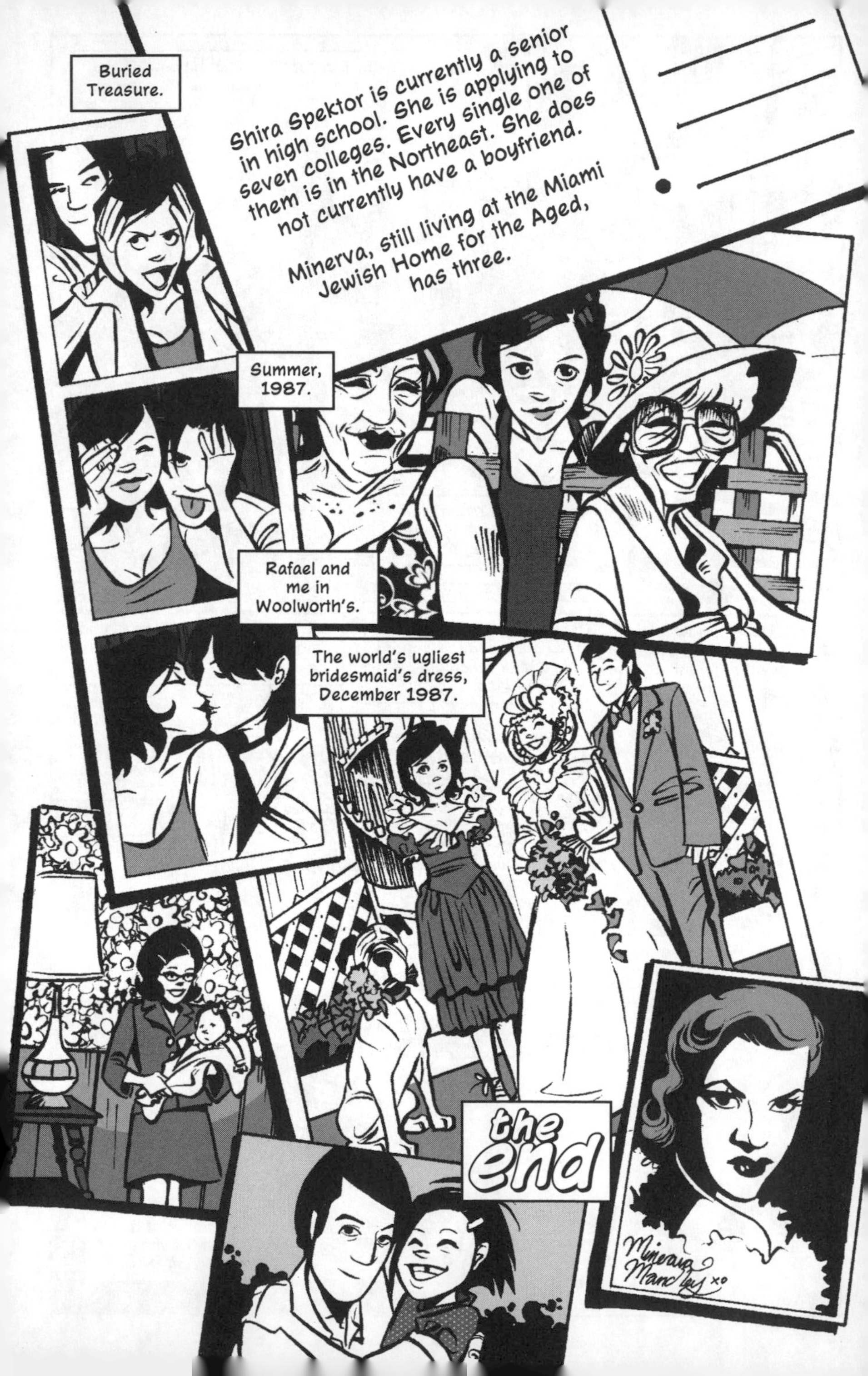
Buried Treasure.
Shira Spektor is currently a senior in high school. She is applying to seven colleges. Every single one of them is in the Northeast. She does not currently have a boyfriend.
Minerva, still living at the Miami Jewish Home for the Aged, has three.
Summer, 1987.
Rafael and me in Woolworth's.
The world's ugliest bridesmaid's dress, December 1987.
the end
Minerva Manchley xo

ALISA KWITNEY

Alisa is a former Vertigo editor and the
author of six prose books and the graphic
novel *Destiny: A Chronicle of Deaths Foretold*.
She currently lives with her family in
New York's Hudson River Valley but is still
an Upper West Sider at heart.

JOËLLE JONES

Joëlle lives and works in Portland, Oregon. Her comics debut was in the 2005 anthology *Sexy Chix*, and she has since gone on to work on the graphic novels *12 Reasons Why I Love Her* and *You Have Killed Me.*

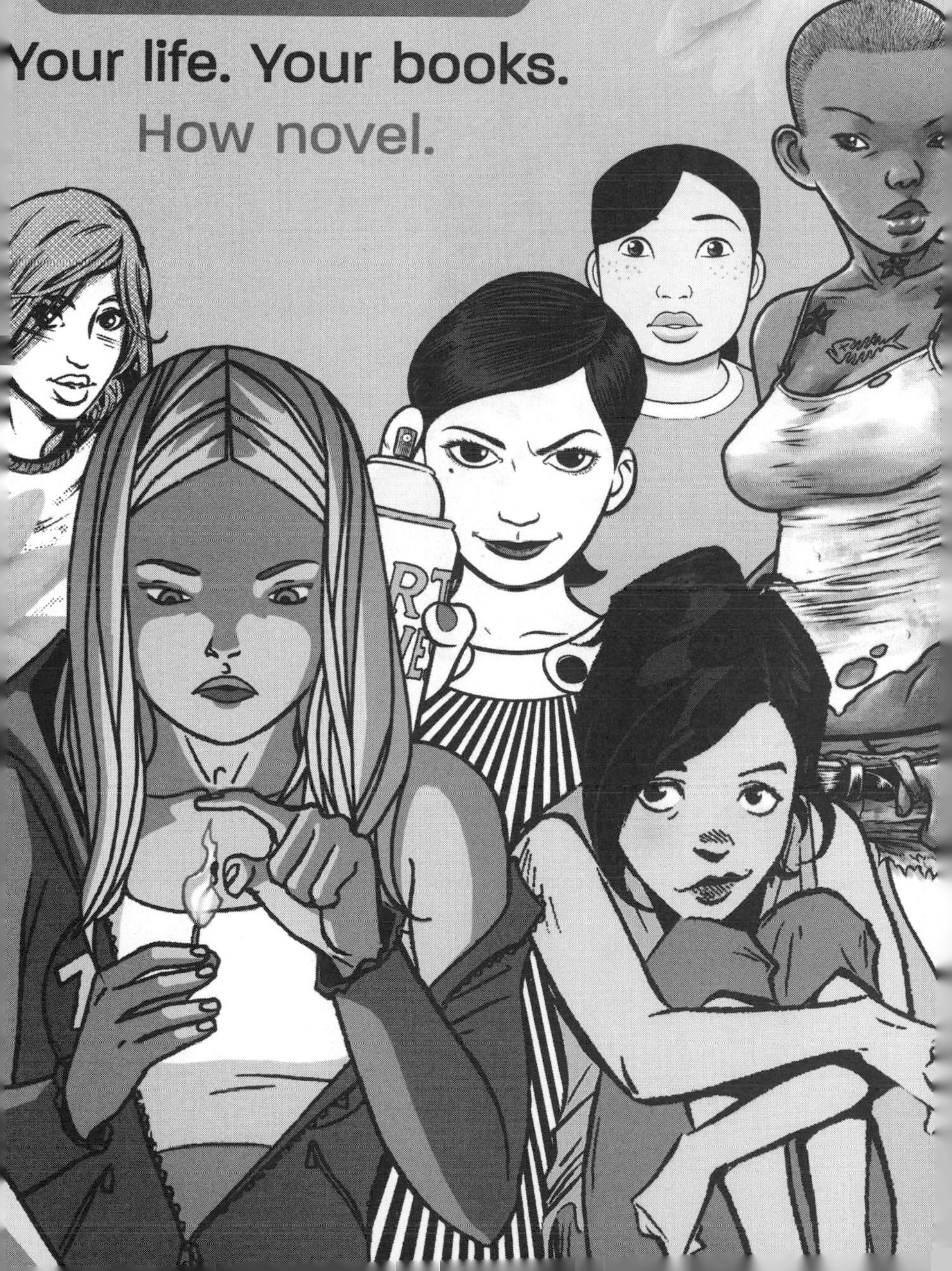

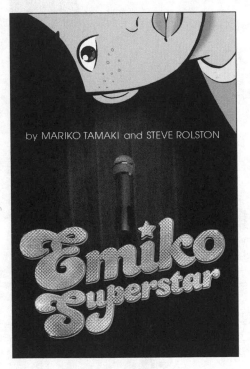

by MARIKO TAMAKI and STEVE ROLSTON

Written by novelist/performance artist
MARIKO TAMAKI

A "borrowed" diary, a double life and identity issues fuel a teenager's quest to find

herself before she cracks and commits social suicide. Watch Emi go from dull

suburban babysitter to eclectic urban performance artist — compliments of one

crazy summer.

By MARIKO TAMAKI & STEVE ROLSTON
AVAILABLE NOW ■ Read on.

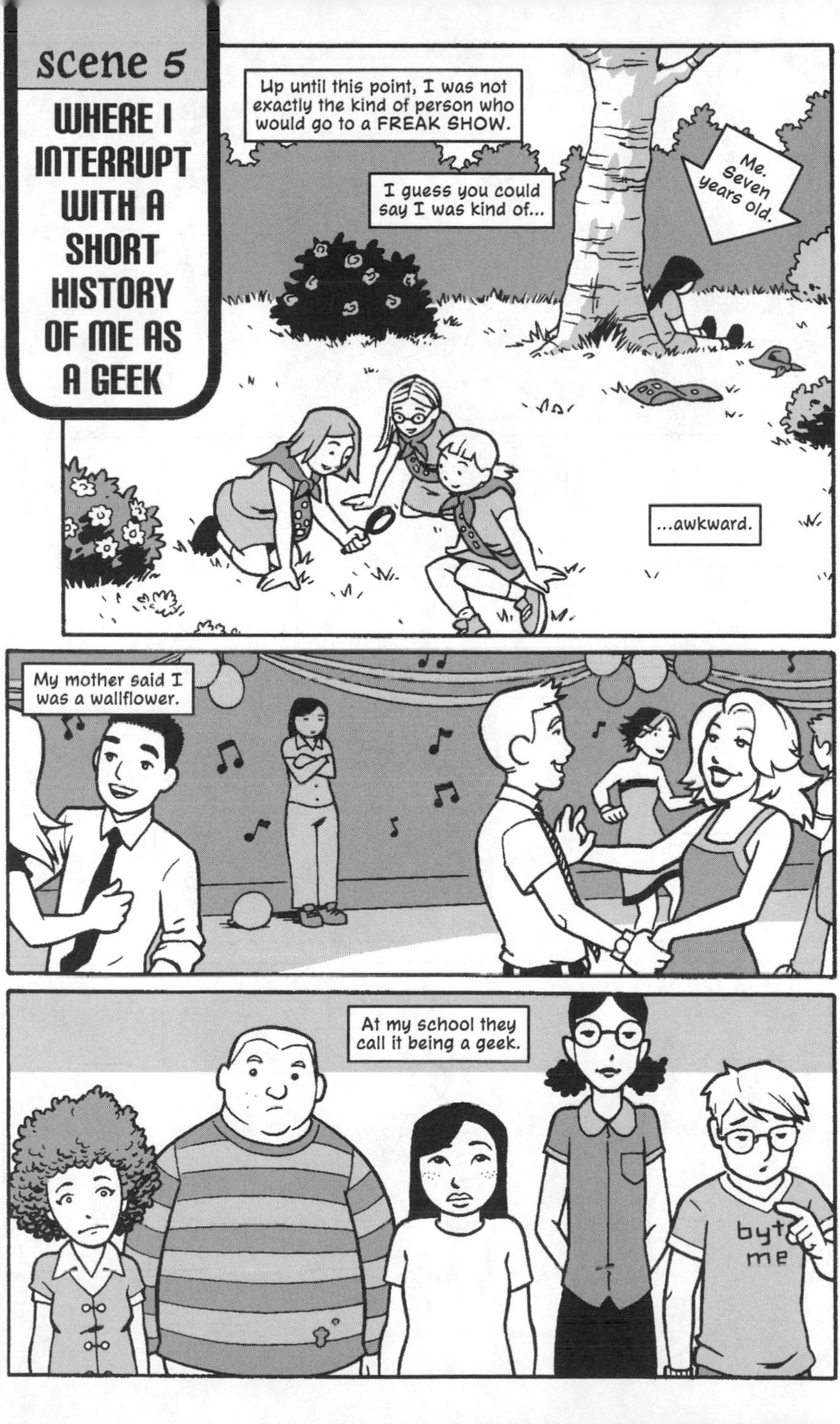
scene 5
WHERE I INTERRUPT WITH A SHORT HISTORY OF ME AS A GEEK
Up until this point, I was not exactly the kind of person who would go to a FREAK SHOW.
I guess you could say I was kind of...
Me. Seven years old.
...awkward.
My mother said I was a wallflower.
At my school they call it being a geek.
byte me

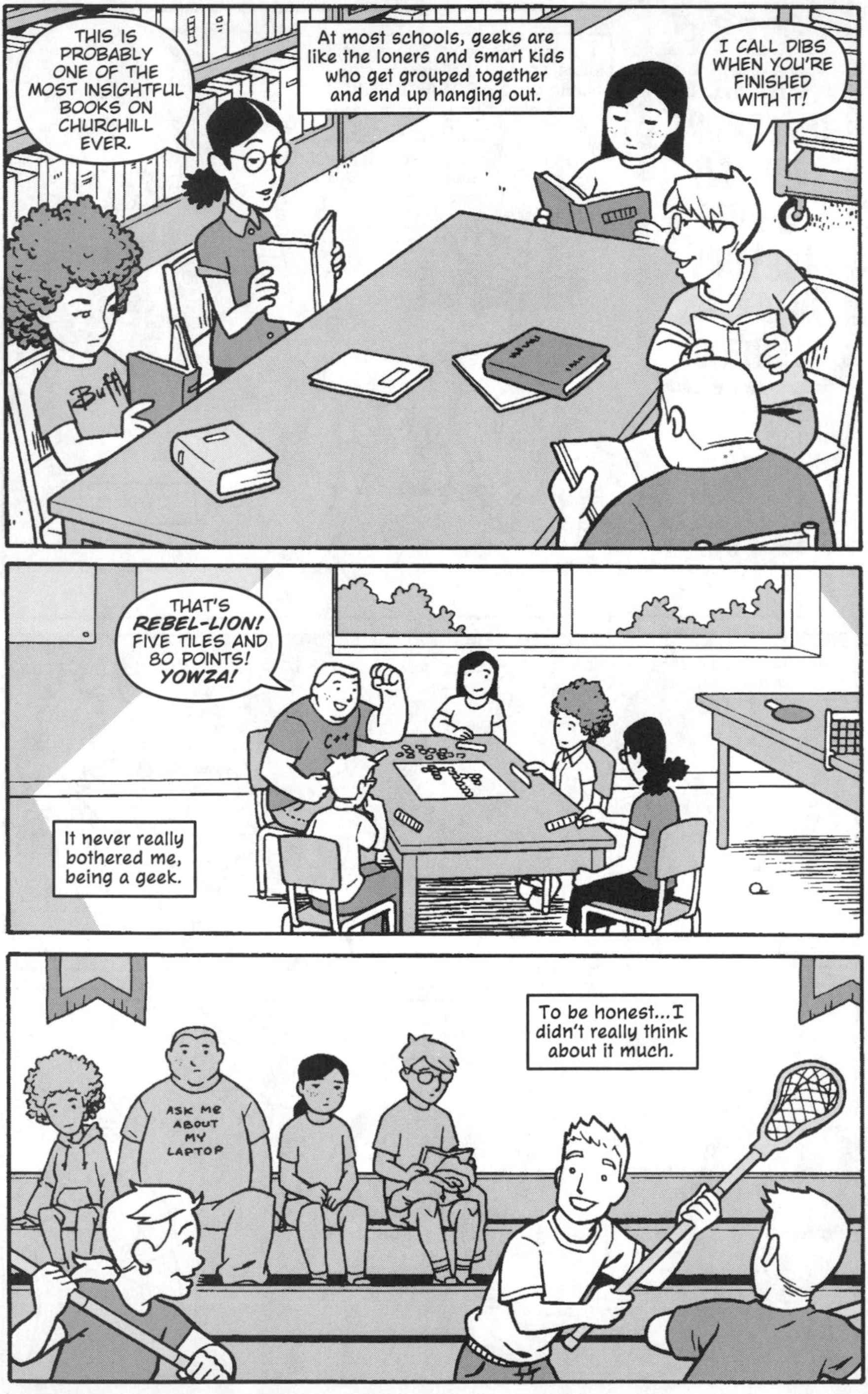
THIS IS PROBABLY ONE OF THE MOST INSIGHTFUL BOOKS ON CHURCHILL EVER.
At most schools, geeks are like the loners and smart kids who get grouped together and end up hanging out.
I CALL DIBS WHEN YOU'RE FINISHED WITH IT!
THAT'S ***REBEL-LION!*** FIVE TILES AND 80 POINTS! ***YOWZA!***
It never really bothered me, being a geek.
ASK ME ABOUT MY LAPTOP
To be honest...I didn't really think about it much.

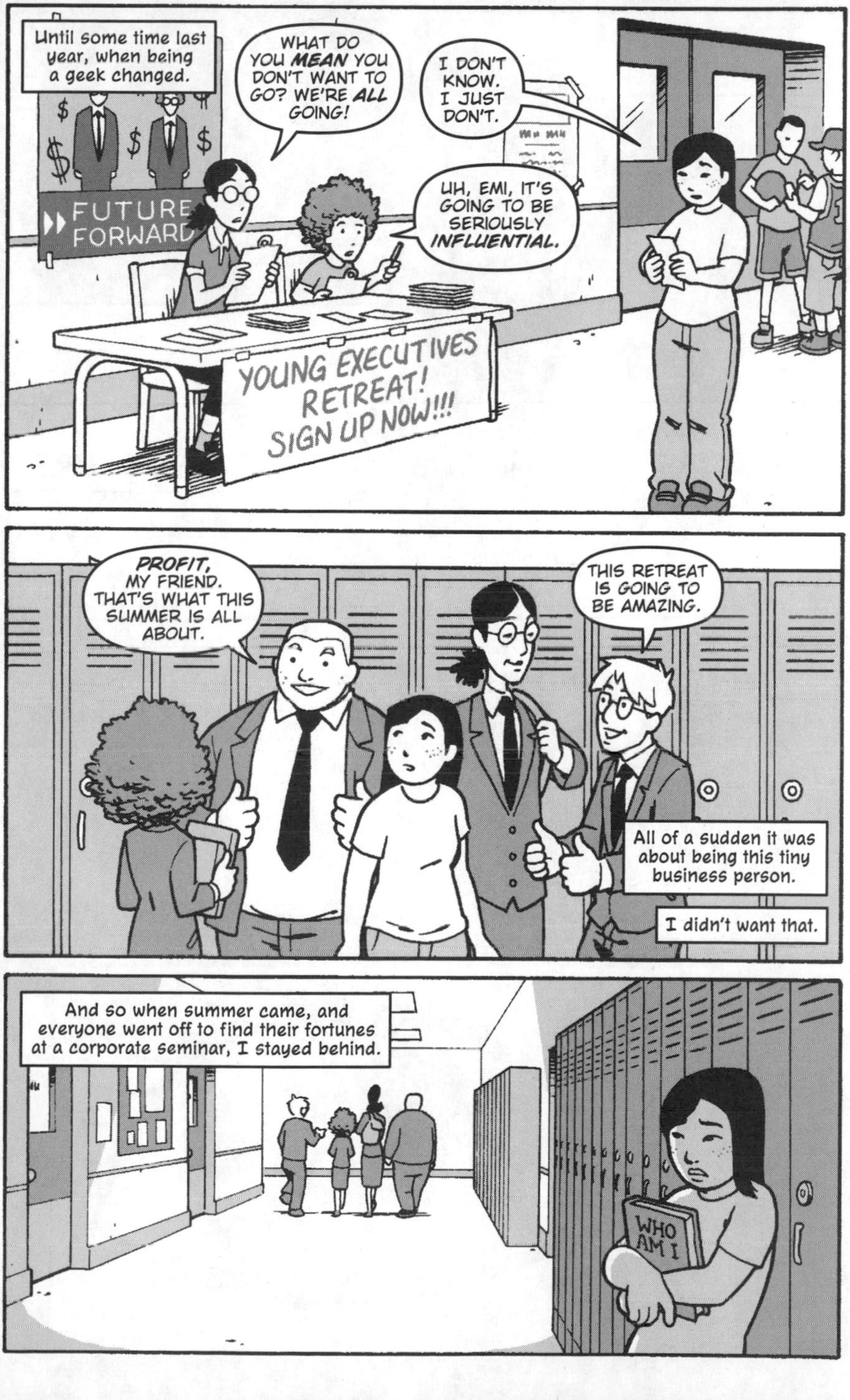
Until some time last year, when being a geek changed.
WHAT DO YOU MEAN YOU DON'T WANT TO GO? WE'RE ALL GOING!
I DON'T KNOW. I JUST DON'T.
UH, EMI, IT'S GOING TO BE SERIOUSLY INFLUENTIAL.
FUTURE FORWARD
YOUNG EXECUTIVES RETREAT! SIGN UP NOW!!!
PROFIT, MY FRIEND. THAT'S WHAT THIS SUMMER IS ALL ABOUT.
THIS RETREAT IS GOING TO BE AMAZING.
All of a sudden it was about being this tiny business person.
I didn't want that.
And so when summer came, and everyone went off to find their fortunes at a corporate seminar, I stayed behind.
WHO AM I

I was at what this book I found described as a "classic crossroads."

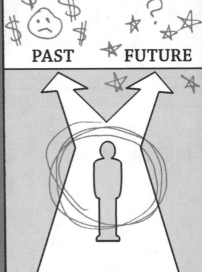

Where one thing gets left behind...

PAST   FUTURE

...and something else gets spotted in the distance.

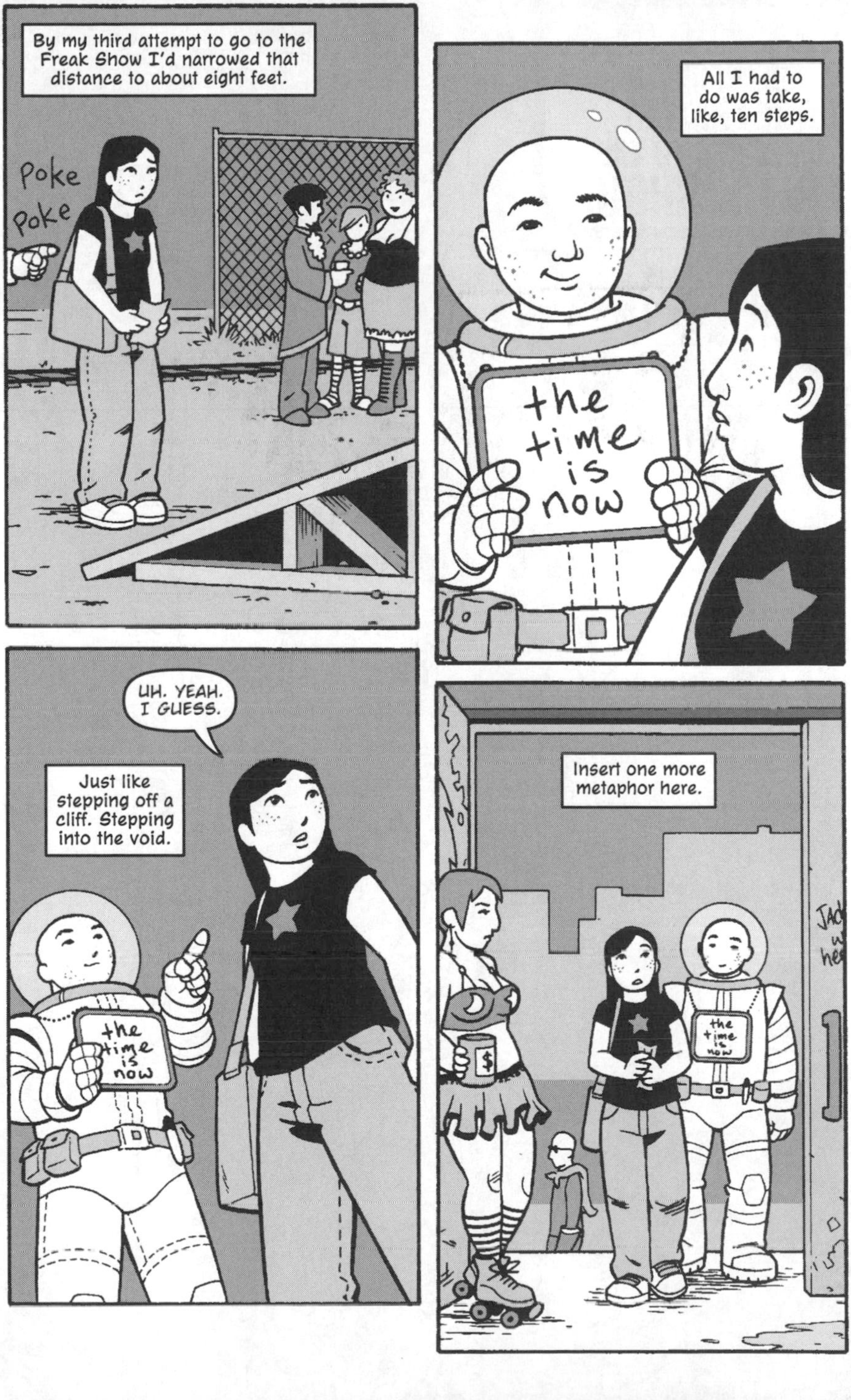

By my third attempt to go to the Freak Show I'd narrowed that distance to about eight feet.
Poke
Poke
All I had to do was take, like, ten steps.
the time is now
UH. YEAH. I GUESS.
Just like stepping off a cliff. Stepping into the void.
the time is now
Insert one more metaphor here.
the time is now

scene 6

WELCOME TO THE FACTORY, WELCOME TO THE FREAK SHOW

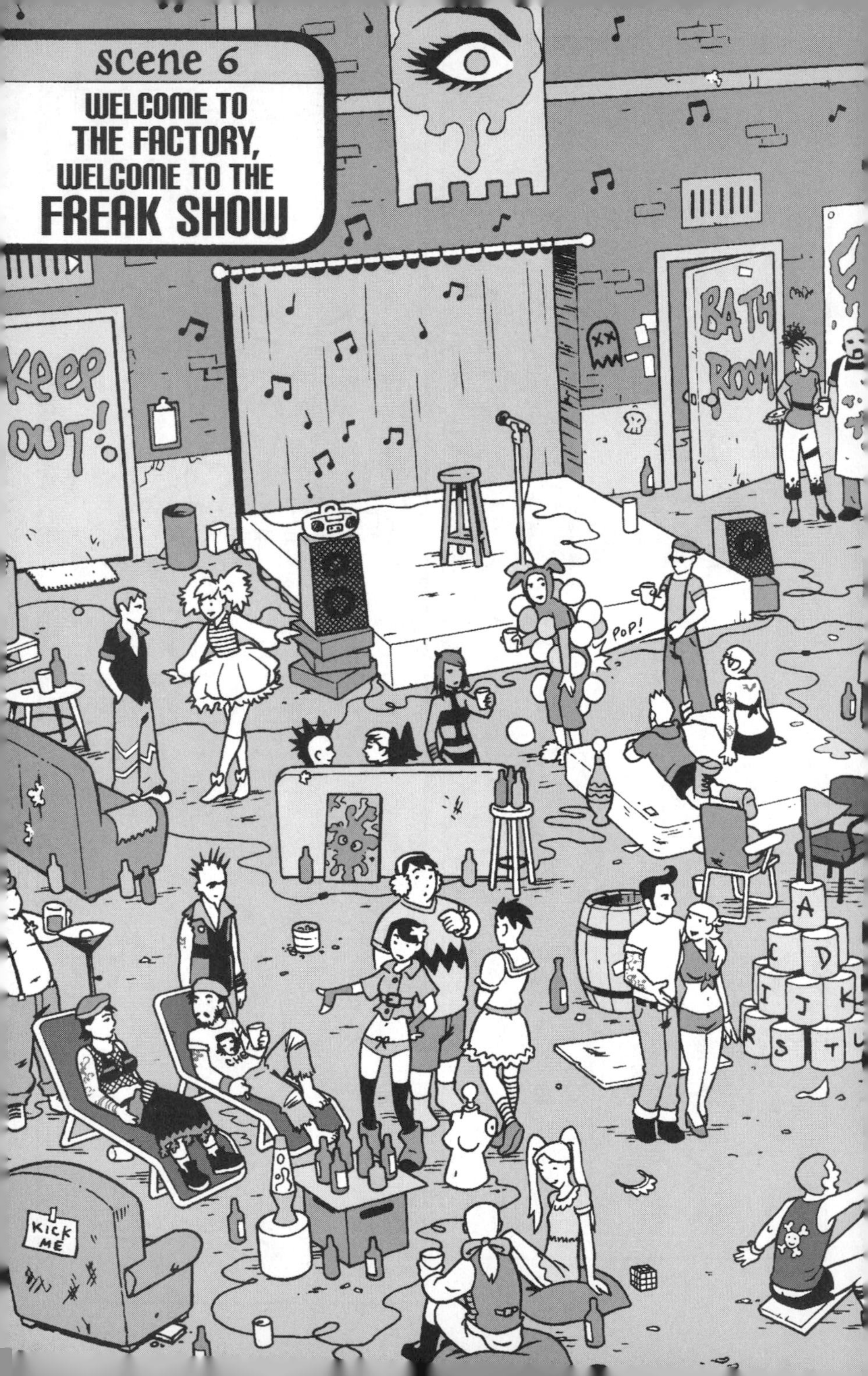
KEEP OUT!
BATH ROOM
POP!
CHE
A
C D
I J K
R S T U
KICK ME

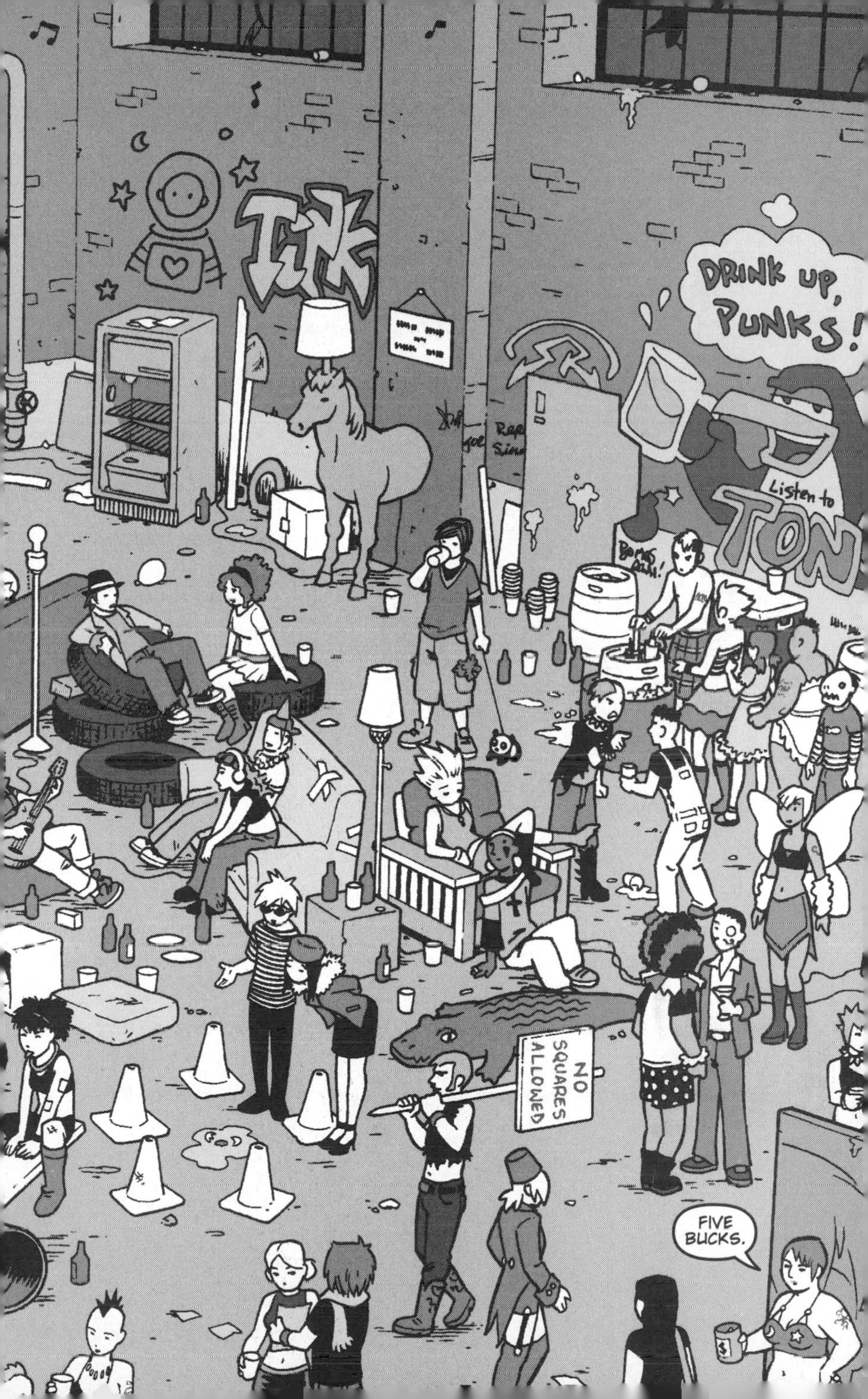
DRINK UP, PUNKS!
Listen to
TON
NO SQUARES ALLOWED
FIVE BUCKS.

By the highly acclaimed author of *Boy Proof* and *Beige*

JANES ♥ LOVE

by CECIL CASTELLUCCI and JIM RUGG

ART SAVE

The second title in the PLAIN JANES series finds the coolest clique of misfits playing

cupid and becoming entangled in the affairs of the heart. P.L.A.I.N., People Loving Art In

Neighborhoods, goes global once the art gang procures a spot in the Metro City

Museum of Modern Art contest. And the girls will discover that in art and in love,

general rules don't often apply.

By CECIL CASTELLUCCI & JIM RUGG
AVAILABLE NOW ■ Read on.
The following pages are not sequential.

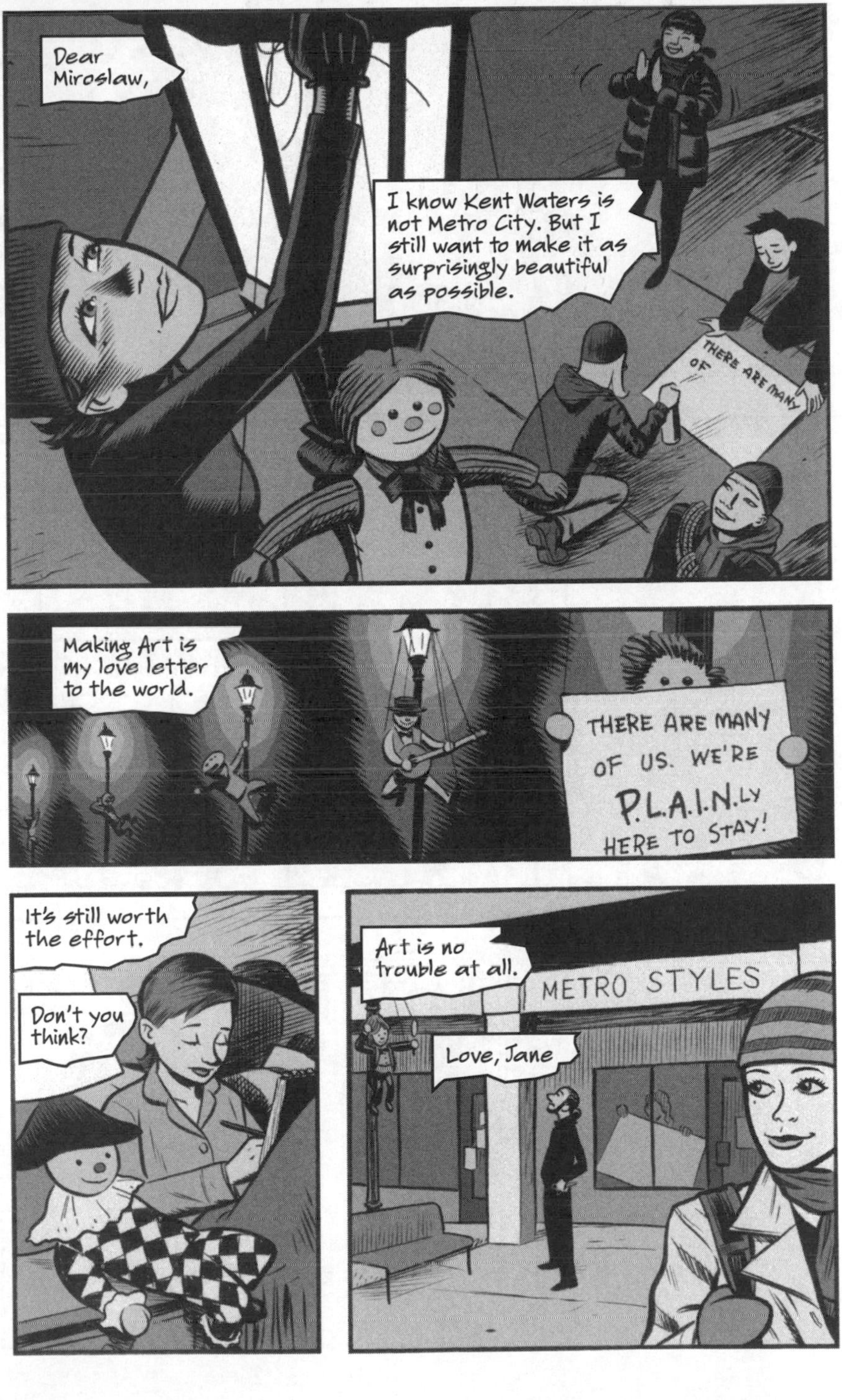
Dear Miroslaw,
I know Kent Waters is not Metro City. But I still want to make it as surprisingly beautiful as possible.
THERE ARE MANY OF
Making Art is my love letter to the world.
THERE ARE MANY OF US. WE'RE P.L.A.I.N.LY HERE TO STAY!
It's still worth the effort.
Don't you think?
Art is no trouble at all.
METRO STYLES
Love, Jane

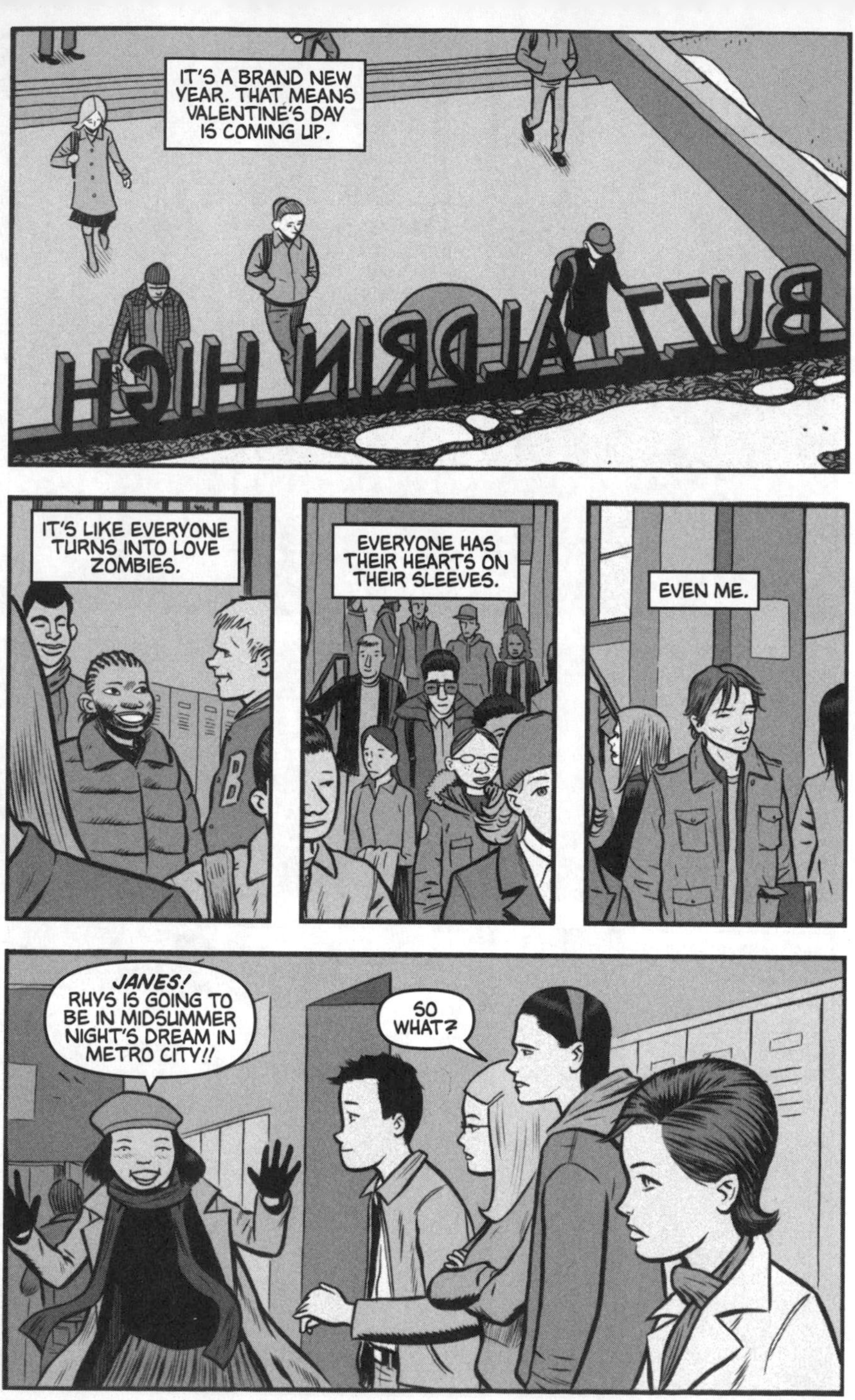
IT'S A BRAND NEW YEAR. THAT MEANS VALENTINE'S DAY IS COMING UP.
IT'S LIKE EVERYONE TURNS INTO LOVE ZOMBIES.
EVERYONE HAS THEIR HEARTS ON THEIR SLEEVES.
EVEN ME.
JANES! RHYS IS GOING TO BE IN MIDSUMMER NIGHT'S DREAM IN METRO CITY!!
SO WHAT?

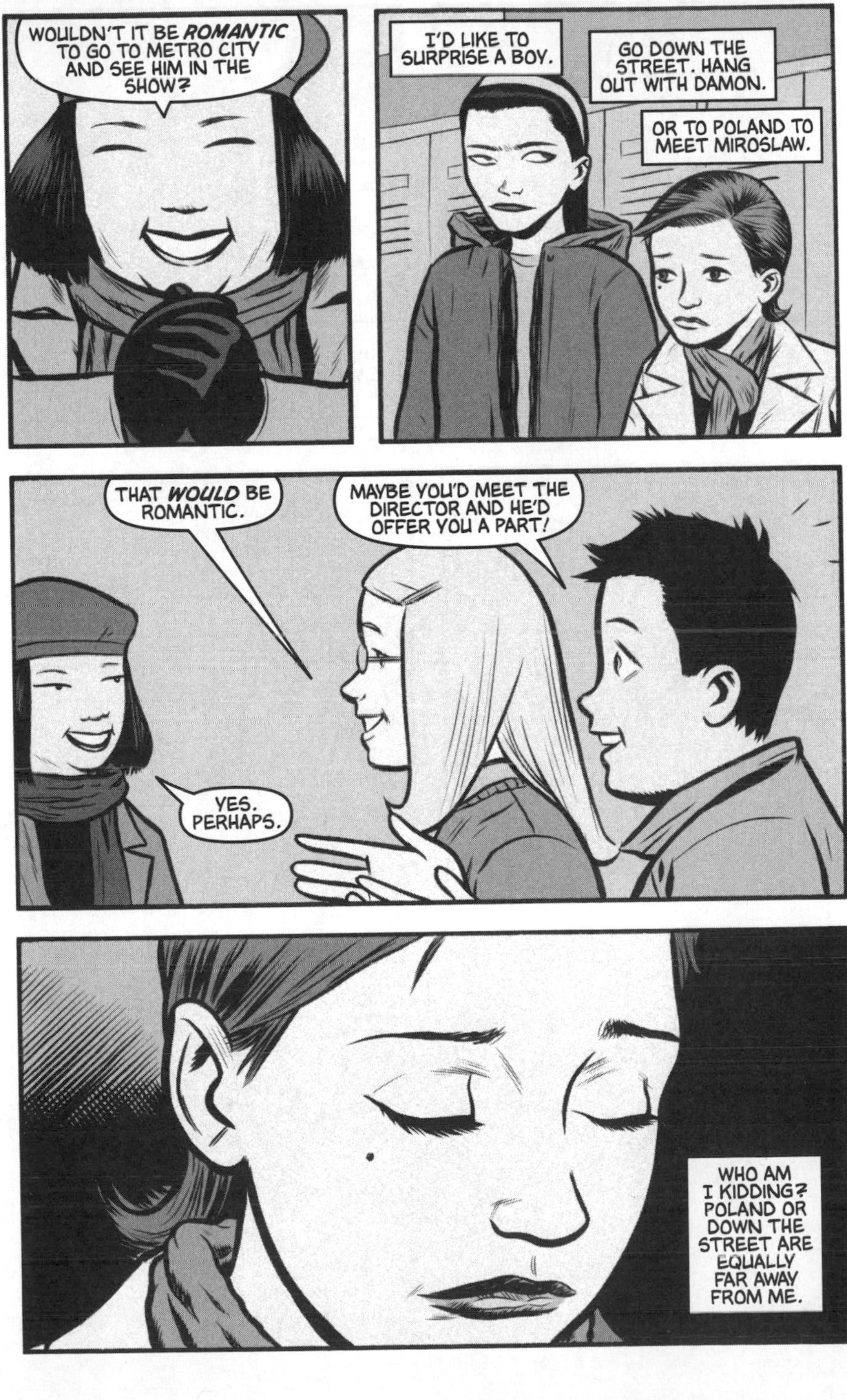
WOULDN'T IT BE ROMANTIC TO GO TO METRO CITY AND SEE HIM IN THE SHOW?
I'D LIKE TO SURPRISE A BOY.
GO DOWN THE STREET. HANG OUT WITH DAMON.
OR TO POLAND TO MEET MIROSLAW.
THAT WOULD BE ROMANTIC.
MAYBE YOU'D MEET THE DIRECTOR AND HE'D OFFER YOU A PART!
YES. PERHAPS.
WHO AM I KIDDING? POLAND OR DOWN THE STREET ARE EQUALLY FAR AWAY FROM ME.

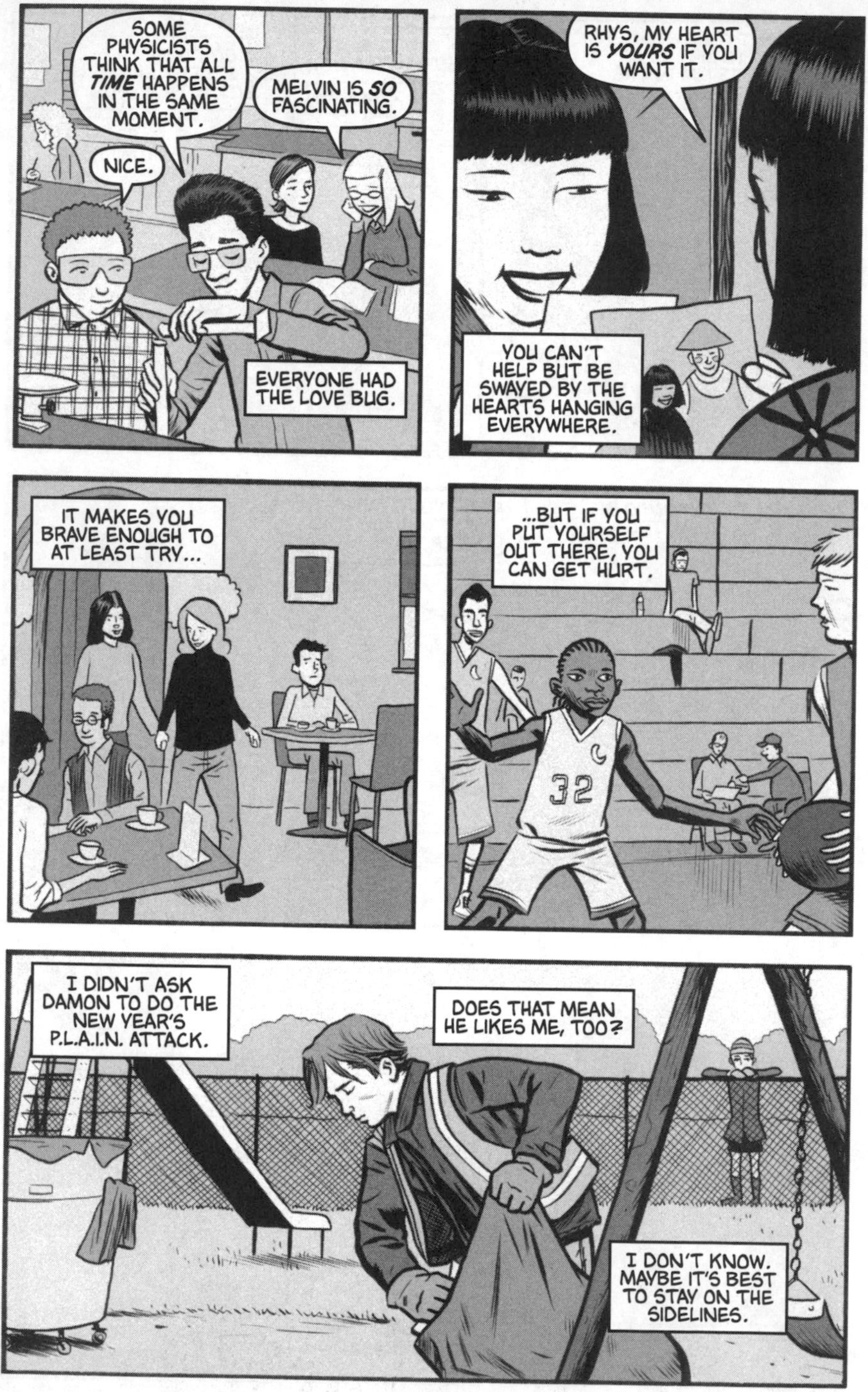
SOME PHYSICISTS THINK THAT ALL *TIME* HAPPENS IN THE SAME MOMENT.
NICE.
MELVIN IS *SO* FASCINATING.
EVERYONE HAD THE LOVE BUG.
RHYS, MY HEART IS *YOURS* IF YOU WANT IT.
YOU CAN'T HELP BUT BE SWAYED BY THE HEARTS HANGING EVERYWHERE.
IT MAKES YOU BRAVE ENOUGH TO AT LEAST TRY...
...BUT IF YOU PUT YOURSELF OUT THERE, YOU CAN GET HURT.
32
I DIDN'T ASK DAMON TO DO THE NEW YEAR'S P.L.A.I.N. ATTACK.
DOES THAT MEAN HE LIKES ME, TOO?
I DON'T KNOW. MAYBE IT'S BEST TO STAY ON THE SIDELINES.

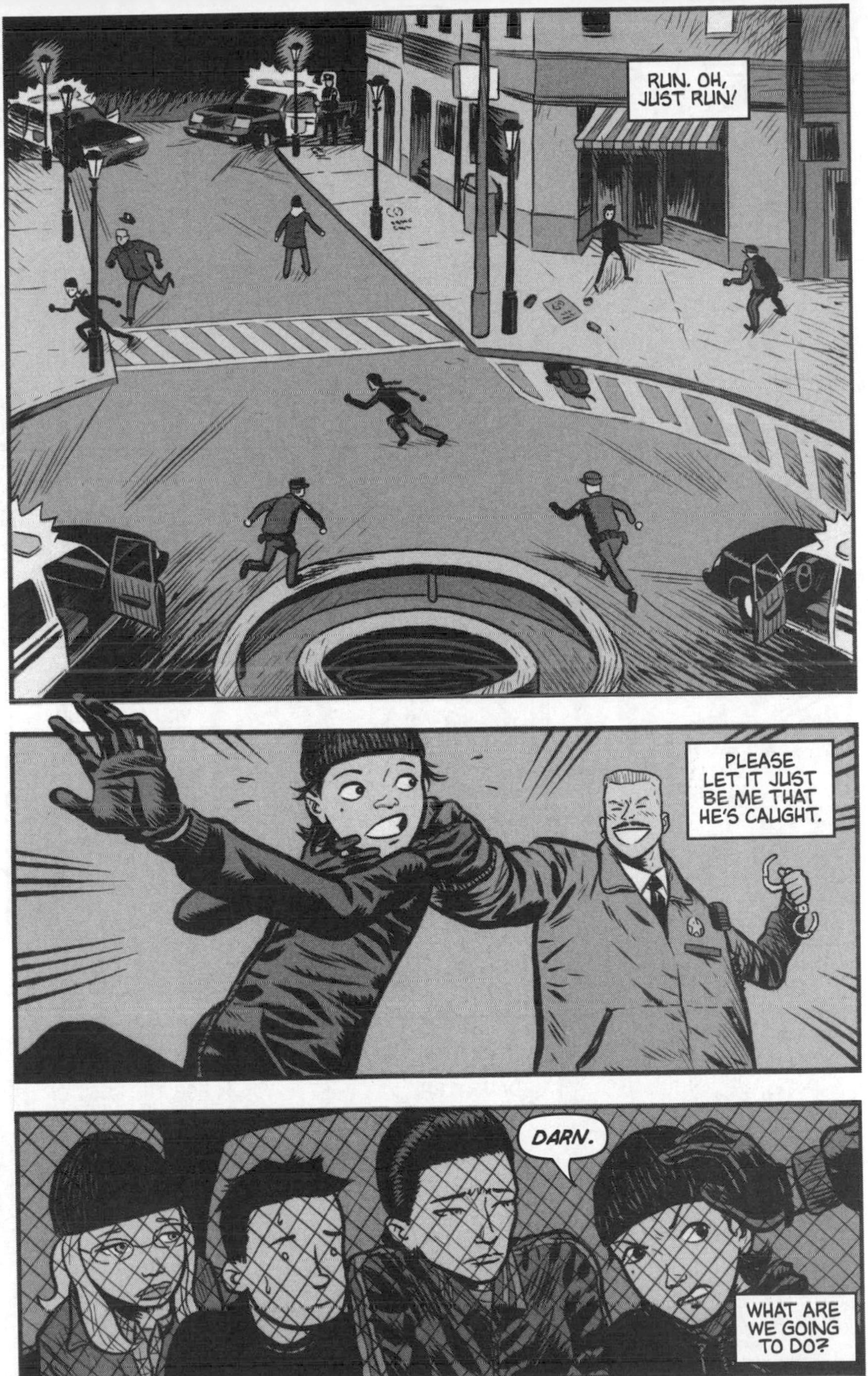
RUN. OH, JUST RUN!
PLEASE LET IT JUST BE ME THAT HE'S CAUGHT.
DARN.
WHAT ARE WE GOING TO DO?

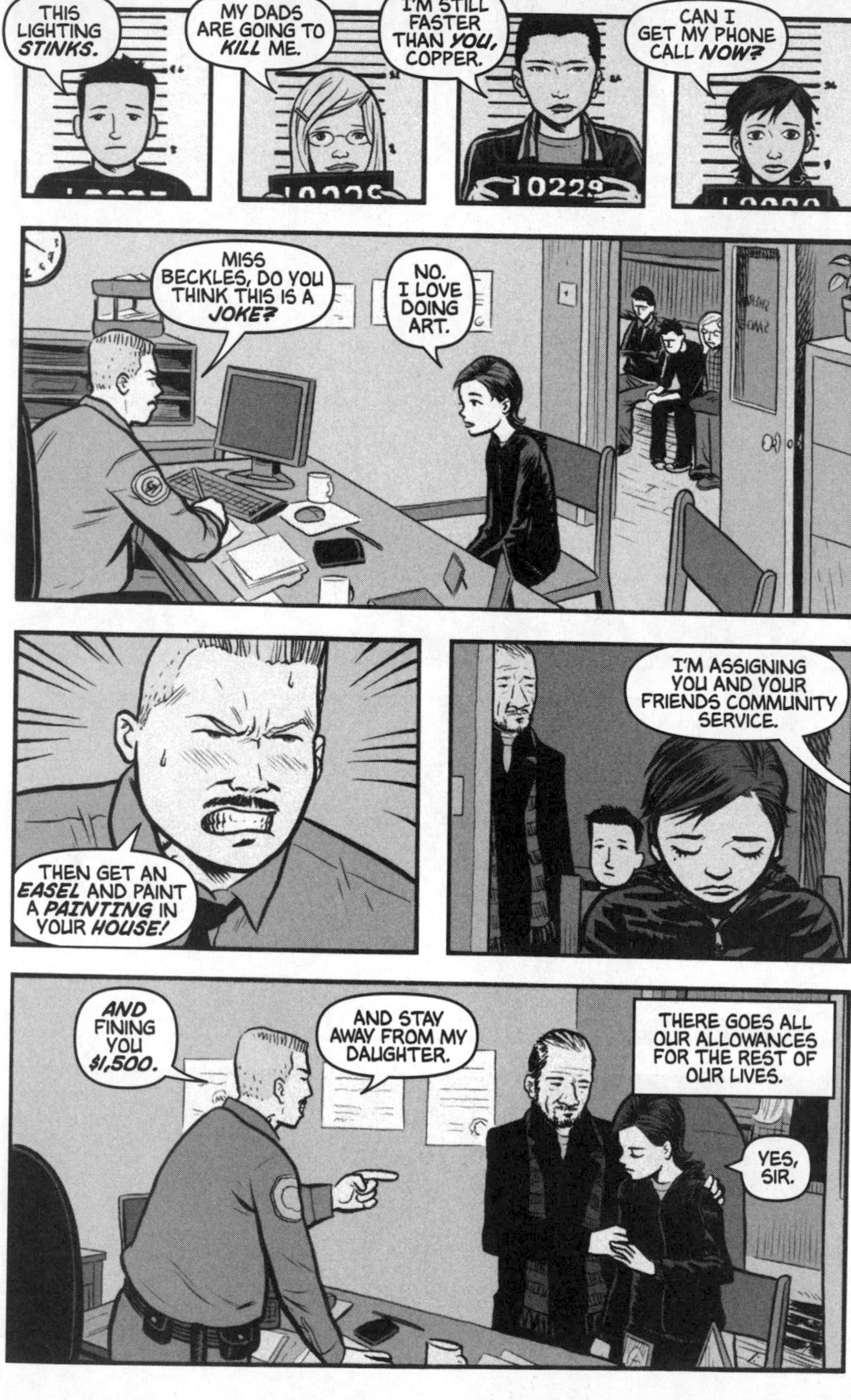
THIS LIGHTING STINKS.
MY DADS ARE GOING TO KILL ME.
I'M STILL FASTER THAN YOU, COPPER.
CAN I GET MY PHONE CALL NOW?
MISS BECKLES, DO YOU THINK THIS IS A JOKE?
NO. I LOVE DOING ART.
THEN GET AN EASEL AND PAINT A PAINTING IN YOUR HOUSE!
I'M ASSIGNING YOU AND YOUR FRIENDS COMMUNITY SERVICE.
AND FINING YOU $1,500.
AND STAY AWAY FROM MY DAUGHTER.
THERE GOES ALL OUR ALLOWANCES FOR THE REST OF OUR LIVES.
YES, SIR.

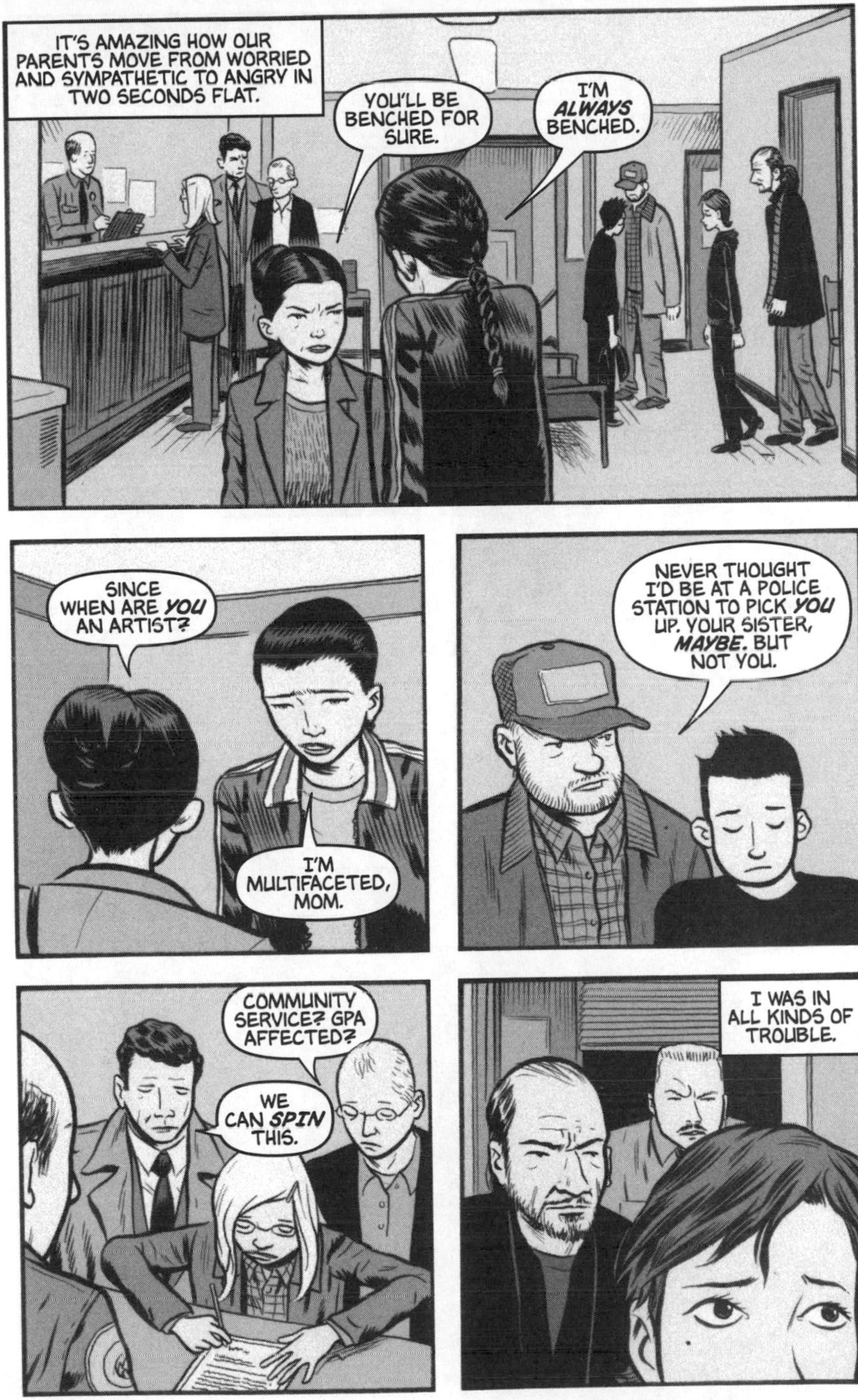
IT'S AMAZING HOW OUR PARENTS MOVE FROM WORRIED AND SYMPATHETIC TO ANGRY IN TWO SECONDS FLAT.
YOU'LL BE BENCHED FOR SURE.
I'M *ALWAYS* BENCHED.
SINCE WHEN ARE *YOU* AN ARTIST?
I'M MULTIFACETED, MOM.
NEVER THOUGHT I'D BE AT A POLICE STATION TO PICK *YOU* UP. YOUR SISTER, *MAYBE*. BUT NOT YOU.
COMMUNITY SERVICE? GPA AFFECTED?
WE CAN *SPIN* THIS.
I WAS IN ALL KINDS OF TROUBLE.

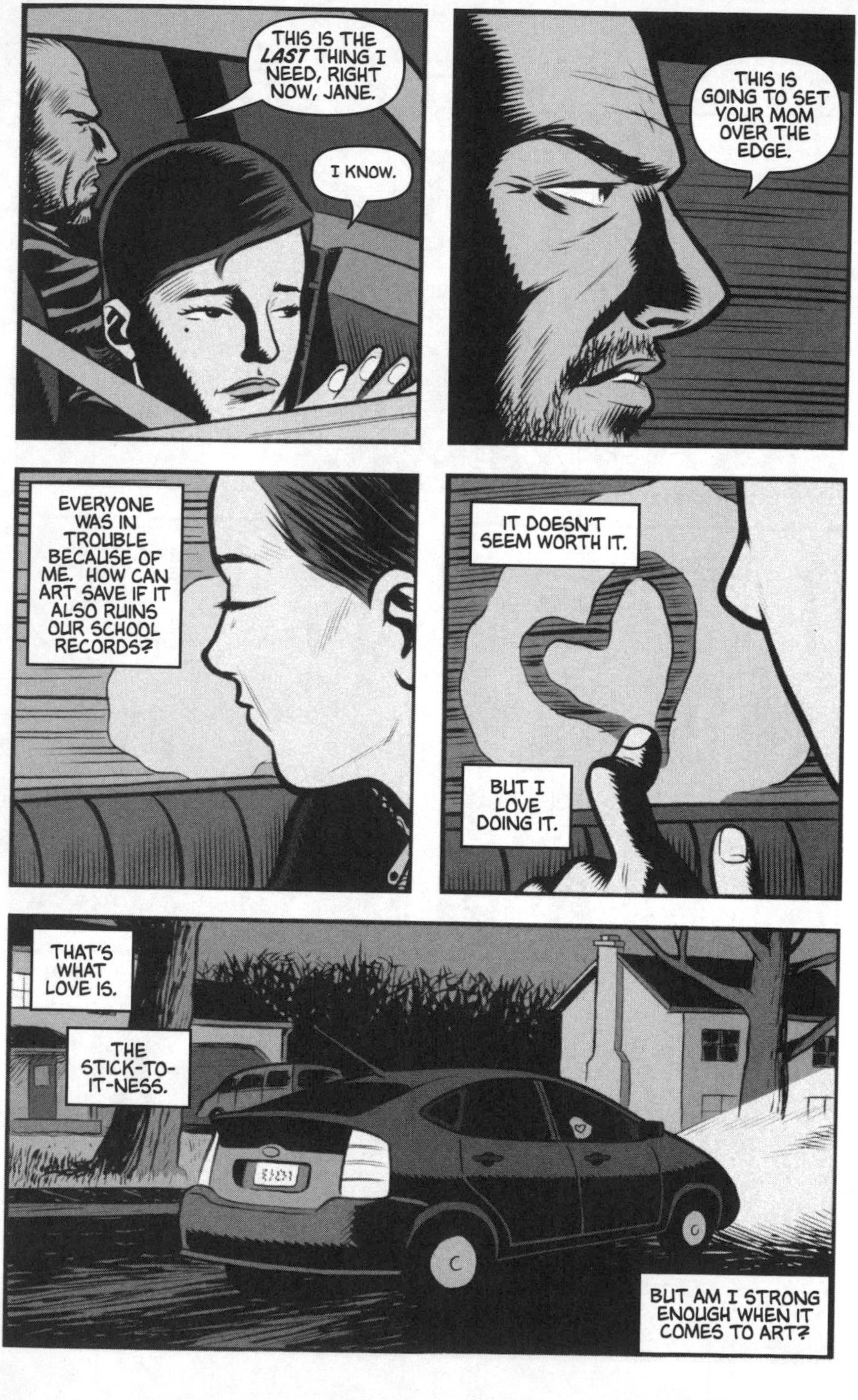
THIS IS THE *LAST* THING I NEED, RIGHT NOW, JANE.
I KNOW.
THIS IS GOING TO SET YOUR MOM OVER THE EDGE.
EVERYONE WAS IN TROUBLE BECAUSE OF ME. HOW CAN ART SAVE IF IT ALSO RUINS OUR SCHOOL RECORDS?
IT DOESN'T SEEM WORTH IT.
BUT I LOVE DOING IT.
THAT'S WHAT LOVE IS.
THE STICK-TO-IT-NESS.
BUT AM I STRONG ENOUGH WHEN IT COMES TO ART?

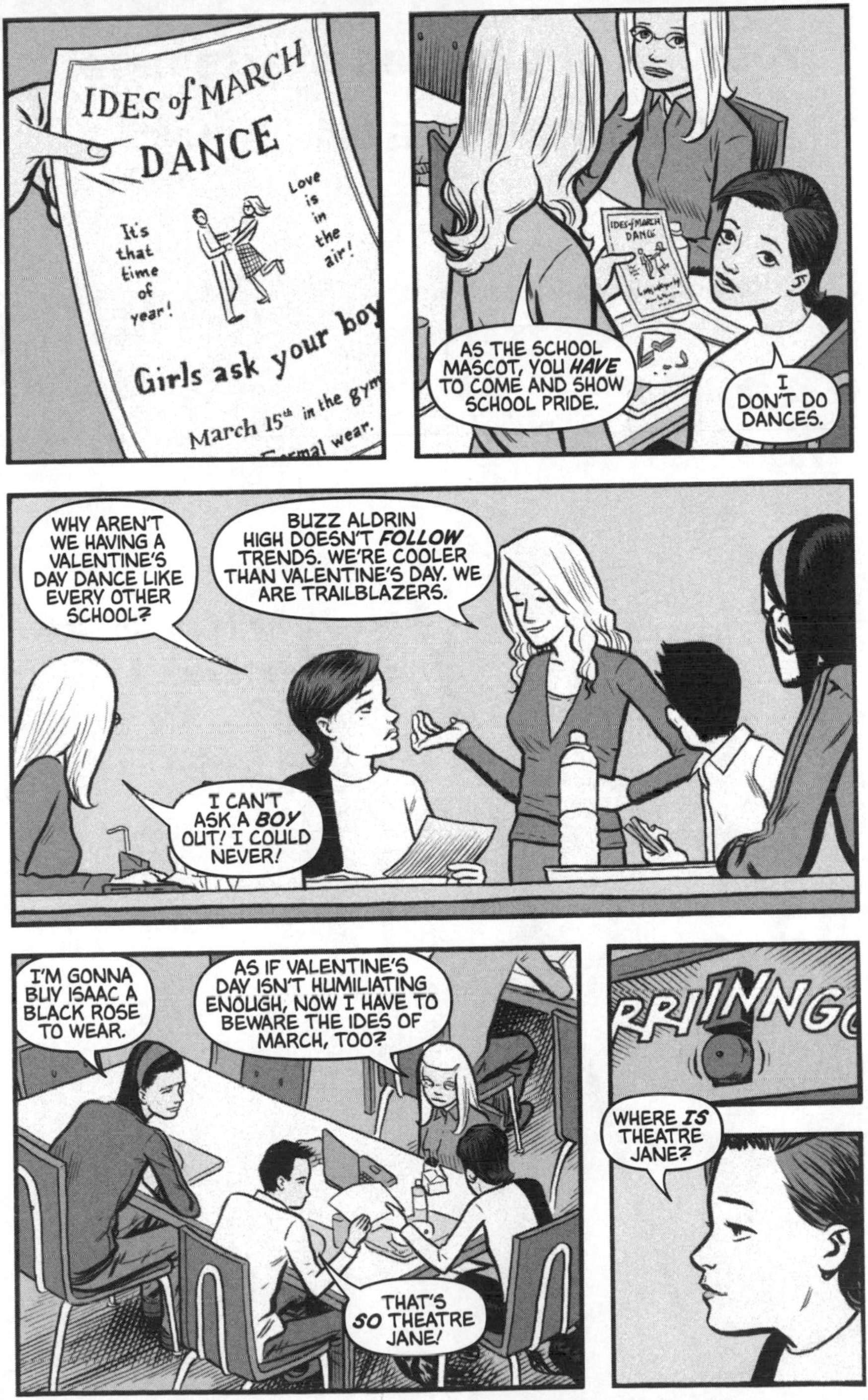
IDES of MARCH DANCE
It's that time of year!
Love is in the air!
Girls ask your boy
March 15th in the gym
Formal wear.
AS THE SCHOOL MASCOT, YOU HAVE TO COME AND SHOW SCHOOL PRIDE.
I DON'T DO DANCES.
WHY AREN'T WE HAVING A VALENTINE'S DAY DANCE LIKE EVERY OTHER SCHOOL?
BUZZ ALDRIN HIGH DOESN'T FOLLOW TRENDS. WE'RE COOLER THAN VALENTINE'S DAY. WE ARE TRAILBLAZERS.
I CAN'T ASK A BOY OUT! I COULD NEVER!
I'M GONNA BUY ISAAC A BLACK ROSE TO WEAR.
AS IF VALENTINE'S DAY ISN'T HUMILIATING ENOUGH, NOW I HAVE TO BEWARE THE IDES OF MARCH, TOO?
THAT'S SO THEATRE JANE!
RRIINNG
WHERE IS THEATRE JANE?

Your life in pictures starts here!

~A DO-IT YOURSELF MINI COMIC~

Write your story ideas here:

Draw your main character sketches here:

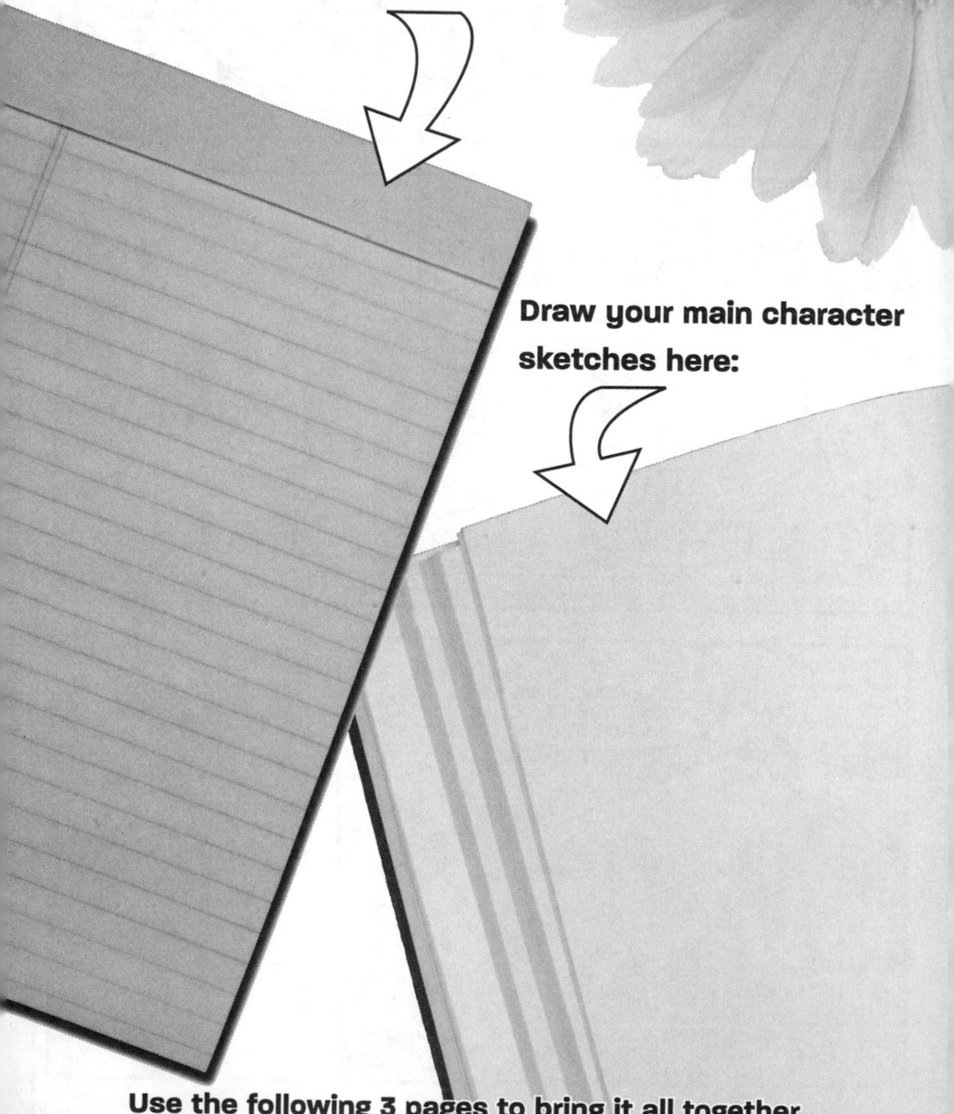

Use the following 3 pages to bring it all together.

TITLE: BY:

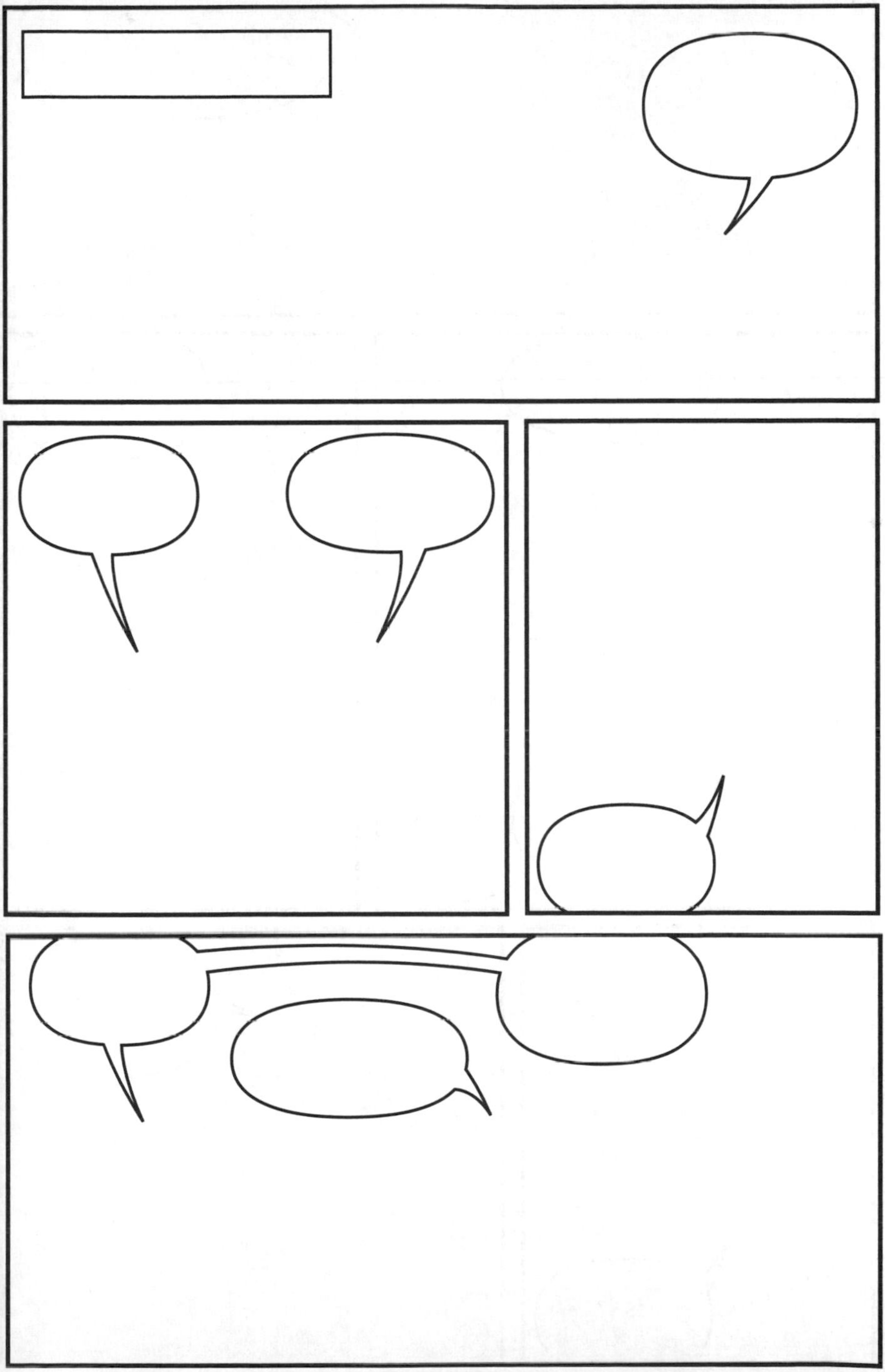

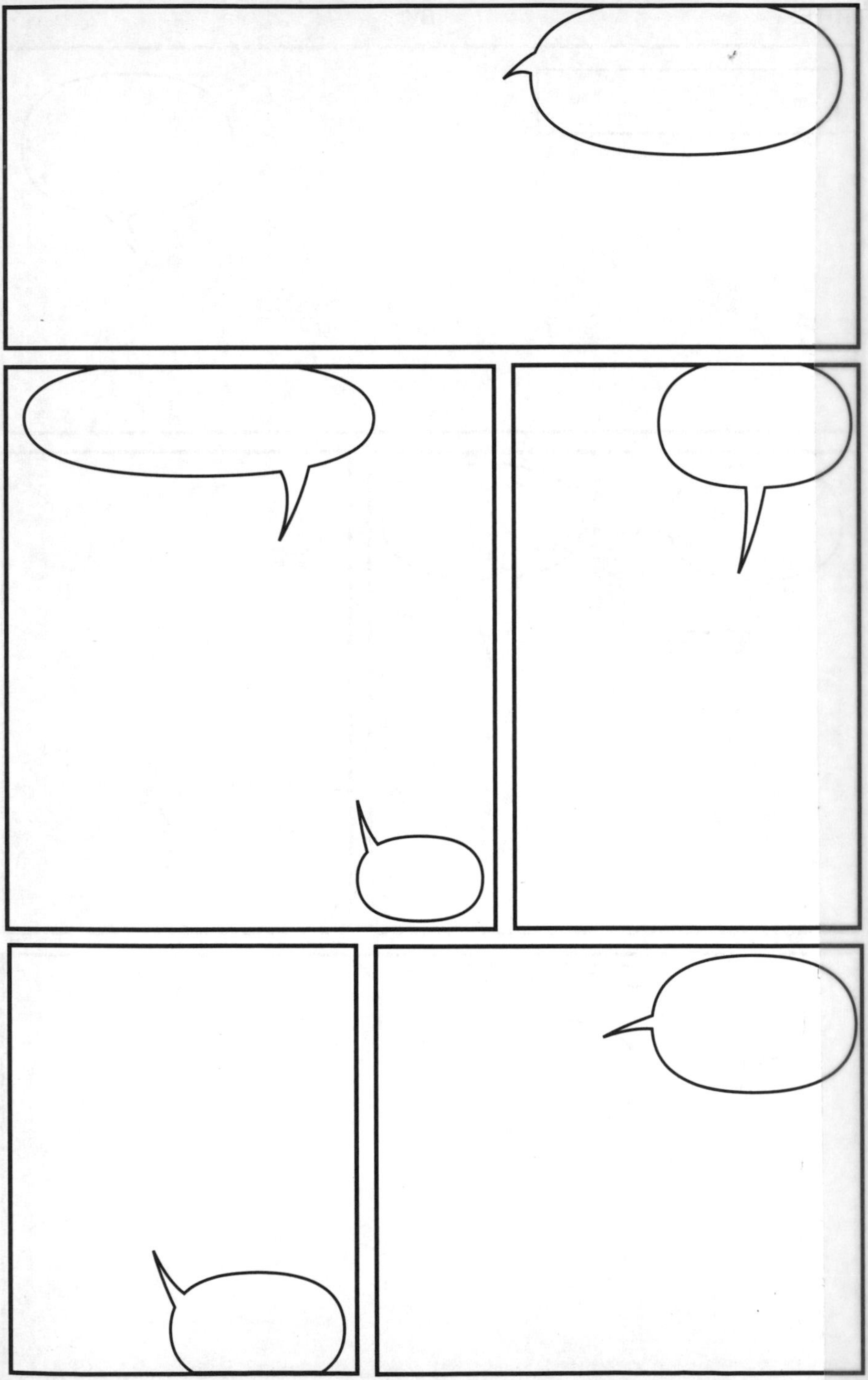

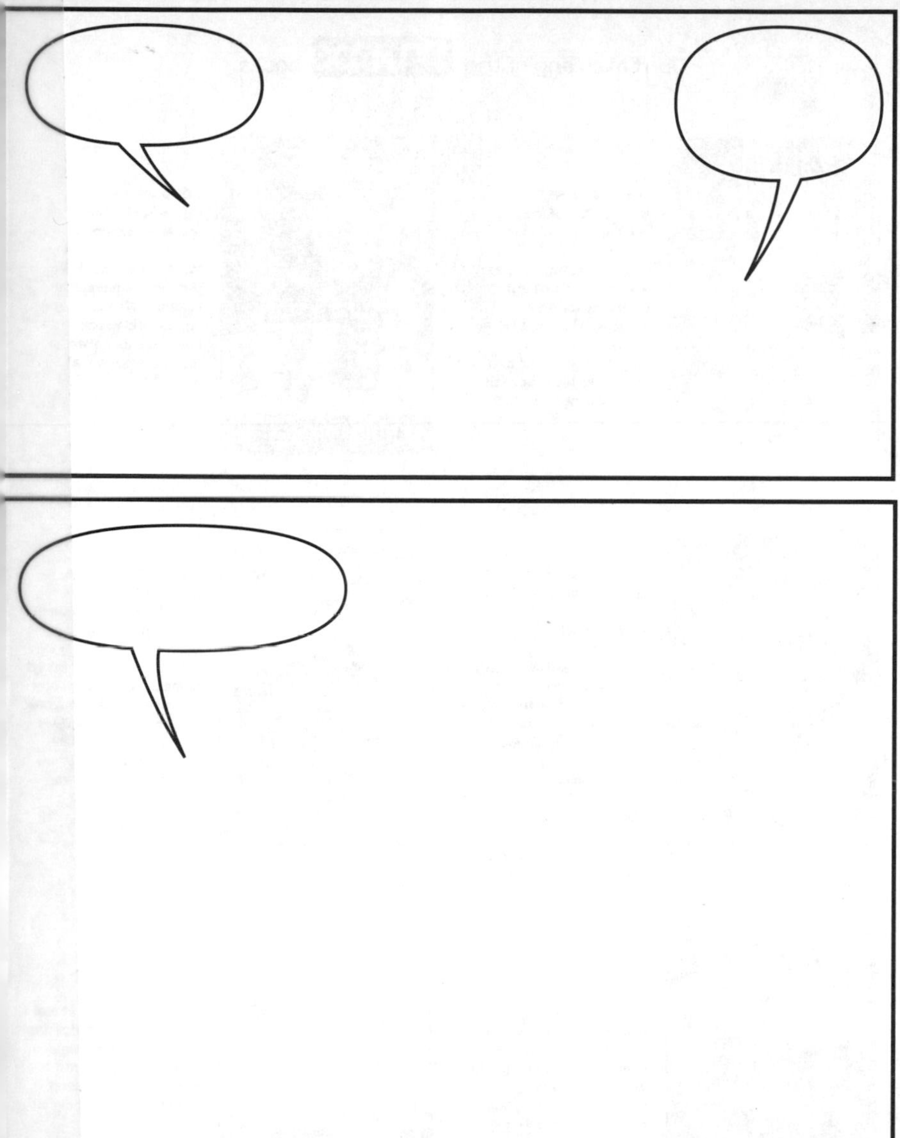

CHECK OUT STORYTELLING TIPS FROM TOP WRITERS AND ARTISTS AT MINXBOOKS.NET

Don't miss any of the minx books:

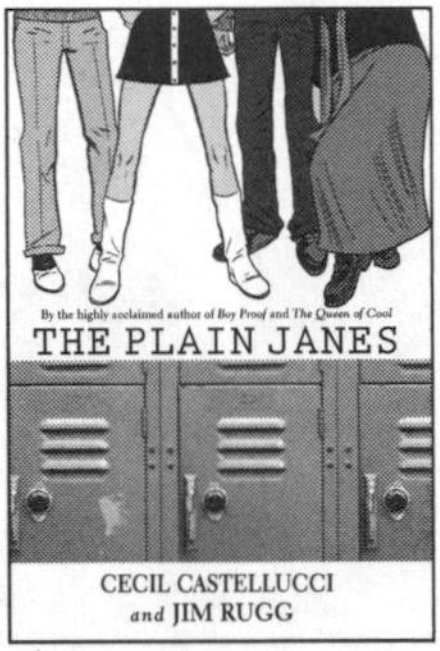
By the highly acclaimed author of Boy Proof and The Queen of Cool
THE PLAIN JANES
CECIL CASTELLUCCI
and JIM RUGG

THE PLAIN JANES
By Cecil Castellucci
and Jim Rugg

Four girls named Jane are anything but ordinary once they form a secret art gang called P.L.A.I.N. — People Loving Art In Neighborhoods. But can art attacks really save the hell that is high school?

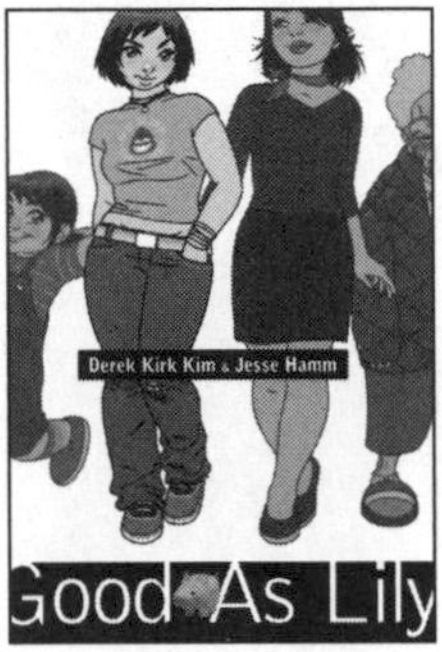
Derek Kirk Kim & Jesse Hamm
Good As Lily

GOOD AS LILY
By Derek Kirk Kim
and Jesse Hamm

What would you do if versions of yourself at 6, 29 and 70 suddenly appear and wreak havoc on your already awkward existence?

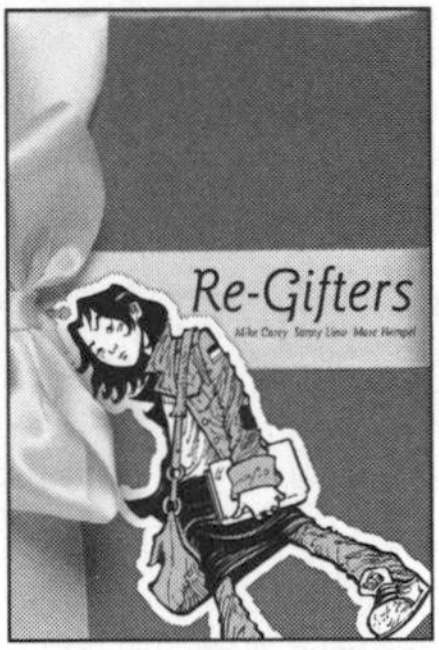
Re-Gifters
Mike Carey Sonny Liew Marc Hempel

RE-GIFTERS
By Mike Carey,
Sonny Liew and
Marc Hempel

It's love, Korean-American style when a tenacious martial artist falls for a California surfer boy and learns that in romance and recycled gifts, what goes around comes around.

YALSA Winner

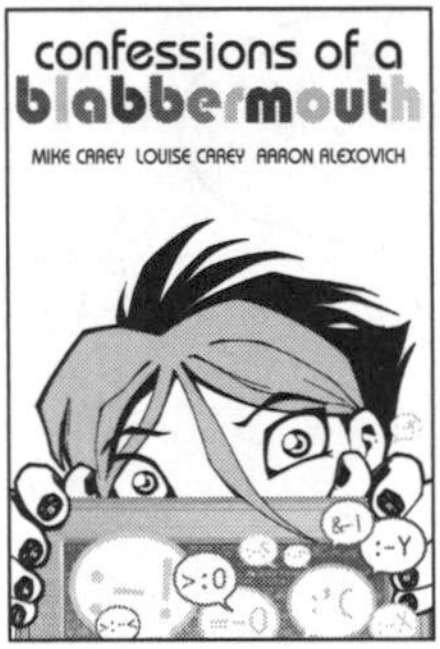
confessions of a
blabbermouth
MIKE CAREY LOUISE CAREY AARON ALEXOVICH

CONFESSIONS OF A BLABBERMOUTH
By Mike and Louise Carey
and Aaron Alexovich

When Tasha's mom brings home a creepy boyfriend and his deadpan daughter, a dysfunctional family is headed for a complete meltdown. By the father-daughter writing team.

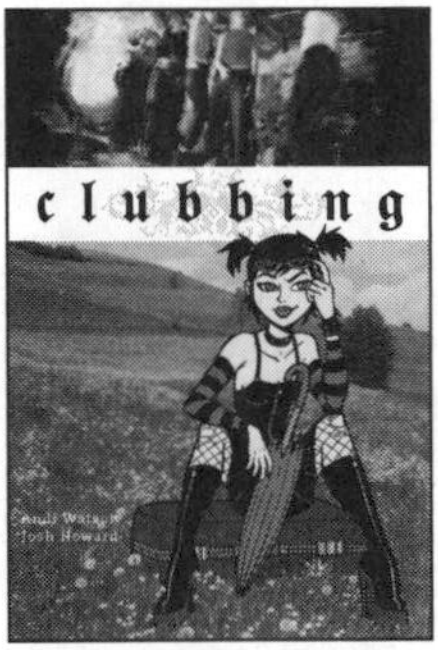
clubbing
Andi Watson
Josh Howard

CLUBBING
By Andi Watson
and Josh Howard

A spoiled, rebellious Londoner takes on the stuffy English countryside when she solves a murder mystery on the 19th hole of her grandparents' golf course.

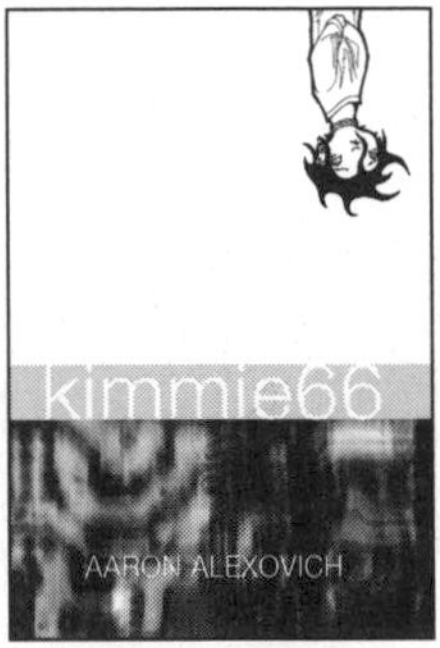
kimmie66
AARON ALEXOVICH

KIMMIE66
By Aaron Alexovich

This high-velocity, virtual reality ghost story follows a tech-savvy teenager on a dangerous quest to save her best friend, the world's first all-digital girl.

Your life. Your books. ***How novel.***
minxbooks.net